Pacific

Ocean

`cus

·Midway

Hawaiian Islands

·Wake

Oahu
Pearl Harbor

Hawaii

·Johnston I.

Eniwetok

**Marshall
Islands**

Kwajalein

··Ponape

·Majuro

Makin·   **Gilbert**

Tarawa·   **Islands**

·Howland

Nauru·   Baker

Abemama·

Solomon

ougainville   **Islands**

adalcanal

·Funafutl

Ellice Is.

Samoa Is.

Fiji Is.

**New
Hebrides**

New Caledonia

G.I. Nightingales

G.I.
NIGHTINGALES

The Army Nurse Corps
in World War II

Barbara Brooks Tomblin

THE UNIVERSITY PRESS OF KENTUCKY

Copyright © 1996 by The University Press of Kentucky

Scholarly publisher for the Commonwealth,
serving Bellarmine College, Berea College, Centre
College of Kentucky, Eastern Kentucky University,
The Filson Club, Georgetown College, Kentucky
Historical Society, Kentucky State University,
Morehead State University, Murray State University,
Northern Kentucky University, Transylvania University,
University of Kentucky, University of Louisville,
and Western Kentucky University.

Editorial and Sales Offices: The University Press of Kentucky
663 South Limestone Street, Lexington, Kentucky 40508-4008

Library of Congress Cataloging-in-Publication Data

Tomblin, Barbara
    G.I. nightingales : the Army Nurse Corps in World War II / Barbara
Brooks Tomblin.
        p.   cm.
    Includes bibliographical references and index.
    ISBN 0-8131-1951-0 (alk. paper)
    1. United States.   Army Nurse Corps History.   I. Title.
D807.U6T66   1996
940.54'7573-dc20   96-1018

CONTENTS

Illustrations follow page 118

PREFACE

My fascination with World War II began in childhood and grew naturally from the memories of the war told to me by my parents, Florence and Sanford Brooks, and their friends who lived through those tumultuous years. My interest in Army nurses in World War II, however, arose in the late 1970s in response to publicity about the Women Air Force Service Pilots (WASPs). Their struggle to gain recognition for wartime service prompted me to learn more about women in the military during the war. I was surprised to learn that among the numerous histories and memoirs of World War II there were so few written by or about women in uniform. My local libraries offered few works about army nurses in World War II, but did include Theresa Archard's and Ruth Haskell's memoirs of nursing in North Africa and Sicily, which only whetted my appetite for more insight into the nurses' wartime experiences. With the exception of Maj. Julia Flikke's book on the Army Nurse Corps, published in 1943 before the war was over, little other information on army nurses was available at that time.

For the next several years I interviewed or corresponded with dozens of WW II women veterans—Army nurses, WACs, WAVEs, Women Marines, SPARS, and WASPs. Their stories and personal memories of the war were fascinating, but in the early 1980s few publishers were interested in a book about women in the military. Then in 1993 Dr. Linda Grant DePauw, founder of the Minerva Center and editor of *Minerva: Quarterly Journal on Women in the Military*, asked me to submit my chapters on the U.S. Navy Nurse Corps in WW II for publication in her journal. The fiftieth anniversary of the Second World War and growing public interest in the role of women in the military convinced me that the history of the Army Nurse Corps in WW II deserved a full-length study.

This book is the result of recent efforts to update the large amount of material I had already gleaned from personal interviews, correspondence with former army nurses, and official army reports. A more thorough search of records in Washington and the unpublished draft of an Army Nurse Corps history at the U.S. Army Military History Institute at Carlisle, Pennsylvania, yielded even more information, as did efforts to contact more nurse veterans, especially African-American nurses who served during the war. Several memoirs of army nurses published in the late eighties have also informed this study, as did the numerous articles about army nursing published during the war in journals like the *American Journal of Nursing*.

I have interviewed or corresponded with only a small percentage of the thousands of army nurses who served during WW II and undoubtedly have missed many wonderful stories and much interesting material. Many of the interviews, as well as the interview form that I sent to former army nurses, did not directly address issues of current interest, such as sexual equality or sexual harassment. The former nurses I interviewed in the late seventies were women of my mother's generation, who often did not volunteer information of such a private and personal nature, and I, being deferential perhaps, did not press them for opinions. Because this study depends on interviews done either during the war or in 1979-80, a more in-depth study of these issues awaits future efforts by historians.

In *G.I. Nightingales,* I have emphasized the experiences of the nurses themselves, quoting them directly whenever possible in an effort to let the women speak for themselves. Their experiences have many common themes because they shared similar experiences nursing in the field, whether it was in India, Alaska, the Middle East, the Mediterranean, the Pacific, or in Europe. In addition to describing the personal experiences of army nurses during the war, I have tried to show how the U.S. Army Nurse Corps mobilized, expanded, and adapted to the demands of a world war while trying to maintain a long-standing tradition of being a nursing corps of unmarried, female, white, volunteer graduate nurses. The pressures of total war challenged and, in some cases, compelled the Army Nurse Corps leadership to modify these cherished traditions.

This study would not have been possible without the interest, assistance, and encouragement of many persons, foremost among them the many Army Nurse Corps veterans who have shared their memories and comments. I am especially indebted to Linda Grant DePauw at the Minerva Center and to Regina Akers at the Naval Historical Center for their research advice, suggestions, and encouragement. The staff of the research branch and library of the U.S. Army Military History Institute at Carlisle, Pennsylvania, the Federal Records Center in Suitland, Maryland, and the Naval Historical Center in Washington, D.C., have provided access to valuable documents and many suggestions for research. The staff of the Alexander Library of Rutgers University, Mendham Borough Library, Morristown Public Library, and Morris Country Library (all of New Jersey) have also been invaluable to my study of World War II and army nurses.

Special thanks is due Prudence Burns Burrell for sharing her memories of the war and for her valuable assistance in contacting African-American nurse veterans, whose stories have all but been neglected. Martha Putney made useful suggestions on the experiences of African Americans in World War II; Army Nurse Corps historian Lt. Col. Iris West provided research suggestions and information on Agnes Rosele, the first army reserve nurse to be inducted into the service in

1940; and Angela Zophy contributed some important comments on the original manuscript.

Financial support for the early stages of this project in the mid-1970s was provided by a research grant from the American Association of University Women, and without their encouragement I might not have pursued my interest in women in the military. Nor would this book have been possible without assistance of the faculty and staff of the Graduate History Department of Rutgers University in New Brunswick, especially the support of my advisors in military and diplomatic history, Richard Kohn, Lloyd C. Gardner, and John W. Chambers II; of my fellow graduate student and now colleague in history, Kurt Piehler; and of Barry Rusnock, who assisted in printing out the final draft. Without John Chambers's guidance, especially his direction of my doctoral dissertation, and without opportunities to teach the military history course at Rutgers University, I would never have understood the role of the army nurse in the American military tradition, nor would I have had the skills to complete this work.

My years of graduate study and research were blessed with continuing support from friends and family. In the Washington, D.C., area, Robert and Pat Trafton and Kay and John Shlaes were generous hosts during my many research trips. In New Jersey, many friends—especially Eileen Cameron, Steve and Elsa Court, Pat Kettering, Susan and Tom Shea, Kathy Stolz, Nancy Sturdivant, Janet Wheeler, and Mary Lou Weller—gave generously of their good humor, enthusiasm, and encouragement, and indulged my interest in all subjects military. I am indebted to my husband, Fred, for his patience and assistance with the intricacies of the personal computer and to my daughters, Brooke and Page, who time and again urged me to continue my research on military women and to complete this work.

1

MOBILIZING FOR WAR

On October 8, 1940, Miss Agnes C. Rosele stepped forward at Walter Reed Army Hospital in Washington, D.C., to be sworn into the U.S. Army Nurse Corps. Rosele was the first of 4,019 Red Cross nurses to be transferred from reserve to active duty on the eve of World War II. At the brief ceremony, Capt. James L. Murchison, adjutant at Walter Reed Hospital, administered the oath, while Edith Starr, a Navy nurse, and Monica F. Conter, an Army nurse, looked on. An Associated Press photographer captured the historic moment as Rosele, in her starched nurse's cap, white uniform, and navy blue cape, raised her right hand and pledged to serve her country.[1]

A trained, experienced nurse registered with the American Red Cross, twenty-four-year-old Agnes Rosele had made the difficult decision to leave private duty employment for a more demanding, possibly less lucrative job as an army nurse. Because as much as active duty held the promise of professional opportunities, travel, and a chance to serve her country, it also meant sacrifice if America became involved in the war in Europe. Our entry into the war was a distinct possibility, as was reflected in President Franklin D. Roosevelt's numerous "short of war policies" and in the Selective Service call-ups which were bringing thousands of men into the armed forces. To care for these new draftees, the U.S. Army was hastily constructing more hospitals and infirmaries at existing and new army bases all over the United States and calling for a corresponding increase in the number of nurses and doctors in the Medical Corps.

Those present at Agnes Rosele's swearing-in ceremony must have been keenly aware of the drama of the moment, but few assembled at Walter Reed Army Hospital that autumn day in 1940 could have predicted that she would be the first of over fifty thousand reserve and civilian nurses to serve as active duty army nurses. Nor could they have envisioned that within four years President Roosevelt would call for a draft of nurses to fill vacancies in the Army Nurse Corps due to a lack of volunteers. Although all of this lay in the future, as she recited the oath Rosele could rely on one certainty—she was taking a solemn vow to uphold the long, proud tradition of the Army Nurse Corps, a tradition that in many ways had begun long before the Corps itself was established in 1902.

Nurses had been serving the U.S. Army in varying capacities since the American Revolution, and although not a part of the Army, had tended the wounded on battlefields and cared for the sick in hospitals in the Civil War and the Spanish-American War. When the latter conflict began in 1898, the surgeon general, George M. Sternberg, was reluctant to use women nurses to care for troops in the field. Instead, the Army tried to recruit and train a hospital corps of young male nurses. However, these efforts failed to provide enough soldiers to tend the wounded and the enormous number who fell ill with various diseases or succumbed to typhoid attacks in the summer of 1898. Few infantrymen wanted to volunteer to join the hospital corps, which promised low pay and even lower prestige. Nor did most Army men wish to forgo the excitement of overseas duty to take up the difficult task of nursing or to risk catching infectious diseases from fellow soldiers.

Unable to recruit more than 6,000 male nurses, on May 10, 1898, the Army began contracting with civilian women nurses to care for the troops. The surgeon general authorized Dr. Anita Newcomb McGee of the National Society of the Daughters of the American Revolution to select graduate nurses for the military service and place them under Army contract at a salary of $30 a month. The nurses went to several army camps in the United States and six went to the newly outfitted hospital ship *Relief,* which sailed from Tampa, Florida for Cuba in July 1898. The *Relief* anchored off Siboney, Cuba, on July 15, following the naval battle with the Spanish fleet and the fall of the city of Santiago. During the next two months the nurses and medical staff of the *Relief* cared for 251 wounded and 1,234 sick military personnel.

Following the battle for Santiago, in which more than four thousand American soldiers became ill with malaria, yellow fever, and dysentery, Gen. William R. Shafter asked the War Department to send him contract doctors and nurses to tend the wounded and ill troops. In response to this urgent appeal, the Army sent 65 doctors and 729 nurses to Santiago. Many of the soldiers were victims of yellow fever, which was little understood in 1898. To determine if the disease was contagious, the Army conducted a series of medical experiments at a camp near Havana using volunteers, including nurse Clara Louise Maas of New Jersey. After twice being exposed to carrier-mosquito bites to determine if the insect could transmit the disease, Clara Maass died of her infection on August 24, 1901, becoming American nursing's first "authentic martyr-heroine."[2]

During the Spanish-American War, over 1,500 "contract nurses" cared for American military personnel in the United States, Puerto Rico, Cuba, the Philippine Islands, Hawaii, and in Japan. When the war ended, the number of contract nurses quickly decreased to 700, and by the following June the number stood at just 210 nurses. Although the Army Surgeon General's Office had established a Nursing Division during the war and had adopted regulations concerning the appointment, duties, pay, and privileges of contract nurses, some of the nurses were under the control of private voluntary organizations. To recognize the need for women nurses in the military and to establish uniform policies, legislation was introduced in February 1899 creating a permanent Army Nurse Corps. The bill was conceived by a committee of influential American women chaired by Mrs. Winthrop Cowdin. The committee's work was supported in part by a donation of $500 from Mrs. Whitelaw Reid. Despite the determined efforts of the committee, this bill failed to pass, but in 1901 a permanent Army Nurse Corps, called at first the Nurse Corps (Female), was established as part of a general army reorganization bill. Nurses were appointed in the Regular Army for a three-year period and could be reappointed provided they had "a satisfactory record for efficiency, conduct, and health." The surgeon general was also required to maintain a list of qualified nurses to act as a reserve in time of national emergency. This pool of experienced nurses, all of whom had served at least four months in the Army, became the official Reserve Corps.

According to an amendment added to the reorganization bill by the Senate, the superintendent of the new corps had to be a graduate of a hospital school. This compelled Dr. Anita N. McGee, who had done so much to support army nursing, to resign in favor of Dita H. Kinney, a former contract nurse and chief nurse at Fort Bayard Army Hospital, who became the first superintendent of the new Nurse Corps (Female).

With the establishment of a permanent Nurse Corps and, in 1908, of a Navy Nurse Corps, the United States had two national nursing services staffed by professional graduate nurses. As nursing historians Philip Kalisch and Bernice Kalisch have noted, "The official establishment of the Army Nurse Corps and the Navy Nurse Corps represented an important step in the professionalization of nursing."[3]

In the early years of its existence the Nurse Corps was small, but by the eve of World War I it had grown to over 400 nurses and 170 reserve nurses. After the war in Europe broke out in 1914, the U.S. Army began a program of gradual expansion, to which the Nurse Corps responded by calling 1,176 nurses to active duty and by assigning the 170 reserve nurses to duty with Gen. John J. Pershing's expedition to the Mexican border in 1916.

The United States' entry into the First World War gave the Army Nurse Corps, as it was redesignated in July 1918, its first official opportunity to prove the value of skilled, graduate military nurses in wartime. American women responded so enthusiastically to the call to the colors that nurse educators feared nursing might be swamped with eager but untrained women. Many of these civilian women signed up for intensive Red Cross first-aid courses in hopes of serving overseas as individuals or with volunteer organizations. Their determination to serve prompted the head of the Red Cross Bureau of Nursing, Clara Noyes, to write, "There are moments when I wonder whether we can stem the tide and control the hysterical desire on the part of thousands, literally thousands, to get into nursing or their hands upon it."[4]

Anxious to protect the professional standards of nursing, in June 1917 Adelaide Nutting, Annie Goodrich, and Lillian Wald formed a committee to organize the American nursing effort. Their committee included Jane Delano, chair of the American Red Cross; Lillian Clayton of the National League of Nursing Education; Dora Thompson, superintendent of the Army Nurse Corps; and Dr. Winford Smith, president of the American Hospital Association. This Committee on Nursing, which became an official part of the U.S. war effort with federal status and financial support, coordinated responses to civilian and military nursing needs. The need for nurses during WW I was critical, not only in the armed forces but also in the industrial and civilian sectors. The Army's requests for nurses kept escalating until the War Department asked for 35,000 women to help the Medical Corps care for the increasing numbers of men conscripted into the Army and sent to training camps all over the United States and eventually overseas. Under the pressure of wartime demands, the Army Nurse Corps increased rapidly, and by June 3, 1918, there were 12,186 nurses on active duty at almost 200 army bases worldwide.[5]

On May 11, 1917, four hundred Army nurses who had volunteered to serve with six general hospitals in the British Expeditionary Force sailed for France. They were the vanguard of many American army units that would eventually come to France as part of the American Expeditionary Force under Gen. John J. Pershing. Although no U.S. Army transports were torpedoed and sunk during WW I, many merchantmen were attacked by German U-boats, making the Atlantic crossing a treacherous journey in 1917. Yet, ironically, the worst disaster at sea for American nurses occurred when the USS *Saratoga* was rammed by another merchant vessel off New York harbor. The *Saratoga,* which was carrying 100 army nurses, personnel, and equipment of the No. 8 General Hospital, sank in less than twenty minutes, but the passengers and crew managed to take to the lifeboats and were rescued.

Those 8,587 nurses who made it to Britain or France found wartime nursing exerted special demands on them physically and emotionally. Army hospitals often had one nurse for every fifty or sixty patients, requiring nurses to work fourteen to eighteen hour days tending men hideously wounded by artillery and machine gunfire. Many patients were also victims of poison gas attacks. One American hospital unit received 600 such patients over a brief two-day period. "These patients were horribly gassed and were pictures of misery and intense suffering," wrote nurse Margaret Dunlop. Nursing these soldiers, who were often seriously burned and unable to breathe, was emotionally draining on the nurses, who could do little to ease their suffering except give them morphine injections.[6]

An influenza epidemic from September 1918 to August 1919 added to the demands of wartime on nursing. Soldiers contracted this virulent strain of flu and so did the civilian population—in such numbers that by June 1919 the American death toll from the epidemic reached 584,452, most of them from pneumonia and other complications. Nurses civilian and military worked long hours caring for the sick. Almost 200 military nurses died from the influenza.

By the end of World War I, the Army Nurse Corps numbered 21,480 nurses. Its members had served in France, Belgium, England, Italy, and Serbia, as well as in Hawaii, Puerto Rico, Siberia, and the Philippines. At home, Army nurses worked in cantonment hospitals and general hospitals, at ports of embarkation, and at other military bases. Three Army nurses won the Distinguished Service Cross and twenty-eight were awarded the Distinguished Service Medal. Military nursing in the United States had come of age, establishing traditions and setting precedents for the future of army nursing.[7]

Among these traditions was the Army School of Nursing, organized in 1918 to train students and ensure the army of an adequate supply of nurses. Annie W. Goodrich, Inspecting Nurse in the Army Surgeon General's Office, was chosen as dean of the new school, which had branches at thirty-one base hospitals from Mesa, California, to Massachusetts. Dean Goodrich's five-month recruiting campaign enrolled 5,380 student nurses in the school's first year of operation.

To meet the school's entrance requirements, student nurses had to be high school graduates, of good moral character, and in excellent physical health. They were given free room and board, textbooks, a monthly allowance of $15, and, after a probationary period, outdoor and indoor uniforms. Their distinctive blue uniforms earned the student nurses the nickname "bluebirds." Living in barracks or tents under what Maj. Julia Flikke later called "Spartan" conditions, the "bluebirds" participated in a three-year course using the newest text, *Standard Curriculum for Schools of Nursing.* They also took part in calisthenics, popularly called "upsetting exercises," and were encouraged to play tennis, basketball, or swim in their spare time. The Army School of Nursing students at Walter Reed Army Hospital organized a basketball team and played in a girls' basketball league in Washington. The school's sporting activities, social events, and societies gave it a collegiate atmosphere. Over its fifteen-year existence, the Army School of Nursing developed many strong traditions, but it did not survive postwar cutbacks and was not revived in World War II.[8]

The Army School of Nursing continued after the war ended and graduated its first classes of 402 students each in 1921. However, the end of the war obligated the Army to allow student nurses who did not desire to finish the course to leave and those who remained were shuttled from camp to camp. With demobilization of the Army after the war, the student nurse training program was gradually reduced to just two hospitals, Walter Reed and Letterman. Dean Goodrich stepped down as director to head the Henry Street Settlement and later became dean of the Yale Nursing School.

In 1920 the Army Reorganization Act authorized relative rank for Army nurses "in recognition of the outstanding services of more than 20,000 Army nurses during World War I." Relative rank meant the nurses now had the status of officers and wore the same insignia, the gold bars of a second lieutenant, and were able to rise in the Army hierarchy to major. The act also allowed Army nurses to take specialized training in subjects like anesthesia at civilian hospitals while continuing on the army payroll. However, the relative rank accorded Army nurses meant that they were not given the full rights and privileges of commissioned officers or pay comparable to an officer in the same grade. This would become a serious issue in the next war.

The First World War had made the American public more aware of the need for nurses and had motivated more young women to enter nursing schools, but the postwar years saw a decline in the prestige of nursing in the United States. This was due, in part, to the fact that almost all American nurses were women and the majority of the leaders in the profession were unmarried, depriving them of the prestige marriage bestowed on women in a male-dominated society.

Despite nursing's lack of prestige, enrollment in nursing schools continued to increase, from 54,953 in 1920 to 77,768 in 1927, but some postwar graduates received inadequate training and many had difficulty finding jobs, especially during the Depression. When graduate nurses could not find employment even as private-duty nurses, they were compelled to work, sometimes just for room and board, as floor nurses in hospitals, a job usually allotted to students. All of this was a serious concern for nursing leaders during the 1930s. On the other hand, the 1930s saw an increase in public health nursing and an improvement in working conditions for nurses in hospitals that benefited from the federal funding of Depression-era programs. These years also saw an increase in health care for the average American and in the number of hospital beds in the United States. With advances in medicine, health insurance, and routine hospitalization, graduate nurses were in greater demand and more nurses acquired specialized skills. All of these factors would prove crucial in the global war to come.[9]

The postwar years also saw the reduction in the size of the Army Nurse Corps, which by 1921 had shrunk to 851 nurses. The Corps' superintendent during these years was Maj. Julia C. Stimson, a Vassar graduate who had been chief of the Red Cross Nursing Service in France and in 1918 had been director of the Nursing Service for the Allied Expeditionary Force. She succeeded Annie Goodrich as dean of the Army School of Nursing in 1919 and guided the Army Nurse Corps for seventeen years, retiring in 1937 to become president of the American Nurses' Association.

The interwar years were a time of quiet routine for army nurses. Separate acts of Congress raised their pay to $70 a month with maintenance, linked retirement to length of service, and provided for disability pay. Most Army nurses enjoyed military life at hospitals like Walter Reed and Letterman, where they had nicely furnished single rooms, their own dining halls, and parlors. At Army posts, nurses took advantage of recreational facilities for tennis, swimming, and horseback riding, and availed themselves of the social life of the post with its teas, card parties, dinner at the officers' club, and formal dances. Peacetime routines meant Army nurses usually reported for duty on the wards at 7 A.M. and were off duty by mid-afternoon. In addition, the Army offered nurses the opportunity to travel abroad and many went to the Philippines or China. They also helped the victims of the Japanese earthquake of 1923.[10]

As the Depression of the 1930s deepened, the Army tightened its belt: one of the first programs to be cut was the Army School of Nursing, which closed its doors in 1933. Four years later, Julia Stimson resigned as Army Nurse Corps superintendent and was succeeded by Maj. Julia Flikke. Two years later, after the outbreak of war in Europe, a state of limited emergency was declared in United States, and the authorized strength of the Army Nurse Corps was raised to 949 nurses. By June 30, 1940, the official strength of the Army Nurse Corps stood at only 942 women, but over at Army Nurse Corps Headquarters Maj. Flikke and her staff of three nurses and three civilians were working feverishly to organize programs to expand the Corps by recruiting new nurses. At first the campaign was very successful; in the peak month of April 1941, 689 nurses joined the Corps. By the fall of 1941, however, interest in volunteering had dwindled as Americans adjusted to the emergency and as the nation's involvement seemed to be limited to being the "arsenal of democracy." When Director Flikke looked over the total number of nurses in November 1941, the figures were alarming: appointments exceeded discharges by only fifteen nurses! At the same time, Congress had extended the length of service for National Guardsmen and Selective Service trainees and the number of new hospitals and cantonments continued to grow.[11]

The number of nurses coming into the Army Nurse Corps (ANC) may have slowed to a trickle, but the need for nurses was mushrooming. With hundreds of thousands of new soldiers and sailors in basic training and "boot camps" across the continental United States, accidents and serious illnesses were everyday events, as were the routine health care needs of young men, many of whom had suffered from years of poor dental and health care during the Depression.

In the 1940-41 prewar period of expansion, the Army tried its best to cope with increasing demands for medical services, demands which were exacerbated by the requirements of military service that recognized only two kinds of status, "full duty" or "hospital care." Soldiers suffering from minor ailments that would be cared for at home in civilian life were required to report for "sick call" and be treated in hospitals or infirmaries until they could be returned to full duty. Fortunately, the outbreak of respiratory disease in the winter of 1940-41 was brief and few soldiers developed the complications that had occurred in the army camps of the Spanish-American War or during the terrible flu epidemic after WW I. However, the outbreak did remind the Army how vulnerable troops living in close quarters could be to infectious diseases. Of even greater concern to military authorities was the accident rate, which resulted in more deaths in this prewar period than disease did and which the army attributed to "the highly mechanized status of the Army, the rapid increase in air activities, and the movement of large bodies of men by rail and truck."[12]

Among the hundreds of nurses to join the Army just prior to World War II was Ruth Evelyn Parks, RN, who described her new army life at Camp Blanding, Florida, to readers of the *American Journal of Nursing* in June 1941. Parks told readers, "Camp Blanding is a product of the emergency. The sense of permanence which everywhere is apparent at regular Army posts is lacking here." She explained that when Camp Blanding was first under construction in November the hospital facilities were housed in tents. It rained almost continuously and the small group of nurses who were the first to work there went about their duties wearing raincoats and heavy shoes. At night they worked by flashlight. The situation took its toll on hospital staff: "Equipment was scarce and hours on duty were long, many of them worked when they should have been hospitalized."

Ruth Parks was candid about Army nursing during this time of national emergency. "In truth," she writes, "I can paint no pretty picture of life in the Army during these days of great stress and urgency. In the loneliness and confusion of a chaotic world one finds much hard work and sacrifice and little peace. It takes a few weeks to adjust to Army life. There is sadness at leaving home and the sense of security which familiar surroundings give one." But even after only two months in the Army, Parks felt she was becoming part of a united group, a team, and she urged readers of the journal to volunteer for the Army Nurse Corps or do whatever they could for the preparedness effort: "Our individual integrity and sense of responsibility is the essence of success and survival of democracy."[13]

Publicity about the need for nurses and articles by new Army nurses like Ruth Parks helped raise consciousness about the demands of wartime expansion, but they did not solve the immediate problem of providing medical care for new draftees. To help meet that demand, the Army changed its official policy by limiting admissions to hospitals to Civilian Conservation Corps workers, veterans, and army dependents. In another necessary but unpopular move the army refused to permit the new cantonment hospitals to build wards for dependents. To ease the stress on medical personnel, the Army also began eliminating elective surgery and confining surgery to emergency cases only. A shortage of beds in Army hospitals was partially overcome by using porches, halls, barracks, and even by placing patients in tents.

Overcoming a shortage of qualified nurses and medical personnel, however, proved a more difficult obstacle. Although the number of nursing school graduates in the United States had risen by 1940, the demands for health and hospital services had also increased. Many new graduates were going into private-duty or industrial nursing, where the salaries and benefits surpassed that of general-duty hospital work; few opted for military service.

When the authorized strength of the Army Nurse Corps was increased to 949, the American Red Cross, which traditionally acted as a reserve for the military services, began an enrollment campaign. Alert nursing leaders like Isabel M. Stewart, who had worked for the National League of Nursing Education (NLNE) in World War I, saw clearly the enormity of the task that lay ahead for professional nursing and urged American nursing associations to meet to discuss the situation.

As a result of her prompting, on July 29, 1940, a conference of representatives from five nursing associations, the American Red Cross nursing service, and several federal agencies was held at Army Nurse Corps Headquarters. Mary Beard was very blunt about the impending crisis. "I have no words to tell you how serious I believe this is going to be, " she told the assembled representatives. Many present realized that in the years since World War I nursing associations had expanded to the point that in any future conflict no one group could direct and manage a wartime nursing program. As nursing historian Mary Roberts has written, "The complexities of the situation and the democratic spirit of the times called for group action." The result of that July meeting was the establishment of a Nursing Council for National Defense with Maj. Julia Stimson as president. The council's stated purpose was to serve as a clearinghouse on nursing, to inventory all the nurses in the United States, to recruit more student nurses, to cooperate with other agencies, and to endeavor to maintain existing standards of nursing education and nursing service.[14]

The council's first project was to make a survey of nursing resources, no easy task considering that the U.S. Census Bureau's 1940 census included student nurses in their graduate nurses' classification. In the end, the state nurses' associations carried out the survey under the auspices and with the financial support of the U.S. Public Health Service. Three-quarters of the nurses surveyed responded to the questionnaires, but of these 290,000 active nurses, only 100,000 were deemed professionally qualified to serve in the military; that is, they were graduate nurses, unmarried, and under forty years of age. Although another 25,000 inactive nurses might later choose full-time nursing services, the survey revealed that the nation clearly needed to train more nurses. Subsequently, American nursing would devote much of its wartime activity to devloping a student nurses' program to provide for future growth.[15]

Without federal funds to increase nursing school faculties and provide more student housing, however, most nursing schools could not substantially increase their enrollments. To meet the need for financial support, Isabel Stewart prepared what was called "The Plan," a program calling for $12 million in federal aid. The request was rejected, but another proposal sent through the U.S. Public Health Service and endorsed by the newly formed Subcommittee on Nursing found acceptance in Congress thanks to the support of Congresswoman Frances Bolton of Ohio, who had been instrumental in securing support for the Army School of Nursing in WW I. Bolton arranged for federal funds for nursing education in the amount of $1,250,000 to be included in the 1942 Appropriations Act. The act, effective on July 1, 1942, provided funds for aid to needy students, for the improvement of facilities and hiring of new nursing faculty, and for refresher courses for trained nurses. To help recruit more nurses, the Bureau of Nursing Information published a bulletin stressing the importance of "good students in good schools." Together with a second appropriation for federal funds, the 1942 act enabled nursing schools to increase their enrollments, to offer refresher courses for inactive nurses, and to hire additional instructors. Thus, on the eve of the war, nursing schools received needed financial support and saw an increase in enrollment of 13,000 student nurses.[16]

While those concerned with the expansion of American nursing were focused on funding for nursing schools and on the recruitment of more student nurses, the Army Nurse Corps was attempting to provide nurses for a rapidly expanding army of draftees and volunteers. Although enlisted men in the Army did much of the actual ward work, the expansion of enlisted personnel in the Army Medical Corps necessitated an increase in the number of registered nurses to train and supervise the inexperienced men. In Washington, Army Nurse Corps Headquarters struggled to meet these demands, and its efforts were greatly enhanced in September 1940, when the War Department gave the director, Maj. Julia Flikke, the authority to call reserve nurses to active duty. This was not an involuntary call or conscription: the reserve nurses were being asked to volunteer for at least one year of service. They were also required to be unmarried, under thirty-five years of age, and able to meet certain physical qualifications. Nurse Agnes Rosele was among the first to volunteer and the first to be sworn into the "short of war" Army Nurse Corps, but by the end of 1940 she had been joined by another 290 reserve nurses. An additional 290 were called up, but this was still far short of the need. Army Nurse Corps historian Lt. Col. Pauline Maxwell attributes this shortage to the fact that many reserve nurses failed the physical examination. She also blames the Red Cross's outdated filing system, which suffered from an excessive number of incorrect addresses in its registry, and she blames the Red Cross's publicity, which stressed that nurses had a "moral obligation" to come forward for active duty. Other nursing historians point to the fact that the Red Cross's reserve nurse list was not a list of nurses eligible and qualified for military service but a national registering body of nurses for which there were no national minimum standards. The effect was to create a Red Cross Reserve composed of nurses essential for nursing services and schools in the United States and therefore not available to serve in time of war.[17]

Despite the shortcomings of the Red Cross system, by mid-1941 the Army Nurse Corps had enrolled enough nurses to staff 165 army posts both in the United States and overseas. By year's end, fifty Army nurses were on duty in Alaska and Army nurses had also been sent to Iceland, but no efforts had been made by the Army to recruit African-American nurses or male nurses. The U.S.

Army's lack of interest in male nurses and black women nurses did not reflect a shortage of qualified graduate nurses in either category. In fact, there were thousands of black graduate nurses in the United States and numbers of skilled, professional male nurses who had been drafted into the military through the Selective Service Act.

African-American nurses had shown interest in joining the Army Nurse Corps as early as 1927, but none had been accepted. When a black nurse applied for admission to the Corps in late September 1940, Major Flikke responded by saying that Army regulations made no provision for the appointment of Negro nurses. In 1940, when approached on the subject of using black nurses, Surgeon General of the U.S. Army Medical Corps James C. Magee, responded that "their employment has been found impracticable in time of peace. You may rest assured that when military conditions make it practicable for the war department to use colored nurses they will not be overlooked."[18]

The American Red Cross, National Association of Colored Graduate Nurses (NACGN) and other nursing organizations protested the Army's policy of excluding African-American or, in the parlance of the day, "Negro" nurses. Mabel K. Staupers, executive secretary of the NACGN, went directly to President Franklin Roosevelt on the issue. She praised Roosevelt for his appointment of Benjamin O. Davis as the first black general officer and then brought Major Flikke's letter to his attention "with the faith and belief that [he would] do something to remove this stigma from the Negro nurse." Roosevelt responded to Staupers's letter by assuring her that the War Department was considering the employment of black nurses.[19]

In fact, in October 1940 Surgeon General Magee had begun to study the use of black nurses and had recommended that they be employed in segregated wards of station hospitals with an average of 100 patients. The following May, all-black wards were set up in Army hospitals at Fort Bragg, North Carolina, and Camp Livingston, Louisiana. In keeping with the Army's steadfast adherence to a separate but equal racial policy, the surgeon general felt that black nurses and medical officers should staff only Army hospitals serving exclusively black troops, but his recommendation was disapproved by the Army General Staff in favor of segregated wards.

Although cautious about the use of black nurses and physicians, the Army was clearly moving in the direction of employing all-black units. By February 1941, the Army Nurse Corps' First Reserve had 117 black nurses registered, and within several months plans were announced to call 185 to active duty. Staupers had been working throughout the winter with Major Flikke and the American Red Cross to promote the use of black nurses and to protest any limitations on their "service, whether a quota, segregation, or discrimination."[20]

Male nurses were equally annoyed with the U.S. Army for not allowing them to join the Army Nurse Corps or to be given appropriate rank and assignments.

Many of the nation's young professionally qualified male nurses were not joining the military voluntarily, but were being called for military service by the Selective Service Act of 1940. Once inducted into the military these draftees discovered their skills and training were not being utilized by the services and they were being assigned to non-medical tasks. A survey of thirty-five graduate male nurses drafted into the army revealed that only 40 percent were serving in medical units.

One of the male nurse draftees who wrote to the *American Journal of Nursing* said that their assignments were "not of a professional nature and the chores they are doing could be relegated to 'lay men.'" Furthermore, most of the draftees were ranked as "buck" privates (all Army nurses were ranked as officers) and only those with previous military service were given rank commensurate with their status as graduate nurses. Although the rules stated that male nurses registered with the Red Cross Nursing Service would be eligible for promotion to technical sergeant after four months' duty if a vacancy existed, in reality few vacancies occurred early in 1941. The author of one letter, H. Richard Musser, RN, said, "Men nurses throughout the country feel that they are being done a great injustice in that they are not rated as women nurses are," and he urged a standardized rating system be instituted to assure professional equality in governmental rankings. However, this recommendation was not carried out and male nurses during WW II continued to serve in the regular army without officer status and often alongside corpsmen with only a minimum of medical training.[21]

Despite the availability of black and male nurses, February 1941 brought a call for "more nurses" from the representatives of the Army, Navy, and Red Cross attending the First Lady's press conference on February 24. Eleanor Roosevelt agreed with the need for nurses and with those present who expressed the belief that "the present emergency is not appreciated to the full by the qualified nurses of the country of whom 33,000 volunteered for service during the World War period." She cited the fact that although 10,000 reserve nurses were qualified for active duty, only half of the 4,000 needed by July 1 had stepped forward to volunteer. Mary Beard, national director of the Red Cross Nursing Service, added, "We know that of those who can and should serve there are 4,000 who will respond to the call, directly they realize how greatly they are needed."[22]

Despite all the Army Nurse Corps' best efforts, however, by October 1941 enrollment of First Reserve nurses was a thousand nurses short of its goal. The *American Journal of Nursing* reported in its November issue that 1,000 nurses would be needed in 1942. The journal's December issue had barely arrived in members' mailboxes when an event thousands of miles away dramatically and suddenly changed not only the projected figures for 1942, but the future of the entire Army Nurse Corps.

2

WAR COMES TO
THE PACIFIC

U.S. Army Nurses at Pearl Harbor
and in the Philippines

 While Maj. Julia Stimson's office in Washington was preparing for a national "emergency," Army nurses overseas in 1941 were going about their daily peacetime routines all but oblivious to the war clouds gathering on the horizon. At bases in the Panama Canal Zone, Hawaii, and the Philippines, Army nurses were thoroughly enjoying the benefits of overseas duty, opportunities to travel, sightsee, and practice their nursing skills in a relaxed atmosphere on Army posts that often featured swimming pools, golf courses, tennis courts, horseback riding, and social activities at officer's clubs. In the fall of 1941, 2d Lt. Revella Guest was on duty at Tripler Army Hospital, where she had been serving since March 1941. She described Hawaii as "beautiful" and her tour of duty as "exciting." Guest remembered the picnics and tours with friends or dates, the formal dances at the officers' club, and said, "We had a lot of fun. I wasn't bored at all." Although the newspapers and news magazines carried detailed war news from Europe and China, she insists that she didn't pay much attention to international affairs before December 7 because "we were too busy having fun. We thought, 'Well, our leaders in Washington will take care of it.'"[1]

Revella Guest was one of about two hundred Army nurses on duty in the Hawaiian Islands at the end of 1941 at hospitals and dispensaries providing medical care for over 50,000 men and 2,588 officers. These nurses were deployed at Schofield Barracks Station Hospital and at Tripler General Hospital. According to emergency medical plan, Mobilization Plan 40, in time of disaster the Army's Hawaiian Department would utilize sixteen civilian hospitals and, in return, would provide first aid to civilian casualties. A preparedness committee chaired by Dr. Harry L. Arnold, Sr., was established to coordinate this unique military-civilian plan for medical care, and plans were also made to convert suitable schools to hospitals. The Army was actually in the process of occupying one such school when the attack came on December 7, 1941.[2]

December 7 was a typical, sunny peacetime Sunday morning on Oahu. Most civilians and many military personnel were still asleep when the Japanese attack took the island by surprise. In addition to the main targets along Battleship Row in Pearl Harbor, Hickam Field, Wheeler Field, Bellows Field, Ewa Marine Corps Air Station, and Kaneohe Naval Air Station on the north shore were bombed and strafed by Japanese planes from six aircraft carriers. Japanese dive bombers hit Schofield Barracks and even strafed cars and other civilian targets on the roads near Honolulu. The attack was swiftly and effectively carried out, and by 0825 most of the damage had been done and casualties had started coming to Oahu's hospitals and aid stations.

When the bombs began to fall, medical personnel put emergency plans into effect. Within twenty minutes of the attack, twenty civilian first-aid stations were manned and receiving civilian wounded, who had been hit by bomb fragments and machine-gun fire. Off-duty nurses and medical personnel were ordered to report for duty, and many civilian doctors and nurses volunteered to help care for casualties.

The U.S. Army Air Corps facility at Hickam Field, completed as a bomber base in 1937, suffered serious damage in the Japanese attack. Aircraft that had been packed wing tip to wing tip to prevent enemy sabotage on the field made easy targets for Japanese dive bombers that began attacking the field's air depot at 0805. Two more attacks, at 0825 and 0900, strafed and bombed the planes, the parade ground, the post exchange, repair areas, and other buildings. Wounded began arriving at the station hospital soon after the first attack, and the staff gave first aid to the casualties, who were suffering from injuries caused by high-explosive fragments and machine-gun bullets. In the absence of enough medical supplies for so many casualties, the nurses improvised, fashioning tourniquets, for example, from belts, gas mask cords, and pistol shoulder straps. However, Hickam Hospital was unable to treat such an influx of seriously injured men, and the injured were evacuated as quickly as possible to Tripler Army Hospital nearer Honolulu.[3]

At Schofield Barracks, the station hospital received numerous casualties from the attack on the barracks and nearby Wheeler Field. Army doctors, including dental personnel, and nurses worked throughout the night to give minor and major surgical care to incoming wounded. Army nurse Myrtle Watson was on duty at Schofield Barracks Hospital that fateful Sunday morning: "We were busy after breakfast wheeling bedridden men onto the second-story porch so they could watch a barefoot football game about to begin. I remember it was about 7:45 A.M. As we stood on the porch looking out at the field, we heard the low sound of planes coming overhead. Some people on the ground and the porch began waving at the planes. Our curiosity was aroused because the planes just kept coming. There was no let up." Nurse Watson remarked to an injured G.I. named Jack standing next to her that the planes did not seem to be our planes, but Jack, "who was a sergeant and knew planes, said, 'Chick, I think we're at war.' I said in a rather shaky voice, 'We couldn't be at war; someone would tell us.' We just stood frozen in our places, staring at the sky as the planes made their runs. The effect was almost hypnotic."

When the explosions began Jack, Watson and the other nurses began wheeling their patients back to safety. Watson had just gone back out onto the porch when, she recalls, "the sound of gunfire and the drone of plane engines intensified. Jack was still out on the porch and I was standing next to him when suddenly he shoved me aside and to the floor of the porch. A line of bullets was cutting a path from the ground and up the side of the building. Two heavy bullets lodged in a door frame, right where my knees would have been. Just a fraction of a second longer, and the strafing would have cut me off at the knees."

Nurse Watson escaped unscathed and began cutting patients out of traction and piling mattresses around their beds to protect them from stray bullets and flying glass. For the next three days, she and the Schofield Barracks Hospital personnel tended to "an inexhaustible supply of wounded and dying men." She says the stream of casualties was so overwhelming that they could not separate the living from the dead, "bodies were piling up like cordwood wherever there was space." She and the doctors and medics were especially appalled by the many wounded men who were missing arms and legs, and those so seriously burned "the medical staff was amazed they were still alive when they were brought in."

For Watson, the "next three days following the attack were a blur of activity." She and the staff worried about another Japanese attack, kept going on chocolate bars and coffee while nursing dying men, giving morphine and whiskey, filling old vodka bottles with hot water to serve as hot-water bottles, checking vital signs, and placing basins under the thin mattresses to catch the leaking blood. "Red became the prevailing color, as blood seemed to work its way into every nook and cranny of the hospital," she recalls.[4]

Many injured military personnel were taken to Tripler Army Hospital several miles northeast of Hickam Field and nearer to Honolulu. The Japanese raid was well under way before many of the personnel at Tripler Army realized they were being attacked. "No one questioned the noise as there had been quite a bit of maneuvering and construction work going on about the hospital and we were accustomed to the blasting," 2d Lt. Julia M. Martin, ANC, told an interviewer. They heard the news from some nurses who had been taking a walk in the park below the hospital and had seen the "rising sun" insignia on the enemy planes. Then a radio blared, "Please turn your radio up and as loud as possible, this is not an Army-Navy maneuver—enemy planes are bombing the island." Nurse Anna Urdu (Busby) was in Tripler Hospital with an infected cheek that morning of December 7, but when she saw a nurse running down the hall to the second floor back porch she followed her. "From there we could see fire and smoke at Pearl Harbor. Something flashed in front of us as the oil tank at the pineapple cannery exploded." When Busby overheard someone call Hickam Field and shout, "My God, the Japanese are bombing Pearl Harbor!" she headed for the nurses' quarters to change into her uniform. As she entered the building, she met a friend carrying a picnic basket, told her what was happening, and added, "No one is going on a picnic today!" Reporting for duty, red face and all, Busby was told to relieve the nurse on duty in the women's ward at Tripler. She worked all day. She remembers, "I was terrified. The corridors were full of wounded. The delivery room was converted into an operating room. That night two boys were delivered by flashlight."[5]

At Tripler Army Hospital, nurse Nellie Osterlund was awakened by the concussion of the bombs. She turned on the radio and heard the announcer tell all military personnel to report to their stations. "I hurried to get dressed, thinking here I am, it's a moment of history, our soldiers are being killed and wounded. I'm a nurse prepared to help care for them," she recalls, but she was so flustered that her fingers were all thumbs, and she struggled to button the many buttons on her uniform.[6]

By the time Osterlund got to Tripler, casualties were already pouring in. Medical personnel were triaging patients, separating them into categories according to the kind and extent of their wounds. 2d Lt. Martin recalls, "Our first concern was to relieve the pain of the wounded. One nurse filled 30cc syringes with morphine sulphate, stimulants, and tetanus, while another went from bed to bed giving hypodermics." The arrival of so many wounded patients taxed Tripler's supplies and personnel to the limit, but fortunately the sulfonamide powder supply was adequate and there was a large supply of blood plasma on hand. Many lives were saved by this emergency care, and Tripler Army Hospital lost only eleven patients out of the 328 cases brought to the hospital on December 7.

Dr. John J. Morehead, who was in Honolulu at the time of attack, reported to the hospital and was restored to temporary active duty in the Army Medical Corps as a colonel and surgical consultant. At Tripler he found numerous casualties, many suffering from shock and hemorrhage. "These did surprisingly well combated by transfusions of blood or liquid plasma. Burns were very rare in our formation; elsewhere they were the major group but fortunately most of them were of the first and second degree variety. When we began work on the morning of the attack there was the inevitable confusion caused by the influx of a large number of cases, but very soon eight operating teams were on duty and most of them operated continuously for eleven hours," recalls Dr. Morehead.[7]

By a strange coincidence, only thirty-six hours before the attack Dr. Morehead had given a lecture on "The Treatment of Wounds, Civil and Military" to an audience of some 300 medical personnel, many of them Army and Navy doctors and nurses. His advice for treatment, based on his World War I experience and on civilian practice, included adequate cleansing, debridement, application of sulfanilamide in the wound, and a heavy gauze dressing and splints if necessary. He strongly advised against suturing of wounds, believing that sulfa in the wound or taken orally would help prevent infection and that a wound left wide open would receive oxygen and prevent the growth of the bacteria causing gangrene. As Dr. Morehead said later, "no one there thought that these principles of treatment were so soon to be put to a large-scale test in a proving ground only a sort distance from the lecture platform."

The medical care of Pearl Harbor casualties proved Dr. Morehead's case for treatment, and he said that the "results were better than [he] had ever seen during nineteen months in France when serving with French, Belgian, and American medical formations." He credits the low postoperative mortality rate of 3.8 percent and the lack of deaths from gangrene to the fact that casualties usually reached a hospital within five hours of being wounded and were given early treatment for shock, adequate debridement with no principle suturing, sulfa drugs, and adequate aftercare. He also cites the early hour of the Pearl Harbor attack, when most personnel were clean and not fatigued, the absence of puttees on the soldiers, the climate of Hawaii, and the absence of flies. In fact, Hawaii proved a wonderful place for servicemen to recover from wounds, especially for the few gangrene cases, who were able to expose their wounds to the bright sunlight.[8]

By sunset on December 7 the influx of patients into Hawaii's hospitals had decreased, but nightfall brought the difficulties of caring for wounded in total "blackout" conditions or of getting back to quarters past jumpy guards "instructed to shoot first and ask questions later." Many of the wounded were anxious about another Japanese attack, as Julia Martin recalled: "One patient had been killed outside a ward and several wards had been hit with shrapnel. A piece had come through the window of my ward, landing on an unoccupied bed. The patient had just been transferred to the Red Cross building."

The Japanese attack on Pearl Harbor resulted in thousands of casualties in a very short time. Most of the military personnel killed were officers and men of the U.S. Navy or Marine Corps, but 229 Army men died on December 7 and another 459 were wounded. Pearl Harbor day will long be remembered as the day America was jolted into war by a surprise attack, but it should also be remembered as a day when American medical personnel, military and civilian, reacted promptly and professionally to this sudden emergency.

In the wake of the Pearl Harbor attack, routine in the Hawaiian Islands turned from a leisurely tropical way of life centered on pineapple and sugar production and tourism to a grimmer existence geared primarily to winning a war. The islands became America's Pacific crossroads, where military traffic stopped and many units staged before going into combat. Troops and supplies poured into the islands for the next three years, and temporary buildings and barracks rose all over Oahu. For weeks after the attack, rumors of a Japanese invasion were rife, and for six months authorities in the islands expected another attack. Accordingly, Hawaii was put under martial law and spent the war years under a military government. The lights of Waikiki Beach went out as "blackout" procedures took effect, barbed wire was rolled along Oahu's famous beaches, a 7:45 P.M. curfew was declared, and the populace began to feel the pinch of rationing and shortages.

Medical facilities continued to grow in the months after the attack as more garrison troops and combat units arrived in the islands. The chief surgeon established hospitals on the outlying islands staffed by nurses from the three main hospitals on Oahu. In addition, in March 1942 the 204th General Hospital came to Oahu, the 165th Station Hospital (S.H.) arrived on Kauai, the 156th S.H. on the big island of Hawaii, and the Twenty-second S.H. set up on Maui. Two more general hospitals, the 147th and 148th, also came to Hawaii from the mainland in the first six months of 1942, bringing total nurse strength to 571 from only 195 nurses on duty in the Hawaiian Department in late December 1941.[9]

One of the newly arrived nurses, Eloise Bowers, received her orders only three weeks after Pearl Harbor. Her group of nurses sailed for Hawaii in early 1942. "The only reminder we were going to war seemed to be frequent, harrowing middle of the night torpedo alerts when reflex action got you to the decks in all stages of dress but always with your life preserver." Under new wartime conditions the normal four-day cruise to Hawaii took eleven days in convoy, zigzagging every few minutes, and escorted by destroyers, but the nurses enjoyed the voyage. "The Air Corps and Marine officers aboard and the nighttime parties were memorable," Bowers recalls.

Like so many new arrivals to Hawaii in early 1942, nurse Bowers was deeply moved by her first sight of the charred hulks of our fleet at Pearl Harbor. Her unit was taken immediately to a civilian hospital quartered in a college to help care for casualties of the December 7 attack.[10] With comfortable quarters in temporary buildings at the college and Waikiki just a five-minute walk away, the nurses enjoyed their new assignment. Mary Donovan, who joined the Army Nurse Corps in 1940, agrees: "We were never 'in the field.' We occupied a school building. The bathroom facilities were less than adequate and meals service was difficult." But, she says, despite the fact they were all young and had never been way from home for such a long period of time (three years) "morale and health were generally good." Donovan says that prominent families in Hawaii held open houses for the nurses and allowed them to use their ranch or beach houses when they had liberty. There were also opportunities for sightseeing, beach parties, tennis and horseback riding.

Nurse Donovan points out that although they were close to Waikiki and downtown Honolulu, "barbed wire and the fact the nurses all had to wear uniforms was [sic] a constant reminder that a war was on." As the civilian population was evacuated to the U.S. mainland and the number of males in Hawaii's already predominantly male population increased, "getting dates," she remembers, "was no problem."[11] Eloise Bowers describes social life in Hawaii as "hectic and unending, since duty was half day in the tropics and the ratio of women and men was at one time 10,000 to 1. Multiple dates daily were common and every day there were parties and dancing at the various officers' clubs around the island." Social events, however, ended promptly at 6 P.M. and no travel was allowed after blackout hours. That posed no problem for the nurses who had night duty, and according to Nellie Osterlund, many of the others spent their evenings playing penny-ante poker. Nurses who served in the islands recall that health and morale were good during the war years except for the last year when the nurses "grew weary." Bowers observed that some of the young officers felt duty in the islands was "too restive and many did not like the lack of seasonal changes and not being able to be 'home for Christmas.'" She also notes, "Ready compliance to military orders rather than medical judgment was a difficult adjustment for many male officers."

In fact, wartime duty in the islands would have been perfect had it not been for the danger of invasion. "In the months before the Battle of Midway we lived in fear the Japanese would return," Osterlund recalled. Bowers and her fellow nurses followed the progress of that naval battle closely, and they spent the time emptying every bed they could and getting ready to receive casualties from Midway: "Supplies were checked and rechecked and then came the early evening when word rippled across the post that 'they' were en route to the hospital." Personnel lined the hospital balconies, which overlooked Honolulu and the sea. From the balconies the nurses could see a long line of ambulances slowly winding up the hill to the hospital. "I remember especially the uneasy quiet of those moments before we met the litters as they were wheeled to designated wards," Bowers says. However grateful the wounded sailors were to be back in Hawaii, they were not ready to discuss their ordeal: "I cannot remember any soldier who talked about what happened during the battle."

Army nursing in Hawaii during the war was not all fun and parties; Nellie Osterlund says the nurses at Tripler Army Hospital worked "seven days week, and for the most part twelve hours a day caring for a "large number of casualties, tropical diseases, and emotional problems due to the war." The patients were assigned to large wards of thirty to forty beds and slept on low cots. Nellie Osterlund recalls that in the temporary hospital quarters set up in schools or wooden buildings they "used to hang intravenous fluids and blood transfusions" from nails in the rafters, and "some of the equipment had been stored since WW I."[12]

Other nurses, however, found that supplies were very adequate, because Hawaii was a shipping crossroads. Capt. C. Elva Collision, ANC, was the chief nurse of the Twenty-second Station Hospital in Hawaii and then at the 204th S.H. on the island of Maui. She recalls that during her six months at the 204th, the patient census doubled from 200 to 400 patients, but that they had few surgical cases and no malaria or tropical diseases from Hawaii. They did receive some cases, however, from other locations in the Pacific. In fact, Captain Collison told an army interviewer that nurses felt they had too little to do at first and some "are very anxious to go further down in the Pacific." Nurse Collison remarked, "We had quite a bit of appendicitis. Sulfa drugs are used with very good results." Mary Donovan echoes this assessment: "Sulfa powder, sulfa crystals, and then penicillin were introduced in the care of patients with infected wounds. Results were truly 'miraculous.'"

For many units, the Hawaiian Islands provided an ideal training place for future assignment to duty on Pacific islands. For example, Hannah M. Matthews, who served at the Thirty-eighth Field Hospital where she was a nurse on the orthopedic wards, was sent to Coco Head in January 1944 to train for duty in the field. In February Elva Collison was sent for training as a nurse anesthetist, and in June 1944 she transferred to a hospital on Kwajalein.

For many Army nurses, wartime in Hawaii held special memories. A highlight of wartime duty for Eloise Bowers was her wedding to an Army officer also on duty in Hawaii. Another was the visit Franklin D. Roosevelt made to her hospital late in the war. Security at the hospital was very tight and all cameras were banned: "A long procession of cars with flags flying arrived at the hospital, where ramps for the President's wheelchair were in place. He wore a long black cape and was obviously a very ill man at this time. It was a shocking thing to observe how frail the Commander-in-Chief had become, but he was wheeled through the wards to shake hands and speak with many of the men in their beds." This was one of President Roosevelt's last visits to the troops. In Hawaii Eloise Bowers remembers, "soon after about noon one day the flags were lowered to half mast as the news of Roosevelt's death was broadcast to all stations."[13]

Across the Pacific in the Philippine Islands, another contingent of Army nurses was on duty when the war began. Despite rumors of war and active hostilities in China, Army nurses and other medical personnel remained on duty in the station hospital at Camp John Hay 200 miles north of Manila and at Stotsenberg Station Hospital at Clark Field near Manila. These hospitals were integral to the defense of the Philippines and were expected to play an important role in caring for casualties when war with Japan started.

The possibility of hostilities with the Japanese had long been contemplated by the American military, but by 1941 little had been accomplished to prepare the Philippine Islands for that eventuality. Defense planners assumed that hostilities would not begin until April 1942 at the earliest, by which time Lt. Gen. Douglas MacArthur hoped that the newly organized Filipino Army and Gen. Jonathan Wainwright's Philippine Division would be sufficiently trained and equipped to meet a Japanese invasion. Most of the 22,000 American and Filipino troops were stationed in or near the city of Manila, and the Far East Air Force under Maj. Gen. Lewis Brereton was stationed at Clark Field.[14]

In anticipation of possible hostilities, Fort William McKinley Hospital, just seven miles from Manila, was staffed with nurses, and tentative plans were made for wards, a surgery, a mess, and storage facilities in the tunnel on the island of Corregidor. By mid-November 1941, Fort McKinley had housing for twenty-two U.S. Army nurses and six Filipina nurses, and the conversion of the post dispensary to a 250-bed station hospital was almost complete.[15]

Two army nurses, 2d Lt. Ruby C. Bradley and 2d Lt. Beatrice Chambers, were on duty at the small thirty-five-bed Camp John Hay Station Hospital near the cool mountain resort of Baguio. Camp John Hay boasted an officers' club for dances, barbecues, and bridge parties, and even a golf course that wound over the hills in front of the nurses' quarters. The town of Baguio was only a short walk away and offered shops filled with native Filipino crafts.

South of Camp John Hay, about seventy-five miles from Manila and adjacent to Clark Field, was Stotsenberg Station Hospital. In December 1941, Chief Nurse Lt. Florence MacDonald, fourteen U.S. Army nurses, and three Filipina nurses served at Stotsenberg, a cavalry post where polo games were the main source of entertainment, along with golf, bowling, and horseback riding. Nurses at Stotsenberg performed routine station hospital duties and staffed a busy maternity ward.

In Manila, Sternberg General Hospital received all the chronic and psychiatric cases of the Philippine Department. The nurses at Sternberg were housed in a "rambling, two-storied, dark, hot building" in downtown Manila, but they took advantage of the proximity of shopping, churches, theaters, restaurants, and the Army-Navy Club, "where swimming, dancing, tennis, and bowling could be enjoyed."[16]

On Corregidor Island in Manila Bay, the Army also had Fort Mills, a ninety-bed station hospital where Maude C. Davidson was chief nurse. Duty on the "Rock" was pleasant indeed, with a beautiful officers' club, a golf course, tennis courts, a bowling alley, a beach house, and a swimming pool. Manila was only a three-hour trip across the bay, but Corregidor had its own well-stocked PX and a native barrio with a good market and numerous shops.

In the autumn of 1941, preparations at these Army hospitals were being made for a possible war, but according to Marie Adams, who came to the islands in October to develop Red Cross services in the hospitals, "there wasn't much feeling of tension or anticipation of war in Manila. The Red Cross had been conducting practice evacuations, blackouts, etc., but in general there didn't seem to be any real concern about the possibility of war."[17]

Adams had come from Fort Ord, California, where war plans were being made in earnest, and she was shocked by the old-fashioned and utterly inadequate equipment at Fort McKinley. The only type of ambulance there, she said, was "a rusty looking conveyance that looked as if it dated from the Spanish-American War." Adams remembered that eight or nine days before the attack on

Pearl Harbor all military installations in the islands had been out on a full war-time basis by order of General MacArthur. The working day was lengthened to eight hours and the medical personnel and nurses were blood typed, issued steel helmets and dogtags, and instructed in procedures in the event of a gas attack. "We went on a full black out from then until the war began," she recalled. "Everyone was jittery and tense during that period."

Word of the Japanese attack on Pearl Harbor arrived in the Philippines about 0630 the same day, which was December 8, 1941, in the Far East. Marie Adams recalled, "I was on duty at Ft. McKinley and had left my quarters to go to breakfast, when a corpsman who was hurrying by called out to me the news. . . . I learned that already hundreds of trucks had left the camp, carrying our troops to their combat positions in the field. By 1200 that day there was almost no one left on the post except the hospital staff and patients."[18]

At Stotsenberg, 1st Lt. Florence MacDonald heard that Pearl Harbor had been bombed and then rumors that Baguio had also been hit by the Japanese. Despite this distressing news, work at the hospital went on as usual, but at 1145, Nurse MacDonald looked out the window and saw planes coming overhead. "They looked so much like our army planes that we said, 'Here are our boys coming in from the morning flight.' We realized in about two minutes that we were mistaken when the bombs began to fall over Clark Field."[19]

Marie Adams was awakened that night at 0300: "The bombs were falling all around the compound, and the air was filled with red tracer fire. The antiaircraft guns were not able to put up an effective defense against the bombing planes because the range of the guns was only about two thousand feet and the planes were able to stay well out of range."

The next morning Adams found the hospital jammed with casualties from Clark and Nielson fields and other localities. She handed out cigarettes and other articles from her patient supplies to the ambulance drivers, who were exhausted from working all night collecting the wounded. Most of the casualties at Clark Field were personnel caught running for cover after the bombs started falling or those at the officers' club and a mess tent, which both received direct hits causing numerous casualties. Many were taken to Stotsenberg Station Hospital, which was soon overwhelmed by the number of cases and was sent additional nurses and doctors from Sternberg General Hospital.[20]

Throughout those first harrowing weeks of war, Clark Field was bombed almost daily. Lieutenant MacDonald recalled that "one day there were 28 alarms. The Japs did not bomb at night. They bombed the quartermaster installations, but not the hospital, barracks, or quarters." Marie Adams also remembered these raids: "We had almost constant bombing, although no more night bombings. However, the nurses and I slept in our uniforms in air raid shelters."

Stotsenberg Station Hospital was built of concrete and fairly safe from bomb damage except for direct hits, but the staff still took cover under desks or beds when the alert sounded. As the weeks wore on, Stotsenberg took on casualties from Iba and Clark fields until "every available inch of space was filled with beds, in corridors, around the porches, and between regular beds."[21]

On Saturday, December 13, 1941, Stotsenberg's personnel and patients were evacuated to Sternberg and its seven "annexes" or small hospitals were set up and equipped in schools and public buildings in Manila. This so-called Manila Hospital center operated only two weeks, with Army, Navy, and former Army nurses who came to Sternberg and volunteered. Nurses from the Rockefeller Foundation in Peiping, who were on board a ship in Manila harbor when hostilities began, also volunteered their services. 2d Lt. Josephine Nesbit, ANC, who became chief nurse when Maude Davidson injured her back in a night raid, noted, "Miss Robinson, who had been one of the head nurses in the Foundation, was 'left holding the bag' together with many civilian American and Filipina nurses, when the military left Sternberg."[22]

Military personnel evacuated Manila on December 24, and two days after their departure, the Japanese landed on Luzon. Overwhelmed by the well-equipped and trained Japanese invaders, the Philippine Army fell back and General MacArthur ordered the defenders to withdraw to the rugged peninsula of Bataan. Manila was declared an open city to spare its destruction. Walter Edmonds wrote, "No word of explanation was given except that Manila was to be an open city. . . . The greatest haste (amounting to a rout) and speed were urged. You couldn't take any more luggage and equipment than you could carry and no specific things were designated to be taken."[23]

A convoy of thirty buses carrying twenty-five American and twenty-five Filipina nurses left Manila around 0600 the day before Christmas. Among the first to reach the new hospital site at Limay was Dr. Alfred Weinstein, who recalled the trip to Bataan: "The jungle on our right grew thicker and more confining with its huge, vine-covered, spreading trees and matted underbrush. . . . Round eyed children stared at us as we turned the car sharply down a winding dirt road heading toward the beach and our new home."

Despite the availability of water and medical equipment, flush toilets, and cool breezes from the ocean, Dr. Weinstein thought Limay was a "lousy" setup. Nonetheless, General Hospital No. 1, commanded by Lt. Col. James Duckworth, served the U.S. Army for six weeks and accepted 1,200 battle casualties in need of surgery. The crowded operating room, with its eight tables, took only major casualties. The remainder, some of which would have been considered major wound cases in civilian practice, were attended by Lt. Willie Perliman and Lt. Jack Gordon, who repaired any wounds that could be handled with only Novocain anesthesia—everything from jagged flesh wounds to amputated fingers and toes. Serving with the medical officers at hospital No. 1's two sites, Limay and Little Baguio, were Lieutenant Nesbit, twenty-five army nurses, twenty-five Filipina nurses, and Lt. Anne Bernatitis of the Navy Nurse Corps. The nurses at

Little Baguio quickly discarded their blue uniforms, which were the same color as the Japanese uniforms, and donned Army Air Corps coveralls, shirts, and shoes.[24]

Back in Manila, those nurses and civilians not evacuated with the U.S. Army tried to celebrate Christmas amid the largest Japanese air raids to date. Tressa Cates, a civilian nurse, wrote in her diary, "The Filipinos have named this day well, Black Christmas. Apparently the Japanese were not guided by international law and ethics. Open City meant nothing to them. They raided the city six times today and four times yesterday. The patients in my ward ate their Christmas dinner under their beds when the bombs started to drop all around us."[25]

Over at Sternberg, the remaining Army nurses tried to celebrate Christmas and to open holiday gifts, among them an order to prepare to evacuate Manila come nightfall. Before midnight, twenty nurses and other personnel sailed on the harbor boat *McHyde* across the bay to Corregidor. At 0700 the next day the boat went through the minefield to Limay on Bataan peninsula, where the party went ashore to set up nursing activities at General Hospital No. 2.

These nurses, who called themselves the "Original 19," were given an immediate introduction to wartime field nursing by a Japanese bomber that flew overhead, forcing them to take cover in nearby trenches. Later that day, the nurses went to the Twelfth Medical Regiment's camp, where they spent the day in foxholes and the night on cots beneath huge mango trees.

Fortified by a breakfast of hot cakes at the Twelfth's field kitchen, the women played hide and seek with enemy bombers all day and were finally transported to the Philippine Medical Supply Depot, where "their big treat was a cleansing bath that evening out in the middle of a winding creek."[26]

Acting under Chief Nurse Clara Mueller's supervision, the nurses set up a mess and made beds. Mary L. Moultrie, who arrived at Limay in late December, described her first impressions of the hospital set up: "There was no medicine, not even a thermometer, and . . . no record of the patients' names. With the help of two of these patients, an American and a Filipino, we made a record of all the patients. When the ward officer was assigned, he and I, with the help of our up-patients began to gather supplies." The surgery, a mess, and four wards were in operation by January 1, when Chief Nurse Josephine Nesbit, American Red Cross worker Catherine Nau, and five medical and two medical corps officers arrived from Corregidor. Vivian Weisblatt, a civilian, also joined the group on New Year's Day as a dietitian. Other civilian women quickly joined No. 2 hospital and offered their assistance wherever needed: doing laundry in three-gallon pails, serving meals to patients, or doing clerical work. 1st Lt. Brunetta Kuehlthau, a physiotherapist, recalled that when she arrived at No. 2 there were about 4,000 patients. "The hospital," she remembers, "was all open and the cooking and serving of food was almost all done out in the open under the trees." Trying to cook and sreve outdoors without screens to keep out the flies, she said, "created some real sanitation problems."[27]

By New Year's Day 1942, Manila had been evacuated of all nurses. Lieutenant MacDonald and her party arrived on Corregidor on December 30. The previous day the hospital had been bombed, despite its clear Red Cross markings, and continuous raids had damaged most of the barracks, officers' quarters, and hospital. Fortunately, most the hospital's patients had already been moved into the Malinta Tunnel hospital. As one PT boat officer later wrote, "That beautiful modern one-thousand bed hospital had been abandoned. There it was, I don't know how much it had cost, as useless to us as a Buddhist monastery."[28]

Florence MacDonald, on duty in the Malinta Tunnel hospital, recalled caring for victims of enemy air attacks: "The casualties were brought into the hospital at night. The wounds, all of which were from artillery or bomb missiles, were quite severe. . . . many of the wounded were pretty badly mangled." All of them, she felt, were adequately cared for in the tunnel; "In fact care that was equal to that in a well-administered general hospital." Malinta Tunnel hospital had enough dressings and sufficient sulfa drugs to prevent many cases of infection. Although water was plentiful, the hospital laundry, done by soldiers by hand, was an ongoing concern.[29]

While the hospital on Corregidor handled an increasing number of air-raid victims, the two field hospitals on Bataan tried to cope with a flood of casualties from the incessant fighting on that mountainous peninsula. The wounded were first sent to General Hospital No. 1 and then evacuated further back to No. 2. As the patient load at No. 2 increased and the front lines grew closer, nurses were transferred from No. 1 to the hospital on Cacloban. On January 23, 1942, two Filipina nurses and thirteen U.S. Army nurses joined the eleven nurses who had gone to Cacloban on January 19.

Dr. Alfred Weinstein vividly recalls those hectic weeks at Limay when hundreds of wounded poured into his hospital by ambulance, bus, and truck: "Exhausted by days of combat, racked with malaria, dehydrated by tropical heat, blood oozing from massive wounds, they flooded the operating tables and littered the floor."[30]

When the Japanese pressed too close to Limay, the staff "spent two frantic days slapping plaster on the fracture cases to make them transportable" and pulled back to Little Baguio near the ammunition and quartermaster depots. Baguio was a "cool, wind-swept" compound several thousand feet above sea level and a mile inland. Here Lt. Claude Froley's crew built an admitting office and sheds to expand the hospital's capacity to 1,000 beds. The nurses' quarters were in a rambling wooden structure in which electricity and plumbing were installed.

When a lull in the fighting developed, some of the officers and nurses at Little Baguio slipped off for picnics of carabao sandwiches and a drink made from limes. The sandy, white beaches near the compound were protected by barbed wire and razor-edged bamboo poles pointing seaward. Offshore, PT boats stood at anchor, but the nurses and doctors swam or floated in Manila Bay oblivious for the moment of the war all around them.

Dr. Weinstein also remembered the budding romances of that period on Bataan: "Romance under these circumstances had an intensity and overpowering quality never experienced in leisurely peacetime life." At least one romance culminated in a wedding, when Capt. Garret P. Francis, DC, and 2d Lt. Earleen Allen, ANC, were married in a field on January 3, 1942.

Little Baguio was even the site of a maternity "ward" when the Chinese wife of a civilian employee gave birth to a baby girl, who was named Victoria Bataana. "She slept in a rataan bassinet made by a Filipino and the nurses scrounged materials and made her a wardrobe." Little Victoria was the darling of the hospital, and her trips from the nursery to her mother at feeding time became the highlight of everyone's day as "medical officers and nurses vied for the privilege of taking her to her mother and patients who could sit up to gaze at her and those who couldn't move demanded to see her, while wistful eyes and soft clucking noises followed her as she passed by." The entire hospital camp "felt lonely and let down" when the baby's mother took her deeper into the jungle to safety. Sadly, the nurses learned after the war that Victoria had died soon after the surrender.[31]

Victoria Bataana had been a bit of hope amid an increasingly discouraging situation, but the nurses and doctors at the hospital also found time to hold a dance in the officers' mess, using an old phonograph and vintage 1920s records for music. For the occasion, the nurses exchanged their khakis for "finery and depleted their cache of makeup and perfume." It was a memorable night, a time to be happy and forget that "death was closing in on all sides."

In sharp contrast, Dorothy Engel remembered the atmosphere of danger that pervaded hospital No. 2: "Little did I dream that I would soon be trying to care for patients on beds set up in the middle of a sandy river bed, that snakes would hang down from the bamboo and mango trees that sheltered us from Japanese bombing. . . that we would always be hungry, always frightened."

The food situation on Bataan soon became critical because, as Lieutenant Kuehlthau told an interviewer, Bataan was "a very barren country" where nothing grew, forcing the army to bring in all food supplies. Soon their diet became "monotonous—rice, salmon, sardines, bread, native peas occasionally, oatmeal with weevils in it, and tea. No butter, no coffee, coarse brown sugar. Only rice pudding and bread pudding for desert, and they didn't have any raisins in them." These food shortages were partly attributable to the fact that the U.S. Army had about 150 days' stock from Manila for fifty to sixty thousand men, but no one had anticipated the mass of civilians who fled to Bataan. The Japanese knew their humanitarian enemy would feed these refugees with food stocks barely sufficient for the army alone. Consequently, in January 1942 American troops went on two-thirds rations, with rice as the foundation of their diet. Bread was baked in jungle bakeries until the flour ran out. Eventually, when rations grew short they rounded up and slaughtered the carabao and horses for meat. Ruby Motley noted, "The boys in the kitchen did a marvelous job, considering what they had to work with. Our equipment, I believe, was the poorest in the world. The equipment we used most was a 50-gallon oil can with the top cut off; this was placed over the fire pit, and in it we cooked the rice that was our main food."[32]

In Bataan's hospitals, the most seriously ill patients received some milk, meat, liver, and vitamins, but the rest of the patients and staff subsisted on fewer rations. Dr. Weinstein lost twenty-five pounds in three months from exertion and the lack of food and sleep. He says that was the average weight loss for hospital personnel and admits that some of the nurses lost more than twenty-five pounds. The effect of poor rations on the soldiers was devastating. As the calorie intake declined from 2,000 calories per day in February to 1,000 in March, the men fell victim to beriberi, night blindness, swelling, dysentery, diarrhea, and malaria. The two hospitals on Bataan were flooded with sick G.I.s, until No. 2 hospital had 7,000 patients and No. 1 another 2,000. To handle the increasing patient load, doctors and nurses were brought over from Corregidor, but the American nurses never numbered more than seventy-eight with an additional five Filipino nurses.

The small number of medical personnel meant that everyone, sick or well, had to care for patients with little or no time off. Nurse Enid Hatchitt wrote, "The days and nights were an endless nightmare until it seemed we couldn't stand it any longer. Patients came in by the hundreds and the doctors and nurses worked continuously under tents amid flies and heat and dust."[33]

The Japanese did not bomb the hospital at Cacloban or Limay, but on March 29, 1942, they hit Little Baguio. Dr. Weinstein recalled that awful moment: "There was no shelter available, no time to run. We hit the dirt and waited, but not for long. The world exploded. I don't know how long we were knocked out. Bleeding from the nose and ears, drums shattered, holding on to one another, we stumbled through the dusty, smoky murk."[34]

The unprovoked bombing destroyed part of the hospital, and a direct hit blew bodies, tin roofs, and iron beds in all directions. Some of the 100 patients who were killed in the bombing were mangled beyond recognition. One body was blown into the top branches of a tree, together with blankets, pajamas, and mattresses. In addition to the 100 patients who died instantly, 150 more were wounded, including nurses Easterling, Hogan, and Palmer, and the chaplain, Father Cummings. Not even wounds, however, kept the nurses from their duties. One nurse spent that entire night watching over a surgical case who had just had shrapnel removed from his skull.

In the days that followed the Japanese attack, more enemy bombers raided Bataan. Although his staff felt that the bombing of the hospitals was deliberate, Lt. Col. James Duckworth argued that it was an accident, "poor bombing on the part of the Japanese," who surely could have destroyed the hospital during the two-month period prior to March 29 if they had wanted to do so. Easter Sunday services were interrupted several times by air raids. By then the Japanese had broken through the defense line on the bay side and were forcing weary American and Filipino troops to retreat.[35] At Little Baguio hospital, mud-stained casualties poured in with conflicting reports and rumors. Finally, at eight o'clock, the nurses were ordered to report to headquarters. Two trucks arrived to collect them and the officer briskly said, "O.K., girls. Orders for you to go to Corregidor on the double. The tug is waiting at Mariveles. Take only what you can grab. No more than a suitcase apiece. Make it snappy. Don't know when the Nips are coming down the road."[36]

Making hasty, tearful farewells, the group of fifty-three Army nurses, twenty-six Filipino nurses, one dietitian, one civilian, a physio-therapist, a Red Cross worker, and five civilian women boarded buses, trucks, and ambulances for Mariveles. Behind at Little Baguio, they left Dr. Weinstein and most of the hospital staff, who had decided to remain with the 1,800 helpless patients.

The convoy of nurses was caught in the heavy traffic of the retreat and did not cover the fifteen miles to Mariveles before the ammunition dumps were blown up at 0200. 2d Lt. Dorothea Daley vividly described their harrowing retreat:

> Finally we got away on a truck with a sergeant in charge. We ran into a convoy of soldiers about ten miles long, all on their way to the wharf at Mariveles. Their officers had told them they were on their own and should get back to Corregidor if they could. . . . The firing kept getting closer and closer. There was shell-fire in it, going over our heads.
> The road was full of civilians and crying children who had gotten lost . . . we were stopped at one place for an hour. I was so tired I went to sleep and somebody gave me a helmet for a pillow.[37]

At six o'clock, the hour of Bataan's surrender, stragglers arrived at the dock, but found it deserted. After two anxious hours, a harbor boat appeared and started to take them on board, but suddenly a Japanese plane flew over and forced the boat to move away. After several similar delays, the nurses all embarked and the boat headed across the bay to Corregidor, dodging enemy aircraft the entire way. Three hours later, the nurses landed safely on the Rock and dashed to the tunnel.

These women were some of the fortunate 2,300 soldiers and civilians who escaped from Bataan that night. Tragically, they were but a small percentage of the total personnel on the peninsula, 79,000 of whom surrendered on Bataan and were forced to march to Camp O'Donnell and Cabanatuan prison camps.

Plucked from the nightmare of Bataan's surrender, the nurses enjoyed a brief reprieve. The hospital was located in a lateral of the 1,400-foot tunnel carved out of Malinta Hill and had wards, a laboratory, a mess, and quarters for the doctors and nurses. Toilets had been installed in the tunnel soon after Manila fell, and they were a vast improvement over the one bathroom that had served the women in the early days of tunnel life. When the 88 women from Bataan arrived, however, conditions in the tunnel became crowded, but two more laterals were taken over and engineers welded together beds in tiers so each woman at least had her own bed. This was essential for the newly arrived nurses, who were exhausted and ill after the strain of the past few weeks.

Life in Malinta Tunnel was fairly amenable in the beginning. Clarke Lee recalled, "For the first few weeks there was still some of the minor pleasures of peacetime life in a big army garrison—a little ice cream or a bottle of Coca-Cola; but they soon became major luxuries and then disappeared altogether." Corregidor went on half rations on January 5, 1942, and then on three-eights rations on March 1. The average soldier on Corregidor described "good chow" then as a piece of bread, a slice of corned beef, a cup of tea, and rice for supper.

The Japanese began shelling Corregidor from Bataan. A single day's gun-fire "did more damage than all the bombings put together," wrote Col. Stephen Melnik. The casualties were not heavy, but they came into the hospital in a steady stream. Dorothy Engel later recalled, "We found that the chief danger was not from shells or bombs but from being knocked down and mashed trying to get back into the tunnel during raids. The air inside was thick with disinfectant and anesthetics and there were too many people. Several times the power plant supplying the tunnel was hit and the electricity was off for hours. It was pretty ghastly in there, feeling the shock of the detonations and never knowing when we would be in total darkness."

Perhaps the worst incident for the nurses occurred on April 24, when a Japanese 240 mm shell exploded without warning amid a group of men outside the tunnel's west portal. As soon as the doors could be opened, litter bearers rushed to aid the wounded. Juanita Redmond wrote, "I wish I would forget those endless, harrowing hours. Hours of giving injections, anesthetizing, ripping off clothes, stitching gaping wounds, of amputations, sterilizing instruments, settling the treated patients in their beds, covering the wounded we could not save. I had still not grown accustomed to seeing people torn and bleeding and dying in numbers like these.[38]

Five days after this tragic incident, the enemy plastered Corregidor with more than 10,000 shells—a celebration of the emperor's birthday. By then General Wainwright was "determined to get as many nurses away from Corregidor as was humanly possible" and he decided to send them off in two Consolidated Catalina flying boats (PBYs). Rumor had it that ill nurses would be flown out, but "able-bodied nurses were sent and the ailing ones who should have gone remained." The nurses chosen to fly off the island felt guilty about abandoning their friends. One nurse, Anne Wurts, refused to go and urged an ill nurse to take her place. This was not allowed and PBY 1 took off with ten officers, ten nurses, and three civilian women. PBY 7 left the Rock around midnight, with ten officers, nine nurses, three women, one soldier, and a priest. Mary Lohr recalls the flight: "We started at midnight. All we were allowed to carry with us were our musette bags filled with toilet articles and a few personnel possessions. At the controls of our plane was Lt. Deatty, a Navy flier. He has since been killed in action."

The flying boats made Lake Lanao on Mindanao safely and were hidden in a cove and covered with branches to prevent Japanese reconnaissance planes from spotting them. After a special breakfast of real scrambled eggs and champagne brought from the Dansalan Hotel, the party waited for the safety of sundown, when they would take off on the final leg to Australia.

When the sun finally set, the first of the two PBYs began taxiing into take-off position, but it suddenly hit a coral reef, which tore a hole in the plane's hull. In a frantic effort to patch the tear, the nurses on board placed blankets over the gash, but to no avail. Water poured into the flying plane's hull and it had to be beached.[39]

Heartsick, the passengers headed for the nearby U.S. Army base to await the Japanese invasion. Two weeks later, they were captured when the enemy seized Mindanao. The second PBY, however, was able to lift off the lake despite its heavy load, which included two army stowaways hiding in the tail. Florence MacDonald remembers their dramatic take-off: "We made four attempts to take off the lake and had to empty our bags and throw away everything that we could to lighten it." Their seventeen-hour flight to Darwin also had its anxious moments: "After we had flown about an hour the soldier with the earphones reported to the pilot that an airplane was following us. Immediately the pilot guided the plane higher and higher. Inside an hour we had lost the plane that was following us. We flew all night over enemy territory. During the trip one of the engines functioned very badly and finally ceased to operate. Early in the morning we landed in Port Darwin."[40]

Meanwhile, back on Corregidor the Japanese were stepping up their attack with round-the-clock bombing and shelling. "Nerves were getting jittery. There were short periods when dynamos would cease working and there was total and utter blackness. The air in the tunnel was still as death, hot, and damp. Nearly everyone had impetigo, some on their faces, some all over their body. The water supply was scarce and frequently there would be none for hours at a time."

According to Maude Williams, a former Army nurse who had resigned before the war broke out but was in Manila with her husband in December 1941, many of the soldiers in the tunnel spent their last days of freedom playing bridge, rummy, and poker, gambling their accumulated pay. Realizing the end was near, the defenders clung to little things: "The smallest and most simple pleasures became increasingly rare and dangerous—an uninterrupted cigarette, a stolen biscuit, a good night's sleep in the open air."[41]

The last nurses to be evacuated from Corregidor left on the night of May

3, 1942, by submarine. The USS *Spearfish,* which had entered Manila Bay by eluding a Japanese destroyer and minesweeper, was the only means of escape for those left on the Rock. General Wainwright saw the group of women off at the dock. It was a hurried departure with no fanfare, for as Helen Summers wrote later, "words didn't count." Those remaining on Corregidor awaited almost certain captivity, yet Chief Nurse Annie Mealer, who Wainwright had specifically named to leave on the submarine, refused to go. "I consider—and still consider—this a truly great act of heroism," wrote General Wainwright.[42]

Twelve Army and Navy officers, eleven Army nurses, one Navy nurse, and one Navy wife were taken off the Rock by boat to the waiting submarine. The *Spearfish*'s skipper, Lt. James C. Dempsey, was taken aback by the sight of the thirteen women, but he regained his composure quickly and tried to hurry the loading of passengers and seventeen footlockers of financial records. The sub crew passed out candy and cigarettes to the boat crew and then *Spearfish* shoved off into the bay and submerged.

Less than two days later, the Japanese landed at Monkey Point on Corregidor. Despite a determined defense, some 600 Japanese soldiers managed to gain a foothold on the island. In the early hours of May 6, 1942, a force of 500 untrained sailors crawled out of Malinta Tunnel in a last ditch-effort to stop the enemy invaders. With raw courage, they pushed the attackers back, but when daylight came and Japanese artillery opened fire, the moment of truth was at hand. General Wainwright knew the cause was lost and feared Japanese tanks might attack the helpless inhabitants of Malinta Tunnel. With a heavy heart, he ordered the Rock to surrender. At noon on May 6, 1942, the white flag was hoisted up the flagpole.

Inside the tunnel, soldiers and 106 remaining women waited anxiously. The Japanese captors had raped and murdered British nurses in Hong Kong on Christmas Eve 1941, and the women on Corregidor had every reason to be terrified. To their immense relief, however, the first Japanese to appear were officers with swords. "They were orderly, though curious about everything." At first only Japanese medical officers were allowed to enter the hospital laterals where patient care went on unabated. Initially, the nurses were not permitted outside the tunnel, and for six weeks their life was a monotonous, secluded one, caring for over 1,000 patients and existing on two inadequate meals a day. Finally, on June 24, 1942, the Japanese ordered the nurses and patients to move to the old Middleside Hospital, which had been hastily repaired. There were no mosquito nets for the beds and everyone was plagued by the insects until the girls could sew netting from gauze, but at least they were out of the tunnel.[43]

By the time the order came to move to Manila, many of the nurses had fallen ill with fever and some could barely walk. The trip began on July 2, 1942, a "hot, sticky morning." "It took the Japs hours to get anything done always. After sitting in the sun a long time everyone had to climb a ladder with countless steps to board the upper deck of the old freighter. It as an exhausting climb in their undernourished, weakened condition," recalled Josephine Nesbit.

The freighter moved across the bay and docked at Manila, where the Filipina women were taken to Bilibad Military Prison and the American women to a Catholic girls school across the street from Santo Tomas University and then, on August 24, to Santo Tomas Internment Camp, where they had their first decent meal in months. Nesbit says, "The fresh pineapple was the first fresh fruit they had eaten since the war began."[44]

At Santo Tomas Prison, the arrival of the nurses from Corregidor caused a stir among the other nurses and 4,000 civilian internees. "We crowded around to greet them," wrote Tressa Cates, a civilian nurse from Sternberg Hospital, "and many others pushed forward to inquire about relatives who had fought at Bataan and Corregidor." The Japanese refused to allow the prisoners to communicate with the new arrivals, but Tressa managed to locate six of them in the bathroom. "Jinny appeared ill and she was naturally worried about her wounded and captured husband. Zest, another one of my friends, was thin and unusually nervous. How good it was to see them."[45]

The Corregidor nurses were quickly initiated into life at Santo Tomas Prison, which was located in the old Santo Tomas University. In the absence of dormitories, prisoners were housed in former classrooms, which were very noisy and overcrowded. Marie Adams said that forty women shared her room and slept on cots barely six inches apart. The internees were kept in the camp and not allowed to leave without permission, but as Lt. Brunetta Kuehlthau said, "I saw no evidence of abuse of the internees by the Japanese" and explained that only members of the committee that ran the camp dealt directly with their captors. The Japanese gave passes to internees who lived in Manila to visit their families and allowed nurses who needed treatment to go to the Philippine General Hospital.

At first the food at Santo Tomas was "fairly good" because they were able to obtain supplies from the outside, including wheat from a Red Cross ship, *The Gripsolm,* interned in the harbor. "When we finally got down to the bottom of the sack, there were actually more weevils in it than cracked wheat, but we ate it, weevils and all." Only the older prisoners and children were served a noon meal, but many of the internees had managed to contact persons outside the camp and were able to buy food. The only mail the internees received came from the *Gripsolm,* which also delivered to each internee one forty-eight-pound Red Cross package consisting of powdered milk, corned beef, Spam, cheese, chocolate, cans of eggs and ham, pork, salmon, and sugar. The medical facilities at Santo Tomas consisted of a sixty-five-bed hospital housed in Santa Catalina dormitory and staffed by Dr. Charles Leach of the Rockefeller Foundation, several medical missionaries assisted by some Filipino doctors, and Army nurses under the leadership of Maj. Maude Davidson, ANC. In addition to this facility, there was a clinic in the main building and a hospital run by Navy nurses for small children. Initially, the camp obtained drugs from the Red Cross bodega or from outside sources, and for the first two years acutely ill prisoners were sent outside the camp. In a fortunate turn of events, the Japanese sent Dr. Cho-Kaito three times a week to Santo Tomas to examine internees to see who was eligible for release. As Adams recalled, the doctor had failed out of the University of the Philippines medical school and was incompetent, and was "therefore easy to 'fix' so that many of the internees got out on trumped-up diagnoses." Santo Tomas camp also had a blood-donor service administered by Adams.[46]

In May 1943, the Japanese sent a group of 800 American prisoners, all young males except for twelve Navy nurses, to a new camp at Los Banos in the hills about forty miles from Manila. When they arrived at Los Banos on May 16, 1943, they learned that the water supply was contaminated and they were temporarily housed in a gymnasium with only four toilets for 800 men. Despite its beautiful setting, Los Banos was no resort—even the healthy young male prisoners expected a difficult internment.[47]

Although conditions at Santo Tomas were far from ideal during the first two years, they deteriorated rapidly when the Japanese military took over control of the camp in February 1944. Instead of "fairly decent" Japanese civilian administrators, Santo Tomas now came under strict military control. Communication with the outside was forbidden, the ration was cut, newspapers banned, and all canteens, restaurants, and shops were closed. From five-minute broadcasts each day picked up on a hidden radio, the internees kept informed of the progress of the war, but often the news was distorted in the retelling. "By the time the news reached me, it had become so mixed and garbled with rumors that it was hard to know exactly what was and what wasn't the truth," Marie Adams said. Naturally the camp officials disapproved of the radio. Adams recalls, "The Japs knew we had it but were never able to locate it." One night, in a desperate effort to find the radio's location, the Japanese guards roused everyone from sleep and searched the entire camp, all eight buildings and 600 shanties. To no avail! The secret radio remained hidden in a coffee can until Santo Tomas was liberated by American forces.[48]

By far the most distressing effect of military control of Santo Tomas was the decreasing food ration. Lt. Brunetta Kuehlthau, working in the main hospital kitchen, recalls: "The Japs took over our 'bodega' or storehouse, with all our reserve food supplies—mostly rice—in it. Then they began to issue the supplies to us in small amounts, as they saw fit." Almost immediately the Japanese cut the internees' meat ration down to the point where the only way the cooks could use it was as flavoring. Kuehlthau says they were also forced to stop serving a noon meal, but she continued to offer "soup, or some other nourishing dish at noon, at least to the hospital patients." As the ration allowance was drastically cut, lengthy debate ensued among the internees about who should receive extra rations. It was decided that some internees responsible for heavy work, such as those who worked on garbage details, in the camp garden, or on electrical crews, should receive extra food.

"The ration allowance declined to a point where it was deficient in minerals, vitamins, and especially in proteins," Lieutenant Kuehlthau said. According to Marie Adams, the ration provided a daily average intake of 1,300 calories in 1944, which fell as low as 800 in November and December, and to 680 during their last month of captivity. She recalls: "For about eight months we had no meat of any kind, just rice and corn, and no fat, except in the form of soy beans, which they gave us toward the end. Part of the time we were allowed to buy carabo milk, in very limited quantities." The internees were also given permission to buy coconuts, from which they extracted the milk. "All cats and dogs in the camp were eaten. Major Bloom ate his guinea pigs," Adams reported. Toward the end of their captivity, meals, if there was firewood, consisted basically of very thin mush and a cup of hot water for breakfast. The Japanese cut off their charcoal supply and the internees chopped up beds, chairs, benches, and anything that would burn. Lunch was soft rice with hot water and boiled greens, and their evening meal was mush or perhaps camotes, a sort of native sweet potato, and boiled greens. Occasionally they served a kind of stew made from what was left of the Red Cross meat-and-vegetable ration. Sometimes the Japanese gave them fish, a small, salted minnow-type fish that the men called "guts and eyes." By January 1945 the average male internee had lost fifty-one pounds and the average woman thirty-two pounds. As one might expect, the number of deaths rose in late 1944 and so did the number of cases of edema and anemia. The starvation diets also brought new cases of tuberculosis and the first epidemics—measles, whooping cough, and bacillary dysentery.[49]

Bruentta Kuehlthau recalled, "Everytime there was an American victory in the Pacific area, the Japs would cut our rations again." Protests were in vain; Kuehlthau remembers, "One of our doctors was thrown in jail because he wrote, 'malnutrition and starvation' as the cause of death on some of the certificates and refused to change it even when the Japs insisted." The reduced ration was not a result of deprivation among the Japanese occupation forces, for Tressa Cates wrote in her diary on October 12, 1944: "We continued to lose weight at an alarming rate. Verbal and written protests from both the medical and executive committee regarding our starvation were ignored by the Japanese. The Commandant repeatedly reminded our leaders that we were on the same rations as Japanese soldiers. We had only to look at the Japanese soldiers garrisoned in camp to learn that this was a lie. All the soldiers in camp were as fat as butterballs."[50]

The new stringent rules and the decreasing supply of food caused considerable tension among the internees, but they did not result in as many mental breakdowns as medical personnel had feared. There were only four or five attempted suicides, but none was directly attributable to camp conditions. Internees at Santo Tomas were treated reasonably well compared to prisoners in other enemy camps. "I was never physically abused by the Japs," Brunetta Kuehlthau said. However, she recalled that on Corregidor, after their surrender, the Japanese "ran through our quarters at all hours" and stole wristwatches, pens, and other personal possessions. Lieutenant Kuehlthau said she had to bow to the Japanese and as head of the kitchen had to stand at attention through staff meetings with her captors. She also recalls, "We witnessed some punishments, such as slappings, of the internees at Santo Tomas for minor offenses; most of the serious punishments were inflicted outside the camp limits." Kuehlthau said some internees "were taken out of the camp for questioning and never returned" and she personally witnessed the Japanese seize a man who had received a bag of food thrown over the camp wall by some friendly Filipinos. The internee and two others were taken out of camp and when they returned "it was evident he had been severely punished. They had to be hospitalized for some time."

That more deaths did not occur at Santo Tomas was largely attributable to the medical and nursing staff, and to a large supply of drugs and medicine sent in by the Red Cross. The camp medical board set up a control system that rationed the drugs and blood plasma so that even in February 1945 Santo Tomas still had plasma on hand, although the supplies of ascorbic acid, nicotinic acid, and liver extract were exhausted.

Fortunately, by early 1945, liberation was near at hand. The first Allied land-based planes had been sighted over the camp in December 1944 and "early in January we heard the news of the landings at Lingayen, and we knew that the time of liberation was almost there. However, we were dying at such a rate that we were afraid our troops might not find us alive. There were twenty-three deaths in December and thirty-two in January. More and more internees were becoming acutely ill with beriberi, pellagra, and just plain starvation," wrote Marie Adams. Most of the internees were suffering from boils, tropical ulcers, or other infections, and "everyone was stooped with fatigue." Their starvation diet caused considerable irritability and Adams recalled, "We were all cross, irritable, and edgy; we argued about things that were utterly insignificant. We were ready to claw each other's eyes out—over nothing at all. We were hungry, we were starved." To this was added the lack of water, which meant that laundry could not be done: "Consequently a patient would sometimes have to lie on the same sheet for a week. The situation in the hospital was horrible. The wards were in an awful condition." The sanitary facilities at Santo Tomas were by then almost nonexistent. For example, in Adams's building, low water pressure meant there were no facilities on the second and third floors, and 1,800 women shared five toilets, but usually only two were operative.[51]

Liberation could not come soon enough. Adams, who weighed only 95 pounds by then, wrote in her report after the liberation, "If we had not been liberated when we were, I believe that the majority of the internees would have been dead within three or four weeks. Considering the amount of work I was doing and the amount of food I was eating, I think that I would probably have lived only another four or five days." To his credit, Gen. Douglas MacArthur was anxious for Allied forces to reach the prisoner-of-war camps and ordered General Krueger's First Cavalry and Thirty-seventh Infantry Division to advance as rapidly as possible toward Manila. Racing toward Santo Tomas at fifty miles an hour, American troops reached the prison camp on the afternoon of February 3, 1945. They were preceded by six bombers that flew very low over the camp and dropped a note that said, "Roll out the barrel. Christmas will be either today or tomorrow." In her diary Tressa Cates wrote: "We suddenly heard the rumble of heavy tanks outside the camp. It was followed by wild cheering and shouting coming from thousands of throats. . . . We watched, we prayed, and listened trembling with excitement. We dared not believe. Not just yet. We had been fooled so many times."

Brunetta Kuehlthau recalled, "Then we noticed a strong light, like a searchlight, at the gate, and someone came running into our room crying, 'There's an American tank at the gate!' We just couldn't believe it." She said the soldiers moved slowly and cautiously for they had no idea where the internees or their Japanese guards were located. Another recalled, "We saw soldiers, tall and bronzed, in peculiar looking uniforms, walking between them on the sides of the tanks. Some of us were dubious they were Americans. Not until we saw the American flag draped over the lead tank did we really believe that, at last, the realization of a beautiful dream had materialized. When we saw the lovely Stars and Stripes our throats constricted and our eyes were blinded by tears."[52]

After thirty-three months of captivity the 3,700 internees at Santo Tomas were free. About 2,300 of them were American, another 800 were British and a few other nationalities. Sixty-six army and several civilian nurses joined in the celebration, embracing the American soldiers of the First Cavalry. Recalled one survivor, "Those American soldiers looked like angels despite the fact their language did not originate in heaven and their wings were tanks. We were too stunned to move. The campus was filled with shouting, cheering, internees mixed with soldiers—the joy and happiness on their faces indescribable." Their joy, however, was short lived: the Japanese had made the camp into an arsenal and fighting broke out. The nurses returned to their patients at the hospital, which had received several direct hits. "To see the torn bodies of people who had waited for this day for so long, only to die or be maimed when their freedom was so close, was almost unbearable," one nurse remembers. The liberation of Manila took weeks, and the liberated nurses worked alongside nurses and medical officers who had arrived from Leyte to assist with the wounded. On February 12, however, seventy-one of the newly freed nurses, a physical therapist, a Red Cross representative (Marie Adams), and one hospital dietitian were flown out of Manila on a C-46. After a stop at Tacloban Airfield to rest, the women were issued new tropical slacks and shorts, fed, and interviewed—and fed again![53]

The other prisoner-of-war camp at Los Banos, however, was still behind Japanese lines, so a special task force was sent to liberate the 2,147 prisoners, Lt. Cdr. Laura Cobb and ten Navy nurses interned there. With only slight losses, American glider and parachute forces dropped in near Los Banos on February 23 and linked up with support troops landing on nearby beaches. They annihilated the Japanese garrison and told the bewildered prisoners to hurriedly pack up two bags of possessions and make their way to waiting amtracs that would take them to the beach and evacuation. Navy nurse Mary Rose Harrington recalled that on the beach they dressed the wounds of a couple of paratroopers. Another nurse said, "Our rescuers showered us with K rations, their cherished chocolate bars, cigarettes, and anything and everything they had. We warned them not to turn over anything they couldn't spare, we had three-year-old appetites."

The first Army nurse to reach the prisoners, Dorothea Davis, wrote, "I was shocked to see the condition everyone was in. The internment camp had been on a starvation diet for more than six months. For three years they had not received adequate food either in variety or quantity, but during the last six months the diet was cut down to practically nothing. The internees were actually dying of starvation."[54]

Meanwhile, in Leyte, the liberated nurses from Santo Tomas were enjoying their new summer uniforms: "We had never worn this ANC uniform before. We strutted and primped, bemoaning our loss of weight and our confusion with the numerous insignia. For three years we had worn the same shirts and skirts, made by the quartermaster on the Rock, . . . but our interest in clothes was stimulated mighty rapidly." Before flying back to the United States, the nurses were awarded the Bronze Star and promoted one grade higher in rank. Sequestered in prison from the world for three years, they left for home and as one liberated nurse wrote: "We have so much to catch up with—to learn—new strides in the fields of medicine and nursing, new techniques which leave us bewildered. The discovery of the new drug, penicillin, and its results amaze us. We have so much ahead of us, so much to see and hear, we are so eager to live again."[55]

3

Across the Pacific

Nursing in the Central Pacific and Southwest Pacific Area

 With the exception of American nurses already stationed in the Philippines, Guam, or Hawaii in 1941, the first American servicewomen to be sent to the Pacific theater during World War II were U.S. Army nurses. They accompanied Army hospital units assigned to the Pacific to care for the first American troops sent to that theater. The early months of 1942 were dark days for the United States and its allies. Combined Japanese land and naval forces had decimated the Asiatic Fleet, captured the British bastion of Singapore, and by March 1942 were poised to strike at Darwin, Australia. They had seized America's island outpost of Wake, were fortifying their airfield at Rabaul, and planning operations to occupy the Solomon Islands.[1]

American strategy in the opening months of the Pacific war focused on protecting the vital lifeline from Hawaii to Australia by securing a chain of islands in the South Pacific. Despite the fact that Australia was at least a month's voyage by sea from the United States and that the poorly equipped U.S. Army was barely prepared to defend the United States, Hawaii, and the Panama Canal Zone, the U.S. Forty-first and Thirty-second Infantry Divisions were rushed to the Southwest Pacific in March and April 1942 . In addition, an Army task force of division size was despatched to New Caledonia, where it arrived in February. Lying 500 miles east of Australia, New Caledonia was to form the western anchor in a chain of bases stretching from the American west coast to the southwest Pacific.

Discovered in 1774 by Captain Cook, the islands of New Caledonia had been French territory since the mid-nineteenth century and in 1942 still retained a French flavor. New Caledonia proved an ideal base for Allied forces, with a large protected anchorage at Noumea and a sunny, mild, subtropical climate. U.S. Navy construction battalions arrived in early 1942 to prepare the islands for American air and ground forces by building roads and airstrips, erecting quarters and warehouses, and establishing water and electrical services on the island.[2]

With the arrival of American troops came the first Army hospitals, the Twenty-seventh and 109th Station Hospitals, Ninth General Hospital, and Fifty-second Evacuation Hospital. These early arrivals were the pioneers, but they represent only the first nurse complement of one evacuation, seven station, and two general hospitals assigned to New Caledonia, which would become the nerve center in the South Pacific area. The islands were the first to receive American Army nurses, and more U.S. Army nurses served on or staged through New Caledonia than through any of the other islands of the South Pacific command.

The islands' first contingent of nurses arrived at Noumea on March 11, 1942, in a convoy from the States. The group included thirty nurses of the Ninth Station Hospital with 1st Lt. Minnie Newell as chief nurse, thirty nurses from the Tenth S.H. under 2d Lt. Mary T. Johnson, and fifty-two women of the Fifty-second Evacuation Hospital led by 1st Lt. Frances E. McClelland. They had departed from the United States without tropical uniforms, but were able to buy suitable lightweight material during a stop at Panama en route to the Pacific. At their next stop, Bora-Bora, the nurses were permitted ashore to sightsee and stretch their legs. Here they found they could trade a piece of lingerie for a bunch of fresh bananas, a welcome addition to their monotonous shipboard diet. While their ship was anchored off Bora-Bora, a sudden rainstorm provided nurses with abundant soft water for bathing and laundry after several weeks of their being confined to using the transport's limited saltwater supply.[3]

Before arriving at their final destination, the convoy docked in Australia, where the nurses broke the routine of shipboard meals with "Big steaks, candy, ice cream soda, and yes, tea." After a short voyage to Noumea, the group left the transport by barge, decked out in their best white hospital uniforms, blue capes, and overseas caps, but to their chagrin no official greeted them on the dock. The only welcoming party was a group of curious local citizens, "their only apparel a sort of gay colorful pair of shorts and flowers in their bleached hair."

Without orders or directions to their billets, the nurses could only settle down on the wharf and wait. In time an Army major arrived to take them to their temporary quarters, which he warned them "wouldn't be much." The group marched off through the town carrying their suitcases and were directed through a gate marked "Home for Wayward Girls." The building was an orphanage next to the French Colonial Hospital in Noumea. Here the newly arrived nurses spent a cold, uncomfortable night on the second floor. Without orders to open their one can of rations, the nurses obediently did without supper and the next day went into Noumea in search of food. The stores were closed, but the women finally got into a U.S. Army mess line using mess kits borrowed from some soldiers. It was their first meal in twenty-four hours! Although their introduction to New Caledonia had been less than encouraging, the nursing report said, "On Sunday we marched to church with a military escort. That was fun!" Three days later, the staff of the 109th Station Hospital opened an American hospital on the orphanage's first floor, and gradually, the other units moved into their sites outside Noumea. Some of the hospitals moved several times.[4]

The nurses and the men of the medical corps assigned to New Caledonia in early 1942 were "pioneers." They lived in tents and battled the mud and insects while they listened to the roar of bulldozers and the ring of hammers as permanent housing was constructed. Eventually, with the addition of the Eighth and Twenty-ninth General Hospitals, and the 331, 332, 336, and Thirty-first Station Hospitals, New Caledonia became an important convalescent center for veterans of the Pacific fighting. Here soldiers and sailors recovering from malaria and other tropical diseases, as well as from combat wounds, could convalesce in cool, comfortable hospitals overlooking the Pacific. On this beautiful island, recovering casualties could swim in the ocean or in the island's many streams, and those able to hike could explore and regain strength lost in the debilitating tropical climate of other Pacific islands.

Army nurse Dorothy Moore came to New Caledonia in November 1943 on board the SS *Noordam,* a Dutch ship, which sailed unescorted from San Francisco. The voyage took three weeks, during which the nurses occupied their time by taking French lessons in preparation for duty on a French island. In recalling the trip, Moore said, "Our ship traveled zig zag to avoid the enemy and at one time there was an alert of an enemy submarine, so the ship altered course for a time. They could only serve two meals a day, but we could buy snacks on board." The ship was "blacked out" at night and the passengers were cautioned not to throw anything overboard lest the litter alert Japanese subs to the ship's presence.[5]

Nurse Moore's hospital was situated about fifteen miles from Noumea, and the nurses were quartered in tents until buildings could be constructed. "Living was primitive during those first months, but our dormitory buildings were fairly comfortable. We scrounged for any kind of furniture besides our cots," she recalled. Another early arrival, 2d Lt. Marisha Doubassoff, wrote of her experience in New Caledonia: "It is hard to believe that the nights can be so cold when the days are so warm. Now that winter is almost gone, we'll have to face something worse than the cold—South Pacific Mosquitoes. Due to improvements, most of us now have floors in our tents. This will help when the rainy season comes back. It's a relief not to have to wade in mud knee-deep right outside our house!"[6]

Although Noumea was a small, modern city, Dorothy Moore says the natives on New Caledonia lived in "grass thatched huts. They went barefoot and wore light clothing. I remember visiting a coffee plantation. Japanese and Tonkinse people also lived on the island." For recreation the nurses had dances and parties in the officers' club and were invited to dances at other units on the island. They could swim in a river nearby and occasionally go deep-sea fishing. Limited transportation kept the nurses from doing much exploring on the island, but Moore says they could go to the northern part of the island for a few days of R and R. She remembers that their morale was good, and although the hospital was not in a combat area, they received casualties from other islands. The main difficulty for the nurses was the isolation. "We were happiest when we were extra busy," she recalled.[7]

The holidays brought additional duties for these Army nurses, who tried to make Christmas special for their patients so far from home. In 1942 they put on white uniforms for the first time since their arrival and sang Christmas carols in the wards. The soldiers declared, "They looked like Christmas angels when they appeared in a burst of glory, none of the soldiers had ever seen them in any outfit but pants and shirts with helmet and heavy shoes. That day the nurses in their whites heroically ignored the mosquitoes."

Every hospital ward tried to have a Christmas tree, and one ward found a real evergreen tree in the middle of a stream and marked it as theirs. But rival groups from other wards also had their eye on the evergreen and in desperation to save "the pathetic little tree" for the Red Cross's main Christmas party it was tagged with a sign, "This tree will not be cut down. By order of the C.O."[8]

In June 1942 more Army hospital units left the United States in a convoy for the South Pacific. The Eighteenth General, 142nd General, and troops of the Thirty-seventh Infantry Division went to New Zealand, where they arrived on June 12, 1942, but the Seventy-first Station Hospital went on to Fiji. The New Zealanders warmly welcomed the new arrivals, opening their homes to the nurses and feting both nurses and soldiers with dances and parties. In Auckland and Wellington, the nurses of the Thirty-ninth General served in naval hospitals until their own units could be set up. These hospitals were in spacious, airy buildings featuring the modern conveniences of hot and cold running water and bathing facilities. Nurses were housed two to a room. When off duty, they enjoyed the attractions of New Zealand's two major cities and the many opportunities for sightseeing on the spectacularly beautiful island.

Gradually, however, these Army hospital units moved from New Zealand to the island of Fiji, where the Seventy-first Station Hospital had been operating for a month. The Seventy-first's nurses, under Chief Nurse 2d Lt. Florence E. Judd, lived for two weeks in the ballrooms of the Grand Pacific Hotel in Suva and then moved to a former New Zealand Army hospital five miles away. Here, the nurses enjoyed what would soon become luxuries for them in the Pacific war—steam heat, sterilizers, electric stoves, and showers. Nurses lived in large, breezy rooms in two-story frame buildings surrounded by manicured green lawns and tropical flowers, which gave the hospital grounds a resortlike setting. Indeed, the island of Fiji is one of great natural beauty, with hills, forests, open grasslands, tropical palms, and wild orchids.[9]

In contrast to the fairly luxurious setting of the Seventy-first Station Hospital, the nurses of the Ninety-eighth General lived in native-type buildings with grass roofs, although the hospital wards were set up in prefabricated buildings at a site near Suva. In July, the 142d General Hospital moved 170 miles to a new hospital site near the village of Nandi on the west coast of the island. The 142d's sixty-one nurses, under Chief Nurse 1st Lt. Regina M. Donahue, worked in wards set up in a warehouse and lived in tents. A nearby river provided water for drinking and washing clothes. Daily tropical downpours made life in the field very uncomfortable until permanent quarters could be built. Fortunately, Fiji's climate is mild and never excessively hot.[10]

West of Fiji, closer to the Solomon Islands, the climate becomes warmer and more humid. Here, the New Hebrides Islands, a group of fourteen large islands and many smaller ones, provided a base for American forces supporting the planned operation against the island of Guadalcanal. The New Hebrides Islands had a reputation of "foreboding terrain, dense jungles, and ferocious islanders," and the U.S. Marines assigned to occupy the islands arrived in March 1942 with some trepidation. The Marines' first sight of Efate, the chief island of the New Hebrides group, confirmed their suspicions: Pacific rollers crashed onto coral reefs and dense tropical growth hugged the seemingly deserted shoreline. "Not a building or work of man was in sight—only dense dripping jungle," wrote Maj. Robert Heinl, Jr. But as their ship rounded the point, the Marines were pleasantly surprised to see "a harbor entrance guarded by several tiny islands and crowned by a completely unanticipated village on the heights to shoreward." The islanders who paddled out in their outriggers to greet the transport ships seemed friendly, but the Marines landed cautiously and bivouacked out of sight of the natives.

The "invasion" of Efate proved a peaceful one, as no Japanese troops were discovered, only hospitable islanders and a few Chinese and French planters and Australian traders. In the island's government office the Marines set up a hospital, which cared for wounded until the arrival of the Forty-eighth Station Hospital in late 1942.[11]

Thirty Army nurses arrived on Efate in mid-January 1943 in the middle of the hot, rainy season. Like the Marines before them, these nurses found their worst enemy was not the Japanese but the malaria-bearing mosquitoes, the stifling heat, and the ever-present mud. Army medical personnel arriving on the island of Efate found a 600-bed Navy hospital already in operation and filled with patients suffering from malaria and dysentery. At this early stage of the Pacific war, most American soldiers, unfamiliar with malaria, were less than conscientious about taking measures to prevent the disease. In addition, a shortage of antimalarial drugs and a woeful lack of construction and screening materials handicapped the malaria prevention program on Efate. In time, American personnel traced the source of the mosquito population to opened coconuts left to collect rainwater, which became breeding grounds for flies and the annoying and potentially deadly mosquitoes. When the coconuts were cleaned up and atabrine, a malarial suppressant, arrived in enough quantities to be taken daily by all nurses and personnel on Efate, the local malaria problem began to abate.[12]

Nurses on Efate lived in wooden buildings until Quonset huts could be erected, and the hospital was set up in tents with improvised equipment. As time went on, their quarters reflected a feminine touch. Curtains and rugs appeared, and the women decorated a large reception room and acquired lounge chairs, tables, a radio, and a phonograph. The nurses were also welcome at the officers' club, which had a "gorgeous view of the harbor."[13]

An even more magnificent natural harbor was to be found on the largest of the New Hebrides islands, Espiritu Santo. "Santo," as it was called by the natives, was a wild tangle of jungle, the least civilized of all the New Hebrides islands, but one with an undeniable attraction to the United States in the summer of 1942. It was only 500 miles southeast of Guadalcanal, which Adm. Ernest J. King had called the "tollgate" of the road to Tokyo. When the Japanese occupied the island of Tulagi in the Solomons in May 1942, Admiral King had ordered Commander of the South Pacific (ComSoPac) Adm. Robert Ghormley to send forces to Espiritu Santo to establish a base for Allied operations against the Solomons. The projected operation against the Japanese in the Solomon Islands was authorized for July 2, 1942, but was moved up when intelligence sources informed the Allies that the Japanese were building an airstrip on the island of Guadalcanal.

To counter this new threat, American troops were sent to Espiritu Santo to build an airfield, which they completed just nine days before U.S. Marines landed on Guadalcanal. This coral airstrip, cut from dense jungle, became the home of the Marine Fighting Squadron 212 and an indispensable field during the seesaw battle for Guadalcanal. In October 1942, Douglas Skytrooper aircraft flew gasoline into Guadalcanal from Santo, and B-17s took off from the airfield to attack Japanese ships threatening the "'Canal."

Espiritu Santo also proved invaluable when it came to caring for the casualties of the bitter combat in the Solomons, casualties who could be flown out of Henderson Field to hospitals on Santo in just three hours. At first air evacuation was done by returning transport planes of the South Pacific Combat Transport Service (SCAT) with medical corpsmen from the marines assigned to each flight. In mid-January 1943, however, an advance party of the first air evacuation squadron arrived in the South Pacific, and at the end of February 1943 flight nurses and the remaining personnel of the 801st Medical Air Evacuation Transport Squadron (MAETS) joined them. By March a group of 25 army flight nurses under Lt. Margaret A. Richey, in addition to Navy flight nurses and corpsmen, were serving with the 801st in the South Pacific. The women were based on Noumea and shared living quarters near Tontouta Air Base with nurses from the Thirty-first Station Hospital.

Navy flight nurse Mae Olson was the first nurse to fly into Guadalcanal in March. Her arrival caused quite a stir: "Officers and soldiers tripped over each other to reach the plane when word went around that a white woman had arrived. . . .

Sure enough, standing in the doorway and looking fresh as a daisy was Lieut. Mae Olson, flight nurse." Only a few months prior to her dramatic arrival on Guadalcanal, Olson had gone to an American Airlines office in Chicago and informed them that she had decided to give up her job as a stewardess to enlist in the Navy. Her arrival was quickly followed by other flight nurses. On the average, transport planes with a crew and two flight nurses made two flights per day into Guadalcanal, and additional runs when necessary. They first flew two and one-half hours to Espiritu Santo, where they awaited their flight to Guadalcanal. The First Marine Air Wing provided a waiting area, with toilet and shower facilities at the base for the nurses. From here the transport planes flew the long four-hour flight to Henderson Field, loaded wounded, and accompanied them back to Noumea.[14]

By then Espiritu Santo had three Army hospitals to care for Marines and G.I.s wounded in the Solomons campaign—the Twenty-fifth Evacuation Hospital, the Twenty-second Station Hospital, and the Thirty-first General Hospital. These hospitals were set up in former coconut groves in one-story, screened Army housing that boasted electric lights, showers, and laundry facilities. Eventually, the grounds were landscaped with tropical vegetation and flowers making them very attractive for hospital patients and personnel alike.

Duty for nurses and other medical personnel on these South Pacific isles was pleasant enough, but no "tropical" holiday—the savage fighting on Guadalcanal sent hundreds of casualties pouring into the hospitals during that fall and winter. Later, the Twenty-third Infantry or American Division sent a "staggering load" of malaria cases to the island. Fiji's milder climate made the island an ideal location for recuperating malaria cases and its hospitals housed a large number of soldiers and sailors suffering from the debilitating disease.

The first hospital to be permanently assigned to Guadalcanal, the Twentieth Station Hospital, arrived in January without its nursing complement, because the 'Canal, with air raids and Japanese snipers, still posed some very real threats, and was judged "too rough" for nurses. The Twentieth S.H. set up in a coconut grove two miles from the beach and, like the marines before them, dug plenty of foxholes for shelter from enemy bombs. Before the arrival of the Twentieth Station Hospital on Guadalcanal itself, army and naval hospitals all over the South Pacific provided care for the sick and wounded G.I.s and Marines from the island. In November, the 142d admitted its first patients from the fighting on the island of Guadalcanal. They had been flown out of Guadalcanal and then brought to New Caledonia in the hospital ship USS *Solace*. Although only seven of the 360 wounded Marines needed major surgery, many of the others had to have their wounds cleansed and redressed under anesthesia, keeping the 142d's operating rooms and nurses very busy.[15]

Army and Navy hospitals in the Fiji Islands also received a substantial number of battle casualties following the American landings in the Solomons in August. For example, on October 27, 1942, the Eighteenth General Hospital on

Fiji received orders to prepare for the arrival of casualties from Guadalcanal. The order meant increasing the bed capacity of the hospital by 500 percent in just twenty-four hours, but when the USS *Solace* arrived the next day the Eighteenth was ready and waiting to receive the 300 patients. One nurse remembered these patients: "All were thin, gaunt, quiet, serious, expressionless, shaken, men in their late teens and early twenties, fresh from contact with the enemy. Rations had been low, water scarce. Mosquitoes had added malaria to their misery. Many of the Navy casualties had been rescued from rafts or from the water after many hours of exposure. Ambulant patients were helped onto trucks and litter patients were carried to ambulances as a division was made between the 18th General and the 71st Station Hospital. Baggage was no problem. . . most had lost all their belongings save perhaps a few letters or a stained photograph."[16]

It was June 1944 before nurses were allowed on Guadalcanal, and even then the hot, humid climate remained an enemy. Nurses of the Forty-eighth, Ninth, and 137th Station Hospitals were quartered there in Dallas huts. Because the Americans had been on Guadalcanal for almost two years, the women had many of the comforts of home, comforts which were unheard of during the early months of occupation. By 1944 there was also an attractive officers' club, and the nurses were allowed to go sightseeing, fishing, boating, and swimming![17]

By spring 1944, however, the front lines of the Pacific war had gone past the Solomons. Bougainville had fallen to the Marines, and the Japanese stronghold of Rabaul had been encircled and neutralized. Enemy-held islands in the Solomons were cut off from the Japanese mainland and had been left to "wither on the vine" while American forces concentrated on a drive across the central Pacific.

While Army nurses were caring for patients in the hospitals in the South Pacific, others were arriving in the Pacific theater for duty at a growing number of Army hospitals in Australia. The first contingent of U.S. Army nurses to arrive "Down Under" debarked in Melbourne on February 26, 1942, and were given an enthusiastic welcome by Lieutenant Fellmeth, an Army nurse who had escaped from the Japanese in Manila on the *Mactan*. One of the very few American military women in Australia in early 1942, Fellmeth was given the assignment of arranging for temporary quarters for the first nurses scheduled to arrive in Australia. "You can never know with what happiness and excitement I went out on the harbor boat to meet the incoming convoy; it was like going home," she said. The 233 new arrivals were housed in 100 hotel rooms and three Red Cross convalescent homes in Melbourne before moving to their new posts. 1st Lt. Olga Benderoff and 120 of the nurses went to the Fourth General Hospital, and the others sailed for New Caledonia on March 6.[18]

By the time the theater's Director of Nursing, Capt. M. Jane Clement, took office, the number of nurses in the Southwest Pacific (SWPA) command had risen to 466. With the addition of fifty-six nurses in June, and counting those attached to two field hospitals in mid-August, Captain Clement could boast that she had about a thousand nurses on duty at various bases and hospitals in the theater. Few nurses served at Base Section One, which was a United States Army Air Force area. Enemy air raids on Darwin in early 1942 had discouraged the buildup of medical support services there. However, in the Melbourne, Brisbane, and Sydney areas, the increasing numbers of American troops necessitated the inclusion of numerous station and general hospitals staffed with Army nurses.

One of the many hospitals to arrive in Australia in 1942 was the Forty-second General Hospital, which arrived on the transport *West Point.* 2d Lt. Ruth Frothingham was on the *West Point,* which had departed San Francisco on May 17, 1942, "destination unknown." Frothingham remembered that the ship was crowded with seventeen nurses assigned to cabins built for two persons: "Deck space was at a premium but it was available to male and female officers, with squatters rights on your own blanket."

The Forty-second General's eventual destination was Canberra, where they arrived after an all-night train ride from the port of debarkation. "Few of us will ever forget our first impressions," one nurse recalls," Australians, Dutch, and Americans having their morning tea in the lobby, a group of Dutch airmen celebrating with one of their members who had just 'Sighted sub, sank same,' the confusion of sixty-five foreigners descending en masse on a comparatively small hotel, our own confusion when we found our luggage had been lost." They were assigned to a modern Australian hospital, but it was still under construction, so they spent their time drilling, hiking, and helping the Australian women with their war work. As many Americans were to find, the Australians were "more than hospitable" and the citizens of Canberra showered the American nurses with invitations to teas, luncheons, dinners, tennis, and picnics. Grace Dick Gosnell, who served in Australia with the Forty-second General, recalled, "The Australian people were very friendly. We had to get used to their different sayings. The food was different from what I had been used to, but I enjoyed it."[19]

From Canberra, the Forty-second General went by train to Brisbane to set up in a Catholic girls school overlooking the city. Ruth Frothingham remembers their arrival at the school, Stuartholme, well: "We immediately began the task of setting up the first floor to receive patients, while occupying the second and third floors as quarters." As officers, the nurses ate in the first floor officers' mess on regular china, not on mess kits, unlike the enlisted men who, Frothingham says, "lived in tents on the hospital grounds and were not so lucky." In time, the nurses moved into new, sturdily built two-story wooden buildings with screened porches. "We still had the old World War I iron cots and thin mattresses," Frothingham remembers, "but didn't need the T-frames for our bed nets now." With the Army personnel in new quarters, the remainder of the school could be used for patients.

Nurse Frothingham, who had joined the Army Nurse Corps at Walter

Reed Hospital in November 1940 from the Red Cross Nursing Service, recalled that Army nursing was similar to civilian nursing, but that the Army nurses had to teach and supervise enlisted men in basic nursing procedures: "In the 42nd General, nurses of the unit worked closely with our corpsmen. . . . It was imperative that these corpsmen be dependable as it was often necessary to assign as many as six 40-bed wards to one nurse, especially on the night tour of duty. Our complement of nurses—60 for a 500-bed hospital—had to be stretched."[20]

Like many hospitals overseas the Forty-second moved around. Eventually Grace Gosnell, Ruth Frothingham, and their fellow nurses ended up in Manila and then in Japan after V-J Day.

Many American nurses serving in Australia during the war were assigned to hospitals in Base Section Two in northeastern Australia, one of the most challenging areas for American personnel in Australia. 2d Lt. Mary Swain, ANC, who spent sixteen months at the Eighteenth Station Hospital near Townsville, told an army interviewer in October 1943 that the climate of Townsville was tropical because it was just north of the Tropic of Capricorn and was very different from Brisbane. Nurse Josephine LeClair, who was the chief nurse at the Thirteenth S.H. outside Townsville, was even more blunt about the weather. When asked about the average temperature, LeClair replied, "About 110." She said it rained for three months a year.[21]

The heat of the Townsville area was especially trying for the Twelfth Station Hospital, which was sent to the fringes of Townsville early in the war. They lived with Aussie families until their quarters could be completed and unloaded equipment from a ship by hand in 90-to 100-degree temperatures.

The Twelfth Station Hospital opened officially on March 29, 1942, and ten nurses from the Thirty-third Surgical Hospital reported for duty on April 14, just in time to help with the first cases of dengue fever. By the end of the month, they had treated 600 cases of dengue, including fifteen officers and ten enlisted men from the hospital staff.

Nursing duty in northern Australia in the spring of 1942 not only meant coping with outbreaks of serious disease, but living with the threat of a Japanese invasion. Rumors of a Japanese convoy headed for Australia abounded in May 1942, and the Twelfth Station Hospital was actually visited by a Japanese aircraft, which did not drop any bombs and was evidently on a reconnaissance mission. No invasion materialized, but the hospital did receive a Navy pilot injured during the Battle of the Coral Sea. At the end of May the hospital also took on wounded soldiers from the fighting near Port Moresby, New Guinea.

Although the U.S. Navy prevented the scheduled Japanese invasion of New Guinea in May 1942, a Japanese submarine surfaced off Sydney in early June 1942 and shelled the city. Nurses of the 118th General Hospital under 1st Lt. Mary G. Sanders had only recently arrived in Sydney when the attack occurred, sending them to air-raid shelters. The nurses were "evidently not greatly disturbed by the attack and proceeded quietly to their air-raid shelters; in fact, two slept peacefully through all the din of the air-raid sirens and the firing of the nearby harbor guns."[22]

Army nurses were not sent to New Guinea until October 1942. Eighteen nurses led by Chief Nurse Lt. Helen J. Gray debarked at Port Moresby just as the Papuan campaign began. They found the hospital set up in two large buildings and numerous tents, with 350 patients already admitted to the wards. The heavy fighting to secure Buna brought an increase in casualties and malaria cases over the next three months. The patients arrived "riddled with malaria, dengue fever, tropical dysentery, and suffering from jungle ulcers." Many had to be carried on native litters through swamps and jungle to the nearest fifty-bed station hospital, and from there taken to one of two grass airstrips at Dobdura to be flown out to Port Moresby.

Hospitals in Port Moresby were not safe from enemy attack, and air raids were commonplace. On November 24, 1942, a Japanese plane descended on the 153rd and dropped four incendiary and four high-explosive bombs. Three soldiers were injured and two tents damaged, but none of the nurses was injured. The danger and hardship of serving in such a forward area did not phase the women, and Chief Nurse Helen Gray wrote to Director Clement, "They showed the enlisted men, officers, and patients that they could take it! I especially wish to commend night nurses Miss [Edith W.] Whittaker and Miss [Jane S.] Goodwin both of whom remained calm and carried out their duties in a manner which brought nothing but praise and admiration from the patients." The wounded and ill G.I.s at the 153rd were very grateful for the nurses' presence, and one critically injured man remarked, "Uncle Sam really looks out for us."[23]

The success of the experiment of bringing nurses to Port Moresby prompted theater officials to send nurses from the Tenth Evacuation Hospital and 171st Station Hospital to New Guinea. The first group arrived in Port Moresby by ship on December 5, 1942, under the command of Lieutenant Gunn, and thirty more nurses followed ten days later. Nurses and staff at the Tenth Evac had 100 beds in operation four days before Christmas. By the end of January 1943, both hospitals had admitted 1,000 patients, most of them from the Buna operation.

Lt. Helen O. Chadburne recalled her first day at the Tenth Evac, which was set up at the Koki mission: "Never have I seen such a mass of suffering humanity than in the ward which housed the most serious casualties. They were on cots on each side of the tent, the soldiers ranging from privates to colonels. Lt. Catherine Desmaris and I went down the line, bathing bodies, dressing wounds, administering treatments, assisting with infusions, and changing beds. Finally at eight o'clock that evening we finished. The most gratifying part came when noticeable difference could be seen in the morale of our men. From solemn, drawn faces we began to see flickers of smiles."[24]

On February 28, 1943, the 153d and the 166th Station Hospitals exchanged hospital sites, the latter returning to Australia and the former to Port Moresby. The theater was unable to adopt a policy of rotating more hospitals to and from the combat area because of the distances involved and because of the expense of such moves. More nurses might have been sent to New Guinea sooner had it not been for a theater policy establishing standards for housing and security for nurses. This new policy gave some commanders an "excuse for delaying their arrival," despite the express statement of the policy that "women nurses were an essential part of the professional services of hospitals." The directive charged hospital commanding officers with providing facilities so that nurses could accompany their units or rejoin them without delay. It stated: "The fact that the area may be subject to bombing or other enemy action shall not be a determining factor in the decision" as to the date the nurses should arrive. There were enough nurses to send to New Guinea, but not enough commanders willing to demand their assignment to the island.[25]

SWPA was not experiencing a nursing shortage; indeed, with the arrival of the Ninth General Hospital during the summer of 1943, the total nurse strength in the theater came to 1,575. By year's end, there were 2,150 Army nurses in the command. With the fall of Lae and then of Finschafen to American amphibious operations, Army hospitals moved westward along the north shore of New Guinea to support the next operations. Nurses moved with them to locations such as Milne Bay and Hollandia. Helen Shriver Brundage was one of the many Army nurses to arrive in New Guinea: "We landed in Milne Bay, New Guinea, at night in the driving rain which continued for weeks and months." Myrtle Arndt Roulston has vivid memories of that first night at Milne Bay: "As the staging area was not prepared for the housing of over 300 females, we stayed on the ship for several hours. Finally after dark in pouring rain, we left the ship to be fed and housed. I use the word 'house' loosely. It consisted of a tent with four cots and mosquito nets, which we had never seen before."

Army nurses came to New Guinea with only their musette bags, and they had to improvise for several days while the rest of their luggage was unloaded. No one had bothered to advise them to pack essential items in their musette bags, but as nurse Roulston puts it, "We were young, laughed and made the best of everything. If anyone became lost on the way to the latrine after dark, she'd yell and we'd answer so she could find our tent—who had a flashlight?"[26]

Some hospitals such as Evelyn Langmuir's had the luxury of ice from an icehouse, but the plant frequently broke down. Operating a hospital in the jungle of New Guinea was a challenge for all personnel and often brought out the creative side of the medical personnel, even the doctors. Langmuir, writing home, reported, "The doctors, too, have hidden talents, such as the brain surgeon who took care of all the plumbing and piped an ample water supply from a mountain stream."[27]

Nurses came ashore on New Guinea in Class A wool uniforms. These were hardly appropriate for the tropics, but their cooler seersucker hospital uniforms were useless in an area where malaria-control measures demanded that all personnel wear long sleeves, trousers, and leggings. Nurses quickly took to wearing men's fatigue uniforms, but as Mrytle Roulston reminds modern readers, "In those days, no lady wore pants and after eighteen months of them, I haven't owned a pair since." Capt. Marian Grimes, chief nurse at the Forty-seventh Station Hospital at Milne Bay, was even more outspoken on the subject of feminine attire. In a 1944 interview she said, "A girl should wear a dress now and then even in the jungle as a reminder that she is still a woman." Captain Grimes felt that not all the nurses wanted to wear slacks and shirts continually and that the nurses should have been provided with uniform clothing more appropriate for the jungle climate.[28]

In New Guinea, laundering uniforms, especially army fatigues, was quite a chore. Helen Brundage explains: "We took our baths, washed our hair, and did all our laundry in our helmets at first." Milne Bay was primitive, or as Nurse Brundage describes it, "nothing but jungle." The nurses lived four women to a tent and ate off picnic tables in the thatched-roof mess tent. "Permanent staples on the table were canned butter (terrible), peanut butter, apple butter, pepper and salt," Brundage recalls. "The food was cooked on army field kitchen stoves and all was canned, dried, or dehydrated. We had no fresh food whatsoever."[29]

Her memories are shared by Capt. Peggy G. Carbaugh, ANC, who told an Army interviewer in September 1944 that the food at her hospital at Nadzab, New Guinea, was "not anything to rave about—bully beef and dehydrated potatoes become monotonous after a few weeks. Fresh eggs are on the menu about every three weeks, but fresh meat is scarce." Carbaugh did not think the nurses suffered from poor nutrition, but she did admit that they lost weight. She blamed the dietitian, who had not taught the cooks to make dehydrated foods tasty: "The cooks with us have never been taught anything about dressing up dehydrated food. All they know is how to add water and stir."[30]

Assigned to a hospital on Goodenough Island, New Guinea, in April 1944, nurse Evelyn Langmuir wrote home that they had reasonably good food, but, she reported, "Money is of no value. There's nothing to spend it on. I'm afraid I'll be a shoplifter after the war." The hospital was set up in tents on a flat, muddy field with a steep, bright green mountain wreathed in clouds behind it. Water was hung in Lister bags on tripods and was used even for brushing teeth. Although the nurses had an office, it was covered with termite dust, which fell from the roof beams like snowflakes.

The area seemed safe, but danger could come from unexpected sources, as Langmuir wrote in a letter home, "One of the gals got bitten on her fanny in the privy. Scorpion or something. She's now in the hospital. Temperature 102." Insect bites were just one of the many dangers of living and fighting in the jungle.

The most serious was scrub typhus, which came from tiny insects that lived in the jungle and especially in the kunai grass. A dread tropical disease, scrub typhus is akin to rocky mountain spotted fever. In one letter, Langmuir told her mother about the cases she was nursing who had scrub typhus: "They just burn up and nursing care is the only help for it, absolute rest, lots of fluids, alcohol sponges, etc."[31]

Marian Grimes, chief nurse at the Forty-seventh Station Hospital at Milne Bay, recalled that most of her patients arrived by ship. While orthopedic surgery predominated, the hospital also saw a number of medical cases: "Dysentery, dengue, and, of course, plenty of fungus infections kept us busy during the first few weeks in Milne Bay region," Grimes remembered. She also mentioned that jaundice was almost as prevalent at Milne Bay as malaria, but that the venereal disease (VD) rate had dropped dramatically in comparison with the number of cases she saw in Australia.[32]

The nurses' quarters on New Guinea were compounds enclosed with barbed wire and having only one entrance. When visiting Air Corps or Navy camps, nurses were required to have escorts. According to Myrtle Roulston, "There had to be at least two couples, and the males had to carry arms—protection from our own troops, not the enemy." Chief Nurse Marian Grimes clarified the policy: "Nurses dislike being under guard at all times, although most of them realize that is done mainly because of colored troops in our area." However, Peggy Carbaugh, chief nurse at the Second Station Hospital at Nadzab, New Guinea, ordered her nurses not to leave their compound without escorts because "a few prowlers, white troops, had been around our area, but no one was hurt seriously." Ironically, the only incident she could recall involved a white soldier in a nearby unit who was found lying next to a cot in the nurses' quarters: "A nurse saw him, and was cut rather severely trying to take his knife. The soldier escaped, but was captured the next day. Negro troops in the vicinity caused no trouble."

Although no official nursing reports mention reports of rape or sexual abuse, an entry for March 28, 1944 in the 166th Station Hospital's daily diary records that the hospital commander, Major Kaufman, returned from a meeting with the base commander and "later that evening met with the Chief Nurse of this organization for the purpose of once again stressing the necessity of enforcing and providing adequate protection of female personnel in this area. Due to recent reports of rape, the Base Commander, Colonel Sandlin, requests that in addition to the directive already published, nurses and female personnel will at no time leave the post at night in smaller groups than two nurses and two officers, one of which will carry a side-arm. Quite jokingly, nurses are being connected with the present popular song, 'Pistol-Packin' mama!'"[33]

The theater policy with regard to security for nurses in SWPA extended also to the Women's Army Corps (WAC) troops. At Oro Bay, New Guinea, WACs lived in a compound surrounded by barbed wire and were forbidden to leave "any area at any time" without an armed escort. Even their dates had to be approved twenty-four hours in advance! According to WAC historian Mattie Treadwell, the WAC staff director for the theater, Lt. Col. Mary-Agnes Brown, appealed to Maj. Gen. James L. Frink about these restrictions, but little was ever done to modify them.[34]

The nurses' comments about "colored" troops in New Guinea referred to the men of the several African-American units stationed on the island. By 1944 the Milne Bay area had become a major port and staging area for Allied operations in the Pacific. Hundreds of American service troops, white and black, worked at Milne Bay, and in April 1944 the all-black 268th Station Hospital arrived in Milne Bay from Brisbane, Australia. Army nurse Prudence Burns, later Burrell when she married Lt. Lowell Burrell, was among the nurse contingent at the 268th. She recalls that they sailed for the Pacific on the SS *Monterey* "without convoy. For two days we were escorted by a Navy blimp and destroyers. After zig-zagging across the Pacific we arrived in Sydney, Australia, eighteen days later."[35]

The nurses spent six months in the Brisbane area while their hospital was under construction at Milne Bay, and because, Nurse Burrell remembered, "the ship that was carrying our enlisted and officers to Milne Bay was shipwrecked on a reef." Lieutenant Burrell thought Brisbane was "beautiful," and she recalled that the black nurses benefited greatly from the friendship and hospitality of Sister Elizabeth Kenny, an Australian nursing sister who had developed a nursing procedure for polio. Burrell had audited several of Kenny's classes at the University of Minnesota. In 1992, Burrell would write, "Some of [Kenny's] relatives arranged trips, luncheons, and other activities for me and my co-workers. In this way we able to explore the city for churches of our choice, restaurants, civic organizations and recreational facilities—a new experience for many of us." Racial segregation was the official U.S. Army policy at home and overseas, but in Australia the local customs did not necessarily include discrimination against persons of color. While some black servicemen and women were not treated fairly, through their acquaintance with civic organizations in Brisbane, Prudence Burrell and her nurses were able to bring about some changes: "We got an enlisted men's club moved from a very unsavory section of the city. To our joy, several facilities that discriminated against African-American servicemen changed their policies."[36]

From Brisbane, the 268th Station Hospital finally moved to Milne Bay, New Guinea, where the nurses lived in prefabricated barracks and slept on beds covered by mosquito netting. They took atabrine daily to suppress the symptoms of malaria, and Prudence Burrell recalls the nurses' health and morale remained good. For entertainment, the 268th enjoyed movies "in ponchos in the rain." Burrell found New Guinea's rain, which she called "liquid sunshine," one of the most trying parts of overseas duty. It was difficult for the nurses to adjust to drenching rainstorms followed by the hot sun and mud—"I fell down daily with my nice ironed khakis."

Rest and recreation were limited on New Guinea for Army personnel, male or female, black or white. Although security precautions taken for women in New Guinea did not entirely eliminate opportunities for dating, there were few places to go on a date in New Guinea. Helen Brundage points out, "We were jungle bound for two years. We had regular G.I. movies, dances, played cards, but had very little reading material. Boats were plentiful and we would have lots of fun on the water, especially for a Kansas girl like me." She does admit that boredom was acute, however, for the patients who had only minor injuries. They had no "home" in which to recuperate and could not be returned to their units until they were fully recovered.[37]

There was little sightseeing in New Guinea, but some of the nurses did visit native villages. Miriam Baker Marken, who spent a year as a nurse at Finschafen and Hollandia, says that once she was permitted to visit a native settlement. The houses were built on stilts. She wrote that "the natives had reddish portions in their black hair, wore very little, and loved to trade anything they could."[38]

Helen Brundage recalls that the natives on New Guinea looked old, even though many were young in years. "They had ornaments in their ears, nose, wrists, ankles and their necks, anything from keys to a Spam can, teeth from animals, bits of copper wire, and I saw one with a bra around his waist going through our trash cans and stuffing 'collectibles' into the cups!" She found the natives unattractive, saying, "They were incredibly filthy, racked with skin diseases, malnutrition, and the effects of chewing beetle nut which left their mouths a brilliant red. It also cost them most of their teeth, which were destroyed by the reaction of the beetle nut juice on the tooth enamel."[39]

Despite the hot, humid climate, the health of most of the nurses on New Guinea was good. Miriam Baker Marken does recall that some of the women suffered from skin trouble known to all World War II veterans of the Pacific war as "jungle rot." These cases were sent back to the United States, but the nurses suffering from common heat rash stayed and tried to cope. "In New Guinea some of us had heat rash over 95% of our bodies," Marken remembers. "Finally we found it helped to apply a 90% alcohol solution to the affected areas."[40]

Myrtle Roulston agreed that health and morale were, in general, acceptable: "Health-wise I would say good—two malarias and two mental patients out of 110 females wasn't bad." As far as morale goes, Helen Brundage concurred: "We were all faced with the same obstacles, since everyone wore the same clothes, ate the same food, and worked the same hours, we all felt in the same boat."[41]

Other nurses serving in SWPA, however, felt that morale suffered from the lack of a rotation policy. Peggy Carbaugh told an Army interviewer, "Morale has been good until recently, but now they want to see the rotation policy apply to them, for they feel they have been over here long enough." She said some of the nurses had only two leaves in twenty-seven months overseas. Capt. Marian Grimes was more candid about the morale of some of the nurses in New Guinea. "I noticed," she said in 1944, "that many nurses are put in hospitals as patients a week after landing in New Guinea. Some of them seem disillusioned and want to go home. They wonder why they came." But other nurses in her unit had high morale, "considering that we were overseas 2½ years with very little work." Grimes said the Forty-seventh Station Hospital had a small recreation hall where they gathered for bridge and refreshments, but that moving pictures became monotonous after a few weeks. She told an interviewer in 1944 that "nurses who have been in a tropical climate for such a long time should be replaced. Even a little leave to the United States would be a great morale builder, for they would be able to see what is going on around home."[42]

In New Guinea, the nurses were not in any immediate danger from the Japanese. The enemy was the climate, the isolation, and the primitive living conditions. Helen Brundage recalls the frightening experience of being quartered in a coconut grove during a hurricane: "The trees were at least 75 feet tall. A hurricane came through and big trees bent by the gale at a 45 degree angle. Each tree was heavily laden with coconuts weighing at least 25 pounds. Our living quarters were supported by slender poles, no sides, but burlap tacked to the poles. We spent most of the long night rolled into blankets under our cots to afford us protection from the dropping coconuts. No one was hurt, although the big blow lasted for a couple of days."[43]

Allied fighting on New Guinea continued to provide the hospitals with casualties as General MacArthur's forces captured Hollandia and then went on to seize Wadke, Biak, Noemfoor, and Sansapor, giving the Allies control of New Guinea at last. Hollandia became an enormous Allied base and the jumping-off point for MacArthur's celebrated return to the Philippines. Evelyn Langmuir's unit moved up to Hollandia in mid-August 1944, and she wrote of her new surroundings, "We are quartered in the middle of an ant hill of activity. Construction of the hospital is going on rapidly, with tractors plowing out the jungle all day and night. The engineers deserve a great deal of credit in this war. They are untiring and efficient and the vast amount of work they have accomplished here in two weeks is unbelievable. Two weeks ago this spot was just a jungle." At Hollandia the nurses lived in "dark, crowded" barracks and had little privacy. There was, however, a good PX at the base and a Coke machine and beautiful scenery. The base was near Lake Sentani and Langmuir described the beauty of the scene with banana, Kapok, and slender eucalyptus trees and a wonderful view of the harbor from the hilltop.[44]

At the Ninth General, she and her fellow nurses were surprised to find their quarters more elegant than at their previous locations—"Comfortable hospital beds with brand new mattresses, pillows, and sheets are a welcome change from the canvas cots we used to have. The mess, which is served in a tent, is just as bad as ever, but it is served in style by waiters. We have plates and cups instead of single metal trays we are used to."[45]

Mrytle Roulston, who served with the Fifty-fourth General Hospital at Hollandia, explained: "We were medical support for the huge invasion. The patients arrived via hospital ship with some first aid. The first month of operation the operating room personnel participated in 750 hospital procedures. Needless to say, we were on duty twelve to fourteen hours a day or until the work was done." Often when the laundry facilities broke down, hospital personnel worked far into the night folding, wrapping, and sterilizing in order to be ready to operate in the morning.

Nurses at Hollandia were quartered twenty-eight to a prefab Quonset hut, but the area was known for rats that carried off crackers at night and for bats that flew over their heads. Roulston recalled, "I'd sit on my army cot with my feet up on the cot and a bath towel over my head while I was writing letters."[46]

As in other areas of New Guinea, the nurses' compound was guarded and they had to adhere to strict rules about dating. As Evelyn Langmuir wrote home, "Young officers began to storm our gates as soon as we arrived, but many had to be turned away because there weren't enough girls to go around." She recalled that there were four rules about going out on a date. Couples were required to go out with at least one other couple, escorts wore sidearms, there was no stopping or going off the main road, and one could only go to approved places. "No swimming yet because the men haven't been ordered to wear suits yet, but they soon will be."

Langmuir said that the barracks were guarded by two sentries day and night in case Japanese hiding in the hills were to wander down to the nurses' area. She related the story of two Japanese soldiers dressed in American fatigues who had come down from the hills two months before and gotten into a chow line: "They took their food, ate it ravenously, and weren't detected until they came up for their second helping of bully beef. No American has ever been known to want more of that particular commodity!"[47]

While U.S. Army nurses were learning to cope with the climate and difficulties of nursing in New Guinea, American forces were conducting a series of amphibious operations in the Central Pacific. U.S. Marines successfully seized the Makin and Tarawa atolls in November 1943, but the casualties suffered in the savage fighting on Tarawa shocked Americans at home. Most of the wounded were collected by corpsmen and immediately evacuated to U.S. Navy hospital ships. When troops invaded the next objective, the Marshall Islands, in February 1944, army hospitals played a key role in providing medical care.[48]

One of the Marshall Islands captured was Kwajalein, where Hannah M. Matthews and eighteen Army nurses served with the Thirty-eighth Field Hospital. They arrived there in June 1944 by C-54 transport plane from Hawaii. Nurse Matthews recalls that the people of the Marshall Islands were "very grateful to be liberated by the Americans. When the natives were brought into our hospital they refused to stay in our beds, but slept on the floor under the beds."

On Kwajalein, Matthews's unit cared for patients from forward areas who were held at Kwajalein until their condition could be evaluated. Then they were sent on by plane to Honolulu. "We received them directly from the battlefield through the field hospital." she recalls. "A plane load or more of the wounded would arrive at midnight every day during the battle to secure the Marianas."[49]

Following their success in the Marshalls, U.S. amphibious forces landed troops in the Mariana Islands in order to build air bases for B-29 bombers that could make the long trip to the Japanese home islands. The actual landings were made on the large island of Saipan on June 14, 1944, but progress ashore was slowed by determined Japanese defenders. During the combat phase of the Saipan operation, the Thirty-first and Thirteenth Field Hospitals and three portable surgical hospitals provided medical care for the casualties from the fighting, which continued for two weeks at the cost of 16,500 wounded. The intensity of the fighting, the rugged conditions on Saipan, and a lack of security delayed the arrival of nurses until the island was secured on July 11, 1944. However, the day after the U.S. flag was raised over Marine Corps General Holland's headquarters, the first Army nurses arrived on Saipan from Oahu for duty at the new 369th Station Hospital. Fortunately, the women had been given instruction in nursing in forward areas, including procedures in landing from transports and amphibious ships, bivouacking, and jungle evacuation. [50]

Five of the original ten nurses sent to Saipan went to a civilian hospital that desperately needed medical help. Plans for the Saipan operation had not taken into account the large civilian population, nor had they anticipated the civilian casualties or the poor medical condition of the natives there. Lt. Wilma R. Kaemlin described the hospital's patients: "No one who has not spent a day in their midst can imagine the horror and misery, the filth and pain and despair through which these people had lived. Many had lain in caves for days with huge gaping wounds of the head and body, with compound fractures of the arms and legs entirely uncared for."[51]

Caring for such seriously wounded patients was complicated by the lack of supplies, for "first priority went to the American armed forces." The hospital lacked cots and adequate supplies, so improvisation became the order of the day: "The patients lay under hastily erected fly tents. Some fortunate few had litters to rest on; others had only a dirty blanket or a piece of straw for a bed." The presence of civilian infants was especially challenging, but the nurses improvised turning dressings into diapers and converting empty plasma containers into baby bottles. Needless to say, the nurses' hearts went out to these filthy, hungry children, who were pampered with baths and new clothes. Gradually, conditions improved as cots, blankets, and supplies became available and as American rations were substituted for a diet of rice, fish, and pickled onions three times a day.[52]

Potable water, however, remained in short supply; Saipan had a water shortage even before the invasion and that meant most patients arrived dirty, clothed in rags, and infested with head and body lice. Wilma Kaemlin said, "Each can of drinking water had to be carried to the individual tents. Rain water was used for bathing. Each day a certain number of patients was given a complete bath, and on alternate days had their hands and faces washed. It was very difficult to keep them clean, especially since their old clothing had to be put on again."

Their dilemma was partly the result of poor treatment by the Japanese prior to the American landings. Malnutrition was common and disease endemic. Hookworm was found in many patients, and nurses who had never seen a case of beriberi saw 499 cases at one Saipan hospital alone. Early admissions to the hospital were in such poor condition that ten to twelve patients a day succumbed to their wounds. The 369th Station Hospital cared for 3,000 civilians by the end of the year.[53]

The nurses' problems on Saipan did not end with the lack of supplies; the local civilians' reverence for flies also created a unique and frustrating problem. The flies had originally been imported to the island to control a pest that attacked Saipan's sugar cane crop and the natives had been taught to consider the insects "sacred." They refused to kill or even brush them off, a serious health hazard on an island strewn with unburied or hastily buried bodies and refuse.

Mopping up continued on Saipan throughout the summer of 1944, necessitating the deployment of more hospitals. When the rest of the 369th's nurses and those of the 148th arrived by air from Oahu in the first week of August, they discovered Saipan was in the midst of an epidemic of dengue fever. The disease was spread by mosquitoes, which bred in the rubble and shell holes as they filled with water from the incessant rain. Army medical personnel were thoroughly exhausted by this influx, 20,000 dengue cases, which did not abate until October 1944.

Living conditions on Saipan remained primitive for the 148th, but more distressing was the real danger of lurking Japanese soldiers who had taken to the hills after the American invasion only to come down occasionally to American occupied areas in search of food. The Army posted armed security guards around the hospitals, but their "friendly fire" could do more harm than good. The 148th's official report noted, "Shooting was the order of the night at all of our guard posts, tracers fired by surrounding units came over our camp area. We were fortunate that we did not kill any of our own personnel or have them killed by stray bullets from other areas."[54]

Saipan's hospitals continued to treat casualties after the island was secured—mopping up operations produced a number of accident victims from hidden grenades, blasting, and jeep accidents. Then in February 1945, the hospitals began receiving the first of hundreds of casualties from the fighting on Iwo Jima. A small, volcanic island, Iwo Jima was needed as an emergency airfield for B-29s, but it was strongly defended by the Japanese, who had dug an elaborate system of caves and tunnels on the island. The 30,000 Americans coming ashore on Iwo Jima found little cover from very accurate enemy mortar fire and suffered 2,420 casualties on D day alone. Many of the casualties from the early fighting were taken off the tiny island to waiting hospital ships, where U.S. Navy corpsmen, doctors, and nurses could give them immediate, professional care in fully equipped wards and operating rooms.[55]

After the initial landings, Iwo Jima casualties were sent to hospitals on Saipan. Caring for so many wounded taxed the medical personnel on that island, who worked day and night during the Iwo campaign. In an effort to treat the hundreds of new patients more efficiently, the hospitals instituted shock teams consisting of doctors, nurses, and enlisted men, who went from ward to ward administering plasma and whole blood. There was a shortage of nurses on Saipan during this period; for example, the 369th S.H. had only eighty-three nurses to care for 1,342 patients.

1st Lt. Kathleen Barrett went overseas with the 39th General Hospital or Yale Unit arriving in New Caledonia on New Year's day 1945. After a short stay the hospital's forty officers, 120 nurses, dietitians, and physiotherapists, and 500 enlisted men were transferred to Saipan. She recalls: "We arrived on Saipan during the middle of the Iwo Jima campaign. Our hospital was not finished yet, so we were loaned out to neighboring hospitals." Barrett describes the six-week Iwo Jima campaign as "the hardest and most gruesome work any of us had ever done." She says the nurses were on twelve-hour shifts and always on call. "We were so short handed, poorly equipped and so horribly overcrowded by the fantastic numbers of patients that it was really amazing that anyone got any care at all." In addition, on Saipan there was a "tremendous water shortage, which made us feel even more helpless, because all the boys wanted after ten days on a crowded hospital ship was a bath. Some of them were lucky to get a backrub before they were evacuated to make room for sicker patients."

This nurse shortage was further aggravated on March 5 by an epidemic of food poisoning. The onset was sudden, "and many people literally fell to the ground ill, some in real pain." Mary Sherman, who served for two years as an Army nurse on Saipan and Guam with the 148th General Hospital, recalls that the hospital was so short of personnel they had to call in a military police (MP) unit to help care for the sick. When the supply of emesis basins ran out, the hospital staff resorted to tin pails and cans. In all, 746 hospital personnel fell ill with food poisoning, including at least nineteen nurses.[56]

When the Iwo Jima campaign ended, nurses on Saipan were transferred to their own compound area on a bluff overlooking a wide bay. Here the nurses decorated their new Quonset huts, planted flowers, and transplanted ferns from other parts of the island. They also enjoyed the maid service provided by diminutive Saipan native girls, which nurse Mary Brennan remembers as "frightened little creatures."

Opportunities for recreation on Saipan were limited. The island's numerous beaches were dangerous to use for fear of Japanese soldiers who held out in caves all over the island for a year after the invasion. Saipan did boast of an attractive officers' club with a dance floor, and as Brennan points out, "as nurses were the only women in the Pacific until late in the war, there were endless opportunities for dating." She also remembers how they improvised taking advantage of the leftover Japanese boats to use for Sunday afternoon excursions on the water. Cast-off enemy equipment, especially wrecked Japanese planes, was fashioned into retractors and orthopedic splints. Helmets were used as basins, plasma cans became forceps jars, and fourteen-inch bomb racks served admirably as bedside tables.[57]

South of Saipan was the island of Guam, which had been captured by the Marines in heavy fighting during July 1944. The island was officially secured on August 10, but some Japanese soldiers held out until V-J Day. They stole supplies, took potshots at the Seabees, and even came one night to watch an outdoor movie! Fleet Admiral Chester Nimitz refused to be intimidated by these enemy holdouts and ordered that Fleet Headquarters be moved from Pearl Harbor to Guam, where Navy Seabees constructed a town that eventually housed 2,500 men.

In December 1944, sixty-three Army nurses arrived on Guam to serve at the 373d Station Hospital, which was set up in a lovely tropical place with coconut palms. The nurses were quartered in pyramid tents, with the usual outdoor latrines and other elements of life in the field. Maj. Minnie Scheer, ANC, reported that the 373d began to receive patients from the Iwo Jima campaign in early March. They came in "hungry, tired and in combat clothes. They had to be fed, bathed, treated and given blood plasma if needed." The hospital also received many patients from the battle to secure the large enemy-held island of Okinawa, but these injured soldiers were "in good shape having [had] prior hospitalization."[58]

The small island of Tinian also cared for patients from the bloody Okinawa campaign and the 374th received their first patients just three days after opening on March 11, 1944. At the end of April, the hospital began receiving several hundred injured from Okinawa and by June 1 had expanded to a 1,000-bed hospital with the addition of numerous ward tents. The 374th's nurses enjoyed picnics and steak fries on Tinian's beautiful beach and dances at the officers' club. Adding to the luxury of life on Tinian was the availability of a Japanese maid for each nurse and a washing machine for every two barracks. On Tinian, too, were roving Japanese holdouts, so nurses were not allowed to leave their compound without an armed escort.[59]

Guam and Tinian were hot and dusty during the dry season, but from January to May rain turned the islands into a mudholes. Continuous rain and mud were also features of life in the southwest Pacific, where fighting continued in 1944 as General MacArthur's forces moved from New Guinea up through Biak and Wadke toward his goal of returning to the Philippines. Evelyn Langmuir went by Landing Craft Tank (LCT) to the old hospital ship *Comfort* for a voyage to the island of Biak, "a hunk of low, flat coral, practically on the top of the equator." P-38s came out to greet the hospital ship, "looping, swooping, and dipping and then lazily soaring like a couple of sea gulls chasing each other." When the aircraft came nearer to the ship the nurses could see "FRAN" written on the side of one of the planes. Frannie Breed was one of the unit's nurses!

On Biak, the nurses lived behind a stockade with heavy metal gates and guards from the military police. They were billeted four girls to a tent, but Evelyn Langmuir wrote home that the latrine was "magnificent" and the laundry and shower facilities excellent. She was soon busier than she had ever been before, caring for freshly wounded G.I.s from the Philippine campaign. Most of her patients were orthopedic cases in casts, who, she wrote, were "much less demanding and more grateful than the local soldiers admitted for minor operations. As soon as they get used to the fact that they are clean and fed and don't have to get up every night at 1 am to get into their foxholes for the regular air raid, they begin to perk up like any rookie, play poker, and tell stories which are punctuated by guffaws."[60]

As soon as the Philippine island of Leyte was secured, Army hospitals were sent there but their nurses' complements were not initially allowed to follow. The first to arrive following the capture of Leyte were seventeen nurses of the Second Field Hospital and ten nurses of the First Field Hospital under the command of the Chief Nurse of the U.S. Army Nurse Corps in the southwest Pacific, Lt. Col. Nola G. Forrest. They sailed in a transport from the Netherlands East Indies for the Philippines, but were caught off the coast of Leyte by a 90 m.p.h. tropical typhoon. Nola Forrest recalled, "During the two days and night we spent in the harbor we had many raids. A Jap Zero was shot down and fell next to our ship. Another Zero fell on a gas tank, which burned brightly during the night. Our ship was silhouetted between the flaming dump and the full moon." Once ashore the nurses went at first to the Thirty-sixth Field Hospital, which was set up in the 200-year-old Filipino cathedral at Palo, south of the city. They were billeted in a very fragile house, so were ordered to sleep on the floor in the cathedral's marble chancel. "No one got any sleep, however, as the Japs came over every five or ten minutes regularly all night. I counted forty raids altogether," wrote Col. Forrest. "With the noise of our 90 mm guns and the ack-ack it was virtually impossible for anyone to sleep."

Within three hours of their arrival at the hospital, the nurses were caring for almost 600 patients, who were "haggard and harassed." The medical department men had been so busy receiving casualties that they had no time to give them individual attention. But Col. Forrest reported, "The next day it was a transformed hospital. The patients were smiling, smoking, and had lost that worried look. They were grateful for the nursing care and many said it was the first bath they had in twelve days."[61]

Despite the welcome addition of Colonel Forest's nurses on Leyte, another contingent of Army nurses was not sent to the Philippines until December 18, when they joined members of the Sixteenth Station Hospital. The Thirty-sixth Evac's nurses also came on the hospital ship *Hope* to join their unit at Palo, where they were reinforced by nurses of the 177th Station Hospital. The practice of assigning a unit's nurses to another hospital was commonplace in the Philippines and by the end of the year 400 nurses were serving at various hospitals on Leyte. There was no shortage of volunteers, because Army nurses in the rear areas were so anxious to care for our wounded in the Philippines that some refused opportunities for rotation in order to accept an assignment there.[62]

Despite the influx of nurses into the Philippines and what one historian called "Herculean efforts to set up more wards," there were not enough beds available to extend the evacuation policy on Leyte. Complicating the medical support further was the next phase of the Philippines campaign, an Allied landing in Lingayen Gulf to liberate Manila and to secure the main Philippine island of Luzon. By January 20, 1945, hospitals on Leyte were receiving an influx of wounded from the fighting on Luzon. To care for so many casualties, the Army began training Filipina women as nurses' aides. High school graduates in good health and of good character, these young women were trained at the Seventy-third Field Hospital on Tacloban and upon graduation were employed in Army hospitals.[63]

When American Sixth Army troops came ashore in Lingayen Gulf on January 9, 1945, medical units and nurses were not far behind them. Army nurses accompanying the landing forces attacking Luzon came ashore from ships in Lingayen Gulf on February 20 and at Subic Bay on February 17. Helen Brundage ended up on duty at McKinley Field in Manila soon after its recapture. She found the city firegutted and without water, electricity, or a sewer system. "The dust was terrible because of heavy military traffic and the lack of paved roads." Nellie Burkholder, who also went to Manila, recalls: "I'll never forget my first day in Manila. I wanted to take a shower and the showers weren't completed, so I put a blanket up between the shower and the dressing area and proceeded to shower. What did I see when I was bathing but a native Filipino above us."[64]

Now all but forgotten, the campaign to secure Leyte and Luzon took almost six months and cost the Americans 10,000 men killed and another 36,500 wounded. In addition to battle injuries, soldiers in the Philippines succumbed to a variety of diseases and noncombat injuries, which created a pressing need for medical support. Unfortunately, however, the U.S. Army's conflicting policies on assigning nurses to forward areas compromised the ability of medical units to give these wounded and sick G.I.s the best care. The Eighth Army's policy of bringing nurses forward "as minimum safety permits" was not shared by the Sixth Army, and prompted the Consultant for Surgery in the Eighth Army to comment, "The casualty load was heavy and the nurses would have contributed greatly to the increased efficiency of all surgical units. As it turned out, they were shuttled about in rear areas, and those complements of nurses that finally caught up with their units did so at a time when the casualty load was low and the unit was on the edge of being inactive."[65]

Army nurses also served on other Philippine Islands—Mindanao, Mindoro, Palawan, Cebu, Negros, and Pana—and with flight-evacuation squadrons. The vast distances of the Pacific and the primitive conditions of many of the combat zones made prompt evacuation of wounded all but impossible until the Army Air Force began medical air-evacuation flights. Patients were flown out of the forward areas to hospitals in C-47 Douglas Skytrain aircraft flown by regular Army crews augmented with medical corpsmen and specially trained flight nurses. The nurses assigned to air-evacuation flights were trained at Bowman Field near Louisville, Kentucky. The first class graduated "with little fanfare and a minimum of military ceremony" on February 19, 1943. Within days, the newly graduated flight nurses had been sent to bases all over the world.

Margaret C. "Peg" Hofschneider was a member of the first class of flight nurses at Bowman Field. She recalls that the training included rigorous calisthenics, forced marches, and close-order drill: "The bivouac was something else. Slit trenches dug, bedrolling, garbage detail, tent pitching, and many more exercises."[66]

At Bowman Field, the nurses were taught the newly developed techniques of evacuating patients by air: "We were trained to load the patients on litters with just the help of our corpsmen," Hofschneider explains. "The plane was refitted to hold 18 litters, nine on each side, three tiers high. There was a small area for walking wounded and room for our rather large, very heavy, medical kit." Flight nurses did a lot of actual bedside nursing, assisted, of course, by corpsmen. "We did whatever we could to relieve pain and suffering, with our limited supplies. Of course we were taught to improvise," Hofschneider adds. With no physician on board these medical evac planes, the flight nurse had the entire responsibility for seeing that her patients were cared for and transferred from the airfield to a hospital.

When Peg Hofschneider graduated from Medical Air Evacuation School, she left for overseas duty. During the month-long voyage across the Pacific, the ship stopped at Bora-Bora for water and the nurses were invited a party at the Navy officers' club there. This was the 1940s, when a "party" meant appropriate formal evening attire, so Peg wore the one long evening dress she had been allowed to pack with her gear: "The dress was red, and while on Bora-Bora I was offered a darling little boy baby for my long red dress. I didn't take him!"

On the voyage from Bora-Bora to Brisbane, one entreprenurial officer quartered in the next stateroom took advantage of his fellow passengers. He had loaded his footlocker with liquor. "No gas mask, no change of clothing, nothing. He made a fortune after we were enroute."

Once in Brisbane the flight nurses enjoyed beautiful accomodations at a hotel in Surfer's Paradise, but were eager to prove their worth and, after a month of prodding, their chief nurse finally allowed them to go to New Guinea. Peg Hofschneider flew the first evacuation mission in New Guinea. She and four other flight nurses were stationed at Nadzab Field in the New Guinea jungle. She recalls, "Dusty, dirty, hot, no food, nothing. I guess the thirst and no food were the hardest to get used to. No cold drinks, no sweets except for the rations we could get."

Although there was no social life and nowhere to go except for the monthly club dance to old records in a juke box, the nurses' morale remained high. "We were young and we made a big lark of the whole thing. We made our own fun and games," says Peg. The girls usually brought "surprises" back from their flights to Australia, but they were not allowed to bring in liquor. When Peg tried to bring an enlisted man a bottle of rum and it exploded in flight, she had some quick explaining to do to her commanding officer.

The American sense of humor did much to combat tensions and the boredom of duty half a world away from home. On one return trip from Brisbane, Peg Hofschneider brought a watermelon back for the enlisted men at her base: "The guys in Brisbane carved 'T.S.' on it. I did not even know what it meant."

Flight nursing in the Pacific was not without hazards however. The aircraft were unmarked cargo planes that brought supplies and mail in, and took patients out. There were no red crosses on the side for protection, the weather was not always good, nor were the aircraft in perfect flying condition. As a precaution, the nurses carried .45 caliber pistols and were trained in their use. As Peg Hofschneider pointed out, flying in and out of New Guinea in wartime was always risky for air crews, flight nurses, and patients. Her best friend was lost in a routine, three-plane flight over the Owen Stanley Mountains: "She was in the lead plane going into the clouds and the plane and crew were never seen again."[67]

Nursing on Army and Navy hospital ships could also be very dangerous duty, especially toward the end of the Pacific war, when Japanese suicide planes attacked U.S. invasion forces. The practice of illuminating hospital ships did not prevent them from being attacked, as the crew of the USS *Comfort* discovered off Okinawa. On April 28, 1945, while steaming fully lit fifty miles off Okinawa en route to Saipan with a load of casualties, the *Comfort* was attacked by a Japanese kamikaze.[68]

The first crewman to spot the attacking Japanese plane was Seaman 1st Class Elmer C. Brandhorst, who was on watch on the bridge. "I saw the plane first when it made its first dive, but it was too dark to identify it as enemy or ours. About ten minutes later I saw it again, coming in dead ahead in a steep dive," he told reporters for Base Hospital No. 18's newspaper. Brandhorst was wounded in the arm and right leg by flying pieces of metal from the plane when it hit the ship's superstructure. In the ship's surgery below, operating teams were at work when the kamikaze hit. The force of the impact hurled the plane's motor through the surgery, igniting oxygen tanks and causing a tragic explosion. On duty on the surgery deck was 1st Lt. Gladys C. Trostrail, ANC. The last thing she remembered before the blast was standing near the entrance of her ward feeling grateful for the peace and quiet following a long day of caring for the wounded. The next thing she knew she was in the galley, climbing onto a dishwasher to escape water pouring into the compartment from broken pipes. She surmises that she had been blown through the bulkhead into the galley by the force of the explosion. An Army sergeant crawled through twisted sheets of metal to lead her to safety.

In the next ward, 2d Lt. Valerie A. Goodman was helping another nurse prepare penicillin injections when the enemy plane hit. Trapped beneath a bulkhead by the blast, which toppled a metal cabinet down on her legs, Goodman could recall little of what happened when the oxygen tanks exploded. The nurse next to her was killed instantly by the explosion. In all, one Navy and four Army medical officers, six Army nurses, one Navy and eight Army enlisted men, and seven patients were killed by the Japanese plane or by the explosions that followed its impact. Another ten patients, seven sailors, and thirty-one soldiers, four of them nurses, were wounded.[69]

Ashore on Okinawa, ten field hospitals were caring for the inundation of American casualties resulting from the tenacious defense of the island by the Japanese. Nurses did not, of course, accompany the invasion forces, but were sent into Okinawa on May 3, 1945. Assigned to the Eighty-second, Eighty-sixth, Eighty-seventh, and Eighty-eighth Field Hospitals, the nurses were in for some rough duty there, where rain and mud plagued American forces and the enemy kept everyone jumping for cover. Sometimes they jumped as a result of "friendly fire." For example, on June 21, a five-inch shell from a Navy gun hit the ward area at the Sixty-ninth Field Hospital, seriously wounding three persons and causing slight injuries to another dozen. Two Army nurses, 1st Lt. Hagoian and 1st Lt. Alice Ray, were among the injured.[70]

Claiming the honor of having the highest patient census during the Okinawa campaign was the Thirty-first Field Hospital which admitted 4,500 patients between April 5 and June 21, 1945. Nor did the nurses' job end with the cessation of combat on Okinawa: medical personnel worked long hours tending Japanese prisoners and civilian victims of a Japanese B encephalitis epidemic as well as vaccinating the 250,000 American G.I.s on the island awaiting the planned invasion of Japan. Many other G.I.s were injured in accidents or while souvenir hunting.[71]

The planned invasion of Japan never took place, sparing Army hospitals on Okinawa and in the Philippines from the task of caring for an estimated one million casualties. On August 14, 1945, following the dropping of atomic bombs on Nagasaki and Hiroshima, the Japanese signed an unofficial surrender and the war in the Pacific was over. Helen Brundage remembered vividly the moment: "We were in Manila and word came to us about two o'clock in the morning. I was on night duty at the time and had a half empty ward, only about 20 occupied beds. The boats in Manila Harbor started to toot their whistles, turned on their spot lights, fired guns, and generally created noise." Helen woke her patients up to tell them the joyous news. Although the nurses on ward duty had no alcohol for celebrations, other servicemen in Manila discovered abundant supplies and within hours MPs were bringing some of the "celebrants" to the hospital. Recalls Brundage, "We dumped them on a cot to sleep off their booze then sent them back to their outfit."[72]

Army medical units went to Tokyo soon after V-J Day. Mrytle Roulston's unit set up in an American hospital three miles from Tokyo, only thirty days after war ended. The nurses were housed in Japanese-style buildings with Japanese plumbing, which was eventually replaced by American plumbing. They enjoyed maid service in Tokyo and even acquired a washing machine. "I couldn't believe it, but I loved it," says Roulston, who was chief nurse at the time. Contrary to rumors circulated prior to our occupation of Japan, she found the Japanese people kind, pleasant, and eager to please. Duty in Japan did not include many opportunities for recreation, but the nurses did have movies and dances and, after years overseas, Roulston finally got six days of R and R at the Fujiama Hotel. "You guessed it—it rained the whole time."[73]

Grace Gosnell was also in Japan, on the hospital ship *Marigold*, where prisoners of war were processed. For her, one of World War II's most memorable experiences was being on the train platform in Yokohama, "when the trains pulled in with POW men, and to see those happy faces and see how they eat and drink some were in pretty bad shape." For Ruth Frothingham, the trip to Japan from Manila onboard the *Marigold* and its arrival in Yokohama on August 30, 1945, also left an indelible impression. The Forty-second General Hospital set up a processing station right on the dock. Frothingham recalls, "One nurse was assigned to each party dispatched to distant prison camps throughout Honshu to evacuate the dispirited and helpless recovered prisoners of war. More than 23,000 were examined, classified, and given every aid and comfort from our facilities on the dock." On September 10, with their "mission accomplished," the hospital moved on to set up St. Luke's hospital in Tokyo.[74]

The *Marigold*, an Army hospital ship, was a veteran of several transpacific runs. Teresa "Rudie" Reynolds was aboard the ship for one trip to Manila and back to the San Pedro hospital in California. By the time she had joined the ship, the war was over, but the Army Transportation Corps was working frantically to get the sick and wounded back to the States. She describes the scene when she arrived in the Philippines in November 1945: "Manila Bay was quite populated with sunken ships that were protruding from the water. When we saw the city it was wrecked. Many bullet-pocked buildings, and large shell marks. Many bridges were out."

In Manila, nurses had an opportunity to visit Bataan and Corregidor and tour the surrounding countryside, seeing typical Filipino scenes of native huts and carabao-drawn carts. Opportunities to date in Manila and on shipboard were practically unlimited, and Reynolds recalls that the *Marigold's* captain was very liberal about enforcement of hours and restrictions that forbade officers and enlisted men (and women) to fraternize with one another: "They just looked the other way if an officer associated with us." The *Marigold* soon became a World War II version of the "Love Boat." Before *Marigold's* voyage was over, fifteen of her thirty nurses were engaged, a fact Reynolds attributes to the number of soldiers who were leaving the service.[75]

For Army nurses like Teresa Reynolds, the end of World War II did not mean their contribution to Army nursing was over. She and hundreds of others served overseas for months after V-J Day, in Army hospitals, on medical evacuation aircraft, and on hospital ships. By December 1945, the U.S. Eighth and Sixth Armies had over 400,000 occupation troops stationed in Japan, with medical support facilities in several locations and two major hospital complexes at Yokohama and Tokyo. The Ninety-eighth Evac opened in Yokohama in early September without nurses, but the nurses of Thirty-seventh General operated with the 161st S.H. at the Totsuka Naval Hospital until they moved to Tokyo to St. Luke's International Hospital. Capt. Lucille S. Spenser and a contingent of nurses from the 364th Station Hospital arrived off Japan on the USS *Hope* on September 22, 1945. Although delayed by a typhoon, they debarked and joined the men of their unit in Kyoto on October 11.[76]

In November 1945, the Army Nurse Corps had a total of 4,000 nurses on duty in the Pacific theater, but as veteran nurses and others with health problems left for the States that number dwindled. For many nurses, duty in the Pacific was over, but the memories lingered. Many who served overseas in World War II would agree with Myrtle Roulston: "I wouldn't have missed it for anything!"[77]

4

THE TORCH IS LIT

Army Nurses Support the Invasions
of North Africa and Sicily

As thousands of American troops were arriving in the southwest
Pacific in 1942, others were being convoyed across the Atlantic to
the United Kingdom in anticipation of a Second Front against the
Axis in Europe. Allied leaders were under strong pressure to go on
the offensive somewhere in the West in 1942. However, after prolonged debate the Combined Chiefs of Staff decided not to launch a cross-chan-
nel attack in 1942, but to mount three separate amphibious landings on either
side of the Straits of Gibraltar in early November. Code-named TORCH, the
operation would be coordinated with a major British offensive in the desert by
the Gen. Bernard L. Montgomery's Eighth Army.[1]

Plans for Operation TORCH included the use of British medical units
and U.S. Army medical battalions and mobile hospitals, but in view of the shortage
of shipping, the antiquated North African transportation system, and uncertain
sanitation and water systems, the medical section agreed to keep medical personnel
and services to an "absolute minimum for the invasion." American medical involvement in the Eastern Task Force, which was assigned to seize the North African port
of Algiers, was limited to four teams of the Second Auxiliary Surgical Group. For
the landings at Oran, however, the Forty-eighth Surgical and Seventy-eighth Evacuation Hospitals were slated to accompany the Center Task Force invasion convoy. A
follow-up convoy would bring the Seventy-seventh Evacuation Hospital and the
Fifty-first Medical Battalion to Oran on D day plus three.[2]

In the absence of recent combat experience in amphibious operations,
medical plans for TORCH were based on manuals and on the experience of the
British during a raid on Dieppe in August. Although that operation had resulted
in an astonishing casualty rate of 50 percent, Allied planners expected only minimal French resistance in North Africa and were not overly concerned about putting nurses and unarmed medical personnel ashore before the beachheads were
completely secured.[3]

In early August the first troop convoys for Operation TORCH left from New York with soldiers of the U.S. First Division and the complement of the Forty-eighth Surgical Hospital, including Army nurses who had arrived at the port of embarkation via train from their camp. Among them was Lt. (later Capt.) Theresa Archard, a longtime Red Cross member who had volunteered in 1940 as an Army nurse. She was at the end of her one-year tour of duty on December 7, 1941, and looking forward to returning to civilian life when she heard the news of the Pearl Harbor attack. Archard didn't believe in war, but she wrote, "as an American I had no alternative except to continue as I had begun a year before." In early August 1942 she found herself on a train going north to a port of embarkation: "In the diner we ate royally. 'Well, it won't last forever,' I said, digging into a steak. 'It'll probably be the last time in ages we eat so well and have so much elbow room.'" No one, not even Theresa Archard, had any idea how accurate her prediction would be that August morning in 1942.[4]

Once at the port of embarkation, the nurses were outfitted for war. Archard reports, "Pandemonium reigned! Three hundred chattering nurses milled around trying to get outfitted. . . . Besides getting us all dressed up to go to war, they had to do a series of innoculations on us, physicals had to be completed, and there was only that day and the next to get the job done." The comments made by the excited nurses included ones like "I don't know what size shoe I take," "What's a bedroll and what do you do with it once you get it?" or "What a lovely mess kit, I've always loved picnics—I'm going to enjoy eating out of this." Needless to say, it was a group of several hundred very naive young women who departed New York for "destination unknown"![5]

On August 5, 1942, loaded down with helmets, gas masks, canteen belts, and hand luggage, the nurses boarded their transport. As they left, Billie Wittler, the chief nurse, bade them farewell, saying, "Good luck to you, girls. You've a tough job ahead of you, but I know you' ll do it well. Be proud to belong to the Army Nurse Corps, and we'll be proud of you. Good-bye and good luck."

With those words ringing in their ears, the first U.S. Army nurses to be sent "into battle" departed. "The gray ships were utterly grim. There was no flag waving. Gone were the bands, the laughter, the shouted good-byes. Not a soul came to see anyone off," Archard recalls. Sailing with nurses from other hospital units, the Forty-eighth Surgical Hospital's nurses were anxious about the wartime crossing. "Deep inside me I was scared. My imagination conjured up fantastic images of floating mines, dive bombers, and submarines. I knew what it meant not to see land for days on end, and now we were to be at the mercy of those predatory vessels. It would take more than a soda bicarb to ease the heavy feeling in my stomach," Archard wrote later.

Once at sea, the nurses were told they would be part of the Forty-eighth Surgical Hospital, a field hospital or mobile surgical installation divided into three units to facilitate movement on the battlefield. Their colonel explained that the surgical auxiliary would always be with the forward unit. "Just how close to the fighting line we will be will depend upon battle considerations. Do I make myself clear?" he said to the girls assembled in the ship's lounge. Lieutenant Archard, learning the Forty-eighth had only twenty nurses with any surgical experience, realized that "they had a lot to learn."

On the voyage across the Atlantic, the nurses passed the time playing Lexicon in the lounge and watching the First Division G.I.s shoot craps and play cards. "Many friendships were formed—and some romances, which later developed into marriages," Archard writes. Although they had no way of knowing it in August 1942, these nurses were to follow the boys of the First Division through two campaigns: "Men whom we grew to like and trust and many of whom we were never to see again after some of these bloody battles."[6]

After several weeks in England preparing for field duty by drilling, going on road marches, and attending lectures, the Forty-eighth was notified they would be departing again for an "unknown destination." Rumors abounded, but the only solid piece of information was that the destination would not be a rainy one—they were told to leave overshoes and rubbers in footlockers which would remain behind in England. After marching to the train burdened with full field packs weighing fifteen to twenty pounds, the nurses boarded a troop train that sped north. Along the way they passed people waving and forming Vs with their fingers and yelling "Thumbs up." At a train station in Scotland, local townsfolk gave them cookies and children asked them for souvenirs, especially American pennies.

From the rail station the nurses went by ship's tender to a troopship packed with American soldiers, who watched and made wisecracks as the nurses struggled aboard carrying suitcases, full packs, gas masks, and helmets. "There they were standing around making wisecracks, and I vowed then and there it would be the last time I ever toted a valise along with the rest of the stuff," writes Theresa Archard. When one nurse fell coming on board and the male spectators broke into gales of laughter, a nurse told the officers off by reminding them that they were officers and gentlemen. After that scolding some of the men came up and apologized.

This time their ship was British and the nurses enjoyed roomy accommodations and excellent meals, even steak and eggs, served by British stewards on tables set with linen. "It was a treat after two months of roughing it." The women passed the time on the voyage sewing Red Cross patches and American flags on their uniforms, playing cards, and gathering around a piano in the lounge each night to sing. Finally, after days of rumors, the nurses learned that their destination was North Africa, a surprise to some. "Why, I didn't know Africa was civilized!" exclaimed one of the women.

As the convoy passed through the Straits of Gibraltar the nurses could see the lights of Tangiers. With D day now hours away there were a lot of nervous comments and fooling around, but Archard recalls, "This fool went on, despite the fact we were going to invade a strange country, care for wounded men, and endure hardships that were as foreign to us as the land itself."

At 2300 hours on November 7, 1942, the assault transports of Center Task Force, carrying men of the First Division who would go ashore at landing beaches in the Gulf of Arzeu, slid into position. The nurses' troopship reached its position off Arzeu in total darkness, but as Archard remembers, "Just before dawn the guns started booming. Explosion followed explosion and the noise was monstrous. This was it! We were invading North Africa and each of us wondered what our part would be." The Allies were about to make their first amphibious landing in the Mediterranean, and American nurses were going to part of that historic invasion.

For hours, the women watched as soldiers and supplies went ashore in boats that drew up alongside their transport. Before disembarking into landing craft, the nurses were told to leave their helmets untied and their shoes unlaced in case they were hit. "If we were hit and had to go overboard, we were to slip out of the pack and kick our shoes and helmets off. Then we would have a chance to save ourselves," Archard recalls. She was with the last unit to leave: "It was horrible gazing down at the swaying ladder, our helmets like iron on our heads, full packs on our backs, our shoes untied, and the roar of the guns around us. Suddenly there was an especially heavy explosion and then, somehow, . . . we were in the commando boat. If Florence Nightingale would see us now!"

Their landing craft touched down just off the beach near the village of Arzeu, and the nurses had to wade ashore in armpit-deep water, except for "some of the good looking girls" who were carried onto the North African shore by the enlisted men, proving, Archard concludes wrily, that "a pretty smile could get you anywhere, even off a commando boat during an invasion!"

Because medical personnel and nurses were forbidden to carry weapons, they were at the mercy of "anyone with a gun," and sought shelter behind a sand dune fifty yards inland. Lt. Ruth Haskell made her way to shore through the cold water: "I staggered over a stretch of beach and dropped down under the steps of a cottage about a hundred yards away. It was then I heard for the first time the ping of a sniper's rifle which, on this occasion, kicked up a chunk of sand on the path along which I had trodden."

It was a chilly, gray morning, Archard remembers: "Cold, tired, wet, and afraid we wondered what on earth was coming next. Some of the boys started to dig foxholes, using the metal part of their helmets as shovels." Unable to light fires on the beach, the women shivered, watched the invasion craft moving toward shore, and listened to the big guns "booming in the direction of Oran."

After an hour or so, the nurses found shelter in some beach houses deserted by the local inhabitants. "The walls dripped, the windows had been smashed, and stories were already going the rounds of the dead Arabs who had just been taken off the premises, along with the filth and junk that had kept them company." Between the excitement and the invasion noises, the women had trouble sleeping that night on the cold tile floors. At midnight Lieutenant Archard, now chief nurse of the second unit, was asked to choose five nurses to go to a French hospital to care for wounded. The Army would not risk sending more than six of the nurses. After a harrowing ride, the six women—Archard, Kelly, Hornbeck, Haskell, Atkins, and Krusic—arrived at the crowded hospital, where wounded and dying American soldiers, civilians, and French military personnel lay on litters. Ruth Haskell describes her first sight of our wounded lying on litters on the floor in rows: "There were pools of blood beside some of them, where dressings had not been changed since the first shock dressing was applied in the field. I don't know how the other girls felt, but I experienced at once a violent anger—bitter, surging anger—against a people that out of greed and power and lust would cause such things to happen to young manhood."

On the way upstairs to the operating room, Haskell was asked by a wounded man for a drink of water, and when she knelt to give him a drink from her canteen he said, "My God! A woman, an American woman! Where in heaven's name did you come from?" Like many American G.I.s, he was shocked to see American nurses, for many had no idea that the women had landed with the invasion forces.

Upstairs, Theresa Archard remembers, "the operating force was going full blast, working by flashlights held by our ward men. Everywhere you walked there were wounded soldiers. Very little sedation could be given them—there was so little to be had. One medical chest from the ship was all they had to work with." Rolling up their sleeves, the doctors and nurses worked all night with no food or hot coffee to sustain them. The next day the rest of the units' nurses left the beach just as it was strafed by an enemy plane. No one was hurt. "We were leading a charmed life and prayed it would continue," Archard concludes.

At the hospital, supplies were short—unloading of the transports in the harbor had temporarily ceased because of enemy fire—so the nurses shared their rations and water from their canteens with the wounded men. "Hygiene! What do germs mean at times like that?"

There was some confusion ashore and a certain lack of organization that resulted in some of the nurses being sent to the French hospital, while others "milled around the barracks not knowing what to do." Lieutenant Archard quickly put them to work converting a French barracks into another hospital. It was a slapdash affair, with French capes pilled on wooden cots and only some non-potable water to clean the floor, but it would do for the lightly wounded casualties who arrived throughout the night.

The hastily converted barracks proved less than a safe haven, however, as snipers fired in through the windows. Evelyn Hodges was particularly annoyed that snipers would fire into a hospital, and Archard recalls, "I had to restrain her from going out to give them a piece of her mind. Nurse Hodges did manage to get to the door, but a corpsman "grabbed her and pulled her down to the floor just in time; a bullet ripped through the door where she had been a moment before."[7]

When the Forty-eighth's two units switched places later that evening, Archard found conditions in the hospital as miserable as before, with numerous patients, no water for washing, and no supplies, not even food rations. The nurses shared their three days' C rations with those wounded men "who could eat such things as beans, hash, and stew." The wounded lay in bed with dirty blankets thrown over them. "They had two-day and three-day beards, blood and dirt caked on their faces," Archard remembers.

While the Forty-eighth Surgical Hospital was coping with inadequate supplies in a civilian hospital, the First Medical Battalion was giving first aid and collecting casualties from the main attack on Oran and its outskirts. Although enemy resistance was not heavy, the Eighteenth Regimental Combat Team engaged some French forces at St. Cloud, and Combat Command B, which had landed at Arzeu and seized Tafaroui Airfield, fought off a French counterattack on D day plus one. On November 9, columns of the Twenty-sixth Regimental Combat Team, which had landed west of Oran on D day, closed in on the city. The next morning the French agreed to a cease-fire.

Following the surrender of Oran, the Thirty-eighth Evacuation Hospital moved inland from Arzeu, where it had landed on November 9, to St. Cloud to care for casualties of the fighting there. They also sent some of their surgical teams to a civilian hospital in Oran which had been taken over by the First Division Clearing Company to care for soldiers and civilians wounded in the attack on the harbor. The Thirty-eighth was reinforced on D day plus three by the arrival of the Seventy-seventh Evacuation Hospital, which took over responsibility for about 300 patients at the civil hospital.[8]

The following day, transports finally got supplies unloaded and nurses at the Forty-eighth Surgical Hospital went straight to work with G.I. soap and water to scrub the hospital and make up cots with clean linen. As more hospitals opened and the Allies gained control of the city, the nurses had time to walk about and explore Oran. Nurses who spoke French, such as Theresa Archard, conversed with the local inhabitants, who invited some of the nurses to their homes for meals. Archard was especially impressed by the children in the streets, who "were thin and hungry. It didn't take them long to discover that Uncle Sam was a fabulous Santa Claus. We had only to appear in the streets and the singing would break out, 'Choclat, chewing gum, bon bon, okay, okey, dokey.'"[9]

On November 21, 1942, another convoy brought more army nurses, including fifty who had been assigned to the Ninth Evacuation Hospital. Roberta Love Tayloe, a Virginian who had trained at Garfield Memorial Hospital in Washington, D.C., before the war, wrote about their arrival at Mers-el-Kebir in her diary: "A beautiful moonlit night with those big stars, occasional guns in the distance. The harbor had many ships, all put to bed for the night. Oran has an exotic look from here. I'm anxious to see it!"[10]

The next afternoon, the nurses went to the Clinique General in Oran and had their first taste of life in the field—"C-rations straight from the can." They were also initiated into life in a war zone by a series of air raids. Nurse Tayloe wrote, "There were a number of air raids that night, and such a racket! It seemed to me we meet ourselves coming and going on those narrow stairs going to the shelter in the basement." The nurses were not injured in the air attacks, but their supply ship, with all the unit's medical supplies, was hit and sunk. A sergeant in arms was "among the missing." "So sad—it brought the war closer than ever," she noted in her diary.[11]

After two weeks in Oran, the nurses were taken by truck to a hospital that was set up in a field about forty miles from the city, near Tafaroui Air Base. The most memorable feature of their new home was the mud. "As one officer called it: 'A Sea of Glue.' It was muddy, but after a rain, and it did this often, it was really something. Why, even your shoes would come off," said Roberta Tayloe. The hospital area, which was set up entirely under green tents, was a shock to many of the nurses: "Here we were, in Africa, forty miles from the nearest town, in a sea of mud and raining like mad. No heat, no electricity, or plumbing, phones, mail, or even a newspaper and no place to buy one. If you were hungry too bad. Not even a place to buy a chocolate bar." Tayloe and her roommate, Nurse Keats, sat on the side of their damp bedding rolls inside their tent and "just laughed and laughed."[12]

After several boring weeks near the air base without casualties to care for, two days before Christmas the Ninth moved by truck to Tlemcen, eight miles west of Oran, to an area under water from a torrential rainstorm. Nurse Tayloe recalls, "We had to find stones to put our belongings on, to keep them out of the water after our tents were pitched." Christmas Day dawned bright and sunny, so she walked into the town with three of the hospital's medical officers for dinner. That evening they celebrated their first Christmas away from home: "Bad on everyone, but worse on the ones with little children, and several who had not ever seen their babies." The arrival of Santa Claus bearing a big bag of mail, their first in three weeks, cheered many, but when the turkeys failed to arrive they ate a Spam dinner. The turkeys, which were eventually delivered, were enjoyed for New Year's.[13]

In Arzeu, the Forty-eighth Surgical Hospital's nurses were determined to have a Christmas party for their patients, many of whom had never been away from home during the holidays. The Germans had cleaned Oran out of Christmas decorations before they left, but with a little ingenuity and some help from "light-fingered" corpsmen, the nurses found a real fir tree and made tin tree ornaments from old plasma cans. "What a beautiful tree! It nearly reached the ceiling and we had plenty of homemade ornaments to lavish upon it. When it was decorated our guests could hardly keep their eyes from it!" writes Lieutenant Archard.[14]

The nurses fashioned over 700 Christmas stockings from G.I. sheets and a supply of red serge discovered in the old French barracks. It had apparently been used for making red sashes for French uniforms. Midnight mass, attended by all nearby military personnel and by the patients, even those on litters, was celebrated on Christmas Eve before an altar decorated with purple bougainvillea. Afterward the guests enjoyed songs, hot cocoa, and cookies. The next morning, Captain Carney played Santa in a red suit fashioned "out of that red serge, trimmed with cotton batting to take the place of ermine. I held my breath hoping the suit would hold together throughout the festivities. It had been made entirely by hand," Archard remembers.

Despite the stockings filled with small gifts the patients longed for mail from home, but as of Christmas morning none had arrived. Then as if by magic the electrifying news spread: "Mail, girls, bags and bags of it, Come and get it!" The nurses shared their letters and presents with the patients. "We laughed, we cried, and acted like children," Archard recalls. "The presents helped us—it was a beautiful Christmas."[15]

After the holidays, the fighting moved east into Tunisia, and Algiers became a rear area, but thousands of troops, new medical units, and supplies to support the campaign poured through its harbor. Among the new arrivals was the Twelfth General Hospital. 2d Lt. Billie Wittler, ANC, remembers their arrival and the truck convoy with armed guards that took the Twelfth General's nurses to their destination, Ain-el-Turk: "The sun was shining, we could see peddlers with oranges and dates, there were lovely French villas with flowers of every color and description, and steps leading down to the beautiful, blue Mediterranean." The scene seemed idyllic, but the reality of the North African winter soon struck, with weeks of rainy, cold weather. They "rarely saw the sun after that first lovely day."[16]

The Twelfth General Hospital set up housekeeping in a cluster of filthy abandoned seaside buildings only inhabitable after cleaning with hot water heated in small cans over little fires. "Mostly we used ice cold water which turned our fingers blue and took vigorous rubbing before it did any harm to the dirt and grime." Coming from large American hospitals "improvisation" was only a word to many of the nurses, but they soon learned to scrounge for jars, tin cans, cigar boxes, or mirrors—anything useful. Cans were as valuable as gold in North Africa in 1943 and were cut down and used for soiled dressings, made into bath basins, or used to carry food to mess halls.

At first, the Twelfth General had no mess hall and the nurses ate in a park, usually in the rain. Billie Wittler recalls, "The first morning we saw real oatmeal and honest-to-goodness American coffee was a memorable one. Even Spam tasted delicious—at first!" Feeding the hospital's growing number of patients was a time-consuming process which was complicated by the shortage of white-enameled dishes and of silverware. "It was not unusual for the day nurse and corpsmen to be doing K.P. at nine o'clock at night."[17]

Standard procedure at the Twelfth was to bathe and shave each new patient upon his arrival and shampoo his hair once during his stay. The nurses were not only responsible for patient care, but also made it their job to try to raise patients' morale: asking them about their families and assisting soldiers who were unable to write letters home. With a nurse's eye for details, the women even made certain each patient had money and a complete outfit before he was discharged. The nurses also gave the men candy and cigarettes, often purchased from their own PX rations.

As the rainy season ended, living conditions improved in North Africa and softball games became a nightly occurrence at the Twelfth. Everyone acquired a suntan on the lovely beach below the villas and nearby units gave parties. Nurse Tayloe recalls, "We were lured with attractive invitations telling us how many handsome young officers would attend, and how much food they had and what good music."

The amenities and pleasures of Ain-el-Turk and of nursing in rear areas were not shared during the Tunisian campaign by nurses of the many field and evacuation hospitals that followed American forces into Tunisia. These semimobile units, housed entirely under canvas, began to move out of Algiers shortly after Christmas to provide medical support for three U.S. divisions that were assembling near Tebessa in preparation for a large-scale offensive. Among the forward hospital units were several medical battalions, the Forty-eighth Surgical Hospital, and the Ninth and Seventy-seventh Evacuation Hospitals.

The Ninth Evacuation Hospital departed by train on January 14, 1943. Tayloe remembers, "We were six to a compartment, no heat and no light, and the cars of the train did not connect! Many of the windows were broken also." The nurses slept on the seats, baggage racks, and the floors, ate in messes set up in railroad stations or consumed C rations on the train, and yet managed to survive thanks to the numerous Arab urchins who sold them oranges, fresh eggs, and lemons en route. After a stop in the city of Constantine, the hospital moved by truck convoy 125 miles through what the Army came to call "Stuka valley" for the amount of strafing done by German Ju87 Stuka dive bombers. When they reached Tebessa, the Ninth set up in a pine forest and carefully marked the hospital area with red crosses painted on white sheets. Roberta Tayloe writes, "Kas and I prayed the Arabs would not steal . . . the white sheets on which the red cross was placed."[18]

Lt. Ruth Haskell of the Forty-eighth Surgical Hospital remembered their five-day journey to the forward area just after New Year's Day 1943 and their arrival at the hospital, which was so completely camouflaged to protect it from enemy air attack that at first all she could see were weeds. The nurses left the trucks and were led by enlisted men to their bivouac area. No lights were permitted, not so much as a flashlight or a match, and she remembers, "We started off slowly behind them, stumbling over the roots of trees and into depressions in the ground until our eyes became used to the intense darkness." The air was cold and the ground was like ice, but the nurses had nowhere else to sit and wait until the ward tents were set up.

Bereft of bedrolls (which had not yet arrived) the nurses spent a long night wrapped in their coats, sleeping on the cold ground. Haskell was lucky, she was at least fortified by a dram of warming Scotch offered by a friend who had been given a bottle on the train! "I had been brought up in a cold climate all my life, but have never suffered from the cold as I did in the few hours that passed before the welcome voice of Captain Sutton was heard exclaiming outside the tents, 'Your bedding rolls are here!'"

The day following their arrival, the women were allowed to explore their new surroundings, including the modern city of Constantine, before leaving by truck convoy for Tebessa. Lieutenant Haskell remembers the "joys" of traveling with the troops, especially the problem thirty nurses in coveralls had with calls of nature. They finally decided to rig an enclosure with four blankets, but Haskell "still maintain[s] the Army should fashion G.I. gals' coveralls."[19]

The hospital area at Tebessa was so scattered that the nurses' tents were three-fourths of a mile from the mess hall. Haskell vividly recalls their first night at Tebessa: her tent was on a hill at a 45 degree angle and she rolled right off her cot. Theresa Archard explains that the angle was the idea of an Army expert in natural camouflage. He thought that between the angle and the trees and natural vegetation the nurses' tents would be difficult for the enemy to spot. When morning came, fifty-eight "disgruntled nurses were ready to tear that expert to bits," Archard writes. Doris Brittingham bellowed, "Heavens to Betsy, do they think we're mountain goats?"[20]

The nurses' complaints prompted the colonel to relocate the tents to level ground, but Tayloe remembers that their situation remained grim: "It was bitterly cold, with snow on the ground, and we had no fires or lights. Even candles were taboo. We were in bivouac and could expect no quarter from the enemy. We stayed in bed most of the day to keep warm. We lay there fully clothed, complete with mufflers, gloves, and knitted caps. Our shoes were the only articles removed." For a week the Forty-eighth remained in bivouac and the nurses kept busy sewing a large red cross from sheets. They assumed the Germans would respect the Geneva Convention and not bomb the hospital if it was marked by a red cross.

Soon, however, both the Ninth and Forty-eighth were receiving casualties. Roberta Tayloe recorded the moment in her diary: "We started with a few patients, but by morning the tent was full. These young soldiers in Army pyjamas, with bandages on heads, arms, legs, and bodies, to say nothing of all the casts, had three blankets each. They were very quiet, a few cries here and there, a few soft moans, and snores of all kinds. It was bitter cold; no hot drinks for late arrivals, and some had not eaten for some time. Nor were there any more blankets." Later, the hospital was issued potbellied stoves.

By January 26, Nurse Tayloe had charge of six tents and five medics: "We were so rushed, the doctors and our O.R. [operating room] people working around the clock, snatching an hour or so when they were about to collapse." The cold weather turned rainy, with a gusty wind that pulled up the tents' stakes, exposing the wounded on their cots to the rain and cold. In her desperation to provide fuel for one of the stoves in her tents, Tayloe grabbed some wood from a group of enlisted men. She expected a lecture from the colonel the next day, but all he said was "If you must take the men's wood, order them to carry it for you!"[21]

The Forty-eighth Surgical Hospital moved forward on January 28, 1943, to Feriana, a small town of about 1,000 inhabitants, stucco houses, and olive and lemon groves. The hospital was moved into barracks that had just been vacated by German troops and were clean and ready for occupation. No sooner had the hospital set up than casualties began pouring in from the fighting at the Faid Pass and from the Maknassy area only fifty miles west of Feriana. The Germans had unexpectedly attacked the U.S. II Corps near the Faid Pass on February 14, 1943, and their advance threatened several American medical units. One company of the 109th Medical Battalion was captured and an officer from the Forty-seventh Armored Medical Battalion and four ambulances of casualties were also taken by the Germans.[22]

Following heavy American losses at Sidi Bou Zed, General Eisenhower and General Anderson decided to withdraw those Allied troops but to hold Feriana and the newly constructed airfield at Thelepte. The positions at Sbeitla and the Kasserine Pass were also ordered held.

The German advance and heavy fighting threatened to overrun the Forty-eighth Hospital's section at Feriana "about thirty miles from the front." Theresa Archard noted on February 14, 1943, "The troops are withdrawing. Huge formations of Mark IV and Mark VI tanks with their 88 mm guns had surrounded our infantry at Sidi Bou Zed, west of Faid Pass. Warning came we might have to pull out in a hurry." Orders arrived for the hospital to evacuate its patients, but two were too ill to move. Once again the nurses gathered up their bedrolls and were taken to their "G.I. limousines" and evacuated back to the Seventy-seventh Evacuation Hospital near Tebessa. Archard wrote, "We were in the middle of a convoy that was withdrawing. If the Jerries chose to come over we would just have to take it. Nurses had no business being in with the troops. It was a chance we took." The convoy made it to Tebessa without incident and the nurses were warmly greeted at the Seventy-seventh Evac, which to the nurses' surprise had electric lights in the nurses' tents. Lieutenant Archard and her fellow nurses were a bit envious: "Ever since our landing in Arzeu we had used candles. Our dynamo would only serve the operating room and wards." Feeling safe and secure, the nurses bedded down at the Seventy-seventh for a good night's sleep, unaware they were directly in the path of a planned attack by the German general Erwin Rommel, who wanted to strike the Allies at Tebessa on his way to Bone.[23]

Under pressure from the German advance, American personnel at Thelepte withdrew from the area after destroying thirty-four aircraft and 60,000 gallons of aviation gasoline. At the Ninth Evac, Roberta Tayloe knew something was up, as she confided to her diary: "We hear more guns than usual and patients are being evacuated right and left. Many more planes are overhead. The rumor is German Panzer tanks have broken through the Kasserine Pass." By lunchtime on February 17 they learned that the Germans were bombing the airport and were told to be ready to leave within the hour.

The nurses were quickly loaded into trucks, Roberta Tayloe writes, with one male officer to each truck: "and off we went, not being sure we would make it or not—much chatter that the whole lot of us would be captured." After a rough trip over rocky trails in open trucks, the nurses arrived cold but safe at the Seventy-seventh Evac at 3 A.M. Tayloe fell exhausted onto a cot only to discover the next morning that she was sharing her bunk with a black widow spider![24]

The route to Tebessa had indeed been vulnerable to a German breakthrough, but the Italian high command ordered General Rommel to confine his attacks to the north and not in the direction of Tebessa. On February 19, the "Desert Fox" ordered his Twenty-first Panzers to strike through the Sibla Gap, and the Afrika Korps, supported by the Tenth Panzer Division, to attack the Kasserine Pass.

The Kasserine Pass was defended by U.S. Engineer Corps troops and some hastily assembled reinforcements. Despite rain and fog, the Germans advanced on February 20 along the road to Tebessa, forcing the Nineteenth Engineers to withdraw. Late in the afternoon, Axis troops poured through the pass and across a bridge, but fortunately for Allied units in and near Tebessa, Rommel halted his troops momentarily in anticipation of an Allied counterattack. After much thought, General Rommel decided not to pursue the Allies at Hamra and seize Tebessa, but to make his main thrust toward Le Kef via the town of Thala.[25]

While the battle of Kasserine Pass raged, Theresa Archard's Forty-eighth Surgical Hospital had moved all over the Tebessa area trying to stay close to the fighting, but not so close as to be overrun by the Germans. Moving from Bou Chebka to Youk-les-Bans, the Forty-eighth set up and within hours admitted 600 patients, more than three times their capacity.

Feeding the overflow patients was almost impossible; the nurses and enlisted men "worked like beavers." When a kitchen tent caught fire and the flames outlined the hospital in the darkness, everyone held his or her breath. The Germans would never see their protective red cross in the dark and might well shoot first and ask questions later. Into this tense scene came the first of the nurses from medical units evacuating from the Kasserine Pass area. They had escaped, but all of them were worried about the soldier patients who had remained behind.

The Ninth and Seventy-seventh Evacuation Hospitals had left the Tebessa area in the nick of time, and on February 20 they relocated in the Ain Beida-La Meskiana area on the road to Constantine. They were soon joined by the Thala section of the Forty-eighth Surgical Hospital. Casualties from the battle kept all of these hospitals very busy: II Corps figures ran over 300 killed and 3,000 wounded. Losses of equipment, fuel, and ammunition amounted to more than the Allies had stockpiled in Algeria and Morocco combined, but shipments from the United States in March helped make up for the materials lost in the battle.[26]

On February 23, 1943, the Germans withdrew from Thala and resumed their former positions. Almost a month later, II Corps, now commanded by the colorful George S. Patton, attacked enemy positions in the south, followed by an Eighth Army offensive against the Mareth Line. This time the Americans seized Gafsa and Maknassy. Just three days later, the Forty-eighth set up several miles from Gafsa in open desert just cleared of German mines. Seriously wounded men were brought to the Forty-eighth from clearing stations and collecting companies, and those in need of surgery were taken straight to operating rooms. During the final phase of the Tunisian campaign, the Forty-eighth's ten operating tables were filled day and night. According to the official Army medical history, "The 48th Surgical Hospital's facilities were wholly inadequate for the steady stream of casualties from the three divisions operating in the El Guettar-Maknassy sector during the final drive." Fortunately, many of the hospital's admissions were able to be removed to evacuation hospitals 100 miles to the rear and those patients who were ambulatory were fortified for the journey with soup, crackers, and coffee at the hospital's "cafeteria."[27]

Thousands of casualties were evacuated from the front during the Tunisian campaign, and the necessity to make room for freshly wounded men forced the Seventy-seventh Evac and Ninth Evac to send their existing caseloads back to the United States. This measure, while expedient, resulted in the evacuation of many soldiers who would otherwise have been able to return to duty. Most of the wounded were evacuated by rail and road, although in the El Guettar-Maknassy area the rough terrain forced hospitals like the Ninth Evac to rely on litter carries. Unable to move safely in the daytime, the medical corpsmen and their patients waited in slit trenches until nightfall before beginning the long trip back to aid stations and hospitals. Although there are no statistics for litter carries, those for rail and road tell the story: 1,740 patients evacuated by road and 1,052 by rail in the south from January 16 to March 16, 1943. In the north of Tunisia another 5,628 injured men were taken out in just one month's time from April 10 to May 15.[28]

Unfortunately, the rail system in North Africa consisted of one narrow-gauge line, so despite the use of hospital trains that ran from Souk Ahras to Algiers, a great many wounded soldiers had to be flown out by aircraft. The patients were taken to holding units and then by ambulance to airfields where C-47 transport planes waited to fly them to Algiers. Each aircraft had a capacity of eighteen litters or twenty-four ambulatory patients, and many C-47s carried a flight nurse supplied by the 802d and 807th Medical Air Evacuation Squadrons.

The concept of air ambulances was not a new one to the U.S. Army, which had envisioned the use of flight surgeons and aircraft for the evacuation of wounded as early as 1921. By 1940 an air ambulance battalion was proposed and in May 1942 a medical air evacuation squadron was activated at Fort Benning, Georgia. The idea of including trained flight nurses originated in 1932 with Lauretta M. Schimmoler, who envisioned registered nurses serving in air ambulances or on transports. Her efforts to convince the Red Cross of the usefulness of her Aerial Nurse Corps failed in 1940, but they did attract the attention of Army Air Surgeon General Grant. He developed the concept of military flight nurses as part of Med Evac squadrons. On November 30, 1942, the U.S. Army made a nationwide appeal for graduate nurses and airline hostesses, ages 21 to 35 and physically qualified for flying, to volunteer for appointment to the Army Nurse Corps and into the air evacuation units. The first units were hurriedly trained at Bowman Field, Kentucky, by the 349th Group. Each squadron had a headquarters unit and four flights with one surgeon, six nurses, and six medical technicians per flight.[29]

One of the early graduates of Bowman Field was Lt. Henrietta "Mike" Richardson, who had flown as a hostess for Western Airlines before joining the Army Nurse Corps. She had grown to dislike flying, but was chosen for flight nursing because of her training and experience as a stewardess. Lieutenant Richardson recalls the training at Bowman Field as "rigorous" and said it included bivouacs and a jump from a forty-foot tower into a pool. She graduated in the first class at Bowman and left there on Christmas Eve 1942 by train for Camp Kilmer, New Jersey, where she boarded a troopship bound for Oran and Algiers. Her squadron, the 802d, was assigned to North Africa, and the other squadron, the 801st, to Guadalcanal.[30]

Life in North Africa proved even more rigorous than at Bowman Field. "Mike" Richardson says, "The water was polluted so they said we'd have to brush our teeth with champagne!" The nurses slept in sleeping bags on cots and kept their meager water ration in their helmets under their cots. "If we had an air raid and had to put our helmet on we lost our water ration," Richardson recalls.

Flying between Algiers's Maison Blanche Air Field and the Tunisian airstrips near the front was not without danger. Lieutenant Richardson's most memorable flight from Tunisia was with a neuropsychiatric patient on board. The fighting in Tunisia had produced an unexpected number of psychiatric disorders, but medical personnel discovered 58 to 63 percent of these were actually battle fatigue cases and could be returned to duty if they were given heavy sedation and transferred to a rear-line evacuation hospital for awhile. Air evacuation proved the fastest and most efficient means of handling such cases. On this particular flight, however, Maison Blanche Airfield was so fogged in that the plane had to circle the field and the pilot made several passes at the runway while firetrucks and crash trucks waited on the field. Despite the wear and tear on everyone's nerves, including those of the neuropysch patient, the C-47 finally settled down safely on the runway and no one was injured.[31]

The most dramatic example of the dangers of army flight nursing in the Mediterranean during WW II occurred in November 1943 on what was supposed to be a routine flight from Sicily to Bari, Italy, to evacuate soldiers wounded in central Italy. Pilot Thrasher had barely reached cruising altitude when the large transport ran into a violent thunderstorm. For over three hours the plane flew through thick clouds, unable to communicate with home base, while the thirteen Army flight nurses on board prayed for better weather and a safe landing in Italy.

Finally, Thrasher saw what he thought was an Allied airfield through a break in the clouds; but when he began his approach to the field, anti-aircraft guns opened fire on the plane and the nurses spotted planes on the field below marked with Nazi insignia. Chased by enemy flak and two fighter planes, Thrasher climbed into the cloud cover and safety, but after an hour the plane was running out of fuel and he again decided to land. This time the plane touched down on a small field in the mountains and came to a stop in the mud. The crew and nurses were met by some friendly local people who informed them they were in German-occupied Albania.

"For two days the party hid in a farmhouse where they were fed on water buffalo, slept on the floor where chickens pecked at their feet, and made their way among the herded goats at night to the only sanitary facility, a hole in the ground." The nurses' shoes wore out wandering for days in the mountainous terrain toward the coast, and one party was saved during a snowstorm only by practicing the survival training they had been given at Bowman Field. After walking through knee-deep snow, being chased out a village by strafing German planes, and being forced back because of German troop movements, one party of the downed flyers and nurses was told to go to an airfield where they would be rescued by four American transport planes. To the party's crushing disappointment, the transports flew over but refused to land when they saw two German tanks on a hill near the field. Although many were sick, including two with jaundice and one with pneumonia, they made their way back to the Adriatic coast. After a seven-day march, they were rescued by a British motor boat. Their guide, Lt. Gavin Duffy, praised the nurses, saying, "Those nurses were brave. They showed no signs of fear, even in the tightest spots." Nurse Agnes A. Jensen writes, "It all sounds exciting now, but looking back on it I think perhaps the cooties and fleas we all picked up caused us the most hardship." A second group of three nurses who had gotten separated from the other party wandered for four months in Albania, aided by Yugoslav partisans. They managed to avoid German patrols and finally made it safely to Twelfth Air Force Headquarters on March 25, 1944.[32]

In late April 1943, as the final phase of the Tunisian campaign got underway, more hospitals moved to the front, which was now concentrated in northern Tunisian between Bone and Mateur. Taking advantage of experience gained in the North African campaign for this final drive to Tunis, the medical section located the semimobile 400-bed hospitals with attached surgical auxiliary teams just behind the front lines, with evacuation hospitals supporting them in areas to the rear. These preparations for the final drive to Tunis required some hospitals to travel long distances. For example, the Eleventh Evacuation Hospital came 1,000 miles from Rabat to its new site nine miles south of Tabarka. An advance party of the Fifteenth Evacuation Hospital made a 660-mile trip to Tebessa without incident, and five days later the nurses and other personnel arrived by rail. From the windows of the crowded French passenger cars, the nurses watched the scenery and the Arab and French inhabitants of the area. The scene gave the trip "a tourist" aspect.[33]

The Fifteenth set up under canvas about forty miles behind the front lines, in an ideal location on level ground "solidly covered with grass and bordered by cactus stubble." Although the area was bordered by mines, there was sufficient space to erect the hospital's tents—within eight hours of their arrival the Fifteenth Evac was ready to admit patients. During the next nine days the Fifteenth received 104 patients, but as the fighting moved to northern Tunisia admissions dropped to almost zero. Soon the Fifteenth was on the move again. By now they had established an efficient routine for taking down the entire hospital, loading it onto trucks, and reassembling it rapidly in a new location. The journey from Sbeitla to Bedja, however, proved an arduous one because Army troops formed a solid line of traffic, forcing the Fifteenth's convoy of fifty-four vehicles to detour back though Tebessa then north to Souk Arras, Lamy, and east to Roums-es-Souk. They "traveled over tortuous mountain roads under total blackout conditions for the first time. The route was unfamiliar and although a small portion of the convoy was lost for a time, the 227 miles were covered without accident."

As soon as the Fifteenth Evac reached its destination eleven miles north of Bedja, the enlisted men went to work to set up and to prepare to receive the first of 311 casualties. Only eight miles from the nearest enemy position, the Fifteenth began admitting patients only seven hours after its advance unit arrived. The wounded were mainly from the combat teams of the First and Thirty-fourth Infantry Divisions, assisted by the First Armored Division, which were advancing in a northeasterly direction toward Mateur. For two weeks, the nurses and doctors of the Fifteenth kept up a frenetic pace as patients poured into the hospital. A total of 1,042 patients were admitted during this two-week period. The hospital's report states that they received, almost exclusively, battle casualties requiring surgery of "every classification." Among the casualties admitted to the Fifteenth was Lt. Gen. Lesley J. McNair, commanding officer of Army Ground Forces, who arrived on April 23. McNair was hospitalized for three days at the Fifteenth Evac until he could safely be evacuated to a rear area.

The Fifteenth Evac's stay at Beja was a memorable one; after all, the hospital's personnel were new to the front lines. As their report summed it up: "The experience at Beja served as an acid test of the capabilities of the surgical staff. Many new and unfamiliar surgical problems arose, and with the realization that we were relatively inexperienced, we felt that the job was well done."[34]

On May 4, 1943, Mateur fell, and American forces were poised for the final push to Tunis. Because the Fifteenth Evac was not in position to support the drive, it was ordered to pack up once again and move forward. On May 6, the hospital was ready to move out. In less than five hours it was settling in at a new site some twelve miles west of Mateur. Their former location was quickly reoccupied by the old Forty-eighth Surgical Hospital, which had reorganized as the 128th Evac. Also handling casualties as the Allies closed in on Bizerte and Tunis was the 750-bed Thirty-eighth Evacuation Hospital. During this final phase of the campaign, the Seventy-seventh Evac remained back at Morris, near the coastal city of Bone, to handle casualties evacuated from more forward areas.[35]

The fighting during the final two weeks of the campaign resulted in numerous casualties, and the mountainous terrain made evacuation of wounded back to hospitals exceptionally difficult. In desperation, the Ninth Evac resorted to mules, which carried litters in tandem. They also used the nearby rail line by fitting two half-ton trucks back-to-back over the rails. All along the II Corps front, the terrain made evacuation by ambulance or even jeeps difficult and medical battalions began using front-line troops and even cooks and clerks as litter bearers.

Meanwhile, in the rear areas, other Army hospitals were waiting to receive wounded soldiers evacuated from the front. Margaret Willauer, who joined the Army Nurse Corps in February 1942, spent five months at an Army hospital in North Africa and then served aboard a hospital ship making seven trips to England and two voyages to the Pacific theater. She says that her most memorable experience of the war was her soldier patients, "Their loyalty, bravery, uncomplaining attitude, and patience."[36] Among the nurses caring for injured G.I.s from the fighting in Tunisia was 2d Lt. Catherine M. Rodman, a surgical nurse attached to one of the auxiliary surgical teams. She told an Army interviewer about her arrival in North Africa: "We left here [the States] February 28, 1943. We had meetings aboard ship and talks and things like that. We became familiarized with our team, the function of the team, and we were asked what we would like to have, orthopedic, general, etc. Most of the girls were surgical girls, trained in surgery." After a few weeks in Casablanca, Rodman's surgical teams moved to Rabat, Morocco, where they drilled, did calisthenics, and listened to lectures before being sent out to help with surgery in various hospitals in Algiers, Tunisia, and even in some British hospitals.

A British hospital, the Ninety-eighth British General Hospital at Chateaudun on the plain of Constantine, provided the site for one of wartime medicine's dramatic moments. One April day in 1943, Professor Alexander Fleming arrived at the Ninety-eighth to test his new miracle drug on British patients. The assistant matron, Ursula Dowling, informed Miss Thorpe, the matron, of the arrival at the hospital of a mysterious stranger: "He's wearing a panama hat and khaki shorts and he hasn't got his knees brown yet." Professor Fleming applied his new drug, called penicillin, to a soldier suffering from gas gangrene. The soldier was, in the matron's words, beyond the help of modern medicine, "but to the astonishment of the staff at the 98th BGH, this man recovered." Penicillin was still expensive and in short supply, but it soon "revolutionized the treatment of wounds and death from sepsis was reduced to an amazingly low level."[37]

In addition to caring for sick and wounded G.I.s, Army hospitals and medical personnel were responsible for German prisoners who had surrendered to Allied forces by the thousands. Some POWs were taken by ship to the United States in the company of wounded American soldiers, but Army nurses were not usually assigned to tend the wounded on these trips. On one such voyage across the Atlantic in 1943, however, 2d Lt. Yvonne E. Humphrey, ANC, discovered she was the only woman aboard the ship. The Army had mistakenly assigned her to the ship as a medical officer: "When I reported to the ship the Commanding Officer was amazed to find that I was an Army nurse. There were no women patients aboard, and, as a matter of fact, they really had no accommodations for women," Fortunately for Lieutenant Humphrey, the vessel had been a coastal steamer before the war and not all of its cabins had been converted to troop spaces. Humphrey had a private room with a shower all to herself for the voyage, which she described as uneventful: "We never saw the feather of a single sub, and we decided Jerry knew there were some Nazis aboard and was therefore leaving us alone."[38]

Although not assigned to the ship as a nurse, Lieutenant Humphrey soon found her skills were needed because the ship's medical staff consisted of just one medical officer and nineteen corpsmen. When a German prisoner developed appendicitis she gave the anesthesia for the operation, nursed a very ill hospital corpsman, and stepped in to care for a severely burned patient whose second degree burns had crusted over. "The corpsmen were afraid to touch this case," she says, "so I took it over, for certainly an experienced nursing hand was needed to spare this boy as much suffering as possible."

Lieutenant Humphrey found that most of the German prisoners were "polite, orderly, and cheerful"—possibly because, as they told her, Hitler would soon come to occupy the United States and they would be glad to be there to greet him! She recalls that the Germans were young, most of them between nineteen and twenty-two, and had been in the military for two to five years. Although she did not speak German, nor they English, she was able to communicate with them using signs and gestures. The prisoners were given a good meal of meat and potatoes when they arrived on board the ship and provided with an ample supply of cigarettes. "Our men treated them with dignity and respect, if not with warmth and enthusiasm," she writes.[39]

While Yvonne Humphrey was sailing to the States, the war in North Africa was ending. With the surrender of German and Italian forces in the II Corps sector on May 9, 1943, and of all remaining Axis troops three days later, the Tunisian campaign officially came to a close. In the struggle, Army hospitals had played a vital role, admitting 6,730 patients during the fighting in southern Tunisia and another 8,629 patients between April 10 and May 15 in the north. When hostilities ceased, 275,000 Axis troops surrendered and had to be located and taken care of in camps. The prisoners included the patients and personnel of two German field hospitals, which continued to operate until May 15 under the supervision of the Fifty-first Medical Battalion.[40]

The U.S. Army's need for medical care did not stop after the surrender, so the Ninth Evac remained in the Tunis area as a station hospital caring for as many as 100 outpatients a day. By May 1943 there were a number of U.S.Army hospitals in North Africa, including the Twelfth Evac, which set up near an A-20 bomber field at Souk-el-Arba. "The hospital went up so rapidly that one thought someone had waved a wand or rubbed Aladdin's lamp," wrote nurse June Wandrey in her diary. A native of Battle Creek Michigan, Wandrey had enlisted in the Army Nurse Corps shortly after Pearl Harbor and was assigned to the Mayo unit in Rochester, New York, although she was under the age limit of twenty-two years. "They need surgical nurses so badly," June explained to friends. Throughout her months overseas, June kept a diary and filled it with candid comments about duty in North Africa, Italy, and France. She also wrote frequent letters to her family describing North Africa—the scorching heat and strong wind, the Stukas overhead, swimming in the Mediterranean, and bargaining with Arab boys for sweet, "blood-red" oranges, or being given a pair of curved, polarized sunglasses by an Italian prisoner. Wandrey had been on her own since the age of sixteen and resented the restrictions placed on nurses during the North African campaign. When a P-38 pilot friend of hers was killed dive-bombing Tunis, she took a walk along a mountain stream to be alone and mourn, but returned to the hospital to find she had been restricted to her tent. In her diary she wrote, "The army's running a nursery school. If you don't tell Gruesome and Chewsome when you're going, you're a naughty, naughty girl."[41]

For the thousands of young German and Italian soldiers that passed by Wandrey's hospital after the surrender, World War II was over, but for others the struggle to control of the Mediterranean had just begun. Serving in Italy and on the Italian-held islands of Sicily, Sardinia, and Corsica, they waited for the Allies' next move. The question was where the American and British armies would strike next, a decision Allied planners were discussing even before the conclusion of the Tunisian campaign. After considering their options, the Allies decided their next objective would be a joint amphibious landing on Sicily on July 9, 1943. Code-named HUSKY, the operation would put Gen. George Patton's U.S. Seventh Army ashore on the southern coast of Sicily, while Gen. Bernard L. Montgomery's Eighth Army landed on three main beaches to the east. Medical plans for Operation HUSKY included sending attached medical units, supplemented by special supplies of blood plasma, morphine syrettes, and extra dressings, ashore on D day, followed by one 400-bed evacuation hospital per division. Planners decided that no fixed hospitals would be brought to Sicily until the island had been conquered. Until that time, casualties would be evacuated to North Africa by sea on troop carriers, hospital ships (or LSTs, Landing Ship Tanks), and by air.

After a stormy voyage from various ports in North Africa, American and British troops came ashore on Sicily on the morning of July 10. At first, the attackers met only light resistance from the Italian defenders, many of whom surrendered in large numbers, but German units assigned to hold the island fought back tenaciously. In the American sector at Gela, on Sicily's south coast, Italian tanks of the Livorno Division and German panzer tank units penetrated Allied lines and almost reached the sea before they were stopped by General Darby's Rangers and men of the "Big Red One" First Infantry Division. With the American beachheads then secured, General Patton sent his II Corps north to Termini to cut the island in two, while Gen. Lucian Truscott's Seventh Army broke free and advanced quickly toward Palermo in northwest Sicily. In eastern Sicily, however, British forces were slowed down in heavy fighting against the Germans, who kept General Montgomery from attaining his main objective, the city of Catania, which was the key to seizing Messina and the Straits of Messina, which formed the Axis's only escape route to the Italian mainland.[42]

The first American hospital unit to begin operation in Sicily was the Eleventh Evacuation Hospital, which opened on July 15 at Licata. Col. Raymond Scott recalled that the unit's four medical officers, sixty nurses, and eighty-eight enlisted men arrived in Sicily by Landing Craft Infantry (LCI): "They almost beat the infantry in and called themselves the 'Commandos.'" Another early arrival in Sicily was June Wandrey, one of dozens of nurses crowded twenty-four to a compartment on board the LCI crossing from North Africa. "During the night, a violent storm tossed our little craft around like a cork, even the pack mules got seasick too," June writes. The LCI took the nurses right into Licata harbor: "A number of sunken vessels were cluttering up the harbor. Some fishing boats were blown out of the water and were sitting upright on land." The nurses' arrival surprised the harbor master, who was expecting the Tenth Field Artillery, not ninety-eight nurses.[43]

The women were quickly welcomed to Sicily by an air-raid warning that proved a false alarm, but they did witness an aerial dogfight between returning Allied planes and German fighters. One American plane was shot down. June Wandrey had a friend in an antiaircraft (AA) battery who took her in his jeep to the downed aircraft: "The pilot was okay," she remembers. "He gave me his parachute as a souvenir, and I used it constantly. We were never issued pillows."[44]

Within two hours of touching Italian soil, her unit was caring for casualties. She says the hospital was located between an ammo dump and a makeshift airfield, "just a bomb's drop from the harbor." Here, in a stubble-riddled field teeming with "fleas, lizards, mosquitoes and ants," they pitched their tents. The nurses soon discovered that their most serious problem at Licata was a shortage of potable water and they were rationed one canteen of water a day from a guarded water trailer. This meant that the nurses had to bathe in a nearby sulfur creek. "Sulfur doesn't suds and my skin felt awful," Wandrey writes. "All of the hospital's bloody linen was washed by hand in a scant amount of water. Then it was hung to dry on the shrubs or scattered about on the ground to dry in the sun."

From the very beginning it was evident to all that Sicily would not be a vacation spot. Coming ashore with the first invasion forces meant that the nurses had to learn to dig foxholes, to expect bombs to fall nearby, and to eat cold C rations. They also learned to adjust to the frequent air raids. "Air raids became routine. At first I'd peek out of my pup tent to see who was getting the worst of it. After awhile, I'd just cradle my helmet in my arms and try to go to sleep again. We needed all the rest we could get," Wandrey writes.[45]

Despite the primitive conditions and bombs dropping all around them that first day Colonel Scott says of the Eleventh Evac's nurses, "They were a happy group of girls in spite of the fact they were hard put for food, had no water except in the canteens, and slept in half-shelter tents." By the next day, however, the men had the hospital tents set up and the unit began receiving its first patients, 900 cases in three days. The Eleventh cared for casualties at that location until Palermo fell and also received II Corps patients when the Ninety-third Evac moved from Gela on July 21. For those patients, this meant a rough four-hour ambulance ride from the Fifteenth Evacuation Hospital at Caltanisetta.[46]

The Fifteenth Evac was one of the first hospital units to arrive in Sicily, wading ashore at Gela on D day plus four (July 14, 1943). Unlike the invasion forces, the hospital personnel enjoyed an uneventful 24-hour voyage on an "unusually calm sea." After marching through the town of Gela, they bivouacked in a burned-out wheat field two miles north of the town. Without their vehicles which had not yet arrived, the Fifteenth could not unload its equipment from LSTs on the beaches. Here confusion reigned, and the Fifteenth Evac discovered that no provision had been made for moving nurses or baggage. In fact, no one knew exactly which ship contained their equipment. In desperation, the hospital sent some of its officers out to the ships to determine where their equipment was located and to supervise its unloading.[47]

Lt. Mary Hawalt was one of the nurses assigned to the Fifteenth Evac. She recalls their arrival in Sicily: "Yes, we went in the invasion and landed at Gela. We waited there for a few days. Incidentally, I and eighteen of us left there and went up to the clearing station for three days to work at the front lines." On July 20, the unit finally moved from Gela west through Licata and then north to Caltanisetta, where they set up on a plain bordered by wheat fields. Utilizing skills honed during the Tunisian campaign, the Fifteenth quickly unloaded tents and equipment, each truck rolling into its preassigned area. An advance party had staked the exact location of each tent the day before and in three hours the basic unit of the hospital (three ward tents, a supply and mess tent, and nurses and doctors' quarters) was up and ready to receive patients.

Injured and sick G.I.s soon began pouring in to the Fifteenth Evac, which was supposed to be a 400-bed semimobile hospital. Mary Hawalt says, "we were way over at Caltanisetta. I tell you what we did. These medical units, the 51st Medical battalion, came in and helped us out most of the time in bed capacity because we didn't have the beds." According to Hawalt, most of the patients admitted to the hospital at Gela or Caltanissetta were not battle injuries but soldiers suffering from diseases, mostly malaria. The unit's annual report bears her out: only 154 of the cases admitted to the hospital during its stay at Caltanisetta were listed as injuries and 583 were listed as disease cases. As the Fifteenth Evac's staff had quickly learned in North Africa, "maintaining a specific policy of hospitalization during combat would be virtually impossible" in Sicily. At Caltanisetta the Fifteenth did manage to evacuate most of their patients after four days, but such evacuations involved "the use of rough winding mountain roads and took over four hours one way by ambulance."[48]

It took several days, however, from the time the Fifteenth arrived at Caltanisetta for the rear area hospitals to be set up, ambulances from the Fifty-fourth Ambulance Battalion to arrive, and the route to be designated. In the meantime, the Fifteenth had every bed filled. Those patients who were expected to be able to return to their units within ten days were taken back to the Eleventh Evacuation Hospital near Agrigento, and the cases that required longer treatment were flown out of the airfield near Agrigento to hospitals in North Africa. Informal air evacuation from Gela had begun on July 14 using available aircraft until the 802d Medical Air Evacuation Squadron could arrive to take over the air route using transport planes equipped with a flight nurse and a medical technician. In all, between July 10 and August 20 the Army evacuated 5,967 men by air from Sicily and another 5,391 by sea.

During the early stages of the Sicilian campaign, an equal number of patients were evacuated by sea from Gela, from Licata, and from Scoglitti over the beaches or from the small harbors. The Ninety-third was set up at Gela to serve II Corps and the Eleventh Evac at Licata to support Seventh Army. When General Truscott's troops reached Palermo, the facilities of that port city became available for use by American medical units as a staging area for sea evacuation. The Ninety-first Evac set up in a University of Palermo clinic and was reinforced on August 6 by the Fifty-ninth Evac.

Capture of the port of Palermo enabled the Americans to open a coastal sea evacuation route, and on August 1 a captured Italian train permitted the army to transport wounded and sick GIs from the 128th Evac at Cefalu directly to Palermo and on to waiting ships. Although the larger ships could come into the Palermo harbor, the docks were in no condition to be used to load patients, so they had to be taken out to the ships by landing craft and winched on board. The hospital ships *Acadia* and *Seminole* took on American patients, and three British hospitals ships and five hospital carriers evacuated their wounded. The latter were shallow draft vessels that carried six water ambulances each and could evacuate wounded from the beaches or small harbors. 1st Lt. Muriel M. Westover, ANC, was a nurse on the *Acadia*: "We sailed into Palermo three days after it was taken and got the casualties . . . from that battle." Muriel explains that the ship made trips back from Palermo to Oran and Bizerte, except once, when they received so many patients they returned to Algiers.[49]

The rapid advance of American troops in Sicily required maximum mobility from Army hospital units, and each division clearing station had to have at least one field hospital unit adjacent to it and a 400-bed evacuation hospital within ambulance distance. Those casualties that were too seriously injured to be evacuated were operated on by attached surgical units at the field hospital before being sent back to an evacuation hospital. Lack of suitable hospital sites, limited shipping space, and front lines that moved constantly meant that during the Sicilian campaign hospitals tended to be overcrowded. Less serious cases were sent immediately to Palermo and often evacuated back to hospitals in North Africa. For 166,000 troops committed to Sicily, the U.S. Army had only 5,000 beds. In fact, only one 750-bed evacuation hospital was sent to Sicily, the Fifty-ninth Evac, which landed at Palermo on August 6, 1943.[50]

The advance of Truscott's "Trotters" was so fast that units like the Eleventh Evac were soon on the move again up the coast to a new site. Traveling forty-two miles from Licata, they set up briefly at Agrigento. June Wandrey described the scene to her family in a letter written on July 19, 1943: "We're high up on a hill with mountains on all sides except one, and that has the sea. Ancient cities with old and modern ruins are perched on two of the mountains. . . . This was originally a grain field and the stubble is quite high. My stockingless legs are scratched to shreds." She told her family that she had just cooked her supper over canned heat, but that the cocoa had boiled over and the bouillon water spilled because the ground was so lumpy. She and some of her fellow nurses were anxious to do some sightseeing, so they took an ambulance into Agrigento on a watermelon-gathering expedition. Wandrey says they found a Sicilian who spoke French and were able to buy several large melons, but one nurse who wanted a bathing suit could find only an old woolen knee-length suit with wide bands of color. "Expensive, too, only twenty dollars. The suit looked like it came from a Smithsonian exhibit," writes Wandrey.

After four days near Agrigento the hospital went by convoy to Palermo. "The men are complaining about moving so often, packing and unpacking a hospital unit, and pitching all those tents," Wandrey wrote to her family.[51] According to the official report, however, the nurses and other medical personnel learned to adjust to life in the field. Colonel Scott explains, "After several days, there was no particular glamour. Every night the Germans came over with planes and we rolled into fox holes. As the flak came through the tents, nurses wore helmets constantly. Everyone was frightened at first, but later paid no attention to it. Bombing and strafing are like thunder and lightning—the thunder scares you and the lightning kills you if it hits—if it doesn't—! During the bombing there was comradeship; everyone joked and laughed."[52]

The hospitals moved frequently during the campaign to secure Sicily's northern coast. Sometimes they were even ahead of the engineers repairing the coast's narrow, twisting road. June Wandrey remembers one particular move: "One night in my topsy turvey Sicilian world, we got a rush march order in the middle of the night. Our ambulance was creeping along in a blackout, hanging on the side of a mountain. I was sitting with the driver to help him see the road. Squinting in the dark I thought I saw a soldier with a gun beside the road and I told the driver to stop. I stuck my head out the window and said, 'We're looking for a place to set up a hospital.' The guard exploded, 'My God, women, the bridge is out ahead, we're waiting for artillery.'" She adds, "We had a terrible time turning around."[53]

Transportation in the interior of Sicily meant tortuous mountain roads, dust, and heat. Lt. Theresa Archard and the nurses from the Forty-eighth Surgical Unit, which had learned the ropes in North Africa, also served during the Sicilian campaign. But nothing had prepared the nurses for the terrain of Sicily. Archard vividly describes their twelve-hour trip from Licata to Cefalu: "Starting from Licata on the seacoast, we traversed the island from south to north. That journey was endless, up and down mountainsides, around curves that shut out of sight the rest of our convoy, through miserable little towns. The people seemed scared until they saw the Red Cross bands on our arms. Then they shouted, 'Americanos, viva Americanos!'" In every small town and village Sicilians ran out of their houses to greet the passing American convoy "and to watch us in amazement—women dressed as men, nurses!"

Night fell, and the convoy rolled on without headlights toward Cefalu. Archard and the nurses opened their U rations and ate the spaghetti cold, right from the can. "We were in strict blackout. It was the dark of the moon, and those trucks were steered by guesswork. Over the hills, bumping up and down on the hard seats, the blankets forever slipping, we wondered how long the journey was going to last." At one hairpin turn in the road, the trucks had to go forward, back up, then go forward again. The driver of Archard's truck "was cussing for all he was worth."[54]

Despite the roads, the nurses arrived safely in Cefalu at three o'clock in the morning. But instead of falling exhausted into their cots, the women discovered that the tents were set up "sans cots": "What did it matter?" asks June. "Spreading the blankets on the ground, arranging the musette bag, kicking off the G.I. shoes, in no time at all we were dead asleep."

When morning came Lieutenant Archard and the other nurses were greeted by a hot breakfast and by orders to move from the empty tents to the nurses' "area," a beautiful lemon grove set in soft sand. "In our G.I. shoes, which were much too large, with the blistering heat and the touch of malaria most of us had, plowing through that sand was going to steal what little pep we had left," Lieutenant Archard thought. And energy was going to be needed, for by afternoon the patients were arriving by ambulance and by the truckload.

Soon the nurses and medical personnel were back to working twelve- and fourteen-hour shifts. The nurses were longing for the arrival of their baggage, with those cool seersucker uniforms, but the baggage truck had gotten lost and they had to endure more days in their soiled overalls. At least at Cefalu the women had a beautiful beach nearby and "could take a dip every so often."

Their hospital now boasted an eighteen-bed ward for brain cases, which were treated by two brain specialists, and another ward for sucking chest wounds. But most of the patients admitted to the hospital at Cefalu were evacuated within twenty-four hours. "There was not much chance to get to know our patients— two or three days and they were gone," Archard recalls. Nonetheless, when they came to the receiving tent, patients were given a warm greeting by the Red Cross worker, Maybelle Kahle, who "made a tremendous difference in the atmosphere of the hospital." She dispensed cigarettes, Red Cross supplies, and cheer to each newly arrived patient. Although determined to see every patient, she finally had to give up and get some sleep. "She gave in, but not without a struggle," writes Lieutenant Archard.

Local Sicilians also came to the hospital in their gaily decorated carts to sell melons and grapes, and Italian prisoners of war were employed as laborers and litter bearers. Their assistance was greatly needed, for "the weather grew hotter by the minute and more patients were coming in; this time the medical cases exceeding the surgical. Those boys were very sick. The infantry had holes in their shoes by now." Conditions in the operating rooms at the hospital were especially difficult. "The blackout was complete. We worked by flashlight, the sides of the tents rolled up to let in some air. Planes were fighting fiercely in the distance, the roll of the barrage getting worse as the night wore on. Catania would be taken very shortly. 'But there won't be a building left' was the prophecy."

At least the meals were improving: they were getting some meat and a few tomatoes, green peppers, and onions. Still, in the summer heat everyone was growing weary. Even the nurses and doctors were getting sick, and Archard writes, "We were tired from plowing through that loose sand, tired of trying to keep track of the empty beds for the receiving ward, and tired of drinking chlorinated hot water. We were tired of looking at tired faces—we were just plain tired."[55]

The Sicilian campaign was exhausting for everyone, the heat proving as bothersome as the retreating Germans. On July 30, June Wandrey wrote to her family, "It's incredibly hot. The last time we bivouacked four nurses played bridge. Visualize our tent with the top full of flak holes, slime trails on the canvas left by snails at night. We sat on our army cots, used the ground for a playing surface. Each of us was in our underwear. With the temperature a usual 103 plus, we had our laundry pails filled with sea water in which we soaked our feet. Around our head and neck we had a small, wet hand towel."

As the Germans pulled back along the coast toward the Straits of Messina, the Americans pursued them and evacuation hospitals were sometimes located only a few miles from the front lines. Wandrey wrote, "We were so close to the lines we could see our artillery fire and also that of the Germans. The Jerries have poor aim today. Shells landed in front of us and behind us." The hospital was so overwhelmed with casualties that even the dentists were doing minor surgery and all cases, American or German, were treated according to the strict rules of triage. "Belly or chest wounds take precedence over orthopedic surgery or simple debridement," Wandrey writes. Naval casualties from ships bombed offshore added to the hospital's case load and the auxiliary surgical teams "work non-stop 'til the shock wards are emptied of patients."[56]

The work of caring for so many seriously wounded patients was emotionally draining on the medical personnel. In a letter to her family, June Wandrey confided: "Working in the shock wards, giving transfusions, was a rewarding, but sad experience. Many wounded soldiers' faces still haunt my memory. Many of us shed tears in private. Otherwise we try to be cheerful and reassuring. I've seen surgeons work for hours to save a young soldier's life, but despite it they die on the operating table. Some doctors even collapsed across the patient, broke down, and cried. There are many dedicated people here giving their all. Very tired." Although most of the nurses came down with malaria, Wandrey reported that the symptoms were seldom reason enough to stop working: "We had to work with temperatures of 103 or more. The G.I.s frequently offered me their cot, saying I looked worse than they felt." Male patients with malaria were often evacuated to Africa, but "the nurses stayed on duty in Sicily."[57]

When Catania finally fell to British forces on August 5, the Germans withdrew toward Messina and the Straits that separated Sicily from mainland Italy. The U.S. Ninth Division, with assistance from Montgomery's Seventy-eighth, continued to press Randazzo, but the British failed to take advantage of their air and naval superiority to close rapidly in on the straits and cut off the Axis retreat. Along Sicily's north coast, American troops slogged eastward, attempting to reach Messina from that direction, but could not make sufficient progress to trap the fleeing Germans.

As the front lines changed, Army hospitals moved up to be nearer the fighting. On August 7, the Ninety-third Evac moved to San Stefano, about thirty miles from Cefalu. The Eleventh Evac went to Brolo on the same day. Half of Lieutenant Archard's nurses moved to San Stefano and the other half remained at Cefalu. Packing up the hospital tents and equipment in the scorching Sicilian heat, she recalls, was a chore: "The corpsmen were out in that blazing sun putting up tents, pulling them down, perspiring, short-tempered, thinner by twenty to thirty pounds. The dreadful heat was taking its toll." Many of the nurses had lost weight and all of them were atabrine yellow.[58]

Archard, twenty-five nurses, and the Red Cross worker went by truck along the coast past waist-high geraniums, overturned tanks, and ruined houses to the town of San Stefano. Here the tents were already set up and occupied by very ill G.I.s. The nurses went right to work, bathing patients with hot water from their Lister bags, giving them clean pyjamas, and sending them to new cots with fresh sheets.

During the Sicilian campaign, from July 10 to August 20, 1943, American hospitals admitted a total of 20,734 American patients, 338 Allied soldiers, and 1,583 civilians. Of those 13,320 were sick, 5,106 were battle casualties, and 2,308 had noncombat injuries. In general, American sick and injured soldiers received excellent care during the battle to secure Sicily. Cots were not always available in sufficient quantities at some locations, but according to Lt. Mary Hawalt, medical supplies were adequate. The only problem she recalls was the availability of diphtheria antitoxin: "We had some diphtheria and diphtheria antitoxin over there was impossible to get ahold of. We had to wait as long as forty hours one time before some of it arrived." She explains that the Fifty-sixth Evacuation Hospital had used the supply of antitoxin from the medical depot during an outbreak of diphtheria in Palermo.[59]

On September 8, 1943, the Italians surrendered to the Allies. In the towns and cities of Sicily the local population poured into the streets and town squares to celebrate peace. Unaware of the surrender, June Wandrey and her fellow nurses drove into the town of Corleone and were surprised to see crowds of people: "They mobbed us. The jeep would barely move. An Italian couple took them up to a balcony and they waved to the cheering crowds . . . all the church bells were ringing. It was soul inspiring. Lights came on in house windows that had been blackened out for ages because of the continued air raids." Some of the crowd entered a church and brought out two of their oversized saint statues on a candle-rimmed platform and started a procession. Italians came up and pinned money on the saints' robe and when two G.I.s who were absent without leave got hold of band instruments the procession's music tempo changed. June says, "It was a night to remember."[60]

Not only were the Italians celebrating the end of a difficult campaign, but also their relief after years of Fascist rule under Benito Mussolini and of semi-occupation by German troops. The weary men of Hitler's Wehrmacht, however, had managed to escape across the Strait of Messina on barges right under the Allies' noses. By the morning of August 17, 1943, the Germans had successfully evacuated 55,000 troops, over 9,000 vehicles, and 163 guns from Sicily to the mainland, from which they would continue to fight the Allies until the end of World War II.[61]

5

FIFTH ARMY FIRST

Nursing in the Italian Campaign

 With the Allies firmly ashore on the island of Sicily, Allied planners could turn their attention to the next objective in their strategic plan to attack the Axis's "soft underbelly." On July 17, 1943, Gen. Dwight D. Eisenhower, buoyed by the early successes of the Sicilian operation, decided that the Allies should give serious consideration to an invasion of the Italian mainland. In Washington, Army Chief of Staff Gen. George C. Marshall seconded Eisenhower's choice, stressing the early capture of the Italian capital at Rome. Restricted in their choice by the need to keep the invasion beaches within range of Allied fighter aircraft, they selected a half-moon sweep of beaches along the Gulf of Salerno south of Naples. Here, amphibious task forces would land the U.S. VI Corps near Paestum and the British X Corps north of the Sele River. Code-named Operation AVALANCHE, the Salerno landings were set for September 9, 1943, preceded by a British landing at Reggio on the Italian "boot."[1]

Medical plans for VI Corps's part in Operation AVALANCHE were made by the Corps's surgeon, Col. Jarret Huddleston, and by Col. Joseph Martin. They included four Army medical battalions, the 261st Ambulance Battalion, and the Fourth Medical Supply Depot, which would bring in extra dressings, litters, plasma, blankets, atabrine, and biologicals. Each of the two American divisions would have the support of 400-bed and 750-bed evacuation hospitals and four field hospitals. When the beachhead was secured, these hospitals would be joined by six 500-bed station hospitals and four 1,000-bed general hospitals. Also included in the invasion operation plan were nine teams of the Second Auxiliary Surgical Group, who would go ashore as part of the assault wave. Army nurses for the evacuation hospitals would go ashore on D day plus two.[2]

Operation AVALANCHE was executed as scheduled. The assault waves reached the Gulf of Salerno on the evening of September 8, a calm, bright moonlit night made more peaceful by the radio announcement of an armistice with Italy. The news set many anxious soldiers' hearts at ease, for they now expected to walk ashore into the arms of friendly Italians. Instead, as the troops of the 141st and 142d U.S. Infantry Divisions waded onto Italian soil, they were met by intense enemy fire sweeping across beaches strewn with land mines. Heavy enemy fire from tanks and 88s on D day even prevented some Allied landing craft from beaching. On Beach Blue, one battalion was pinned down for twenty hours.

German opposition to the landings resulted in many Allied casualties. In the American sector, Army corpsmen barely had time to give the wounded first aid and hide them in foxholes or ditches. A couple of collecting companies from the 111th Medical Battalion did manage to set up near the town of Paestum by late afternoon on D day. Of the clearing companies assigned to the Salerno operation only two from the 162d Medical Battalion were in operation that first day. By dawn on D day plus one, the Army was able to put additional first-aid stations ashore, and by using "ambulances, jeeps, trucks, and hand-carried litters," casualties were collected and assembled on the beaches for evacuation. Salerno's beaches were exposed to enemy aircraft, artillery, and machine-gun fire, which did not distinguish aid stations and medical personnel from combat troops. In fact, one crippled German plane landed and exploded near a clearing station. The 120th Medical Battalion report notes that newly arrived patients "displayed unusual agility in jumping from operating tables into foxholes." Medical personnel, including Navy corpsmen and medical officers, managed to evacuate 678 wounded to transports offshore on D day and D day plus one. In view of the stiff German opposition to the landings and of the dangers faced by medical personnel on the beaches, the decision not to include nurses in the assault waves was a wise one.[3]

Ironically, however, hospital ships standing off Salerno were no more immune from enemy bombing than they had been off Sicily in July, and Army nurses once again found themselves "in harm's way." Among those units assigned to the Salerno operation was the Ninety-fifth Evacuation Hospital's nursing complement, which embarked for Italy on the British hospital ship *Newfoundland* at Bizerte on September 10. According to the nurses' report, "We saw many German and Italian prisoners in Bizerte. They were poorly dressed, and an ill-nourished looking lot, but seemed always to be in good spirits. This was true, especially of the Italians. The German prisoner is, in G.I. parlance, always inclined to be an 'arrogant cuss.'"

After a short voyage, the *Newfoundland* came into the Gulf of Salerno on the morning of September 12 and a message was sent ashore that the nurses had arrived. "We could hear artillery fire and several times heard planes overhead," the report continues. "Several other hospital ships were nearby and at noon we had our first taste of real war when a bomb landed near our ship." The near miss prompted officials ashore to order the hospital ships out to sea and postpone landing the nurses until Monday morning. Although anxious to rejoin their units on the beachhead, the nurses could only be patient and wait. To pass the time they "played cards and sang songs, and visited with British nurses and doctors on board the ship." At 0500 on September 13, more German bombers came over. "There was no mistaking our ship. Three or four other hospital ships were nearby. The ships were lit up like Christmas trees. The large red crosses on the ship's funnel and every small green light around the ship was burning."

Despite its clear Red Cross markings, *Newfoundland* became a target for German bombers and at 0515 took a direct hit from a German bomb. It was a terrifying moment for the Army nurses and other personnel on board: "All around us walls and articles of furniture were piled high. It was pitch dark. Nurses with their tiny flashlights were calling to each other and searching for articles of clothing." When the hospital ship caught fire, the nurses were ordered to report to their abandon-ship stations. The nurses' report describes the scene: "Orderly and surprisingly cool and apparently ready for what was ahead of them, the nurses one by one climbed the stairs to the deck and took their places at their boat stations. From there on the British sailors took over, constantly ribbing us about tea and a late breakfast that had been promised us the night before, they helped everyone of us over the side into our life boats." From the boats they could watch the ship burn. A total loss, it was later destroyed by gunfire.

All of the American nurses made it safely off the *Newfoundland* and were taken back to Bizerte. But this time the tables were turned; instead of being caregivers, the nurses found themselves tagged as "survivors" and sent to the Seventy-fourth Station Hospital at Mateur as patients. "Several of the girls needed hospital care. The rest of us rested up and slept for the first time in several nights." The experience of being bombed and abandoning ship had taken its toll on the nurses' nerves, and one wrote, "They might have dispensed with their watch aboard the ship that took us back to Bizerte. We heard every noise and watched closely and rather fearfully any planes going overhead."[4]

Newfoundland was not the only hospital ship to serve off Italy. Making her wartime debut at Salerno was the *Shamrock*, a former Ward Line vessel that had just missed duty as a hospital ship during World War I. When the United States entered World War II, the need for hospital ships brought the *Shamrock* back into government service as an Army hospital ship. In addition to the 202d Hospital Ship Complement and her crew, the *Shamrock* had a number of Army Nurse Corps nurses.[5]

Sally Weaks remembers the day the nurses joined at Camp Kilmer, New Jersey. It was the Fourth of July 1943: "They were all newly graduated nurses, new in the army but very enthusiastic over an assignment to a hospital ship. With one exception, they had never been on a ship and few had even seen the ocean. Twenty-nine nurses, one dietitian, and one Red Cross worker sailed as there was no room to carry more women on the ship."

Although newcomers to Army life, the nurses were given two months of intensive overseas training, including swimming, abandon-ship drills, and the use of life preservers. "It was all done in a spirit of fun and we were certainly none the worse for having the training," Weaks recalls. Then on August 19, 1943, the nurses boarded the *Shamrock* and joined the 202d Hospital Ship Complement. The ship was dirty, the workmen were still in possession, and all was in a state of confusion, but the nurses and staff got down to business immediately, cleaning wards, checking supplies, memorizing plans to evacuate the ship in case of disaster, and learning to manage in life boats.

On September 4, 1943, *Shamrock* finally sailed, and after four days of stormy weather and abundant seasickness, life on the hospital ship settled down to a routine described by Sally Weaks: "We made hundreds of muslin wrappers to sterilize surgical equipment. We sorted instruments and set up surgical trays, treatment trays, infusion sets so as to be ready to function as soon as possible."[6]

When the *Shamrock* finally arrived in the Gulf of Salerno, Allied forces were still locked in a deadly battle for control of the beachhead. Once off Salerno, the hospital ship's nurses and crew were anxious to receive their first wounded from the battle raging ashore but, to their disappointment, learned the ship could not enter Naples harbor. They could only stand by and wait: "Each night the *Shamrock* was alerted and received orders to cruise around outside the blackened out harbor. There was little activity those nights. We sat on the open decks in the humid darkness and stared at the distance where the mountains should have been. Most of the night we could see the glow of flares and gun flashes."[7]

Finally, on the afternoon of September 25, the *Shamrock* took on its first group of wounded. "Many of us watched the landing barge ploughing across the harbor cutting a wide circle around the ship before tying in. Then came the announcement that sent everyone to his post at a trot—Medical Department! Stand by to take on patients." Slowly, each litter-bound wounded man was hoisted aboard the ship from the landing craft. Sally Weaks recalls, "Everyone forgot the heat of the afternoon, the uneaten chow, all other activities, to get those wounded boys to bed and make them comfortable. Many of these first patients came directly from the battlefield. Their clothes and their records were still smeared with blood and their boots frosted with mud. Some of them had only the everyday medical tags which had been tied to their clothes by the medics."[8]

Ashore on the Salerno plain, evacuation hospitals were also coping with the onslaught of wounded from the bitter fighting for the beachhead. The Ninety-fifth and Sixteenth Evacuation Hospitals landed on D day, but both required time to assemble their equipment, and initially both hospitals were without their nursing complements, which had been on board the *Newfoundland* when it was bombed.

Operating without their nurses proved only a temporary inconvenience—after resting in Bizerte following their ordeal on the *Newfoundland*, the Ninety-fifth Evac's nurses returned to the Gulf of Salerno. On September 24, 1943, they waded ashore uneventfully. The hospital's nursing report noted: "We climbed into trucks once more on Red Beach near Paestum, Italy, and joined our officers and men. They looked like ghosts of their former selves. They had been working night and day." The notations in a hospital diary during the days at Paestum are worthy of note: "Sept. 13, 1943—The fact that our nurses are not with us is costly." Again on September 15, 1943—"The fact that our nurses are still not with us has proved a serious handicap to our medical and surgical staffs." The nursing report adds, "It was a happy bunch of individuals that set to work together the next morning. Tales flew thick and fast."[9]

The Ninety-fifth Evac's nurses found the hospital set up under canvas as usual, but closer inspection revealed the addition of a preoperative, or shock, tent and a postoperative tent where the same surgical team cared for patients following surgery. This new arrangement reflected the fact that the caseload at Salerno was predominantly battle casualties in need of surgical care before being evacuated back to the Zone of the Interior. A nurse serving with an evacuation hospital in Italy describes working in the field in a letter to the New York *Herald Tribune*:

> You are horrified at first when you realize the grimness of it all. Horrified that you, a trained nurse from a civilized country, a nurse used to American standards of medicine and hospitals and living in general, can set up a place so primitive to be used to save human lives. . . . Your professional equilibrium is thrown topsy-turvy for a few minutes when you see the first wounded men brought in and you haven't the white-walled operating room to care for them. You see them lifted on a litter to the operating table, dirty clothes and all. You remember how a surgeon at home would use ten or twelve sheets and as many as twenty-seven towels to do one little appendectomy. Here he would amputate a leg in half the time with a maximum of six clean towels.[10]

Working for the first time in their new beige seersucker uniforms, the Ninety-fifth Evac's nurses helped care for a record number of patients at Paestum—2,443.

By the time the Fifty-sixth Evacuation Hospital arrived at Salerno from North Africa, the beachhead was secured, Allied troops were advancing inland, and the hospital area at Paestum was quiet and out of harm's way. Not so the port city of Naples, which the Allies finally captured on October 1, 1943. They found the city destitute: the departing Germans had deliberately wrecked the port, polluted the city's water supply, destroyed the spaghetti factories, and piled hotel furniture in the courtyards. Allied salvage experts, with the experience gained in Palermo and Oran, rushed into Naples and reopened the port. Finding delayed-action bombs proved more difficult. One exploded at midday at the Naples central post office, injuring a number of Italian civilians.

Fortunately, Army nurses and medical personnel entered Naples soon after its capture. The Ninety-fifth Evacuation Hospital went to work in buildings belonging to the "23rd of March" hospital, named "for the date of the inception of Fascism in Italy." The hospital's chief nurse reported, "The Germans had destroyed the water and electric plants before they left Naples, and our equipment was not adaptable to buildings without these facilities. Nurses, doctors, and corpsmen worked twelve hours a day from Oct. 9th to Oct. 19th." Most of the hospital's patients were surgical cases, many from mine and bomb accidents in and around Naples. Not even hospital personnel were immune from these nasty delayed-action bombs and booby traps—in November, one of the Ninety-fifth Evac's enlisted men was killed in a mine accident in the city.[11]

While salvage experts and other military units worked frantically to repair Naples, additional hospital units were being transferred from Sicily to the Italian mainland to support the Allied drive up the peninsula. Among them was June Wandrey's unit, which crossed the Straits of Messina on DUWKs on October 22, 1943. DUWKs were amphibious vehicles that could carry fifty men or 5,000 lbs of equipment, but "comfy they're not" Wandrey wrote to her folks. The nurses bivouacked overnight at Reggio di Calabria and the next day began a trek north by DUWK. "We spent many days in convoy, over rugged mountain roads with hairpin turns," writes Wandrey. "To make each curve the DUWKs had to back up and that slowed us down to a snail's pace. All along the way we bartered for fresh eggs, chickens, potatoes, and fruit to supplement our awful C rations the Army furnished."

After a five-day journey, the nurses arrived in Caserta and set up a 400-bed hospital in an Italian-German barracks "heavily camouflaged by scenes of tall trees painted on the building." Nurse Wandrey, assigned six wards of patients, cared for them under total blackout conditions, for German aircraft frequently raided the area. She recorded her impressions at the time: "I can hear Gemans go overhead time after time and then you hear the bomb as it bursts. You just keep doing whatever has to be done. There is no place to hide. No bomb shelters. I'm so very tired. Three and a half hours of sleep wasn't quite enough for me. Suppose I'll ever be able to sleep again?"[12]

By early October the Germans had skillfully withdrawn from the Salerno plain and had formed a defensive line across Italy from Sorrento to the Adriatic. The British pursued them to the Trigno River and the Americans took Avellino, but forces were abruptly halted at the Volturno River. By now it was autumn, and constant rain turned the inadequate road system into a morass of mud. The result was a nightmare for Allied medical personnel trying to transport and care for the wounded. Ambulances were unable to move closer than five miles to the front because of the mud and shellfire, so medical evacuation depended on litter bearers, mules, and even breeches buoys on steep slopes. Many times it took as long as twelve hours to get wounded men to casualty clearing stations.

Although well aware of the dangers and inconveniences of having hospitals so near the front, the Army decided that the rugged conditions of the Italian campaign justified the risk. Consequently, in mid-October, the Ninety-third Evac was sent from the relative safety of Paestum to Montilla, and the Ninety-fourth went to Avellino and then to Piano di Caizzo, north of the Volturno River.[13]

At the end of November, the Ninety-fifth Evac and Tenth Field were ordered up to the little village of Capua. The Ninety-fifth Evac's nursing report describes their situation: "We set up our hospital for the fifth time and began the real work as an evacuation hospital. The battles were being fought around the mountain heights near Cassino, not far away. Artillery fire can still be heard plainly during the day and the sky is brilliantly lit up at night. Groups of bombers fly overhead night and day, and the battle casualties are coming in." The Ninety-fifth's staff, including nurses dressed in army fatigues, field jackets, and field boots, worked long hours caring for wounded, hungry soldiers arriving from the fighting near Cassino. With a well-earned hint of pride, the Ninety-fifth's nursing diary notes, "A sign, 'When did you eat last?' is significant, and is placed outside our receiving tent door. Hot soup, sandwiches, and coffee with a good warm fire and the best medical attention that we Americans can give is to be had by these boys once they reach our hospital."[14]

Among those serving near the front in October 1943 was 2d Lt. Catherine M. Rodman, ANC, a surgical nurse assigned to a team composed of one major, a captain, a lieutenant, anesthetist, a nurse, and two corpsmen. The Second Auxiliary Surgical Unit also had shock teams, neurosurgical, maxiliofacial, and orthopedic surgical teams that were sent out to various hospitals to perform surgical work. Rodman was assigned to the 400-bed Thirty-eighth Evacuation Hospital near Venafro. "We got up there before they had taken Venafro. We were established quite near the front lines, near the Clearing Station. I don't know how many kilometers we were down from there but I do know we could hear the artillery fire going day and night. You get accustomed to the sound. We were right near the main road and tanks went by," Rodman told an Army interviewer in August 1944. She remembered the weather was freezing cold and the terrain was "volcanic earth, split, and when it rained it just seemed like quicksand. The mud was so bad that when you did get stuck in the mud you had to have someone pull you out." The Thirty-eighth was set up in hilly terrain under tents, but, Rodman reported, "It didn't do any good to dig a ditch because it would be filled up with water and flood your tent every time it rained. There wasn't any lumber in that part of the country. I always carried my floorboard. I had a floorboard made in Africa and I took it everywhere with me."[15]

As fall gave way to an early winter, living conditions for soldiers and medical personnel worsened. Now, in addition to battle casualties and accident cases, Army hospitals near the Cassino front saw an increasing number of frostbite victims. "We had an inflow of a lot of medical cases of frostbite. In that region, it was so cold, they had to stay in trenches so long when they were trying to take that big hill over there. The boys had to stay in that water and there was a lot of frostbite." Lieutenant Rodman's surgical team also operated on many battle casualties: "We did a lot of head cases. It depended on the action up ahead. One time they had that new bomb that they were using whatever it was. It didn't kill them instantly. It sort of hits them in their legs, arms. We did a lot of amputation up there of extremities. We had a tremendous lot of them." She explained that the new bomb appeared around Christmas time, but that the type of surgical cases they saw "depended on the type of artillery or drive ahead. There was no fixed ratio of any kind." Lieutenant Rodman pointed out, however, that the hospital always had plenty of plasma and a blood bank that stored whole blood donated by surrounding troops: "On certain days when they needed blood they would ask for volunteers and these boys from the infantry and different units came in."

Surgical teams saw a great many infected wounds at the Italian front, but in 1943 penicillin was not available to fight infections. Rodman's interview reveals the methods the teams could use: "We did use sulfa a great deal. The troops used sulfa themselves in the tablet form when they were hurt. It certainly saved a lot of lives and infections. They did have a gas gangrene anti-toxin which they gave to patients. It helped sometimes; sometimes it didn't. We did amputations in those cases. We had to clean them out if [we] could. Some of them were very extensive."

Using surgical teams that were temporarily attached to evacuation and field hospitals proved an efficient system in Italy. As Lieutenant Rodman explained, "We trained our own corpsmen and we were just like a little family. We worked with the surgeon and we could tell just what he wanted. We familiarized ourselves with his work so we could give him just what he wanted. We got along well together." But as to training she said, "Well, we had our basic training but you learn by experience you know. You jump in a foxhole and you learn to do it in a hurry in combat. We had no basic training in the States at all. I got my complete training in Rabat and we did get good training."[16]

In early November, the VI Corps had advanced up Route 6, but it could not crack Monte Cassino and the Bernhardt Line. Although heartened by these hard-won advances, including the capture of San Pietro, VI Corps' Gen. Mark Clark realized that his forces could not reach Frosinore in time for a planned Allied landing at Anzio, which was scheduled for mid-December. General Eisenhower agreed with Clark, and the operation, code-named SHINGLE, was cancelled.

Meanwhile, at Fifth Army hospitals in Italy, nurses and medical personnel tried to celebrate the holidays. Two days before Christmas, June Wandrey wrote to her family complaining about the weather: "I have to wear my wool-lined field jacket. As soon as the sun sets, the cold is vicious. Will I ever be warm again? It doesn't seem like Christmas-time without snow. We wallow through mud instead, and it's not very pleasant. It's the poor soldiers I worry about who have to bail water out of their foxholes, and don't get to take their shoes off for days at a time. Trench foot is terrible. The suffering of our young men is awful."

On Christmas Day 1943, she wrote about the arrival of Red Cross packages for the patients and the appearance of Italian civilians who brought fruitbars to the injured and ill. She and her two wardmen sang carols for the patients;

"Then," she wrote, "we tucked them in their cold, hard cots. The men never complain. You can't help loving all of them."

On Christmas night a windstorm blew down many of the hospital's tents, caused others to leak badly, and put the stove pipes out of joint. Wandrey worried about her charges: "Many of the patients are only 18 and 19 years old. They had to grow up too fast and fight for America. Many are homesick and scared about their wounds."

Fortunately, Wandrey was able to get away briefly from the mud and hospital routine for a visit to the island of Capri. She spent the night at a beautiful hotel in a room with furniture and real beds and "an inner spring mattress. All I've slept on since I came to North Africa was a cot and a lumpy bedroll under me or sometimes just the ground." Although they had to leave the next day to catch the ferry back to the mainland, the much-needed respite from war was obviously greatly appreciated, " 'Twas lots of fun being . . . cared for, if only for fifteen hours."[17]

While Fifth Army hospital personnel and patients tried to salvage some holiday joy amid the ravages of wartime, at Allied headquarters high-level commanders continued to debate the future of the Italian campaign. When General Montgomery's gloomy views about the campaign reached the ears of the British prime minister, Winston Churchill, he decided to revive the Anzio operation, an amphibious left hook up the west coast of Italy. Working his charms on Ike and his staff, Churchill finagled the retention of fifty-six much-needed LSTs in the theater and that convinced the Americans to go ahead with the Anzio landing.[18]

The operation, code-named SHINGLE, intended to land 110,000 men from the British First Infantry and U.S. Third Division at the seacoast towns of Anzio and Nettuno. Medical plans based on an expected casualty rate of 10 percent of the assault troops and 5 percent of the other troops, included the Fifty-second Medical Battalion, the Thirty-third Field Hospital, and the Ninety-third and Ninety-fifth Evacuation Hospitals, which would care for nontransportable casualties.

The SHINGLE forces sortied on the night of January 21, 1944, and the first waves hit the beaches as scheduled the next morning. To everyone's surprise the troops waded ashore unopposed. Gen. Lucian Truscott's Third Division quickly moved inland, rounding up dazed German defenders, while U.S. Rangers took the town of Anzio and prevented the enemy from blowing up the mole in the tiny harbor.

The Second Platoon, Thirty-third Field Hospital came shore at H hour plus six and units of the Ninety-third and Ninety-fifth Evac soon followed, but both quickly came under enemy fire. Although there were no injuries, ward tents were shredded by shell fragments and it became apparent that the entire Anzio-Nettuno beachhead area was a prime target for the Luftwaffe and German artillery in the hills above the town. In an effort to provide a safer hospital site, both the Ninety-third and Ninety-fifth packed up their gear and moved to a field two miles east of Nettuno, while the newly arrived Fifty-sixth Evac cared for their patients.[19]

Nurses came up to Anzio from Naples on board LCIs on January 28, 1944. Rumors about the dangers of the journey had reached many of the nurses, and they boarded the landing craft with some apprehension. The Second Auxiliary Surgical Unit's diary records the scene: "We knew it had possibilities of being more than 'just another boat trip' as even the hospital ships had been having trouble in these waters recently—and although we were laughing, joking, and apparently happy, there was a nagging thought in the back of each mind which constantly reminded us of the members of our unit who had been along this same route less than a week ago." The landing craft arrived off Anzio the next morning. The Second Auxiliary Unit's nursing report describes their arrival: "While debarking at Nettuno, twin city of Anzio, about 10:30 A.M., Jerry planes circled overhead. Finally when all were ashore, we were rushed hurriedly away from the port leaving luggage behind. The port was bombed shortly after we left. None of us really thought about being scared, as we still had not been 'Baptized in the fire.'"

They soon would be, for German aircraft had arrived over Anzio on D day and were seldom absent during the coming days and weeks of the Anzio campaign. The beachhead was also the target of enemy artillery, especially the big guns they called "Anzio Annie." The Second Auxiliary Surgical Group diary repeatedly refers to enemy air raids and shelling:

January 29th: Air raids—finished our lunch under the table.

February 3rd: All nurses restricted to hospital area due to shelling of Anzio and Nettuno. Rumors are that nurses may be evacuated from the beachhead, but nurses did not want to go.

February 5th: Beachhead really a hot spot. Shellings and air raids constantly. 2nd Platoon of 33rd Field Hospital moved today because of shelling in their area. No one injured.

February 8th: Shelling too close for comfort.

February 10th: Our worst day yet. Shelling in our area.[20]

2d Lt. Inis M. Kaufman, who arrived at Anzio on D day plus six, paints a vivid picture of the air raids and shelling: "It was like a perpetual Fourth of July fireworks display, each night at Anzio. You could see the flares and the ack-ack tracers. . . . Then there were the occasional planes falling in flames, the heavy concussion of artillery fire—I'll never forget the crashing of those 90 millimeter AA guns of ours!"

Lieutenant Kaufman arrived at Anzio a veteran of two Allied invasions, but recalls, "It was the first time we nurses didn't have to wade ashore. At

Casablanca, and [during] the invasion of Sicily, a group of Army nurses of which I was a member unloaded from our LCI a few feet from shore and had to wade to the beach." The nurses found their hospital tents already set up by the determined enlisted men, who had worked night and day despite constant artillery and strafing. Chief Nurse Lt. Blanche Sigman told a *Servicewoman* magazine reporter that at the time of the nurses' arrival, "We were offered a house with a bomb-proof roof in which to sleep, but we are staying in the tents so we can be near the patients during air raids. All the girls wanted it that way."[21]

And air raids there were! Virginia Barton, a nurse with the Ninety-fifth Evac, recalled one air raid: "Jerry came over one morning strafing while we were at breakfast. Everyone slid under the table. I had always heard that when you were hit all you could feel at first was something hot and sticky. Sitting under the table I felt something real hot hit my neck. Reached up and it was sticky. I started yelling, 'I'm hit!' One of my friends looked and had a big laugh. The hot cocoa turned over and was dripping through the crack in the table on my neck."[22]

On January 30, the Fifty-Sixth Evacuation Hospital arrived and in its first thirty-six hours admitted 1,129 patients. Protecting patients and staff from shell fragments proved nearly impossible in the low ground of the hospital area. Attempts to dig out the hospital wards and cots below ground level often failed because the water table was only a foot down. In desperation, sand bags were used to build walls around the tents, but even they were inadequate protection against direct hits, as a tragic incident on February 7 showed.[23]

The Ninety-fifth Evac was bustling with activity that fateful day. Ambulances were bringing in freshly wounded soldiers, the X-ray tent was overcrowded, and operating rooms were filled to capacity. Suddenly, an enemy plane streaked across the sky with a Spitfire in hot pursuit. As the desperate German pilot jettisoned his bomb load to gain speed and altitude, his five personnel bombs came crashing down on the Ninety-fifth Evac. Clouds of dust rose from the tents and as the explosions went off chaos reigned. In one tent Lt. Blanche F. Sigman and 1st Lt. Carrie T. Sheetz had just finished giving a patient plasma. Bomb fragments killed both nurses instantly and a bullet ripped through the tent, mortally wounding Lt. Marjorie Morrow, ANC.

In another ward, a patient was miraculously saved by his brother who was visiting him at the time and threw himself on top of the wounded man's cot. The visitor was killed by bomb fragments, but his brother survived. In a similar incident a litter bearer carrying a patient into the operating room (OR) tent instinctively shielded the wounded G.I. on his stretcher when the bomb exploded. He too was killed instantly.

Inside the OR, Lt. Col. Howard Patterson was probing a soldier's skull for shrapnel when the antiaircraft fire began. The surgical team coolly continued to operate until a bomb fell close by the tent, sending hot fragments whizzing through the tent. Nurses and medical personnel in other tents at the Ninety-fifth also reacted calmly and professionally to the attack. When the shelling stopped, they immediately assessed the damage, checked for new casualties, and then began cleaning up debris and transferring surgical cases to other units better able to care for them: the Ninety-fifth was crippled. The X-ray equipment was declared a total loss, twenty-nine tents were destroyed, and much of the equipment was damaged. The hospital's commanding officer, Colonel Paul K. Sauer, was wounded, as were sixty-four other personnel. Three nurses, two medical officers, a Red Cross worker named Esther Richards, fourteen enlisted men, and six patients were killed. No amount of effort could return the Ninety-fifth to peak efficiency, so on February 9 the hospital traded places with the Fifteenth Evac at the Cassino front.[24]

By deftly switching these two mobile hospitals, the Army was able to provide uninterrupted medical care on the beachhead, despite almost continual enemy artillery shelling and harassment by the German Luftwaffe, which exacted its toll on Anzio's hospitals and reminded everyone on the beachhead, veterans and newcomers alike, that no one was safe. The very day of the Fifteenth's arrival, enemy artillery fire hit the Thirty-third Field Hospital, killing two nurses and one enlisted man and wounding eleven others. The nurses were Chief Nurse Lt. Gertrude Spelhaug and 2d Lt. LaVerne Farquar, known as "Tex," who were off duty at the time the shell exploded. Red Cross worker Ruth Y. White wrote later, "Fragments hit the generator including the operating tent, plunging all the tents into darkness. Concussion knocked the medical personnel off their feet. Patients became frightened; they could not move, but lay on their cots and worried about the nurses." Urged to go to the foxholes, the nurses refused: "There is not a single one of us who will let this shelling of hospitals chase us off the beach. We are here to stay."[25]

The shelling set the hospital's generator on fire, igniting nearby tents (including the operating room where Major Mason and his surgical team were in the middle of an operation). Because even a small fire is a potential disaster for a hospital entirely housed in flammable tents, this fire brought everyone running. Firefighters from the Fifty-sixth Evac rushed to the scene to contain the blaze and extra litter bearers arrived to carry patients to safety, some still connected to I.V. bottles of blood held by corpsmen. Thanks to this quick response, disaster was averted and the Thirty-third was back at work the next day.

The shelling continued without let up for weeks. Jeanne Wells, who volunteered to leave the Twenty-first General Hospital at Naples for temporary detached duty at Anzio, recalls, "We were taken there by a British hospital ship with red crosses all over it. Nevertheless, when we reached the bay near Anzio the shells started coming all around us. This scared us to death, but finally we got to the shore by small boat." Lt. Dorothy F. Meador was nonplussed about the shelling: "I thought I had seen the worst. We were all so seasick that we did not worry much about the bombs. But I did not count on my tent catching fire this morning. The stovepipe blew down during the night and nobody noticed it till the flames burst."[26]

Jeanne Wells soon discovered the shelling of hospital sites was neither sporadic nor accidental: "There was shelling day and night. We were required to wear helmets all the time and fined if caught without them. At night when awakened during an air raid, I would wake Sally and she would reach down and put it over her head and go back to sleep. I was not that relaxed and able to sleep." She adds, "One early morning I heard the shelling and got out of bed to look outside and see what was going on. When I went back to my cot I found that a piece of shrapnel had pierced through my cot!"[27]

Other nurses were not so fortunate. On February 12, a nurse at the Fifty-sixth was wounded during an air raid and five men at the Fifty-second Medical Battalion and Third Division clearing station were hit. A Second Auxiliary Surgical Team's nurse recorded in her diary:

> February 12th: At 9:00 PM, air raid . . . dropped anti-personnel bombs all around us. (20 holes in Lt. Mary Campbell's and my tent). One nurse injured at 56th Evacuation Hospital. The 'Anzio Express' or 'Whispering Pole-cat,' as many call the big gun, has really been throwing the shells into the harbor the last few days.

> February 15th: Everyone's bed is placed down in his foxhole. Some raids lasted 45 minutes tonight. One Liberty ship in harbor was hit. No work tonight, which is fine for it is too 'hot' for the patients for us to work here.

> February 16th: Artillery is so heavy this morning that it sounds as if they are in the tent next to mine.[28]

The situation on the Anzio beachhead improved little over the next few weeks, for the Allies were confined to an area only fifteen miles wide by seven miles deep. There was no "front line" at Anzio, no safe rear area in what the soldiers came to call "Hell's Half Acre." Here, combat troops were dug in next to support troops; antiaircraft guns, maintenance shops, ammunition and gasoline dumps, and an airstrip were so close to one another that artillery fire intended for legitimate military targets often fell on medical areas.

Attempts to enlarge the beachhead repeatedly meet stiff German resistance and resulted in heavy casualties. One one occasion, the Germans nearly drove to the beach but in a "touch and go" battle, using every spare man from the town and port the Forty-fifth Division was able to contain the enemy attack. The effort cost the Forty-fifth Division 400 men killed, 2,000 wounded, and 1,000 missing. Naturally, these casualties kept Anzio hospitals frantically busy. In her diary, a nurse of the Second Auxiliary Surgical team wrote: "February 17th: 'Snowed under with work.' February 20th-28th: 'Everyone working very hard, often 24-hour shifts.'"

The number of casualties at Anzio prompted the Army to depart from its usual medical procedure and require all beachhead hospitals to perform operations. For example, in one twenty-four-hour period at Anzio, the Ninety-fourth Evac, with the aid of auxiliary surgical teams, performed 138 operations. For Jeanne Wells, the nursing at Anzio was "depressing, as we had to care for the wounded from the front lines. These patients had brain injuries, mental fatigue and almost every kind of injury possible. The surgeons would spend hours doing brain surgery and the patient would die soon after." She remembers caring for one patient who had a small non-magnetic object in his eye that caused him to go blind. "He asked me if there was any visible injury and there was not, so he decided not to tell his wife that he was blind."

Hospitals in the Anzio-Nettuno area also cared for civilian patients. "Most were displaced persons. The authorities were trying to evacuate as many civilians as possible, as it was too hard to care for wounded civilians and soldiers. Many of the civilians would not leave their homes." Wells especially remembers "a little girl about five years old with a fractured arm who was all alone. There were natives coming into the ward looking for family members and a young woman found her daughter. It was a most emotional reunion."[29]

During the fighting in February, the Germans also suffered heavy casualties and by March were exhausted. Except for one sharp unsuccessful attack against the U.S. Third Division on February 29, by the spring of 1944 the struggle for Anzio settled down into a prolonged lull.

While the VI Corps and the British clung tenaciously to Anzio beachhead, Allied divisions made one futile attempt after another to breach the Germans' winter line, which barred the route up the Liri Valley to Rome. Each new battle brought fresh casualties for the frontline hospitals; some of them were veterans of Anzio who had been moved inland to be near the Cassino front. Wounded poured into Fifth Army hospitals that winter and early spring of 1944. Not all of the patients were injured in combat. Many suffered from trench foot after days, even weeks, in wet socks. The symptoms of trench foot—red, swollen, painful feet—came on quickly when the man's circulation was curtailed as he lay motionless in damp foxholes. The first cases showed up in mid-November 1943 in Italy and rapidly increased from 305 cases in November to 1,323 in December and even more in the first months of 1944. The treatment for trench foot was bed rest, warmth, and elevation of the feet. All this meant that the soldier would be out of action for as many as 45 to 70 days.

"War neuroses," or combat fatigue, cases were also common during the Italian campaign; in fact, 15 to 20 percent of all battle casualties in Italy were caused by exhaustion brought on by lack of rest, improper food, and the noise and tension resulting from enemy shellfire. The usual treatment for combat fatigue was to bathe the patients, feed them, and send them to bed for two days with sedation if necessary. Except for the serious psychiatric cases, most were returned to their units after four days of rest. Army nurses in charge of psychiatric patients often sought creative ways to improve their patients' morale. For example, Nurse Virginia Barton taught her patients to knit and crochet. "I had them making bedspreads, etc.," she recalled. Barton also tackled the problem of low morale at her hospital in 1944: "On Christmas 1944 mail was not coming through and patient morale was at low ebb. I managed to obtain a Christmas tree from General. Had my psych patients start making ornaments for the tree out of old electric bulbs. Before long the entire hospital was involved in the project. And what a Christmas we had out of leftovers!"[30]

Not all Army nurses cared for American patients, as Roberta Love Tayloe discovered when her unit was assigned to care for non-English speaking patients— French soldiers, Arabs, and others serving with the French army. She found the Ghoums the most interesting of her foreign patients: "These people are fearless and can move without a sound. We had guards around the unit but they came and went as they pleased." The Ghoums had a savage habit of cutting off the ears of their enemies and wearing them on a necklace around their neck. American hospital policy was to remove the necklaces from Ghoum patients upon admission and put them away in a safe place where non-French patients would not see them. Tayloe recalled the shock one of these ear necklaces gave an American medic from the south who awoke and saw a Ghoum necklace on the cot next to his: "He came into the tent I was in at the time screaming, 'Nurse, nurse! I have been hexed, I have been hexed!'" She said that it took a doctor and a tranquilizer to calm the poor soldier down.[31]

Although not routinely in danger of being injured or attacked while serving at most Fifth Army hospitals during the winter of 1944, the women were vulnerable to occasional attacks by emotionally distraught American G.I.s or by German soldiers. June Wandrey related the story of one nurse in her unit who went to the latrine tent in the middle of the night during a storm: "As she walked through the opening flap, she heard someone move. She turned on her flashlight. In the corner was a soldier. She didn't recognize his uniform. The soldier hit the nurse over the head with a sharp rock, leaving her with a gash in her scalp. She screamed and fell backward unconscious into the rain, but eventually regained consciousness and was able to stagger back to her tent." The attacker's identity was never determined and the hospital did post a temporary guard around the nurses' tents, but June Wandrey realized that they could not spare the personnel for long. "I have my ears so tuned they can detect the brush of a hand on the tent canvas. Will I ever learn to sleep again? soundly? I think not," she wrote to her family after this incident.[32]

With the Italian campaign mired in a stalemate along the Gustav Line, the Anzio front settled down to await the warm, dry weather necessary for success in central Italy. For the troops and medical personnel at Anzio, the lull brought no real rest from air attack or fire from "Anzio Annie," but spring did allow games of baseball, fishing, and swimming off Nettuno's beaches. Soldiers holed up in the trenches and caves at Anzio enjoyed listening to the radio's "Axis Sally," who played jazz tunes and related crude propaganda in a sexy voice. In Nettuno, off limits catacombs bars featuring black market wine sprang up and the lull even led to a few romances, which bloomed among the beachhead's G.I.s and Army nurses.

One such romance led to Anzio's first beachhead wedding, when 2d Lt. Genevieve Clark, ANC, married 1st Lt. Thomas G. Rose before an altar made of 105 ammunition cases "covered with pine boughs and flanked by peach blossoms and narcissus arranged in steel helmets." Chaplain Maj. Lloyd E. Langford performed the ceremony before 300 nurses, soldiers, and officers who sat on ammo cases and kept their steel helmets nearby in case of air attack. After the wedding the happy couple used a trench knife to cut their huge pink wedding cake decorated with doves and two silver wedding bands! The newlyweds, reported *Servicewoman* magazine, "refused to disclose the most tantalizing secret of the entire affair—where they were going to spend their honeymoon on Anzio's one mile square beachhead."[33]

Happy moments were few and far between at Anzio that spring of 1944, and newly arrived hospital units quickly realized Anzio was far from being a peaceful, little resort village on the picturesque Italian coast. When the Ninety-fourth Evac set up north of Nettuno on March 21, 1944, the German Luftwaffe gave them an official greeting: "We had our first air raid at 2000 hours that night; the flak was very heavy and fell into several areas of the hospital." This raid proved the rule, not the exception. A barrage of 150 shells fell on the hospitals on March 12 with no damage, but two days later twelve patients and two officers were killed and seventy-five men wounded at the British 141st Field Ambulance. The Fifteenth Evac was hit by tank shells on March 21, 1944—four patients were killed.[34]

These incidents were only a prologue for more severe air raids to come. On March 29, the Germans bombed the hospital area north of Nettuno. 2d Lt. Inis Kaufman was on night duty in one of the wards when the air-raid alarm went off. The whir of approaching enemy planes was heard and then, she says, "a tremendous explosion shook the hospital, the ground beneath the tents shook violently and all the lights went out." She was thrown to the ground and thought she had been hit, but realized the pot of water she had been boiling on the pot-bellied stove had spilled on her back when she fell. She was unhurt, but a young patient sitting in her deck chair had been sprayed by shrapnel—her windbreaker draped over the chair was riddled with holes.[35]

Medical personnel calmly cared for men rewounded in the attack. The Fifty-sixth Evac was hard hit, three officers, fourteen enlisted men, nineteen patients, and a nurse were wounded and four patients were killed by the attack. Over at the Ninety-third Evac, three enlisted men died and thirty-one others were wounded in the same bombing. The air attack prompted some grimly amusing responses from the patients. When the German planes came over, one soldier got up out of his bed, walked to the camp headquarters, and demanded to see the sergeant major. "I want to be transferred to another hospital, right away!" he insisted.[36]

These frequent shellings and air raids prompted the Army to remove the recuperating wounded as soon as possible from the beachhead to make room for fresh casualties. The low water of Anzio's harbor prevented hospital ships from docking there, so patients had to be taken out to the ships by landing craft or by LSTs. A total of 28,860 American and 9,203 British soldiers were evacuated from Anzio in the four months of the campaign.

Army nurses were not usually on board LSTs as attendants, but they were part of the staff of hospital ships that plied between Anzio and Naples or North Africa. Hospital ships like the *Seminole* shared much of the same danger as warships off Italy and were sometimes targets of air raids. One of the nurses on board, Lt. Margaret Jennings, ANC, recalls, "As we were blacked out I suppose they had no way of telling that we were a hospital ship. In any case, they gave us the works!"[37] Lt. Lois Thomas adds, "They strafed us first." Then came the most frightening moment as the German planes unloaded their bombs. The *Seminole* was near missed by three bombs that jarred metal fittings loose. Fortunately, no real damage was done except to everyone's nerves.

Many officials felt that the morale boost and the excellent medical care given our G.I.s by clean, well-supplied hospital ships more than justified the risk they took in entering combat areas. Lieutenant Thomas remembered how delighted the G.I.s were to be served fresh fruits and vegetables and milk as a treat. One fellow exclaimed in amazement when he saw his breakfast of orange juice, toast, and real soft-boiled eggs, "No! Eggs with shells on them!" The soldiers were, by and large, in good spirits, and Lois Thomas wrote, "All the boys want is to get back to their outfits. We had one lad who was about the most completely wounded man I've ever seen . Both legs were broken, an arm was fractured, he had lost both eyes, and he had chest, abdominal, and scalp wounds, but he still talked and still hoped".[38]

War correspondent Ernie Pyle, who left Anzio on a hospital ship, wrote: "There was no blackout at all. Nobody was ever dirty or cold. Cabin windows had no shutters. The wounded got beautiful treatment. They lay on mattresses and had clean white sheets—the first time since going overseas for most of them."[39]

When spring arrived, the soggy Anzio plain finally dried up, allowing Army engineers to dig in the hospitals and hospital personnel to breathe easier. This lull in the fighting also allowed the nurses short periods of duty in Naples and Sorrento as a relief from the strain of frontline nursing. In Anzio and Nettuno, Allied troops basked in the glorious Italian sunshine and swam in the sea. Everywhere on the Italian front, soldiers rested and trained for the final push to Rome, and at Anzio, the VI Corps grew to an impressive strength of seven divisions.

Then on May 23, 1944, the big breakout from Anzio began. Preceeded by an impressive artillery barrage, the U.S. Third Division battled its way toward

Cisterna, sustaining 950 casualties in one day of combat. Tanks of the First Armored Division advanced on Velletri. The Germans gave ground slowly, however, and fought fanatically along the Albano railroad line. During the early fighting, hospitals supporting the breakout from Anzio beachhead remained at Nettuno, but on May 26, a platoon of the Thirty-third Field Hospital moved up to Corli. In the next week the Thirty-third moved to Velletri. Most of the casualties were given first aid and emergency treatment on the scene by the casualty clearing stations that tried to keep up with our rapidly advancing troops. Wounded were then sent back to the hospitals at Nettuno.[40]

The Ninety-fourth Evacuation Hospital began receiving its first casualties from the new offensive at 0600 hours on May 23. "All that day, that night and into the next day, casualties came in fast and heavy. We received a large amount of German POWs. The hospital worked at top speed and everyone pitched in and helped. Our turnover of patients for the three days, the 23rd, 24th, and 25th of May, was the highest that we experienced all year," the annual report stated.[41]

As the roads to Rome opened, the Allies began rolling through the Alban hills into the valley past truck gardens, walnut groves, and fields of red poppies. June Wandrey's unit, now attached to the Third Division, started its move toward Rome on Memorial Day 1944. She writes, "Over strange terrain, driving blackout at night, passing tanks and other armor on narrow roads, and then establishing our hospital in pitch-dark was an operation we had done numerous times before. Our units leap-frogged each other en route. . . . In the push from Corli to Rome, I stepped out of the OR for a few moments one night just to change the scene. Heard Jerry coming and got behind the biggest tree I could find. He strafed the full length of the road in front of our hospital tents."[42]

Operating near the constantly changing front lines was dangerous for medical personnel, as Wandrey discovered one night when she and five other nurses were traveling up to the front by ambulance. They could hear German planes overhead and put on their steel helmets "in case of strafing." Searching in the blackout for the hospital convoy, the nurses decided to drive on two more kilometers when they met an oncoming jeep. Wandrey recalls, "We could hear small arms fire. The one occupant had a fit when he found we were nurses. 'For God's sake—take'em back,' he yelled at our confused driver." Wandrey and the nurses turned around and, despite heavy fog, were able to make it to a clearing station where they were given blankets and litters to sleep on and directed to a cave in the distance. She told her folks, "Other soldiers were also sleeping in the cave. Soon I'll be an authority on different kinds of snoring." After a half hour, they were awakened and led to their hospital site. "Numb from the cold and fatigue, we curled up on the ground and went to sleep. This field nursing business isn't for the faint of heart," she mused.[43]

On the morning of June 4, 1944, the first American combat units reached the outskirts of Rome. With them were General Martin, Colonel Pierce, and

Lieutenant Rhodes of the Army Medical Corps, looking for a hospital site. They were stopped a mile from the Italian capital by infantry clearing Germans from the streets. The next day the threesome entered Rome and selected a hospital run by the sisters of the Good Shepherd.

The Ninety-fourth Evac's personnel entered the city the next day and were greeted by thousands of Italians crying "Viva Americans." The enemy had quickly departed and the hospital personnel found leftover coffee and dirty dishes at Buon Pastori Hospital. Four nurses from the Second Auxiliary Surgical Group were among the first nurses to enter Rome: "It was a thrilling and triumphal entry. For the first time in history, Rome had been captured by forces entering from the south. Within the city, huge crowds cheered and flowers were strewn in the path of liberating armies."[44]

June Wandrey's hospital was the first to enter Rome and set up in a building formerly occupied by the Germans. Except for some dead patients left behind by the Germans, the hospital was the cleanest she had seen in Italy in sixteen months. She records these impressions: "Even the people look civilized and wear clean clothes. Ever since we've been overseas, the natives have stood outside of our mess tent and watched us eat, waiting for the scraps we might leave. It spoils my appetite seeing the hungry look on their poor faces."

Like many Allied personnel, Wandrey and her fellow nurses took advantage of being in Rome and went sightseeing and visited the Vatican. One of her Catholic friends went to see Pope Pius XII, but was disappointed "when he was upset that she had come into his presence wearing pants," Wandrey recalls. "How sad that in his elegant surroundings he knew nothing of the life of a combat nurse. Maybe he thought she wore white silk hose and white starched uniforms in the mud fields where she lived."[45]

With the fall of Rome, the nightmare of Anzio and the Gustav Line ended, but the price had been a heavy one. In five months, American hospitals at Anzio had cared for 33,128 patients, of whom 10,809 were battle casualties, 18,074 were illnesses, and 4,245 were other injuries. Beachhead medical personnel had suffered 92 killed, 387 wounded, 19 captured, and 60 missing.[46]

Approximately 200 Army nurses took part in the Anzio campaign. Two of them were the first women to receive the Silver Star for meritorious duty. Army doctors, nurses, and corpsmen in World War II were often called upon to face danger and discomfort, said one historian, but "none of these experiences, in their length or intensity, offered a pale similarity to what they were called upon to face at Anzio."[47]

After the capture of Rome, the Italian campaign entered a new phase as the Germans retreated north. For the Army nurses, the capture of Rome was a dramatic moment, but hardly the end to the war. As one nurse expressed it, "Our Army had begun to make progress, and that could only mean one thing—the hospital would be on the move." The Ninety-fifth Evac, for example, followed the fighting north, having the honor of being the first evacuation hospital to cross the Gargliano River. The nursing report explains, "We traveled through many shell-torn, bomb-battered towns on the way to Itri. The signs of war were everywhere evident, many shell holes marking the fields, discarded and abandoned equipment littered the highways, but there was little time for sightseeing."

The Ninety-fifth set up in a "lovely valley" where the nurses went to work immediately caring for wounded from the fighting. After the shortest stay in the Ninety-fifth's history, they moved on to Cori, near enough to Anzio for them to see the "beautiful pattern the tracer bullets made against the sky, when the enemy bombers came over at night." While at Cori, some of the nurses were able to revisit the Eternal City on a three-day pass: "We were billeted in the Excelsior hotel and the hotel rooms were a most welcome treat after so many months spent sleeping on cots."[48]

A veteran of many months in Italy, in early summer 1944 the Ninety-fifth Evac was pulled out of active service and went into bivouac to prepare for the invasion of southern France. New hospitals arrived to take its place. The diary of the Twenty-seventh Evacuation Hospital, which came to Naples on May 17, 1944, paints a vivid picture of its introduction to life at the front: "Through dust and dirt, bombed villages, past bivouac areas and French and English field hospitals we moved steadily to the village of Maddaloni near which our hospital area was located. We turned off the highway into a freshly plowed field, ankle deep with dust. Gusts of wind whipped into blinding, choking clouds. We saw a few dark ward tents and knew that this was to be our 'home.'. . . The sound of the guns in the direction of Cassino was angry and loud and seemed to be very close to us."[49]

However, the Twenty-seventh soon learned it would be serving in a unique capacity, a 1,000-bed hospital devoted to the care of French Army casualties: "We were soon surrounded by Arabs, Moroccans, Ghoums, and Senegalese. Very few native Frenchmen were among the patients. We learned to know that these Colonials were human, in spite of their dirt and filthy clothes and in spite of their language that sounded so unfamiliar. We found they were grateful, cooperative, and appreciative patients. Their evidence of gratitude for the smallest attention encouraged us to do all we could for them."

The French colonials found the regulation of having a mosquito netting over each cot a "silly American custom," but they dutifully arranged the netting. The nurses soon realized, however, that no amount of effort could keep the colonials' heads under the netting: "As many times as you would pass down the row of cots and arrange the net the patient would put his head out and carefully tuck the net around the rest of his body, cheerfully grinning, his white teeth shining in the dark." The colonial soldiers also tested the nurses' and corpsmen's resolve by their ignorance of sanitation and hospital routine. "Latrines were a novelty and were only an unnecessary custom. Pajamas were clothes to wear in the daytime and to take off at night when they crawled into bed. Sheets were a temptation to wrap around their bodies in the familiar Arab style. No wound was too serious or painful for them to remove the dressings from and proudly show to a fellow patient."[50]

Some of the nurses on duty in northern Italy had the unique experience of caring for Japanese-American patients. Roberta Tayloe wrote, "They are the best patients I have ever taken care of, and that in my whole nursing career. Most are badly wounded, but they never complain. These lads frequently were trying to sneak out to go back to duty, so afraid they would not find their company. We had to censor their mail. Always a great embarrassment to me; they were writing home—to one of those camps where all were moved, U.S. citizens or not, for the duration. They would write a tiny scratch: Having a good rest, play cards, don't worry, home soon!"[51]

While several Army hospitals went on to serve in southern France, others, such as the Ninety-fourth Evac, continued to care for wounded in the last, and less well known, phase of the Italian campaign. After Florence was taken by Allied forces, the Ninety-fourth moved to Pratalino, about eight miles north of the city, to set up in the buildings of an Italian sanitarium; "badly mauled by artillery and small arms fire, half of its windows were out and the building was full of rubble." For the next month, the Ninety-fourth cared for 3,995 patients, 71 percent of them surgical cases. According to the hospital's annual report, "This period of 32 days was the busiest sustained in the history of the hospital, even exceeding the stay at Anzio."[52]

Some evacuation hospitals during this phase of the campaign found unusual quarters, for example, the 170th Evac set up in a stadium in Lucca, Italy, on November 24, 1944. They were anxious to leave their former site near Viareggio, which was within the range of German guns, and "on one occasion a shell landed in the hospital area, killing one patient instantly and injuring two of the hospital personnel." At Lucca the 170th set up under tents on the stadium field, where they spent five months caring for a variety of patients, from battle casualties to malaria, hepatitis, venereal disease, and trench foot cases, a total of 4,931 in all. The winter of 1944 proved to be an unusually cold one, but the engineers winterized the tents with framing, floorboards, and oil stoves. Two medical officers even had found local artisans to install brick fireplaces with marble mantles in their tents.[53]

Although the fighting in France was dominating the headlines, the war in Italy was by no means over. In the town of Pistoia north of Florence, the Seventieth General Hospital was housed in a barracks-style building. Nurse M.E. Revely recalls: "It had been a school for aviation students from Brazil. We were pretty comfortable here and our patients were in buildings too. We had a lot of German prisoners working in the hospital and we employed many natives." Revely says she joined the Army Nurse Corps in 1942 at the suggestion of a woman at the registry in St. Louis, who said, "Revely, what are you doing around here doing private duty? Why aren't you in the army?" After training in the United States, she went overseas to Oran with the Seventieth General and arrived in Italy in time for Thanksgiving dinner. Revely found the German prisoners at Pistoia "very nice. They were not different than people of German descent I had known at home. They treated me like a queen and I bought my ration of beer at the P.X. and gave it to them." She remembers the German prisoners had their own chaplain who celebrated Sunday morning mass. "We liked to go to this mass because the men sang and had such pretty voices."[54]

In northern Italy, Army hospitals continued to care for combat casualties and ill or injured G.I.s even when the temperatures remained below freezing for most of January and two feet of snow covered the hospital area and tents. Hospital personnel at the Eighth Evac bought stoves in Florence and, with Yankee ingenuity, rigged saw blades to a reclaimed jeep motor to cut wood. Trees were not plentiful in Italy, and the heavy snow made some wooded areas in the mountains inaccessible, but the Eighth Evac kept their saw in operation and "the tents were kept warm enough to be livable during the cold weather."[55]

The new year of 1945 found Nurse Eugenia Kielar in Ardenza at the Sixty-fourth General Hospital. On January 13, she wrote to her father, "Rumors are that this is to be a long war and I feel like taking out my citizenship papers here in Italy. On the 21st of February we'll have been overseas eighteen months. And to think I was afraid the war would be over before I joined the army!"[56]

With spring, however, came the final phase of the Italian campaign. For nurses at hospitals like the Fifty-sixth Evac, spring meant warm weather and optimism about an early end to the war. April 1, 1945, was Easter Sunday, and for the Fifty-sixth Evac it "was entirely different from our Easter of 1944. Steel helmets of the year before were forgotten, it was a bright spring day, the mountains of the Gothic Line seemed to be so close we could touch them, and there was reason for rejoicing because deep in everyone's heart was the feeling that the coming offensive would end the war in Europe and that this Easter would be the last in Europe and possibly the last Easter we would spend fighting a war."[57]

A big Allied offensive broke the Gothic Line, and on April 21, 1945, Fifth Army troops finally entered Bologna, the key to the Po Valley. The big push meant hospitals supporting Allied troops had to move up as well. Despite the difficulty of moving a 1,100-bed hospital, men and women of the Fifty-sixth Evac "entered into the problem with considerable enthusiasm because Jerry was on the run." They took down the tents and buildings, and soon "only the budding grapevines and piles of equipment graced the landscape. Curious groups of Italian civilians lingered around the edges of the camp wondering what we would leave them for use in their homes."

The Fifty-sixth Evac journeyed to Bologna by truck convoy, past mountains bristling with German gun emplacements and devastated little villages. In the words of its annual report, "Signs of a terrific siege were in evidence everywhere. No one could view the scene along this route without sensing a great inner sadness. This was especially true for those of us who had cared for the soldiers who had so gallantly attempted to break through to Bologna in September, October, and November, 1944. The war for those men had indeed been a hell on earth and now we were seeing one of the reasons why."

After a long day's journey, the Fifty-sixth arrived in Bologna, passing through the city at sundown to "wildly cheering throngs" of civilians. The hospital convoy then stopped at their new site in one of Mussolini's stadiums and had just bedded down early when the sound of German planes was heard in the distance. Soon the stadium and nearby area were under attack by the Luftwaffe, which "strafed and bombed the highways and troops areas near us. Although we could see their tracer bullets and clearly see the bomb explosions, none of the hospital personnel were injured. Jangled nerves, dirty uniforms, and a practically sleepless night were bad enough," the report noted.

The Fifty-sixth set up in Bologna and was soon receiving American casualties and hundreds of German prisoners. "Their impending defeat was made more apparent when scores of unguarded German ambulances drove into the hospital area and disgorged their patients and then turned in at our Motor Pool. Captured German medical officers and corpsmen worked beside our own personnel in caring for the sick and wounded prisoners."

By the last week of April, the Allies were moving rapidly northward. Verona, Feltre, and Bolzano were captured. "It was now a battle of mopping up the towns and the battered remnants of Von Vietinghoff's once proud and powerful German and Italian armies," writes the Fifty-sixth's historian. The Eighth Evac was the first evacuation hospital to cross the Po River, receiving the first of 150 casualties at Verona near the end of April. For four days the injured flowed into the hospital and then on May 2, 1945, all enemy resistance ceased. The war was over![58]

At the Sixty-fourth General Hospital, Eugenia Kielar writes, "There was much rejoicing in the area. Big guns were booming all day and men were screaming as they went by in trucks. Most of the girls were hitting the bottle—starting early in the afternoon, so you can imagine their condition by evening time." Like many of the nurses, the end of war in Europe brought rejoicing but new worries. In a letter to her father on May 7, 1945, Kielar confided, "And now everyone is worried about being sent to the Pacific and we are not excluded!"[59]

V-E Day meant the war was over, but not the work of caring for the wounded, the Italian civilians, and the German prisoners. The weather remained cold, and from the hospital area the Alps were clearly visible, still covered in snow. After the surrender of the German army, the Allies had the problem of caring for thousands of German troops. "It was an impressive sight to see the once proud and conquering Wehrmacht and S.S. Truppen going by, loaded in trucks and vans like so many cattle," recorded the Eighth Evac's report.[60]

Adding to the confusion at war's end were the thousands of Italian civilians who "suddenly decided to go somewhere other than where they were located. Roads were crowded with civilians, men, children, and infants in arms, on foot, bicycles, wagons, and old cars and dilapidated trucks." Army hosptials were kept busy caring for many accident victims, a result of the numerous refugees, heavy traffic, and military vehicles operating at high speed in a sometimes reckless fashion. Cases included a German ten-ton trailer that overturned, sending fifty Germans to the hospital. In a bizarre accident, eighteen Italian civilians were hospitalized and many were killed when refugees rummaging in an abandoned German ammunition dump for wooden boxes set off an explosion.

The Eighth Evacuation Hospital's annual report declared that May 1945 was the most interesting, "if not the most important, month of the war in Italy." They admitted 2,183 patients, 592 of them accident victims, including accidental gunshot cases. "With the breakup and surrender of the German Army, unfamiliar weapons fell into the hands of the Allies as captured material and souvenirs. During the month of May, forty-two soldiers shot themselves, and thirty-one more were shot by their buddies, while handling enemy guns, usually pistols."

It was not all work for the Eighth Evac during the early "postwar" period in Italy, however, as a liberated stock of German liquor also found its way to the hospital, "sufficient to have an excellent champagne party for the enlisted men, and to provide a dash of cognac for all personnel." In June 1945, the Eighth Evac opened a small hospital on the south shore of Lake Garda, an ideal spot for swimming, boating, and fishing. Several boats with outboard motors were found and "a few individuals became proficient in aquaplaning." Many other Eighth Evac personnel began acquiring a tan and the work load was light enough for nurses and others to enjoy plenty of recreation time and to avail themselves of rest camps in France, Italy, and Switzerland. The nurses were treated to additional trips to Salzburg, Athens, and Cairo.[61]

This leisurely pace of hospital duty was typical of many Army hospitals left in Italy, but not of all. Although the Fifty-sixth had anticipated being sent into "rest bivouac" in northern Italy after the war, "where," according to its annual report, "we could revive our Sports and Educational programs and do some sightseeing," they moved instead 250 miles to Udine near Trieste. "The area was beautifully situated. The Carnine Alps to the North and the Julian Alps to the East afforded a magnificent panorama. The surrounding countryside with its spring flowers, cornfields, quaint villages, and numerous clock towers was very picturesque." The area was hardly peaceful, however, because "Italian and Yugoslav partisans were parading impressively through the streets and countryside, heavily armed with rifles, pistols, knives, and grenades, and red scarves." The situation was very tense and rumors of armed clashes and artillery duels abounded.

To impress upon the partisans the fact that the Allies meant business about a peaceful solution to the "Trieste problem," tanks were sent to patrol the streets, and formations of Allied aircraft lifted into the air each evening to fly over

(*Above*) One of the first units of African-American nurses accepted for active duty in the Army Nurse Corps poses for a group picture at Camp Livingston, Louisiana, November 6, 1941. Prudence Burns Burrell. (*Below*) Captain M. Jane Clements, chief of U.S. nurses in the Southwest Pacific Theater, and a group of nurses outside her office at the 171st Evacuation Hospital, Port Moresby, New Guinea, January 5, 1943. National Archives

(Above) Army nurses Lt. Violet Bartholomew, Lt. Geniveve Cox, Lt. Helen G. Blything, and Lt. Corace Ludkins arriving in France in a DUWK driven by Machinist Mate 2/class Leo Arzie, June 24, 1944. National Archives. *(Below)* Army nurses inspect the still smoldering ruins of Laugarnes Hospital in Iceland following an early morning fire on March 23, 1944. National Archives

Army nurses Ceclia Brychta, Susan Cove, Mary L. Morehead, and Lillian M. Pickergill pose on the steps leading to their Quonset hut quarters on Adak Island, Alaska, in 1943. National Archives

Mail call for nurses at the 268th Station Hospital in the Southwest Pacific. Chief nurse 1st Lt. Birdie E. Brown watches as Lt. Inez Holmes hands Lt. Prudence Burns Burrell a letter from the first batch of mail to reach the 268th overseas in 1943. National Archives

China-Burma-India Theater nurses Lt. Martha Toulme, Lt. Phyllis Gay, Lt. Mary Jane Healy, and Lt. Margaret Dannis went looking for stores open for Christmas in 1944 but found only temples and pagodas in northern Burma. National Archives

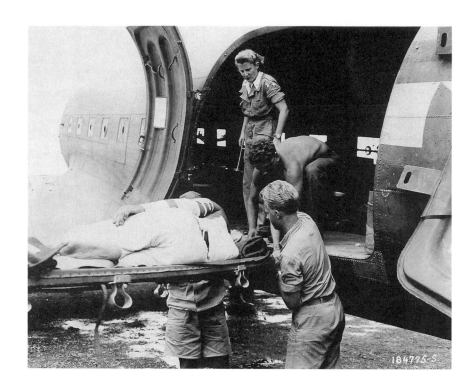

(Above) Air evacuation nurse Lt. Rial Smith watches while a soldier wounded in the fighting on Bougainville is unloaded from a plane for transfer to a base hopital on Guadalcanal in the South Pacific Theater in 1944. National Archives. *(Below)* "Off duty" nurses in Assam province, India, fill their canteens from an army Lister bag, August 1943. National Archives

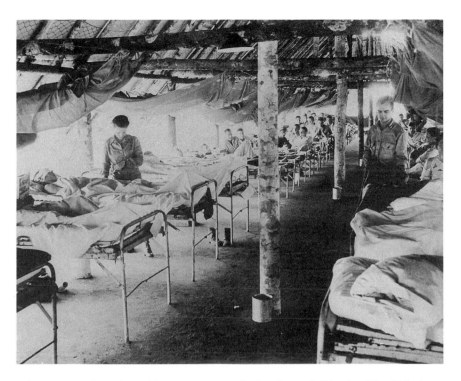

(Above) Surgical ward, 306th Station Hospital, Goodenough Island, 1943. U.S. Army Military History Institute. (Below) Army nurses marching in Southern Devonshire, England, in 1943. U.S. Army Military History Institute

Army nurses Lt. Madonna Nolan and her sister Lt. Agnes Nolan were wounded when their hospital ship was hit by Nazi bombers off Salerno on September 13, 1943. U.S. Army Military History Institute

the Yugoslav line. This display of martial power prevailed and the 56th soon settled down to a more peacetime routine with education and sports programs. The balmy weather brought out softball enthusiasts and a nine-team intramural league was formed. Volleyball games were popular among the officers and badminton games attracted the nurses. Patients gathered in a Red Cross tent to make fudge or popcorn, to listen to records on the phonograph, or to have a cup of coffee from the coffeepot that was kept going day and night. In short, a peacetime routine had begun to set in and those lucky enough to have accumulated enough "points" looked forward to redeployment and going home.[62]

According to Eugenia Kielar, a nurse needed seventy-four points to be sent back to the States. She was well under that critical number and slated to be sent to the Pacific, but wrote to her father, "I consider myself pretty lucky when I look around at the other girls with one or two points less than the critical seventy-four who are headed for the same place as me. That would be really hard to take, I think." Kielar and her fellow nurses from the former Sixty-fourth left Italy on August 17, 1945. They had orders to report to the South Pacific after a period of leave at Camp Sibert, Alabama. Kielar spent the ten-day voyage across the Atlantic playing cards. She remembers, "We were a pretty disheartened group that first day at sea. But a miracle happened on the second day out. An announcement came over the loudspeaker that Japan had surrendered and that we would be going home into New York harbor. The troop ship almost jumped out of the ocean with joy!"[63]

The war in the Mediterranean had been a long one, and Army nurses had been an integral part of every Allied campaign in the Mediterranean Theater of Operations (MTO). In the words of the Fifty-sixth Evacuation Hospital historian:

> It was difficult to believe that the long bitter struggle which had started at Fedhala, French Morocco, and that had traveled doggedly across North Africa to Bizerte, then to Sicily, Paestum, Cassino, Anzio, Leghorn, Florence, Bologna, the Po River, Verona, Milan, and Bolzano was now concluded. No longer would torn, maimed, wounded and dying American soldiers be passing through our hospital. No longer would the angry chatter of machine guns or the horrifying crash of artillery shells pierce the atmosphere. No longer would that ominous throbbing hum of Luftwaffe planes chill us. We were jubilant with the victory, but in our hearts was an inner thankfulness to God that it was over and we were safe. We saluted those of us who were alive, and drank a silent reverent toast to those of our comrades who couldn't make it.[64]

6

TO THE RHINE
AND BEYOND

Army Nurses in the European
Theater of Operations

 Many nurses sailing for distant shores early in World War II were destined for U.S. Army bases or airfields in Great Britain. Our buildup of medical personnel in the United Kingdom was so gradual, however, that a nursing section was not established in the European Theater of Operations (ETO) until July 21, 1942. When the ETO's chief nurse, Capt. Margaret E. Aaron, reported for duty, she found only 359 nurses in the theater, half of them serving at two Army hospitals, the Tenth Station and Fifth General, in Northern Ireland. The Thirtieth General was the only Army hospital in England at the time, but civilian nurses were serving at two American hospitals. Some of these American nurses were convinced to enroll in the Army Nurse Corps, but others elected to return to the United States or to join the American Red Cross.[1]

One of the first Army hospitals to cross the Atlantic for duty in the United Kingdom was the Second General Hospital, an affiliate of Columbia Presbyterian Medical Center in New York City. When the hospital was activated, the nurses were sent to Fort Meade, Maryland, for basic overseas training, which included lectures on gas warfare, airplane identification, and military courtesy, and, of course, drills. Chief Nurse Lt. Marjorie Peto recalls that they were issued gas masks and blue uniforms in the Army's two sizes, "too large and too small," and quickly settled into military life. Fortunately, the food at Fort Meade was excellent—"fried chicken, juicy steaks, and succulent shellfish from the Chesapeake."[2]

By May, however, life on the post at Fort Meade was becoming unbearably dull and the Second General's nurses were getting anxious to go overseas. To the station hospital commander's everlasting credit, he turned the gym into a roller rink and found 100 pairs of skates, which at least kept the nurses busy until their long-awaited orders for overseas came in June.

As luck would have it, the Second General boarded the troopship *Duchess of Bedford* on June 30, 1942, the hottest day of the year, when the thermometer reached 98 degrees F. Burdened with canteens, gas masks, overcoats, and steel helmets, dressed in blue wool uniforms, and carrying suitcases, the perspiring nurses must have had second thoughts about the glamour of wartime service.

The *Duchess of Bedford* sailed in convoy, its destination unknown to most of its passengers, including the 4,000 men of the U.S. First Infantry Division. Would it be Alaska, Australia, or Iceland? No one knew. Days passed. The nurses read, played cards, sang, and speculated on their destination. When the convoy reached Liverpool on July 12, 1942, speculation was over and the eager nurses rushed to catch a glimpse of bomb-damaged Liverpool crowned with barrage balloons. Wartime England was a shock to the nurses, who discovered their new bivouac area was "disgustingly dirty, cold, and dismal—a prison-like set up." To make matters worse, the townsfolk viewed this invasion of Americans with suspicion. In turn the Americans were surprised at the "shabbily dressed" Britons and their Spartan living conditions—a shortage of food, soap, and hot water, and no central heating.[3]

In an even more serious vein, the Second General Hospital's nurses realized that they were located near the city of Birmingham, a favorite target of the Luftwaffe. The first noisy air raid brought everyone at the hospital outside to watch until the horrified local guard shooed them inside to safety.

A group of nurses under Lt. J. Ada Mutch, who had joined the Army Nurse Corps in February 1942 "to the delight of her family and friends," went from the Second's bivouac area in England to Northern Ireland. Mutch recalls that they traveled to Scotland by train and went by ferry across the Irish Sea. "After a three-hour trip we landed at Larne. Almost all of the nurses were seasick, but they managed to get off and into another train." The exhausted party reached their new home at 1 A.M. and after a quick meal gratefully flopped into beds already made by the patients—and short sheeted![4]

Chief Nurse Mutch and her nurses found 500 patients in the hospital recovering from hepatitis. "With no medical or nursing equipment we set up a wonderful occupational therapy workshop for the men," she recalls. They also devised a way to make milkshakes for the patients by combining eggs and powdered milk.

After five months in Ireland, Lieutenant Mutch and her nurses rejoined the Second General in Oxford, England. The unit, which consisted of 500 enlisted men, fifty doctors, and 105 nurses, and twelve dietitians and Red Cross workers, was assigned to Churchill Hospital. Here they cared for American G.I.s who met with the usual accidents and illnesses compounded by the blackout and by the damp English weather, which led to many respiratory infections and pneumonia cases. A few North Africa battle casualties were treated and some Air Corps casualties, often victims of frostbite resulting from flying at high altitudes in unheated bombers.

The Second General received many distinguished visitors at Oxford, including First Lady Eleanor Roosevelt, who made the rounds of the wards. Despite the threats of many bored patients to use her visit as an occasion to complain about the food and the mean nurses, the first lady's questions were greeted with polite answers.

The nurses at Churchill Hospital also acquired a mascot, a lovable puppy they named Sooner—"because he would sooner have been with the nurses than anyone else." Sooner pulled the usual puppy stunts like running off with shoes and the nurses spoiled him with treats of creme de menthe, gingersnaps, and bones. Actress Merle Oberon, at Churchill with the USO, took one look at the mixed breed pup and declared that his father was obviously an airedale.[5]

For most American nurses, life in wartime England had pleasures as well as hardships. Many bought bicycles and rode all over the countryside or went sightseeing and visited London. Alice Howard recalls attending a military tea at Buckingham Palace: "It was a beautiful occasion, quite informal, giving us an opportunity to talk freely with members of the Royal family." Yet the nurses were not tourists and as the months went by they grew homesick, especially around the holidays. Fortunately, the American Red Cross established a club in London which, according to ETO Chief Nurse Aaron, was "tastefully decorated and furnished in a very home like manner." Here nurses on leave could dine on excellent meals in the cafeteria, have tea every afternoon, and attend dances or see movies. On their first Thanksgiving Day overseas some lucky American nurses went to the club for a real turkey dinner with all the trimmings.[6]

By January 1944 there were 4,644 nurses in the ETO, serving with eightyeight different medical units and organizations. Among the hundreds of newly arrived Army nurses was Eula Awbrey, who came to the U.K. in October 1943 on board the liner *Queen Elizabeth*. She was dreadfully seasick on the voyage, but with the wisdom of hindsight imagines much of her nausea was from the fear of the unknown. She recalls, "Those abandon ship drills really got to me. Antiaircraft practice from the ship's guns did not help my psychological state either."

After arriving safely in Scotland, Awbrey's nursing unit was whisked south by troop train to Wales, where they set up a station hospital. "Throughout Great Britain blackout was observed. The Germans were bombing as a daily routine. For that reason the troop movements were strictly guarded." Wartime in Wales meant food shortages, vegetable gardens everywhere, and air raids. Awbrey writes, "Almost every night we could hear the bombs going off in Liverpool, England, and see the flash of anti-aircraft fire, the 'ack-ack' and tracer bullets reminding us of our own Fourth of July displays. But this was war and we were saddened as we wondered how much damage and loss of life was happening under that bright display." She also worried about the lack of orange juice and vitamin C for the children, and recalls, "Milk was also in short supply. Actually—all food was in short supply." 1st Lt. Rose K. Farley remembers the English weather: "We were stationed at bases in England where it was darn cold in winter and we'd steal coal for the pot bellied stoves to keep warm. The rats were so bad we'd hang our precious nylons by strings from the rafters so the rats couldn't eat them."[7]

From Wales, Lieutenant Awbrey's unit moved to a hospital in Midhurst, England. They were near a town, but always took the precaution of walking on either side of the road in case a German plane swooped down to strafe them. "It was not considered too romantic if one wanted to hold hands on a date," Aubrey remembers. "It was more like a forced march, but easier to fall into the ditch on the side of the road if it became necessary." Despite the cold, damp English weather and shortage of fuel, the nurses enjoyed Sussex and took advantage of opportunities to visit English tourist attractions such as the Roman ruins in Bath and the city of Chichester.

In late April 1944, Eula's hospital moved to Weymouth in Dorset in anticipation of the invasion of Europe. Everyone knew an invasion was coming, but the exact date was a carefully guarded secret. "We were guarded by several anti-aircraft guns positioned along the coast near us. D-day couldn't be too far away."[8]

For six months prior to D day, more Army nurses arrived in England than there were hospitals to receive them, so many went to staging areas to train and wait for the invasion. The nurses resented the repetition of old training programs, sometimes taught by unqualified instructors, and also complained about the uncomfortable staging areas, which lacked recreational facilities. The build-up for D day was a trying period for most military personnel, and the U.S. Army tried to occupy nurses by assigning them to inspect Red Cross clubs, help in convalescent homes, administer venereal disease programs, or to assist training of enlisted men and WACs at various dispensaries.[9]

Among the 10,000 Army nurses in the theater in 1944 were sixty-three African-American nurses, the first to be assigned to the ETO, six months before their black colleagues in the Women's Army Corps. Upon arrival in England the nurses were given a three-week orientation and training program before being assigned to the 168th Station Hospital in Warrington, England. This unit had originally been an all-white hospital assigned to Iceland before the war and then transferred to England. Lt. Dorothy Smith felt that, by then, the nurses had been overseas too long. "They are the most unhappy group I have seen," she told an interviewer. "The 168th is an old unit and has been together for a long time. The thing they resented chiefly was being transferred without any reason." When the white nurses were disbanded and sent to other places in England, their places were taken by black nurses. Lieutenant Smith was candid about the reaction of the 168th's personnel to this change: "I know this didn't sit highly with any of us—white Medical officers and white enlisted men working with colored nurses.

The 168th was changed to an entirely prisoner of war hospital and the colored nurses arrived on 19 September 1944; we departed the same day." The selection of the 168th to receive black nurses was done by lot from all of the 750-bed hospitals in the United Kingdom and a plea to have the nurses under white supervision was honored by allowing the white chief nurse and operating room supervisor to remain.

Athough the 168th had been earmarked to receive POWs in July 1944 prior to the black nurses' arrival at the hospital from a basic training course at Schrienham, many in the African-American community felt the assignment of black nurses to a German prisoners-of-war hospital reflected the Army's official policy of segregation. This policy followed African-American soldiers, WACs, and nurses to England, as did racial discrimination, even though the English did not practice segregation. The Army Nurse Corps was clearly not immune from negative racial attitudes; for instance, in ETO Chief Nurse Aaron's official report she cited an example of travel inconveniences suffered by white Army nurses on the Continent: "An extreme case where 100 nurses were assigned to ship's quarters with male negro officers."

On August 4, the 168th was changed to an exclusive prisoner-of-war casualty hospital, and gradually the 731 American patients were transferred. On August 25, the first train of German prisoners arrived and by September 4 the hospital had admitted 1,141 seriously wounded POWs. Twelve days later, the white nurses departed, with Chief Nurse Frances K. Crouch and the operating room supervisor Lt. Marjorie Truax remaining to supervise the sixty-three new black nurses. The 168th was told that the nurses had been "specially selected, highly trained and educated," but in reality, although twelve of them were veterans of the Twenty-fifth Station Hospital in Liberia, only thirty-two had volunteered for foreign service and only a few had any postgraduate training. Nonetheless, when the two white nurses left in December 1944 Nursing Director Aaron reported, "These negro nurses with constant guidance did very good work, and continued to give excellent nursing care after Captain Crouch left the unit." Contrary to the impression that these black nurses cared only for German prisoners of war, the 168th actually reverted to an American convalescent hospital on December 6, 1944. By late December, the 168th had transferred its prisoner-of-war cases to the Eighty-second General and had 1,431 beds occupied by Americans.[10]

In the U.K., however, segregation was neither custom nor government policy, and black nurses quickly discovered that Red Cross clubs, leave areas, and schools in England were open to persons of color. This was an advantage for African-American military women in some respects and a detriment in others. Black nurses could be grouped together at one hospital in job assignments that reflected their skills and training, and the nurses "were found to be a conscientious group of willing workers," but their social life in England suffered because the 168th Station Hospital was not located near a concentration of black American troops. "No negro officers could be recruited for dances or parties, and, too, with the absence of racial discrimination in England, it was difficult to find many negro officers who were interested in associating with negro women." This sad fact of life in wartime England was shared by black WACs, and it is ironic in view of the fact that the first requisition of black WACs for the ETO was rejected by Colonel Oveta Hobby. She felt the requisition had "been . . . plainly for morale purposes," to provide companionship for black troops. Hobby and the Secretary of War's civilian aide, William H. Hastie, felt that sending black WACs overseas for such a purpose would discredit the unit.[11]

With the new year of 1944, Allied officials began finalizing plans for the upcoming invasion of France, which included the deployment of twenty-five U.S. Army hospitals to support the landing and follow-up campaign. Although Allied planners decided not to include nurses in the actual D-day invasion, plans called for them to rejoin their units after the Normandy beachhead was secured. The decision to employ WAC units on the Continent, however, was debated; officials feared for the women's safety and questioned their ability to adjust to field conditions. Doubters worried that "fighting men would worry so much over the WAC's safety that their effectiveness would be impaired." Those in favor of sending WACs to the Continent pointed to the success of female nurses at the front in the North African and Italian campaigns and argued that living conditions in France could not be more dangerous than in London, which was being harassed by German buzz bombs. Citing the success of nurses and WACs in the Fifth Army in Italy, the WAC staff director recommended that they be sent to France and assured officials that the WACs themselves were "eager to go." In the end, her arguments convinced theater officials to allocate WACs for duty on the Continent.[12]

In the spring of 1944, hospitals destined for the coming invasion of Europe were ordered to the Hospital Center at Circencester, where several thousand nurses were billeted in Nissen huts and took part in a rigorous field training program that featured ten-mile hikes in full field equipment and lectures on digging pit latrines and using a Lister bag.[13]

The experience of one hospital was typical of many others. The Thirtyninth Field Hospital was given alert orders in May and told to be ready to move with six hours' notice. Accordingly, hospital personnel and nurses moved into bivouac in a field, set up in pup tents, and waited. Not wishing to unpack and establish a mess tent, the Thirty-ninth ate "out of doors." The kitchen was kept as simple as possible, with only one stove, and the cooks served the food over a counter made of rough timber.

As the weeks wore on with all personnel restricted to base and no orders to move out, the boredom and tension of waiting took its toll on everyone's nerves. Fortunately, the nearby Eighty-third Service Group sponsored shows four nights a week, and in the daytime the men and women of the Thirty-ninth played baseball. The unit was divided into two teams, the "Regulars," who had been playing other teams locally, and the "Gas House Gang," made up of volunteers. While baseball games might seem a trifling affair with an invasion under way, the unit's history claims that the "Gas House Gang" won half of its ball games and the diversion was crucial to the hospital's sanity during the tense wait to ship out for the "Big Show."

Finally, on June 12, 1944, the Thirty-ninth Field Hospital received the long-awaited notice to move out for France. At 1630 a tense, expectant group of nurses and G.I.s climbed into 2.5-ton trucks and headed for the D day plus five staging area, which reportedly had been hit by low-flying German aircraft a few nights prior to their arrival. To everyone's relief the staging area proved safe and "very comfortable," with excellent food, cots with mattresses, and even showers.

On June 14, the Thirty-ninth boarded LSTs at Portsmouth and made an uneventful crossing of the English Channel, which had been rough from storms but was now smooth. The next evening the LSTs landed on Omaha Beach, and amidst some confusion, the unit drove off through the dark into the unknown: "German planes raided the beach area as the unit was leaving, and the sky filled with the gigantic spectacle of ack-ack tracers and exploding shells. Everyone huddled together in the trucks, not knowing whether to expect strafing, the hail of descending flak or sniper fire." After an anxious ride, the Thirty-ninth's personnel arrived in Transit Area No. 5 where someone using a covered lantern managed to find a hedgerow for the nurses to hide in.

Having survived their baptism of fire on the shores of Normandy, the Thirty-ninth Field moved the next day by truck to R and R strip No. 1 near St. Pierre de Mort, where they set up under canvas, one of the first field hospitals to operate in France after D day.[14]

Other medical units were also near the front in Normandy shortly after D day, but none initially included Army nurses. On June 6, and for several days after the invasion, military hospitals at the beachheads were operated exclusively by medical officers and enlisted men assigned to naval beach parties, medical battalions, and the Engineer's Special Brigade. They collected wounded and gave them first aid before evacuating them to ships waiting off shore. The first Army nurses to care for casualties off Normandy were on the hospital carrier *Naushon,* which arrived off Omaha Beach at 1900 hours on June 7, 1944. First Lt. Ruth G. McGowan and five Army nurses assigned to the Twelfth Hospital Train unit were on board the *Naushon* as she took on casualties evacuated from the beachhead by small landing craft. The hospital carrier spent the night of June 7 off Omaha beachhead and then departed for Southampton with 150 patients, "many of them with serious wounds."[15]

There were also U.S. Army nurses on a second British hospital carrier, the *Lady Connaught,* which did not arrive off Utah Beach until two days after the landings because two other carriers in the convoy had struck mines and they had been "subjected to a very heavy air raids throughout the entire night." *Lady*

Connaught was ordered to anchor the night of June 7, but resumed her short voyage to the beachhead where she arrived the next morning. Her medical personnel went ashore to treat the wounded, "despite heavy air activity, flak, and shrapnel," and the following day the hospital carrier departed for Southampton with 450 patients. She returned on June 11 to Utah Beach for another 500 injured men.

The Army's reluctance to expose nurses to the dangers of the Normandy beachhead lasted less than a week. Officials quickly decided that nurses were too integral to the functioning of a field hospital to be excluded and Army nurses were ordered to cross the Channel to rejoin their units. On June 10 they began arriving in both of the American sectors. The first nurses to reach Omaha Beach were from the Fifty-first Field Hospital, followed by nurses assigned to the Forty-fifth Field Hospital and the 128th Evac, who came ashore at nearby Utah Beach. Claiming the honor of being the first Army nurse to wade ashore from the 128th Evac was Lt. Margaret Stanfill, a veteran of the Arzew landing in North Africa in 1942. Scarcely half an hour later she and her fellow nurses were joined by nurses from the Ninety-first Evac and Forty-second Field Hospital. According to the official Army Nurse Corps history, the first nurses to actually care for D-day wounded were the nurses from the Forty-fifth Field Hospital, who "waded ashore in waist deep water and were on duty twenty minutes after arriving in a field hospital unit other than their own."[16]

The experience of the Ninety-first Evacuation Hospital was typical of the numerous frontline Army hospitals in Normandy. Veteran of the North African and Sicilian campaigns, the Ninety-first Evac spent the six months prior to D-day in Totworth Court, 100-room mansion at Falfield, England. Here the unit trained, organized ward equipment, and went on road marches to toughen the personnel up for their next campaign.

On June 5, 1944, the Ninety-first and the nurses of the Forty-second Field Hospital marched two miles to the railroad station and boarded trains for their overseas staging area at Camp Hursley. After dinner in a nearby mess hall, the nurses bedded down for the night and tried to sleep. The next day at breakfast they heard that D-day forces had come ashore in Normandy, The unit's nursing history captured the feeling of their D-day preparations:

> There was an air of excitement, and many planes were overhead. Our English money was exchanged for French francs. The next day, life belts, K rations, etc. were issued. Many of the nurses attended church services during the day . . . at 5 a.m. the trucks arrived, taking us to the docks at Southampton. Nurses were dressed in fatigue suits, with the impregnated suit over that, wearing combat jacket, helmet and life belt, carrying gas masks, musette bags, and rain coat. . . . Nurses were not expected and caused some confusion. Early in the afternoon it started to rain . . . never have the nurses looked worse. Rain coats were donned, hair became damp, and make-up disappeared.[17]

At 6 P.M. the soaked nurses and medical personnel finally boarded the troopship *Thomas Wolfe* and anxiously climbed down the steep ladders to the two holds that would be their quarters for the Channel crossing. The ship sailed in convoy on June 9, 1944, only three days after the Normandy invasion. In late afternoon they arrived off Utah Beach and were taken to the floating pier by landing craft and from the pier by truck to the Forty-second Field Hospital area. While the men of the Ninety-first unloaded equipment and pitched pup tents, the nurses went right to work caring for battle casualties at the Forty-second, which was set up only two and one-half miles inland, near the scene of heavy fighting. By 2200 hours the hospital had admitted 300 casualties, with another several hundred lined up awaiting admission. Four surgical teams labored throughout the night in the operating room to save the seriously wounded, and the following day extra teams were called in to attend to the backlog.[18]

Many of the field and evacuation hospitals in France experienced a similar influx of patients during the first week after D-day. Ashore and in the process of setting up was the Fifty-first Field, which landed at 2300 hours on June 11. Janice T. Goers-Reilly remembers anxiously waiting in the transports offshore for orders. Then the Fifty-first Field's nurses were finally sent to Omaha Beach. "I will never forget watching the soldiers come ashore, falling to their knees in thankfulness for being alive," she writes. The Fifty-first sent its nurses and one platoon to establish a hospital unit at a site near an airfield. Nurses from the Fifth, Twenty-fourth, and Forty-first Evacuation Hospitals also arrived in Normandy and joined the Thirteenth Field at its hospital site. While awaiting a reunion with their units, the women were temporarily quartered in tents set up for them by the Thirteenth's enlisted men.

The Ninety-first opened for business on the evening of June 11, 1944, at its Bouteville, France, location and in thirteen hours had admitted 261 patients. Most of these admissions were serious cases requiring surgery, which meant that the unit's doctors, assisted by auxiliary surgical teams, spent all of their time in the ORs. This left the nurses and technicians to administer plasma, give medications, and start blood transfusions. It was a heavy work load, and the hospital handled 2,142 cases during the next seventeen days.

Other evacuation hospitals cared for a similar number of battle casualties in the weeks after D-day. By June 21, all ten of the 400-bed units assigned to the First Army were ashore and set up to receive patients.[19]

Capt. Jean Truckey, ANC, whose hospital arrived in Normandy on D-day plus ten, described the scene: "On the third night we had 275 new patients lying on the ground outside the receiving tent, awaiting admissions. . . . Days and nights of hard work, of seeing all cots filled with injured soldiers, of evacuating them to England as soon as their condition permitted to make room for the ever-increasing casualties . . . the tense three days, when all wards were filled and the evacuation system was at a standstill. Planes were grounded and the road to Omaha beach was denied us because to bridge to Carentan was out." Her unit cared for 5,300 patients during this period in Normandy, 2,300 of them surgical cases. "It was gratifying to know that the death rate was never over 1.2%," she said.[20]

Many of these injured G.I.s were flown or taken by sea back to Army and Navy hospitals in England. Mary Virginia Desmaris, a U.S. Navy nurse, remembers the first D-day casualties: "They were fresh battle casualties that had been given only first aid and sulfonamide routine in France and aboard the LSTs which brought them into Southampton, England. . . . Each casualty had a 'battle treatment' tag attached to his jacket. Many had their clothing cut away by field first aid men and, being wrapped only in blankets, the tags were tied to an extremity." Desmaris was in the operating room as an anesthetist. She recalls the grueling conditions: "There was no time for meals or rest. The line of casualties was endless, it seemed. If the case was a particularly difficult or severe one another surgeon aided the doctor to lessen the length of time on the table. . . . I worked that day, as did all the staff, until 3 A.M., then had a sandwich and coffee and three hours of sleep."[21]

Some hospitals did not receive patients from the D-day invasion for several days, but all service personnel in England felt the excitement of the invasion. Lt. Eula Awbrey recalled June 6, 1944: "It was really an awesome sight to see our planes going overhead into France, and know the Channel was filled with our naval vessels carrying our troops—many of them to die on the beaches before we could establish a beach-head." Her hospital received its first casualties a few days after the invasion: "They did not come directly to us, but were triaged on the docks after being unloaded from the naval vessels. Then they were brought to our hospital by ambulance." According to Lieutenant Awbrey, the experience of caring for freshly wounded soldiers confirmed the value of the hospital unit's training back in the States: "We learned that our hospital really worked in combat situations. We were glad that we had the many trial set-ups and dismantling experiences in Texas and the desert."[22]

Evacuation of battle casualties from Normandy to hospitals in England saved many lives and was accomplished in part by the newly organized Medical Air Evacuation Squadrons (MAES), which began arriving in England during the summer of 1943. Jean Foley Tierney was a nurse with the 806th MAES. She recalls, "It was really a pioneering job we were doing, and along with a squadron in Africa and one in the Pacific we were establishing a new concept in medical history."[23] Air evacuation as a routine method of handling casualties was an untried concept in 1943-44, and the air evacuation squadrons keenly felt the need to prove their worth.

In the heavy fighting after D-day, the 806th MAES was given ample opportunity to show the value of flying severely wounded soldiers to rear-area medical facilities. The 806th's personnel were trained at Bowman Field, Kentucky, and came overseas in July 1943 on the SS *Thomas H. Barry*. They came to

Liverpool and were assigned to Welford Park, where the nurses enjoyed exploring the English countryside on bicycles. In November, the 806th made history when Lt. Jean K. Bartholomew and a surgical technician evacuated twelve patients from the ETO to the United States. This was the first transatlantic medical air evacuation from Europe. The 806th spent November flying 213 patients from Northern Ireland to England in the first organized mass evacuation of injured by air.[24]

On June 11, 1944, the 806th made its first evacuation from Normandy with Lt. Grace Dunham as flight nurse, a flight that took eighteen litter patients off Omaha Beach. During June, July, and August, the 806th, in conjunction with the Thirty-first Air Transport Group, evacuated 20,142 patients from France, proving the value of medical air evacuation.

After a tour of duty in Scotland from which its members routinely made flights across the Atlantic in C-54s, the 806th moved to Orly Airfield near Paris. Here the nurses were quartered in what their report called a "lovely building." Jean Tierney recalls the building in more realistic terms: "It had everything—except heat, hot water, and window panes (the warmest place was outside in the snow!)" From Orly Airfield, the nurses made many flights across the Atlantic, usually stopping at the Azores, where Tierney remembers, "We enjoyed the warm weather and hot water and got our washing and bathing done." The trips to Newfoundland and the Azores in C-54s were twelve-hour flights. "We carried 18-20 litter patients. These were usually men paralyzed because of spinal injuries. On one of the flights to the Azores, we lost an engine some 350 miles out to sea. There were some doubts that we would not have to ditch and the next few hours were harrowing. We made it safely, however, only to find on reaching the Azores that there was a 90 mph crosswind on the runway."[25]

Flight nursing was a demanding job. As the only nurse on board the med evac plane, each of the women had a great deal of responsibility. Most soldiers had never been on a plane before and were naturally nervous, many got airsick, and undoubtedly a few suffered from claustrophobia resulting from lying on litters in tiers of three on both sides of the plane. As Tierney points out, decisions about patient care on the flight were all up to one flight nurse. As an illustration, she relates the story of one flight from Prestwick, Scotland, to the Azores in 1944. A patient went into shock and showed signs of hemorrhage. The nurse in attendance, Lt. Wilma R. Vinsart, recognized the symptoms and was able to administer morphine and put the patient in a shock position. Her quick reaction may have saved the soldier's life.[26]

In addition to the support of medical air evacuation squadrons, the American troops struggling to break out of the Normandy peninsula had the support of a growing number of Army hospitals. Lt. Eula Awbrey's Twelfth Field Hospital, with twenty-one officers and 150 enlisted men, embarked for France on June 25, but to the nurses' horror there was no embarkation personnel roster for them. The chief nurse, Capt. Claudia Draper, quickly typed one up, but by then the rest of the outfit was on an LCI in the English Channel. "We felt abandoned and were forced to take another boat across," Awbrey remembers. Carrying full packs and wearing heavy rubber raincoats against the ocean spray, the nurses waded ashore on Omaha Beach on June 27. "Once on the beach, we were told to move rapidly up an incline to a rendez-vous point where we were able to pause and take a breather." Instructed to march to an evacuation hospital, the nurses passed dead soldiers and abandoned equipment. "We were guided along by soldiers left to hold the beachhead. We were reminded to stay on a narrow path because the engineers had not had time to clear the area of mines. We were safe only on the narrow path," Awbrey says.[27]

Their brief stay at an evacuation hospital was marked by a enemy welcome to France. "Jerry came over and strafed between the tents of this hospital, disregarding the Big Red Cross which was displayed in the center of the area." From the beachhead Awbrey and her unit were transported in vehicles of the Sixty-eighth Medical Group to take over the French naval hospital in Cherbourg, which had been recently abandoned by the Germans. During the siege of Cherbourg the Germans and two captured American doctors had tried to tend 1,000 wounded German patients and 150 American POWs. When the Twelfth Field's nurses arrived at the hospital they found a large quadrangular building dating from the 1860s: "There was no water supply, the mess hall was filthy, and the stench from the head and the garbage was so vile that we could not even think of eating! For our first few meals, we ate K-rations on the front lawn. It was healthier."[28]

The Americans were greeted at the hospital by a wounded SS officer with his arm in a cast. He was in charge of the Allied and German wounded still at the hospital after the Sixty-eighth Medical Group had evacuated the American prisoners and all transportable German patients. As Eula Awbrey entered, the SS officer gave her a look filled with hate and arrogance. "Even in defeat he acted superior," she recalls.

A member of the operating room team, Awbrey describes the former German operating room: "There were dirty instruments everywhere, dirty linens were thrown around, and arms and legs even filled the trash cans! It took a great deal of effort to get that mess cleaned up enough to do any surgery there." The Twelfth Field's commanding officer also described the condition of the hospital in his report: "The sanitary facilities were virtually non-existent—bed pans and urinals were used again and again without being cleaned. . . . no attempt had been made to provide any form of laundry facilities and the filth was evident. The stench which emanated from these wards is one that can never be dismissed from the minds of those who worked therein." Much of the filth was the result of a lack of running water from a broken water system, which the Americans quickly repaired, but the rest, including a number of unburied bodies found on the hospital grounds, had resulted from a breakdown in discipline at the hospital during the siege.

The Twelfth Field Hospital had, in fact, moved into Cherbourg before the city had been liberated and the Germans continued to shell the city from two small islands. "When we heard shells going over (especially at night), we called them screaming mee-mees because they emitted a screaming sound as they passed overhead."[29]

Lieutenant Awbrey's hospital unit was one of several American units that cared for approximately 1,500 German wounded in three hospitals in Cherbourg found by the American troops when they seized the city. The Sixty-eighth Medical Group managed to send 1,380 German patients well enough to travel to the United Kingdom via Utah Beach. The other prisoners of war were sent to one hospital to be tended by German medical personnel under American supervision. The Twelfth Field Hospital opened as a small general hospital on June 30 to care for American casualties from the Cherbourg area and to provide housing and meals for other medical units en route to assignments in the upper Cotentin peninsula.[30]

By July 1944, American medical units were arriving in Normandy in increasing numbers. The Seventh Field Hospital opened in Osmanville near Omaha Beach in early July, the Eighth Field Hospital at Montebourg, the Ninth at Tourlaville, and after a delay waiting for "misdirected equipment," the Seventy-seventh Evacuation Hospital opened near St. Mere Eglise on July 15. Army field and evacuation hospitals in France were organized to function as one large hospital or three smaller ones. The three hospitalization units or platoons were organized to act independently if necessary and a headquarters platoon was responsible for their administration. The field hospital usually consisted of twenty-two officers, eighteen nurses, and 190 enlisted men. Auxiliary surgical teams were attached to each platoon as needed. Although she came overseas with the 101st Evacuation Hospital, Kathryn C. Singer was a surgical nurse and was assigned to the Second Mobile Army Surgical Hospital (MASH). She recalls, "We moved every 10 days to two weeks. You improvised in almost any phase of life in the field. If you can imagine setting up a sterile field inside a large sloping-sided tent you may get a picture—we fixed sterile sheets to the canvas with towels, padded rough boards under sheets to keep instruments in place. It wasn't easy at times to keep your balance as the canvas floor was coated with water, mud, blood, etc.— even with combat boots." Field hospitals sent separate platoons forward to be near the division clearing stations, but as the Army broke out of the Normandy peninsula and began advancing rapidly across France, medical units had difficulty keeping up with the clearing stations.[31]

For the nurses, the rapid Allied advance meant frequent moves. For example, Lieutenant Awbrey's second platoon moved on to a site at Valognes and set up under canvas. Here they were quartered three nurses to a tent and, Awbrey recalls, dug foxholes alongside the tents: "They were so accessible we could just roll from our cots into the foxholes until the strafing or bombing was over."[32]

During the First and Third Army's breakout from the Normandy penin-sula in July and August, hospitals trying to keep up with the Allies' advancing forces found themselves very close to the fighting. On June 28, the Ninety-first Evac moved to Point l'Abbe and began operations on July 3. In fifteen days they cared for 2,549 patients under what the unit called "trying circumstances" near the front, kept awake at night by the loud artillery fire. The Ninety-first's report states, "The Germans made several attempts to counter-attack in this vicinity for a period of four consecutive days. Both day and night, fox holes were used. . . . Artillery barrages became continuous throughout the day and night; small arms fire was clearly audible within a short range of the hospital. Enemy artillery shells fell all around the hospital area but fortunately none landed within our area."[33]

Other field hospitals in Normandy were near the fighting as Allied forces tried to break enemy resistance at St. Lo. There were also a number of large gen-eral hospitals arriving in Normandy soon after D day, because the Advance Sec-tion had planned to send twenty-five general hospitals into French cities in the first ninety days of the campaign. In early July the Fifth General, with fifty-eight officers, 102 nurses, and 500 enlisted men, left Tidworth, England, for Omaha Beach and its location near St. Lo, only to discover upon its arrival that the site was still in German hands! Fortunately, Army officials proved they could be flex-ible and ordered the Fifth to bivouac at Osmanville while a new site on a low-lying field at Carentan was being prepared for their use.

The Second General Hospital was also one of the units bivouacked about five miles behind the front lines at Carentan. The unit's advance detail had dug foxholes and for the first few nights they proved useful indeed. Lt. Col. Marjorie Peto writes, "Some of the nurses had been through fairly rough stuff in London, but most of them admitted they were paralyzed with fright the first few nights in Normandy when all hell seemed to be breaking loose in the sky. . . . Some of the nurses spent the first nights in foxholes while ruefully recalling a department store advertisement in a home newspaper the Christmas before, 'Pillows for foxholes.'"[34]

The precaution of seeking shelter in foxholes proved judicious when one night six enemy planes were shot down and a Ju88 bomber crashed near the hospital, missing the area by only one-half mile. The first night in France a shell hit the officers' latrine but failed to explode. A sign was posted on it that read, "Beware! Unexploded rocket bomb."

The rain and subsequent "ankle deep" mud and the mosquitoes made life miserable for nurses and patients. Army engineers tried their best to put ce-ment foundations under the hospital tents, and when the Fifth General's cement floors were completed, they invited the Second General over to dance and served local French cider—in helmets!

Amid the horror of war there were occasional moments like these and other memorable ones like the Second General's first Sunday in France, when the nurses attended mass in a local village church: "It was packed to the doors with

American soldiers in dirty fatigues, field boots, and helmets. They occupied all the pews, the choir loft, and they stood in the aisles. Guns were deposited in piles on the floor, against the organ, and against the sides of the altar. A corporal asked permission to play the organ and the priest, a bearded patriarch, readily consented. Three times the offering plates were filled to overflowing, certainly never before had the little church such a spontaneous and liberal outpouring."[35]

Until the Second General could be set up, the unit's nurses were sent to evacuation hospitals on detached duty. About two weeks later, they returned to a fully operational general hospital set up entirely under canvas—acres of canvas. Nurses lived in pyramid tents, four women to a tent, and until a mess hall was erected they ate out of doors in an apple orchard fighting off the bees. A few of the buzzing insects were inadvertently swallowed along with dinner!

At first the nurses roughed it with only kerosene lamps at night, nowhere to unpack their clothes, and only helmets to wash their fatigues in. Local women in Normandy offered to do their laundry, but each week they raised the price and asked for more soap, which was such a precious commodity that the nurses preferred to keep it and do their laundry in a brook using stones.

As the summer wore on and the front moved east, the nurses had no more use for their foxholes. By now the Second General had grown into a huge hospital covering sixty acres. Nurses' quarters were near the POW enclosure and the German prisoners could be heard at night singing and playing games. The nurses never feared the proximity of the POWs because they knew the Germans wisely preferred the safety of their barbed wire enclosure to the danger of the French!

The Second General cared for German prisoners, Free French soldiers, and civilians injured by exploding bombs, vehicle accidents, and land mines. American nurses and hospital personnel also cared for German soldiers who were being removed through the normal chain of evacuation. Despite the emotional drain of caring for enemy soldiers, most nurses responded positively and professionally to the POWs. As one nurse explains, she washed off the blood and grime from their faces and changed their soiled dressings: "I didn't see any half-way business in this, if they're not killed someone has to take care of them." Marjorie Peto recalls that the German wounded were especially trying, "for their wounds were infected and they were poorly nourished. Some were very young, they said 18 years, but X-rays of their bones proved them to be younger. They were so foul-smelling and filthy it was an unpleasant task to clean them."[36]

As the Allied troop buildup in France continued, more Army hospital units arrived including eleven 400-bed units and the Sixteenth Field Hospital. The scale of medical care for just the American involvement in France was staggering. For example, to care for the wounded and ill soldiers from its sixteen combat divisions, the First Army had twenty-two evacuation hospitals and six field hospitals. By August 1, 1944, they had treated and returned to duty 23,000 patients and evacuated to the United Kingdom another 56,000 men.[37]

On August 22, 1944, Paris fell to Allied armies—six hours later the Ninety-first Evac moved to Guyancourt. According to its annual report, "Everyone visited Paris and every nurse bought perfume, the officers and soldiers buying their share. Versailles was frequently visited and many souvenirs were bought."[38] Eula Awbrey also visited Paris "in full battle dress—helmet, green fatigues, and high shoes and leggings. We were quite the sensation as we walked into cafes and stores." The nurses were warmly received by the Parisians, who offered to buy them drinks and show them Paris. When the chief nurse for the ETO spotted them, however, they were reprimanded for not being in proper full-dress uniforms. This was quite an order, considering that the nurses' dress uniforms had been rolled up in bedrolls for weeks and they had no way to press them. "Believe me, we looked better in our fatigues. I'm sure that particular officer never spent a day in the field and most assuredly had never had to dive into a foxhole!" Awbrey comments. This is yet another example of the gulf that separated combat personnel from those serving in the rear areas—a disparity so vividly captured during World War II by cartoonist Bill Mauldin.[39]

When Second General Hospital's nurses learned that some WACs and nurses were in Paris, many were envious and even a bit resentful. They were tired of life in the field. Or, as one nurse said to Chief Nurse Peto, "Its the last straw! The last straw! I've worn wet clothes, sat in the mud for meals, been stung by bees, but when the latrine blows down when I'm sitting in it and the place is surrounded by POWs digging in the trenches, Miss Peto, I want to go home!" [40]

Fortunately, as the Normandy campaign wore on, living conditions gradually improved at the Second General and they even acquired a six-hole latrine with a roof. Stoves arrived as the weather grew chilly and grateful Norman farmers brought fruit and heavy cream to the hospital, which helped vary the nurses' diet of Spam and canned corn. Eventually both the Second General's nurses and the soldiers were allowed to make "liberty runs" to Mont St. Michel, Granville, and Cherbourg.

Although occasionally permitted opportunities for sightseeing, none of the Army nurses in France could be spared from duty for long. In fact, more Army medical units and nurses arrived in Europe to support the army as it pushed into Luxembourg. One of the new arrivals was the 110th Evac, which set up in a beautiful meadow. At first the nurses and staff enjoyed the Indian summer weather, but after awhile the rains came. "The meadow became a lake. The cots stood in water, the tent pins couldn't grip the saturated soil, the wind blew the stove tops off the tents and blew the latrine screens down. But they never once stopped receiving casualties," writes correspondent Mary Jose.[41]

Mary Jose, who spent an evening with the 110th Evac's night shift, wrote a revealing story about the experience of army nurses in wartime. The evening shift began at 7 P.M., with Lt. Ann Bunata, the day nurse in post-op, turning her books over to the night nurse, Bett Seib. "We were plenty busy today, but it looks like it will be worse tonight," Bunata said. Over in the shock ward, where the most serious cases were kept, Lt. Wilhemina Tonnar watched carefully over her patients, trying to get their temperatures, respirations, and pulses normal enough so that they could be operated on. "Here is a head and chest case—a bad combination—breathing with a rattle that crackles through the room like a untuned radio, the next man has his belly ripped open with shrapnel; leg splints stick out over the end of the third litter."

In the operating room at ten o'clock, the night shift had already completed twenty-four surgical cases. The surgeons scrub in the hallway, in basins "where school kids used to wash their grubby little fists off." By midnight there are 117 admissions. "Lt. Margaret Grant, the surgical supervisor, checks her patient list, makes sure they are prepped and ready for the surgeons. As one litter comes out, another takes it place." Jose watches them operate until daylight and wonders how the nurses and doctors keep going. Chief Nurse Capt. Georgia Moss says, "We get casualties fresh from the front and take pride in the quick results that show up from our nursing care. We get them in agony and try to make them comfortable. We wash their bodies to relieve them of the dirt and filth of the battlefield. We relieve their minds, too, because they feel the nurse is somebody from home."[42]

Many of these casualties came to Army hospitals not by ambulance but by hospital train. The first operational train in England was received by the U.S. Army on July 2, 1943, but the use of hospital trains on the Continent was slow to develop "because of the small area to which the fighting was limited." Although the main railway line running from Cherbourg to Bayeux was reached by the Allied advance on June 12, 1944, and the railhead at Cherbourg was captured two weeks later, the first train did not pull out until August 5. In the next week, it evacuated 406 patients.

Transportation of wounded by ambulance train proved an efficient, reliable means of evacuation on the Continent, especially when inclement weather kept the medical air evac planes grounded and the long distances made ambulance transport undesirable. The trains ran out of St. Lazare station in Paris to Chef du Pont, Charleroi, Reims, Verdun, Valognes, and Serfontaire. By November 20, 1944, they had transported a total of 73,835 patients, most of them ambulatory. Medical flights normally evacuated litter patients who were less able to withstand a train ride of up to fifty hours.[43]

While the Allied armies were pushing the Germans back toward the Low Countries, Lt. Gen. Alexander M. Patch's Seventh Army was landing along the coast of southern France. From the coast, they were to advance inland and northward to eventually link up with the Allied armies for the final push into Germany.[44]

Once again, U.S. Army hospitals staffed with nurses accompanied the invasion forces. The first nurses to come ashore were attached to three evacuation hospitals, two field hospitals, and an auxiliary surgical group assigned to support the invasion. The first women to actually wade ashore in southern France were 1st Lt. (later Capt.) Evalyn E. Swanson, Lt. Fern Wingerd, and Lt. Gladys Joyce, nurses with the Ninety-fifth Evac and all veterans of the Italian campaign. While the experience of participating in another Allied invasion undoubtedly created anxiety for all the nurses, it must have been especially meaningful for Fern Wingerd, who was among those injured in the devastating February 7, 1944, German air raid on their hospital site at Anzio, in which three army nurses were killed. Although not killed in the attack, Fern Wingerd and Lt. Ruth Buckley were hospitalized and unable to return to work for several months. Recalling their experiences on the Anzio beachhead, the nurses told reporters that "the boat trip and landing were like a summer holiday compared to Anzio."[45]

Captain Swanson was even more candid about their voyage to southern France: "The trip to our destination, which we had subsequently learned to be Southern France, was a delightful cruise, one that would have been most enjoyable during pre-war days, but this trip wasn't meant to be a pleasure cruise. The reminders of war were ever present, for it was the grim business of war that had made this trip necessary."

Their ship, a newly fitted hospital ship, USS *Marigold,* offered the nurses an array of delights they had all but forgotten existed. "We were truly permitted to indulge our appetites with a variety of food such as we had not seen since leaving the States: fresh eggs, choice of cereal, with even potatoes." In addition to meat served twice daily and liberal portions of fresh salads, the nurses were treated to the luxury of unlimited bottles of Coca Cola. "And we drank them as often as our thirsts needed quenching," Captain Swanson recalled with relish in her annual nursing report.[46]

After a pleasant voyage unmarred by enemy attack, the nurses came ashore near the chic resort town of St. Tropez. In sharp contrast to the confusion and sniper fire of the first landing of nurses in North Africa in 1942, Swanson and her nurses were cordially greeted by their commanding officer and by a Red Cross photographer recording the triumphant arrival of American nurses on French soil!

The Ninety-fifth Evacuation Hospital set up near the town of Gonfaron, where Captain Swanson and her nurses discovered "a beehive of activity and the wards literally packed with patients. The operating room was working at top speed and functioning in a way so familiar to [them]." The nurses set to work immediately, but if anyone had any illusions about the Seventh Army's operations being a "champagne campaign" in the beautiful south of France they were quickly brought back to reality. Although these nurses had worked long hours in difficult conditions in Italy, in southern France they faced "incessant work such as the hospital had never experienced. In addition to the long hours nursing patients, the elements contrived to make life a little more difficult. The wind, of almost gale-like proportions, stirred up clouds of fine red dust to make its way into every conceivable place."[47]

Veteran nurse June Wandrey, who also came ashore from the USS *Marigold*, found her hospital set up at Rians. On the twenty-first, she wrote to her friend Ruth, "France is beautiful. Lots of pretty mountains, but they need rain badly. There are many forest fires from incendiary bombs that have been dropped, and the ground is burned to a crisp." Wandrey found southern France similar to Italy, but was amazed when the local villagers brought the hospital patients fresh eggs and melons and would not accept any payment. "In Italy, they were always begging and trying to best us out of our money," she wrote. The French people were thrilled to see the Allied soldiers and nurses. "They came over and grabbed my hand and smothered it with kisses. It was a tearful, touching and humbling experience," recalls Wandrey.[48]

Capt. Evalyn Swanson shares similar memories of the grateful French people, "for they not only volunteered to work around the hospital, but each day came with their baskets laden with food for the patients as well as the hospital personnel." With so much fresh produce available, many of the nurses in their off duty hours turned to cooking in their quarters, "supplementing their diet with fried chicken, french fried potatoes, fresh bread, cheese and unlimited quantities of freshly churned butter. These hours devoted to cooking proved to be a helpful source of evening diversion," Captain Swanson adds.[49]

As June Wandrey's hospital moved north, the nurses were delighted to have their ration diet supplemented with fresh fish caught by throwing grenades into a local river. On August 25 they went swimming, sans suits, in a cold river that flowed down from the mountains. Wandrey found the worst part of campaigning in southern France was the bees: "The bees are so thick around here one can't sit still a minute. They get in your hair, crawl up your trouser legs or shirt sleeves, and then bite."

With the Allied push north underway, the hospital had a steady stream of casualties. Wandrey wrote on September 6, 1944, "I've already worked 14 hours today in the operating tent. . . . We worked and worked . . . three surgical teams operating without stop except for a snack at dinner and supper. Keeping them supplied with sterile dressings, instruments, and sutures kept me busy."

Not all of their admissions were soldiers. Civilians were often wounded during the fighting in France and elsewhere, but the injured children affected the nurses most deeply. One little five-year-old French girl arrived at June Wandrey's hospital with a shell fragment wound in her neck. "Her long blonde pigtails framed her terrified face." The child was chewing Juicy Fruit gum given to her by the ambulance driver "as though her life depended on it. She didn't cry nor have a word to say."[50]

While General Patch's army moved north from southern France, the Third Army was advancing rapidly across the country south of the First Army.

Most units moved forward by truck convoy, but trains were also used to move hospital units like the Second General Hospital, which relocated to the town of Revigny near the Moselle River around Thanksgiving. Here they were quartered in bombed-out buildings. The chief nurse's building had the luxury of a pot-bellied stove and a toilet, but the latter was on the front porch and had to be defrosted with pans of hot water!

At Revigny the nurses acquired a pet dog, a two-month-old puppy they dubbed "Echo." Most of the nurses had been sent out on detached service, but those remaining planned a Christmas party for eighty-five village children. The war had deprived these poor children of a normal childhood. Marjorie Peto recalls that they called Echo "La petite chien" and "sometimes cried as they stroked the little dog; no one ever found out what that was about."[51]

Fall 1944 found the Twelfth Field Hospital on the move as well, from Paris into Belgium, to a beautiful old manor house in Namur, to Huy, and then to Hologne aux Pierre, a small coal-mining town. The hospital was near a zinc factory and Lt. Eula Awbrey recalls that when the German buzz bombs hit, "zinc powder from the rafters would come raining down on everything. In the operating area we put up sheets like a canopy over the operating tables to catch the zinc dust." The buzz bombs were unnerving; no one could predict where they would land: "When they ran out of fuel they dropped immediately, and there was no sound until you heard the explosion. For a moment one then knew she was safe. One of these bombs fell at the door of the hospital and blew the door off its hinges." Some of Awbrey's patients threatened to go back to the front where it was safer![52]

Army hospitals in France and the Low Countries could indeed be dangerous locations in a "total war," where the distinctions between civilians and soldiers were often blurred. Nurses, patients, and other medical personnel were occasionally the targets of enemy artillery fire or strafing aircraft. For example, the Forty-fifth Field Hospital had been set up near Henri Chapelle, Belgium, for three uneventful weeks, but on the evening of October 21 the Germans lobbed twenty shells into the hospital area. The third round hit the staff tent area, injuring an enlisted man, a medical officer, and 2d Lt. Frances Y. Slanger, who died of her wounds five days later. 2d Lt. Margaret M. Bowler, 2d Lt. Elizabeth F. Powers, 1st Lt. Gladys M. Synder, who were attached to the Third Auxiliary Surgical Group, also received minor injuries in the attack.[53]

The news of Lieutenant Slanger's death deeply affected many American military personnel because twenty-four hours before the attack she had written a letter to *Stars and Stripes:* "Sure we rough it. But compared to the way you men are taking it we can't complain, nor do we feel bouquets are due us . . . it is to you we doff our helmets. To every GI wearing the American uniform—for you we have the greatest admiration and respect."

Frances Slanger was buried in the American cemetery near Henri Chapelle, "flanked on either side by the fighting men she served." She was one of sixteen nurses killed in World War II as the result of enemy action. At the time, Lieutenant Slanger was reported to be the first Army nurse killed in action in the ETO, but in fact the first reported case of a nurse "missing in action" was that of 2d Lt. Reba Z. Whittle attached to the 813th MAES in England, whose medical air evac plane was shot down by enemy antiaircraft fire after it had veered off course on a flight on September 27, 1944. Lieutenant White and the flight technician were listed as missing, but in early December the surgeon on the XI Troop Carrier Command reported her status had been changed to "killed in action." Later that month, to everyone's surprise and relief, Lieutenant Whittle and the technician were discovered to be very much alive and being held in Germany as prisoners of war. They had both received minor wounds when their plane was shot down, but were now listed as being in good health. The Germans returned Lieutenant Whittle to the United States in early January, but the flight technician was not released.[54]

Except for these nurses wounded or killed by enemy action, the attrition rate for ETO nurses in the second half of 1944 was fairly low. For example, First Army evacuated thirty-nine nurses for health reasons during this period, Third Army evacuated thirty-seven nurses from May to December, including one death, but fewer nurses became patients on the Continent than in the United Kingdom, and nurses in field hospitals experienced a lower illness rate than those in evacuation hospitals.

By the fall of 1944, the Allied front was 150 miles long, which made the collection and care of injured soldiers even more difficult and necessitated a large number of forward hospitals. Field hospitals were ordered to act as small evacuation units and the evacuation hospitals as transfer units spaced to limit a continuous ambulance run to one tolerable for the patients.[55]

After October 30, when the weather turned cold and damp, field hospitals sought out buildings in which to set up rather than using canvas tents. In many cases getting the wounded out of the rain, cold, and mud into warmer surroundings aided their recovery significantly, especially those suffering postoperative trauma and shock. These cases could in fact make up a large portion of a field hospital's admissions. For example, between June 10, 1944, and December 1944, the Forty-fifth Field Hospital admitted almost 5,000 patients. One-third of these patients were seriously wounded soldiers. The Forty-fifth performed 1,000 major surgical procedures during this period and provided the preoperative and intensive postoperative care required for surgical cases. In one eight-day period in September, the Forty-fifth's seven surgical teams performed over 150 operations on patients with chest and abdominal wounds.

Although these cases sometimes benefited from being in hospitals set up in buildings, many Army hospitals actually preferred to set up under canvas in warm weather because of the ease of laying out the wards and other tents in open fields. In France, however, open spaces brought the serious danger of German mines. One colonel expressed his preference for cow pastures saying, "No dead cows, no mines." As many of the nurses and hospital staff's discovered, using buildings was not necessarily an improvement over canvas, for many were booby-trapped, filthy, and had their windows blown out. Keeping warm became a constant task for many nurses. At Marseilles 1st Lt. Imogene Yarbrough, ANC, remembered that the nurses of the Twenty-third Station Hospital were billeted in a cement barn without heat and for a day without blankets. The small servants' quarters had a little heat. It "would normally seat six people, but forty-five of us gathered to keep warm. Those that couldn't get in either went to bed to get warm or went to the Red Cross in Marseilles." During an interview, Yarbrough noted that "morale was low, the nurses were despondent and irritable. They felt that something could have been done for them." Life did not improve when they moved to Epinal, France, where the third floor of their quarters in a villa was also without heat or hot water. "I believe these conditions could have been eliminated if the commanding officer wanted them eliminated," Yarborough said. "If the C.O. wants to live like Tarzan he usually wants everyone to live that way," she quipped.[56]

In December the staff of most hospitals began making preparations for the Christmas season. At the Second General the nurses were planning a Christmas party—collecting candy from the soldiers for the children, making angels, and cutting icicles and stars from tin cans. Unhappily, a German counterattack in the Ardennes forest on December 16 took the VIII Corps by surprise and threw everyone's Christmas plans into chaos. Advancing rapidly, the Germans penetrated deep into Allied territory and might have broken through to the coast except for the many small units that held out and denied the Germans the use of the roads needed for a successful counteroffensive. In furious fighting, the Germans were denied their objective, the Meuse River, but the Battle of the Bulge caused the Allied high command some anxious moments.[57]

It also put Army hospitals on the alert. On December 16, 1944, reports of enemy activity poured into the office of the First Army Surgeon, Brig. Gen. John A. Rogers, at Army headquarters near Spa. At Malmedy, the Sixty-seventh Evacuation Hospital reported that the town was being shelled and the hospital had received minor damage. Word came that the Germans were also shelling the area near Eupen, where the Second, Forty-fifth and Fifth Evacuation Hospitals were located. General Rogers was later relieved to learn that these German attacks near Eupen seemed local and that commanders on the scene did not consider them too serious, but he decided to evacuate the Forty-second Field Hospital at Wiltz and the 107th Evac at Clerveaux, which was in the path of the enemy advance. The 102d was also ordered to evacuate and by the afternoon of December 17, 1944, Colonel Rogers felt compelled to order the Forty-fourth and Sixty-seventh to pull out all transportable patients and unnecessary personnel. This left one lone hospital, the Second Evac, to care for all of the First Army's wounded in the Eupen area. Nurses from all these hospital units were moved back to safety in rear areas, but some units sent all-male platoons, auxiliary surgical teams, and medical equipment to Bastogne, which was being besieged by German forces.[58]

Two examples of hospitals caught in the sudden German advance near Bastogne illustrate the confusion and difficulties experienced by Army hospitals operating near the front in the midst of this surprise German offensive. On December 17, 1944, a platoon of the Forty-seventh Field Hospital at Butgenbach east of Malmedy observed several odd sights near the hospital but, assured by the Second Division clearing station that the situation was under control, continued to serve breakfast and care for nine seriously wounded soldiers. When the platoon commander saw streams of vehicles, half tracks, and antitank guns moving to the rear, however, he became suspicious and ordered the nurses back to the main clearing station and from there to Malmedy. They joined other nurses from the unit at Spa and were further evacuated back to Liege. One group of eight nurses made the forty-mile trip safely despite being strafed twice by enemy aircraft.

Another group of eighteen nurses being evacuated to the rear from the Forty-seventh's First Platoon at Waimes, however, was sent scurrying from their ambulance by enemy artillery fire. They had to walk or hitchhike back to their unit at Waimes, where the First Platoon had unpacked and set up again for operation. The following day the hospital platoon, including nurses, some stragglers, and the commanding officer of the 180st Medical Battalion, was "captured" by two armed Germans wearing American uniforms. Out of respect for the hospital's protection under the Geneva Convention, our troops in the area did not resist this German takeover and the nurses and four medical officers were allowed to continue to care for their thirty-six remaining patients. However, when the two German soldiers ordered everyone else into trucks for transport to the German lines, one ambulance driver escaped and got word to an American infantry unit which engaged the enemy troops by blocking the road, rescued the hospital platoon, and reopened the road to Spa.

The German advance caused major disruptions in medical care as hospitals were evacuated and patients shifted from location to location. The fighting near Bastogne continued into the Christmas holidays, creating more casualties for the already burdened hospitals. Between December 16, 1944, and February 22, 1945, First Army hospitals admitted 78,000 patients, 24,000 of them with battle wounds.[59]

The Thirty-ninth Field Hospital, already swamped with casualties, hosted the staff and patients of the 130th General, which had been hastily evacuated two days before Christmas. According to the annual report, "The hospital looked like a hotel in the states during the Democratic convention, though grim and tense. No one knew what to expect next. Every available space was utilized, cots filled the hallways, men [were] rolled up in blankets on the floors, even the furnace rooms were occupied." Naturally the hospital staff worked overtime to handle the patient load, and the kitchen staff achieved wonders, feeding five to six hundred people a day.[60]

Two days before Christmas, June Wandrey's unit had moved up to Sarralbe to receive casualties from the Forty-fourth Division. Some G.I.s had found her a thigh-high tree, which she decorated with cut-up Christmas cards. "Then we took all the bright strings and slivers of foil wrappings from our packages and scattered them over the tree like tinsel." But in the middle of their Christmas carol sing an officer burst in the door and told them that the troops could not hold their sector and they should prepare to evacuate.

Wandrey's hospital evacuated safely, but some field hospitals remained near the fighting during the Battle of the Bulge. Nurses at the Fifty-first Field Hospital cared for both American and German casualties. During the Battle of the Bulge some of the Germans infiltrated Allied lines wearing American uniforms, in a violation of international law. Janice Goers-Reilly vividly recalls one such patient being taken off the ward by the U.S. military and summarily shot. She will never forget another seriously injured German prisoner on her ward who repeatedly tried to take his cast off, saying he wanted "to die for the Fuehrer." Although only a slight ninety-two pounds, Goers-Reilly exerted all of her nurse's authority and told him, "No, you're going to live for Uncle Sam."[61]

The 103d Evac was moved up to an old French barracks near Bastogne to await the Allied breakthrough to relieve the besieged 101st Airborne, which had been surrounded by Germans and cut off from Allied supply lines. Inside Bastogne, the American defenders were caring for some 700 casualties sheltered in schools, churches, and homes. On the morning of December 27, the siege was lifted and within twenty-four hours the 103d Evac was brimming over with casualties. The hospital's usual 400-bed capacity was doubled, with the overflow patients going into a big rec room.

War correspondent Mary Jose described the scene: "An Eagle Division trooper sat by the piano by the window, pounding out 'Carolina Moon.' He had a bandage on his head and blood showed through the right temple. Paratroopers with arms in slings, bandages bulging under ripped pants legs hummed when the soldier struck up 'I'll Walk Alone,' and burst out lustily in the chorus of 'White Christmas.'"[62]

The 103d's forty nurses were veterans of the campaign in France, having cared for casualties from Carentan, Coustances, and Avaranches to Viree, Vitel, Chatel, and Metz. By December 1944 they had handled more than 13,000 patients. Chief Nurse Beth Veley was a veteran of the Bataan campaign and was one of the nurses aboard the last plane to leave Corregidor, so she must have felt real kinship with the besieged troopers of the 101st Airborne at Bastogne.

While the 103d Evac was receiving casualties from Bastogne, a truck load of twenty nurses arrived from a general hospital hurriedly evacuated to escape the advancing Germans. One of the nurses described their escape: "The roads were cut off ahead and our hospital acted as a battalion aid station for some six thousand patients. We treated and evacuated as quickly as possible until we got them all out. Then we got ourselves and [the] equipment out. As transportation was at a premium, we left our bedrolls, clothing, and even our Christmas packages with orders that they be burned if the Germans reached the hospital."[63]

Not all Army hospitals during the Battle of the Bulge were evacuated and some managed to salvage their holiday festivities. At the Thirty-ninth, townspeople brought the hospital patients and personnel a gaily trimmed Christmas tree and decorated the foyer with pine boughs, tinsel, and American and Belgian flags. The YWCA presented a pageant and, dressed in colorful native costumes, did folk dances. Gifts were brought to patients and staff, and everyone had a merry time.

At the First AFCS (Air Force Communication Service), the holiday was also celebrated with a fine turkey dinner and on December 20 the enlisted men of the 926th American Engineer Regiment entertained the hospital with a talent show. The First's nurses had been evacuated to headquarters at Charleroi and the patients had been evacuated "just in case," so the holiday was an enforced rest period for the remaining staff.[64] In Holognes, Lt. Eula Awbrey and the personnel of the Twelfth Field's second platoon celebrated Christmas with a beautiful tree decorated with colored ornaments and real candles, "the kind you light with a match. I was so afraid the tree would catch fire. We sang carols and had a lovely time exchanging small gifts," she remembers fondly.

However, the holidays are not so happily recalled by the Twelfth Field's two other platoons, which were located in tents and at a school complex near Liege. One December evening during a dance and reception given by the British, the building was hit by a German buzz bomb, which exploded and showered the partygoers with flying glass, and injured the hospital's commanding officer, Colonel Wulff, and the chief nurse, Captain Draper. On that same night, December 20, a twenty-six-year-old American Red Cross worker, Ann Kathleen Cullen, was killed by a shell that hit the school building. The hospital did not even have immunity on Christmas Day, for just as dinner was being served a trio of German planes strafed a bridge 200 yards south of the tented area. "Everyone ran for a ditch alongside the road. There were no injuries, except scratches and bruises sustained crossing a fence to get into the ditch. This escapade ruined the meal, and Christmas for them," writes Eula Awbrey.[65]

Meanwhile, additional hospitals continued to arrive in the rear to support Allied operations. Some, like the 197th Field Hospital, moved up from locations in France to areas nearer the front. Madelene Bateman was attached to the 197th, which was supposed to set up at Liege, Belgium, but which, because of the fighting during the Battle of the Bulge, had been sent to St. Quentin, France, where it occupied "a former women's and children's hospital which had been occupied by the Germans and which they [had] sabotaged before leaving." At St.

Quentin the nurses "literally scrounged for anything [they] could get 'til a few supplies trickled in." Fortunately, when Supreme Headquarters Allied Expeditionary Force (SHEAF) arrived at nearby Reims, the 127th obtained the necessary supplies.[66]

Among the new arrivals at the front in mid-December was the 166th General Hospital, which, according to Kay Yarabinec, "arrived [in September] on Omaha beachhead. We bivouacked in various cow pastures until the middle of December. The living conditions were very bad during the first three months in France, at which time we had no heat, no running water, and cold food rations." They also suffered from inadequate clothing for their luggage was inadvertently left behind in England. Yarabinec remembers that the nurses had packed their bedrolls haphazardly, without "the constructive advice of experienced army personnel." She concludes, "Needless to say, we didn't have the clothing and items we needed" until December.

Because the 166th set up just before Christmas 1944, one of the nurses' first assignments was to plan the holiday festivities for the patients. Kay Yarabinec recalls, "My plan for entertainment was to dance with each ambulatory patient and play a card game with the patients who were confined to bed. Also, all the nurses and our chief nurse made the round through the wards between 5 and 7 A.M. and sang Xmas carols. It was one of the most moving experiences in my life."[67]

The day after Christmas, life returned to normal routines. At the Second General Hospital the chief nurse and three nurses went to Nancy to join the doctors and staff on detached service. They arrived hungry and tired at Nancy, which had escaped the ravages of war and was a beautiful city, "a little Paris."

The winter of 1945 in Europe was one of the coldest in memory. On January 19, the first hospital train came in from the front plowing through a fresh two-foot snowfall. One nurse writes, "It was bitterly cold, with morphine and plasma freezing, all wondered how the front line medics could work." The wounded were cheerful, but many were serious cases with fractured skulls, severed spinal cords, and faces torn apart by the explosion of hand grenades.[68]

As American forces pushed across the Rhine River in early 1945, casualties mounted. The increase in combat wounded prompted the army to convert the Second General Hospital into an evacuation hospital, where many wounded stayed only for a week at a time. Morale at the hospital was high during this period, however, for the trainloads of 100-200 wounded G.I.s a day required tender care and expert handling. According to Chief Nurse Peto, the work was demanding, but rewarding.

By the end of January 1945, the Allies had retaken most of the ground lost in the Battle of the Bulge. An estimated 75,000 U.S. casualties resulted from the month of bitter fighting, but it was the Germans' "last hurrah." A massive Russian offensive on the eastern front drew the bulk of German divisions away from the Rhine area, and after a determined stand at the Roer River, the enemy slowly pulled back. In March the U.S. Ninth Armored captured a key bridge across the Rhine at Remagen before the enemy could blow it up, and to the south the Third Army crossed the river in landing craft. The final drive into Germany had begun.

As Allied forces penetrated into Germany, Army hospitals were set up to care for the many casualties of this final offensive. H. Jean McIver Kemp remembers going by 2.5-ton truck across France to Trier, which is just over the Belgian border. The 138th was set up in a German Catholic hospital without heat or running water. To the nurses' delight their quarters had real beds with mattresses, but they "walked up and down six flights of stairs to the latrine in a tent outdoors."[69]

When the flow of casualties was heavy, the nurses of the 138th worked at a frantic pace. Jean Kemp recalls that one of the adjustments they had to make was being reconciled to giving those severely wounded soldiers only short-term care. The longest stay at the 138th was only thirty days and many wounded were evacuated much sooner to rear-area hospitals. At the Second General in Nancy, Lt. Marjorie Peto recalls that many patients, especially burn cases and amputees, were flown out to the United States within forty-eight hours.

Medical air evacuation units were very active during the last six months of the war, and flight nurses like Jean Tierney had some unusual experiences. She recalls one flight in early 1945 to Stalag Luft One on the Baltic Sea: "This POW camp had been liberated the night before by the Russians. Meeting the freed airmen and seeing the camp and the conditions in which they lived was a sobering experience. One of the pilots was the brother of one of our flight nurses, and she had not known he was alive until they met on the field."[70]

In February 1945, Eula Awbrey's unit of the Twelfth Field Hospital set up for the first time inside the Third Reich in the Aachen Clinic. "The clinic was flooded in some areas, much of its equipment ruined. There was no electricity or running water. It was a much cleaner facility over-all than what we had encountered in Cherbourg, France, and there were no dead Germans!" she notes. She celebrated her twenty-fifth birthday in Aachen with her future husband, Art Sforza, a member of the 183d Field Artillery. He had arrived for a brief visit and told her the Allies were about to launch a major offensive near Cologne. "I want to emphasize the force of this attack!" Eula writes. "The thunderous force of the bombardment turned a very large statue at a crossroads near Cologne completely around so that it faced in the opposite direction!"

Eula Awbrey was in Brandt, Germany, when she heard of President Roosevelt's death. "Memories of the President came back to me," she writes, "especially the years of the depression when my family and so many others were the poorest of the poor. To me, President Roosevelt had always been a hero." June Wandrey wrote to her friend Betty on April 13, 1945: "President Roosevelt's death was a shock to me. I didn't know he was ill. When I was a student in

Rochester he came to visit his son who was a patient. That's the first time I real-ized FDR was a cripple. The newspapers never had photographs of his disabil-ity."[71]

When the Seventh Army cracked the Siegfried Line in early April, Wandrey's platoon had moved to Partenstein. To keep pace with the rapidly ad-vancing troops, the hospital frequently divided into a forward unit and a holding company of two nurses, a doctor, and four enlisted men that remained behind with nontransportable patients, but in the process the holding unit was some-times left stranded. Once, Wandrey says, "we were left in the middle of an iso-lated field with few supplies, no transportation, and no field telephone." An ambulance was supposed to come back to bring them supplies, but none arrived. "Our troops had the Germans on the run and moved much farther and faster than expected." As the days passed, Wandrey's unit ran out of food and fuel. She used her father's fishing line and hooks to catch some trout from a nearby stream and when an occasional vehicle came by begged gasoline from them to keep the stove going. "The nights were frigid. We had no news of the war and no weapons with which to defend ourselves from rear-running German defectors."[72]

Although the holding unit eventually rejoined the main platoon, Wandrey and her fellow medical personnel were never completely free of danger. German planes strafed and dive-bombed near the hospital, and on April 2, 1945, the Germans attacked a bridge near the village, injuring a number of civilians. Two small children were among the victims which were brought to the American hos-pital, "The little boy's arm was blown off at the shoulder and the little girl lost her leg below the knee."

The Allied drive over the Rhine and across Germany was, in Wandrey's words, "a maelstrom. Everyday was dangerous and difficult. We operated in di-rect support of Infantry Division Clearing Stations and accepted only severely wounded patients and those in shock. Many patients received hours of shock treatment before they could even be taken to surgery." For blood transfusions they turned to infantry volunteers, who received a shot of whiskey after their blood donation and a slip to present to the commanding officer for payment.

The suffering of so many young men, both American and German, was emotionally draining for the nurses. After losing three patients in one night, one field hospital nurse felt she might not be able to go on. Another said, "The hard-est thing for me is to know that every day a sweetheart, wife, or parent, has writ-ten a letter that will never be read." Increasingly, the misery and futility of war became the subject of June Wandrey's letters. When one of her patients, a young enlisted man with an angelic singing voice, died, she wrote her family, "Despite Sammy's desperate battle to live, he slipped away as morning broke. It broke my heart. Desperately tired, hungry, and sick of the misery and futility of war, I wept uncontrollably, my tears falling on poor Sammy's bandaged remains."[73]

Wandrey also felt deep compassion for the severely wounded German prisoners in her hospital's care. She confided in a letter, "It hurts me when these young men suffer so. I'm sure some of them must be unwilling draftees just like our men, taught to kill or be killed. Another six months of this and they can send me to a hospital too."

Indoctrinated by Nazi propaganda to believe they would be killed if captured, and unable to speak English, German prisoners, according to Wandrey, "consumed precious time by resisting everything the nurses attempted to do for them until they learned, then they were often very grateful. One young Nazi, seeing the bloody drainage the doctor was aspirating from his wounded chest, pleaded to be killed outright rather than be bled to death by syringefuls!"[74]

Prisoners of war only added to the nurses and enlisted men's problems. On duty for twelve-hour shifts, the nurses were often responsible for monitoring ten to fifteen transfusions and intravenous infusions, tending to Wangensteen apparatus, calming or restraining delirious patients, planning special diets, and treating burn cases on one ward. Fortunately for these war-weary nurses, peace was nearing as the Allies closed in on Berlin. On May 1, 1945, the Seventh Army captured Munich, and the next day *Stars and Stripes'* readers saw the headlines "Hitler dead." On May 7, 1945, June Wandrey noted in her diary, "Today the unconditional German surrender was signed with fifty-one Parker pens at General Eisenhower's headquarters in Reims, France." The next day was officially V-E Day and Wandrey was in Paris watching the celebrations from a rooftop before descending into the boisterous crowd. She remembers, "French soldiers picked me up, hoisted me on their shoulders, and carried me down the Champs Elysses shouting 'Vive la France, Vive la America.' It was very thrilling. I was kissed by innumerable, exuberant people. Everyone was out on the streets, planes zoomed overhead in huge formations, all the important brass were there. . . de Gaulle . . . and all, and I didn't have a movie camera."[75]

In the city of Nancy, church bells rang, flags appeared on the buildings, and crowds filled the town square. Celebrating G.I.s fired their weapons into the air for joy, but some were injured by stray bullets. At the Second General, the patients went wild with joy, celebrating with champagne donated by the hospital's French employees. Some patients tossed crutches aside and went into town to celebrate. That night the blackout ended and Nancy was bathed in light, children danced in the streets, and the hospital was adorned with red, white, and blue lights.[76]

In Trier, Jean Kemp says G.I.s celebrated V-E Day by requisitioning the contents of a local wine cellar and filling the nurses' five-gallon gasoline cans that were used to hold the water supply with wine. She writes, "When I came off duty at 1 P.M., I filled my helmet with water, intending to wash my face only to find the water red and possessed of the aroma of good wine!"[77]

For many hospitals and for their Army nurses, V-E Day did not mean the end of long hours and hard work. The steady stream of battle casualties ceased, only to be replaced by soldiers injured in accidents or by a new stream of prisoners of war. The 166th General Hospital was among those converted to a hospital to care for POWs. Kay Yarabinec recalls, "The reason was that most Germans ran away from the approaching German lines into American lines to surrender." Many of the Germans were wounded, but nursing German prisoners, she writes, required adjustments: "We had to teach them how to care for their own, because medicine had fallen far behind that of other Western European countries. This was due to the fact that their best physicians and scientists had either fled from Germany or been killed in concentration camps."

Yarabinec says they spent several weeks teaching the German doctors and paramedical staff how to use American equipment and drugs. Because she had grown up in Germany and had come to the United States at age thirteen, she was assigned to act as interpreter between the German and American physicians. She observed that the young German soldiers, who often had a superior attitude, were withdrawn and would suffer in silence without asking for pain relievers. The older wounded soldiers, however, were disillusioned with Hitler and his regime. Yarabinec writes that these patients "were most grateful to the Americans and relieved to be out of the war."

Kay Yarabinec says that the German prisoners "were hard workers and extremely honest," but remembers taking precautions: "While we were teaching the Germans to take care of their own, I had to impress and instruct our own staff, especially our nurses, to follow strict military protocol in their dealings with their German counterparts so that the nurses could maintain control over the Germans and did not jeopardize themselves and their safety. The young German ward attendants were not used to women officers such as American nurses and would have tried anything."

Prior to their unit's conversion to a German POW hospital, Yarabinec says there was an informal atmosphere between nurses and enlisted personnel that would have "precipitated real serious problems had we continued this type of informality while training the Germans." Furthermore, when German nurses finally arrived, they did not enjoy the same officer status as the American nurses.[78]

Eula Awbrey's hospital, the Twelfth Field, also cared for German prisoners of war who arrived at the hospital in very poor condition. She writes, "They were filthy dirty, scantily clothed, and some had no shoes—only rags wrapped around their feet. Many had gangrene from frostbite and needed amputations. They were covered with lice, many had syphilis chancres, some had pneumonia, and all had some degree of malnutrition. Most of them had diarrhea from prolonged lack of food." Many of them died, and even before a doctor could pronounce them dead "their comrades would strip the bodies of their clothing." Awbrey recalls, "We would find them stark naked on their cots." Other prisoners stole food or bars of soap from fellow patients. The Twelfth Field cared for 3,000 of these German POWs before sending them back to rear-area hospitals for further treatment.[79]

U.S. Army nurses and medical personnel also cared for patients in civilian hospitals such as the displaced persons' hospital five miles north of Munich, which June Wandrey's unit inherited from the Sixty-sixth Field Hospital on June 2, 1945. She says that they had 400 patients, all starved, many the victims of torture and punishment. She describes their condition: "Mostly Jewish, these tortured souls hardly resemble humans. Their bodies riddled with diseases. Many have tuberculosis, typhus, enterocolitis, and huge bed sores." Before they could even begin to treat these patients the hospital personnel and nurses had to clean the contaminated grounds, enlisting the help of twenty-five mobile displaced persons. They wore masks, but nothing kept out the stench of years of poor sanitation. Many of Wandrey's emaciated patients died in their sleep and because they weighed so little she carried each corpse to a storage room herself. "Each time, I breathe a wee prayer for them. God, are you there?" she wrote to her family in a letter dated June 4, 1945.[80]

Lieutenant Wandrey also worked at Dachau, where the liberating Americans found 31,432 internees. They were of many nationalities, but mainly Italians, Czechs, Poles, Jews, Slovenes, and Russians. "Many of the young boys who were here and had been here for some years were still the same height as when they came, though now shrunken and shriveled in body tissue, with sad, haunted eyes. None of the horrible pictures of this place convey the stench of rotting flesh. Very sad," she writes.[81] Many of these displaced persons, or DP's, were flown out of concentration camps on army medical air evacuation planes. Jean Tierny recalls, "We landed on most of our flights in Germany, not on regular airfields or runways, but in fields or pastures on the grass. Not many of the DPs spoke English, and I did not speak any of the languages they represented. They were crowded into the plane with a little valise or else all their possessions tied in a little kerchief. Most of them took the flight well but many were frightened of the plane's motion in flight." [82]

The roads of Germany and France were also crowded with refugees, "pulling or pushing small carts or wagons, a constant motion of dispossessed humanity, old and young," a sight Jean Tierney believes she'll never forget. The nurses' contact with the local populace had been somewhat limited during the war, but after V-E Day some hospitals were set up in Austria, where nurses had the opportunity to relate to Austrian civilians. Helen Graves was with the 124th General Hospital at Salzburg and recalls her Austrian hosts: "I felt we were tolerated and viewed by suspicion. They were thrifty, hard-working people who expected to attend to their affairs and wished the same from us while in their country." In Frankfurt, Germany, nurse Vera Fields found that "the natives were definitely hostile. They looked at us with cold, disdainful looks. They made no attempt to speak to us." The situation for Madelene Bateman's unit in Germany "got so bad that nurses were required to be escorted by American military when away from hospital confines." However, in Frankfurt, the peoples' attitude gradually changed as time passed and Vera Fields remembers, "They would greet us in German and smile by the time six months had gone by."[83]

As Europe returned to peacetime and the patient loads diminished, Army nurses had more opportunities for R and R. The French Riveria was a favorite resort and rest area. Jean Kemp, who spent a leave at the Hotel Juan Le Pins between Cannes and Nice, remembers anxiously awaiting the arrival of a new bathing suit. The only one she had with her was fashioned from a seersucker uniform. When four or her friends arrived by train they carried the long-awaited package. "All gathered around to open the box. But what did it contain? Candles and toilet tissue!" Items once in short supply in the ETO, but no longer needed.[84]

Nurses from the Second General also got R and R in Cannes, and Marge Peto writes, "they loved the resort even if conditions were not exactly gala. There were a few lively night spots open and it was in one of the three that they were introduced to the new drink—a 'blood and guts' cocktail!" Peto assumes it was named after Gen. George S. Patton or "just to show how tough every wearer of khaki thought he was." While relaxing in Cannes, the nurses also swam in the Mediterranean on beaches supposedly cleared of mines. Occasionally, however, a mine did float in and one nurse from the 127th General Hospital was seriously injured when she slipped on one.[85]

Travel was limited, but Helen Graves managed a trip to Salzburg, Berchtesgaden, and a spa in the mountains, where, she remembers, "We were entertained with dinner, a musical program, and dancing." While assigned to the 124th General Hospital in Salzburg, Graves lived in a beautiful Austrian chalet, but accommodations for nurses after V-E Day varied. Alice Howard served in hospitals all over Germany, but was stationed for the longest period at Kassel, where the nurses were quartered in homes taken over by the Army.[86]

The big question in everyone's mind after V-E Day was "what next?" Naturally, home was the No. 1 choice on most nurses' list of future assignments. They were tired and homesick; when a joker at the Second General put up signs for classes in Japanese and Chinese, a few of the war-weary nurses broke down and cried. As it turned out, most units were scheduled to go home for demobilization and therefore stayed in Europe for only six months. Still, thoughts turned toward home and many soldiers and nurses began to worry and plot means to bring their "good and faithful" pet dogs home with them. Officially no dogs were allowed back into the States, but *Stars and Stripes* magazine said, "Use your ingenuity."

By December 1945, there were 9,260 members of the Army Nurse Corps on duty on the Continent, serving at sixty-four general, fifteen station, fifty-three evacuation, and twenty field hospitals as ward nurses, operating room nurses, anesthetists, physiotherapists, and dietitians. As time wore on, many medical units were sent home, and numerous hospitals were closed or replaced by fresh units from the States.

The trip home was memorable for nurses and soldiers alike. Vera Fields recollects her voyage home in December 1945, on the *United States,* formerly Kaiser Wilhelm's yacht: "The ship's capacity was 5,000, but the captain was forced to transport 7,500 of us." After three calm days at sea, a storm hit. "The storm struck with such tremendous force that the ship's rudder was broken and we were listing to port," Fields remembers. All personnel were ordered to stand by their bunks to help stabilize the ship. In one unusual occurence, a seaman was swept overboard by a wave only to be washed back on the ship by the next! Vera Fields recalls that she suffered fractures of the legs and one arm, but otherwise survived the harrowing voyage.[87]

June Wandrey also returned to the States by sea, on the old converted cruise ship *West Point.* This time she wasn't at all seasick and to the cook's amazement she consumed an entire carton of maple nut ice cream. After an uneventful crossing, the ship docked at Newport News and the passengers disembarked "into a shabby dirty area—no bands, no flags, no welcoming crowds." They boarded a vermin-infested trooptrain and stared at each other in disbelief, "a load of high-point nurses home from the Big War." When several gray-haired Gray Ladies suddenly appeared with a cheery "welcome home" and brought them trays of milk and cookies, Wandrey recalls, "I choked up because the lump in my throat was so big it hurt to swallow. Tears spilled down my face."[88]

Other Army nurses flew home from the ETO. Lt. Eula Awbrey, Mrs. Arthur Sforza after her wedding in Belgium, was given permission to fly home because she was pregnant and anxious to return to the States. She left Europe by C-47 in August 1945 and will never forget her feelings as she saw the U.S. coastline out the window. Her reaction to the sight of home was echoed by countless returning women veterans: "One of the greatest thrills in my whole life was looking out the window of the plane as it flew up the Atlantic coast and seeing all the beautiful lights twinkling below. No more blackouts! No more war! I was home!"[89]

7

THE END OF THE LINE

Nursing in the China-Burma-India Theater of Operations

 While the Pacific theaters absorbed the bulk of American fighting forces during 1942 and 1943, other Allied troops were waging war against the Japanese in India and Burma. Although the British had committed the most troops to what became known as the China-Burma-India (CBI) Theater, the United States's Lend Lease commitments to China led to an early American involvement in the area. Although not a large force, Lt. Gen. Joseph Stilwell's American troops in the CBI were assigned medical support in the form of U.S. Army medical units and Army nurses. In fact, for two years the only American servicewomen in the China-Burma-India theater were Army nurses.[1]

Prior the nurses' arrival in India, U.S. troops under Gen. "Vinegar Joe" Stilwell had joined British forces in a desperate but unsuccessful effort to defend Burma against Japanese attack. The first Burma campaign failed, and Stilwell led two cut-up Chinese divisions out of Burma to the Indian frontier on what some reporters called a "voluntary withdrawal or even a glorious retreat." General Stilwell was then ordered to assemble and train a new army to retake the vital Burma Road supply route to China. Until it was completed, the U.S. Army Air Force turned to C-47 cargo planes, which began regular flights over the imposing Himalayan Mountains, on the now legendary "over the Hump" air route.[2]

The first American hospital to be assigned to India was the 159th Station Hospital, which sailed on the SS *Brazil* on May 16, 1942, with a medical staff that included Chief Nurse 1st Lt. Dorcas C. Avery and ninety Army nurses. British women and their children had visited or been stationed in India with their husbands or families, but most of the Americans nurses who arrived in India in 1942 knew little about this vast Asian continent. Life in India was an entirely new adventure for Army nurses like 1st Lt. Marie Rowley, ANC, who was among the first group of ninety Army nurses to arrive in India. She and the other nurses of the 159th Station Hospital left New York City in March 1942 for Karachi. "When we were issued our bedding rolls and went aboard the ship that took us overseas, we were ready for anything," Rowley recalls. The 159th debarked at Karachi on May 16. 1st Lt. Eleanor Bradley, ANC, described their new hospital, which was located in the desert eighteen miles from Karachi, as consisting of "one-story, stone buildings. The buildings were scattered, and the hospital area extended for about a mile. Electric lights and fans were in all the buildings. The operating room was air conditioned." Marie Rowley was surprised to learn upon arriving in India that the nurses' quarters were new concrete bungalows and that the hospital was blessed with air-conditioned operating rooms. "But," she adds, "we were in for other surprises—some not so pleasant."

Once inside her bungalow, she "found sand, which was an inch deep over the floor, furniture and bed, had penetrated the locked doors and windows." It also took the nurses a month of determined spraying of insecticide to clean out the variety of insects which had been making their home in the bungalows. The nurses had no kitchen set up at first, recalls one nurse, so "for awhile breakfast meant coffee and bread. There was no ice, so we drank warm water." Eventually the hospital received a refrigerator unit to make ice, but Rowley reported that the Chinese patients at the 159th Station Hospital preferred warm water. "They are accustomed to drinking it hot, and most of them have no intention of changing."

American nurses and other military personnel soon found that water, a precious commodity in India, was strictly rationed. Lieutenant Bradley recalls, "Running water was available, both hot and cold. We were allowed one bucket a day . . . and some extra for drinking and washing purposes." The supply of servants in India, however, was plentiful, and this gave the nurses, who worked seven days a week, eight to twelve hours a day, the luxury of having native "bearers" to clean their rooms.[3]

According to 2d Lt. Lucy M. Wainwright, who also served with the unit, the 159th (later redesignated the 181st General) was a 1,000-bed hospital and was allocated ninety nurses and forty-six medical officers, "but a need for medical officers all over India arose and they just took small groups of four nurses or six nurses, medical personnel, and enlisted men and sent them all over India. Until this year [1943], when the groups came to take their place, there was a time we had only fourteen officers in the whole hospital." The 159th soon became known as the "mother of all American hospitals in India."[4]

As early arrivals, the nurses of the 159th suffered from a certain lack of provisions and an unappetizing diet of British rations, as well as from frequent dust storms and intense heat. 2d Lt. Dorothy Sykes told an interviewer in October 1943, "Karachi is supposed to have the best climate in India. In June and July it hit 120 and 130 degrees. It was very dry. At sundown it is usually cool."

The nurses' meals were based on B rations, but Sykes related, "as officers we were able to go out and buy vegetables and fruits. We could eat anything that you could boil or peel. We had some fresh beef, very little pork, and chicken now and then. The B ration was mostly canned, dehydrated potatoes, Spam, Vienna sausage, and chili." Lieutenant Sykes agreed that the B ration was satisfactory from a nutritional standpoint, but she told the interviewer that some of the girls wouldn't eat the chili and some did lose weight during their time in India. [5]

The 159th's nurses learned to make the best of the army diet and tried to adapt to the oppressive climate and the living conditions in India which were considered so unsuitable for the employment of other American servicewomen that Women's Army Corps troops were not assigned to the CBI until July 1944. [6] There was little the nurses could do about the heat, so they concentrated upon improving their wardrobes and surroundings. They purchased native furniture and colorful material with which to decorate their quarters, and they found local seamstresses to make them two-piece khaki uniforms. In the heat, frequent uniform changes were the rule of the day, so the nurses found "dhobies" or servants to solve their laundry problems, but, as Dorothy Sykes reported, "frequently the clothes would come back unclean." Little, however, could be done about replacing American-made shoes when the old ones wore out. Until more nurses were sent to the theater and adequate supplies could reach far away India, the nurses had to put up with squeaky, ill-fitting native shoes.

Despite the inconveniences of service half a world from home, nurses at the 159th Station Hospital found time to visit some unusual places, for example, a crocodile farm and a leper colony. They also spent off-duty hours taking camel rides, sailing in native Bunder boats, swimming, and going to movies or picnics. [7] At first the hospital had no recreation facilities, but after awhile, Lucy Wainwright explained to an interviewer in October 1943, "We had movies three times a week and now this new group of Red Cross workers that came out in January and February. We have one very good social worker . . . she and two other workers have turned a ward into a recreation room. They have two ping pong tables and a horse shoe set, and some games." [8]

In the spring of 1943, the original contingent of Army nurses in India was joined by nurses assigned to new units, such as the Twentieth General. Under the command of Maj. Mary E. Cornelius, the Twentieth General's nurses arrived in Bombay on March 3, 1943, after a forty-five day voyage from the States. They stayed temporarily at Poona and then began their journey across India. The slow trip on a crowded train was an eye opener to these young American women. The unit's war diary reported on the trip: "The poverty, disease, and filth of the people of India was apparent at all the rail stations. The people seemed always to be traveling and they apparently had no difficulty in carrying with them all their worldly goods. The people as well as their cattle looked small and undernourished. The cockroaches, on the other hand, are of mammoth proportions."

At each rail station, English women turned out to see the American nurses and to give them tea and "V" cigarettes. "After trying to smoke these cigarettes we were not surprised to find that the poorest Indian beggar refused them,"

Mary Cornelius remembers. At Dhubai, the group left the train and went by hospital boat up the Brahmaputra River, eating cold field rations for dinner and sleeping on the open deck at night. The boat stopped at Pandu on March 29, and the women were taken by truck to the American Baptist Mission at Gaubauti. From there they went in small groups to their hospital at Margherita in Assam province, a mountainous jungle region in easternmost India.

The first nurses to arrive at the hospital found conditions primitive: "They were housed in bashas of bamboo construction eighty by twenty feet with bore hole latrines in the rear. The roofs were made of native palm leaves and leaked badly. Ants were everywhere. Under the beds were mounds of white earth carried up by these industrious insects. No screening was available. Birds flew with freedom through the windows and hopped along the floor to gather insects."[9]

At Margherita the nurses slept under mosquito netting as a protection not only against malaria-carrying mosquitoes but against mice, rats, flying roaches, and snakes. In rainy weather, the local water buffaloes occasionally wandered into the nurses' bashas to "dry out." When the animals came in both the front and back doors, nurses inside had to hop on a bed and climb out the windows to safety! Lt. Alma Garside, ANC, who came to the Twentieth General in the early group, remembers particularly the Brahma bull that came stamping down to her basha. A friend called out, "Alma, company's coming!"

Until semipermanent buildings could be built, the nurses lived thirty-three women to a basha. There was only one shower room—the former morgue—and no shower heads on the faucets, so the nurses improvised with shower heads made from tin cans with holes punched in the bottom.

The Twentieth General's nurses arrived in Assam during the rainy season, or monsoons, which begin around April, replacing the cooler, drier weather of winter. The newly arrived nurses were prepared for neither the heavy rain nor the deep mud. Alma Garside says this was because they were assigned to a general hospital, not a field hospital. Therefore they were sent to India with only white shoes and uniforms. "We borrowed shirts, slacks, and shoes from our male officers until appropriate uniforms would arrive," she recalls.[10]

In desperation, some of the nurses bought high rubber boots at native bazaars for "fabulous prices" and others purchased soldiers' raincoats, field shoes, heavy socks, and field jackets from the quartermaster. The attire may not have been very feminine but it was entirely practical, considering the necessity of trudging through deep mud to the wards and mess hall and of standing outside in the mess line in the rain. Eventually the mess acquired the luxury of tables and chairs and the menu of field rations was varied by including fresh meat and vegetables from the nurses' gardens.

The Twentieth General was located near the town of Ledo, where the famous backcountry road to China began. Proposed by the Chinese in January

1942 as an alternative route to the Burma Road now in enemy hands, the "Stilwell road" was to run from Ledo in Assam province. Northern Burma was not in Japanese hands in early 1942, but the threat of enemy attack was always present and the terrain itself was an enormous obstacle. In December 1942, the U.S. Army took over responsibility for finishing the Ledo Road from the British; eventually about 50,000 American troops were employed building the road.[11]

When the monsoons came, trucks bogged down in the mud, bulldozers rolled over banks, and even elephants had difficulty bringing in food and supplies. The rainy weather soaked everybody and everything, causing the disease rate to soar. Poor food and chronic malaria also weakened the soldiers' resistance, and many Allied troops fell ill with diseases like scrub typhus, which caused high fevers, internal hemorrhages, skin lesions, and even death. The only real cure for scrub typhus was the excellent nursing care that the nurses and staff of the evacuation and three general hospitals in the Ledo area gave to sick G.I.s. The first hospital in the Ledo area was built by an American army engineering unit and an aviation battalion of African-American troops, aided by British and civilian laborers, on thirty acres of land between Ledo and Margherita. In mid-January 1943, personnel of the Ninety-eighth Station Hospital arrived with their equipment, but without their nurse complement. They were the first units to operate in the Ledo area, although other hospitals had been active elsewhere in Assam. Four nurses and four enlisted men from the 159th had come out to Chabua in Assam at the terminus of the air ferry route over the "Hump" in July 1942. They were joined in September by nurses and medical personnel of the Ninety-fifth S.H., which quickly set up in order to care for fifty malaria patients already admitted.

As summer came in 1943 and the ground dried out, conditions at Army hospitals in Assam improved. At the Twentieth General, supplies caught up with the hospital and more adequate housing was built. Summer also brought improvements to army life in the Ledo area. United States Organizations (USO) shows began to arrive in Assam, and Alma Garside recalls that the hospital personnel organized an officers' club and were able to purchase rations of beer and whiskey. She writes, "After the 1st year, Army personnel with native help built us better living quarters—double rooms with electric lights and shower houses." She adds that the nurses then went to the native bazaar a mile away and bought furniture to decorate their new abodes.

In India, hospital personnel quickly learned to improvise medical procedures. For example, in an effort to obtain blood for their Chinese patients, some of the Twentieth General's personnel organized a Chinese blood donor unit that went out twice a week to Chinese troops bivouacked nearby to acquire the whole blood needed for Chinese patients. The blood donor sets—tourniquets, solutions, bandages, procaine—were packed in boxes and loaded in a weapons carrier with the donor team. "Leaving at 6:30 A.M., we traveled along the rough and muddy Stilwell Road. . . . Many times we watched the sun come up over the mountains with only the song of the birds to break the stillness," recalls nurse Mary Cornelius.

At the Chinese camp in the jungle, the team would set up in the open or in tents and begin processing donors, taking temperatures to rule out malaria and taking blood specimens for typing. "Lunch was a welcome break," recalls Cornelius. "We took rations with us and ate under the trees, usually with a group of monkeys as an interested audience."[12]

By evening, the donor team would have collected 300 cc's of blood from some seventy to eighty donors and was ready to head back to the hospital. The importance of having whole blood and blood plasma available for Chinese patients cannot be overemphasized. A doctor in a portable surgical unit operating on Chinese casualties in China later in the war reported that many of his more seriously wounded cases died, not from poor surgical care, but the lack of Chinese plasma or whole blood for transfusions.[13]

Caring for combat casualties became one of the main tasks of American hospitals in the Ledo area in late 1943. The Ledo Road had reached Shingbwiyang across the border of Burma in the Hukawng valley by December 1943. General Stilwell insisted that the wounded be evacuated as quickly as possible to field hospitals and that the more seriously injured or ill be flown to the Twentieth General at Ledo. In fact, it was pressure from Stilwell that led to an airfield being built in the spring of 1944 near the Ledo hospital.

One of the units brought to the new airstrip was the Fourteenth Evacuation Hospital, which sent half of its staff there in May 1944, primarily to care for "Merrill's Marauders," who were trained as a combat unit in India and marched into Burma from Ledo. "Vinegar Joe" Stilwell sent Merrill's Marauders and a regiment of the Chinese Thirty-eighth Division to attack the Japanese near Kamaing. The men marched north, survived enemy counterattacks, clawed their way over the mountains, and, on May 17, seized Mitkima airfield. Their brief victory, however, was soon overshadowed by Japanese reinforcements and by heavy rains. Although many of the Americans had not eaten in days and suffered from Nagu sores and dysentery, they were ordered to stay and hold the airfield. Gradually the sick, who were defined as "anyone with a temperature of 103 for 3 or more days," were flown out by a Medical Air Evacuation Squadron to hospitals at Assam.[14] As the Fourteenth Evac history reported: "Many of them were seriously ill and they were so tired, dirty, and hungry that they looked more dead than alive. They suffered from exhaustion, malnutrition, typhus, malaria, amebic dysentery, jungle sores, and many other diseases resulting from months of hardship in the tropical jungle."[15]

While one-half of the Fourteenth Evac's nurses and other personnel was working eighteen hours a day to take care of these wounded Americans, the other half at the parent hospital was trying to cope with seriously ill or wounded Chinese troops fresh from the fighting in Burma, a total of 2,800 men between the two hospitals. According to Agnes Gress, "Each nurse, with the aid of one or two corpsmen, had approximately 120 to 130 patients under her supervision; in the afternoon she had many more. It was monsoon season and the continual rains, oppressive heat, and heavy mud were exhausting. Sometimes the wards were inches deep in water." The women worked hard and were too busy for the traditional midday siesta usually taken in tropical climates.

Gress remembers too that at that time, in early 1944, "wards were filled with malaria, typhus, dengue fever, amebic dysentery, and other unclassified cases. In the contagious wards were TB, venereal disease, small pox, meningitis, and mumps. Isolation technique was almost impossible to maintain." Despite the watchfulness of the nurses, Chinese patients continued to mingle and eat together, interchanging food and dishes. Strangely enough, there were no cross infections.[16]

Dealing with Chinese patients proved exhausting and frustrating for the American nurses: the Chinese did not speak English and had no knowledge of hospital routine or personal sanitation. Capt. Mary Ellen Yeager, ANC, in her nursing report at the Fourteenth Evacuation Hospital, recalled: "They cooked in cans over an open fire all day and half the night. It was not an unusual sight to see the patients rolling noodles; a chicken or duck tied to a 'chong' (bed), or a dead fish or a pile of meat hanging from their mosquito bar wires."[17]

It was also not uncommon for a nurse making her rounds at midnight to discover some of her patients had gone AWOL or had a friend sleeping on his "chong" with him. Chinese patients slept on "chongs," which were beds built for two persons with a partition down the middle. To protect patients from the rain, the staff of the hospital had hung gray blankets over each bed, but one nurse recalled she often hit her head on these protective canopies when they were filled with water. The result was a sudden shower for both her and her patient.

As the nurses learned a little Chinese and grew accustomed to their patients' odd customs they began to enjoy their nursing duties with the Chinese, who were usually very cheerful and many times "clever and quick to learn." Although Army hospitals had little material for occupational therapy, the male Chinese patients "kept themselves busy" and were "skilled in the art of handicraft, sewing, weaving, and knitting."

The staff of the Fourteenth Evac also had to make its own fun, for the hospital was hundreds of miles from the nearest city. As did many of their compatriots in other field hospitals in remote areas, the nurses attended dances, movies, and planned shows and special events. They also planted vegetable gardens, where they raised lettuce, radishes, onions, celery, and tomatoes to add some zest to their monotonous C ration diet of soybean sausages, beef and vegetable stew, and canned hash or beans. The Fourteenth's report also adds, "15 May 1945 was a red letter day, for we were issued our one and only bottle of Coca Cola." Morale remained high, however, at the Fourteenth Evac, although "at times we were home-sick and discouraged." The health of the nurses, even in India's climate, was good; only seven nurses from the Fourteenth were sent home to the United States for health reasons.[18] This low rate of illness was remarkable considering that the climate of India was not conducive to good health and that many American nurses serving there during World War II suffered at one time or another from skin diseases, dengue fever, bacillary dysentery, colds, and even malaria.

Curiously, although India is known for its oppressively hot weather and months of monsoon, the nurses and medical personnel of the Fourteenth Evacuation Hospital also remembered India for its cold weather. "The winter of 1943 was very cold, a damp, chilly coldness that left one almost paralyzed," says Agnes Gress. Sibley stoves were finally issued to each ward, but the small amount of heat they put out disappeared through the thin bamboo walls. The unit had no coal and no saws to cut wood for fires, so the nurses, doctors, and corpsmen bundled up in layers of clothes. According to Gress, "Only the night nurses and the wardmen knew the agony of staying up all night without heat. Often their hands were so cold they couldn't do the necessary charting."

Overall figures on the health of nurses in the CBI during World War II are not available, but as an example one unit in the Ledo area had a sick rate of 767 per 1,000 in its first year in India. The second year the rate rose to 812, but fell their third and final year to 767. The illnesses included a lot of malaria, colds, and dysentery. The pregnancy rate for nurses was 2.9 percent for the CBI or 36 cases out of 12,273 women in the theater.[19]

Because the sick rate, climate, and isolation had an adverse effect on nurses serving in the CBI, in the summer of 1944 the theater began a policy of rotation to replace nurses who had served two years with the 159th or other units in isolated Assam province. Nurses were sent from other areas or from the United States to replace the CBI veterans who went home. The policy was long overdue. Eleanor Bradley, who was overseas thirty-four months serving at the 181st, told an interviewer in 1944, "We were not working as hard as the nurses in the European theater. I feel that the nurses in the jungle should have been relieved sooner." She felt the authorities did not care about the nurses, for although they had come to India "for the duration," a period was announced when they could go home, "but this never happened." "Rotation has been a sore spot with us," Bradley conceded. 2d Lt. Adele Petraitis, ANC, agreed: "After a person has been at a station like this for a long time, one becomes irritable and consequently morale goes down." She felt even a change of station within a theater would have been good for morale.[20]

One of the replacement nurses sent to the CBI was Sylvia Lasser, who joined the Army Nurse Corps in January 1944. She remembers that during the flight overseas there were eighteen nurses and eighteen enlisted men on her flight and that they shared earphones to the radio. She was listening to a musical program when the aircraft's captain came on and ordered the nurses to give their earphones to the men. The soldiers explained that they wanted to listen to a baseball game, which "wouldn't interest the girls." Lasser said the women obeyed as most of the soldiers were youngsters—18 or 19 years old.

After the plane had circled the Azores and made an emergency landing with ambulances waiting, the nurses learned that the "game" on the earphones was an alert of a failing engine and an impending crash landing! The plane landed without incident, however, refueled, and flew on to Casablanca. Here the nurses waited for further transportation to their destination—India.[21]

Lasser served in a field hospital twenty miles from Calcutta, and later on, her tour continued at a station hospital 100 miles from the city. She says that the nurses' bashas had no indoor plumbing—"Honey buckets were emptied by bearers daily." Bearers also kept their quarters clean, but were assisted by "ayahs and sweepers. Each had specific duties. The ayahs, or maids, were usually very friendly, although communication was mostly through sign language. We had clean linen and our uniforms were well laundered and starched." This was a far cry from the bucket laundry system used by most nurses in the Pacific theater, but, on the negative side, the detergent used to launder their uniforms gave many of the nurses heat rash.[22]

In India the heat was a major problem for the women, but according to Sylvia Lasser, "the Chief Nurse adjusted working hours for our comfort." Mary Barbero, who came to the CBI in 1945, adds, "The most difficult part for me was the climate. We had to have a break in our ward hours because of the intense heat. We were issued fans but only the O.R.s had air conditioning."

Fortunately, by the time Sylvia Lasser arrived, Army policy in regard to leaves was a generous one in the CBI, which did much to improve morale. She spent five days in Darjeeling at a rest camp. "Seeing Mt. Kinchinjunga at sunrise" was a truly memorable experience. Darjeeling, in the north central part of India, had been a retreat from the heat and rain of Calcutta for British officials and their families for years. Nadine Lane also went to Darjeeling: "We stayed at Hotel Mt. Everest. Each day we played tennis, went horseback riding, had tea and scones at a British country club, cocktails and dancing at our hotel with American and Canadian flyers."[23]

Travel and sightseeing were easier for nurses on duty in the CBI than for those on the more isolated island bases of the Pacific theater. Mary Barbero points out that "There were always trips to be taken to other areas—plenty of recreation, even golf courses in the tropic areas-swimming pools, hunting in Burma—movies,—shows. The British were friendly and invited us to their club dances—all posts had clubs." Lasser adds, "On Friday evenings the British R.R. officers invited us to their dances—formal—evening gowns, etc. We wore sleeveless, backless gowns despite malaria precautions. One nurse said, 'Oh, the mosquitoes don't bite on Friday night.'"[24]

A golf course provided Barbero with one of her most memorable experiences during the war. While stationed at the 178th Station Hospital, she often went to play golf. She recalls, "A nine-hole golf course was made by the hospital personnel and when I went to tee off one morning there was a cobra curled up on the first tee!"

Officers in India managed to "requisition" jeeps and write phony orders to acquire gasoline to take the nurses on dates. Other outings were all-male affairs, like one Sylvia Lasser describes: "One day (our) male officers took off for a tiger hunt with rifles, etc. as they learned local natives complained tigers were slaughtering and ingesting their chickens. End of day—men returned—saw not one tiger. Good reason to get away from the post."[25]

Because leave policies in the CBI were generous, some of the nurses in Burma were able to visit their husbands or boyfriends by bending the rules. One nurse recalled they would go to the airport, get orders for some fake mission, forge an officer's name, and get passage on an aircraft for Burma. Tragically, in March 1945 this "frequent and well known," but unauthorized, practice of flying to visit beaus, or in some cases to attend dances, resulted in the single most devastating loss of Army Nurse Corps nurses during World War II. On March 4, a plane carrying sixteen Army nurses, a Red Cross woman, and ten air officers crashed at Ledo, killing everyone on board. The nurses, who came from the 172nd, 69th, and 18th general hospitals, were buried in the American cemetery, and memorial services were held at each unit.[26]

Initially American medical support in Burma was provided in forward areas by the Seagrave Unit at their hospital at Momau east of Bhamo. The 803d MAES, however, made numerous evacuation flights out of Burma, especially from the recently captured airfield at Myitkyina. Flying into the field could be a harrowing experience, as one MAES crew discovered on May 18. Responding to a call for an evacuation plane, it landed at Myitkyina and was parked on the field when a Japanese aircraft dove on the field with guns blazing. Lieutenant Rogers, who was loading patients at the doorway, was injured, but one of the crew pulled 2d Lt. Esther M. Bauer, ANC, to safety. The crew quickly bandaged their wounded, loaded patients, and took them to Shingbwiyang and Ledo before returning to the base at Chabua, where the injured crewmen were taken by ambulance to the Eleventh Station Hospital.[27]

Army ground nurses did not come to Burma until the Forty-eighth Evacuation Hospital came to the Myitkyina area in September 1944. They set up in a grove of tall trees along the banks of the Irawaddy River and opened for business in October. With its heavy work load, the Forty-eighth needed all of its sixty authorized nurses and welcomed the addition of nurses from the Twenty-fifth Field Hospital and Eighteenth General. Nine hundred of the hospital's 1,000 beds were occupied by December. Half of their patients were Chinese and many suffered from battle wounds and/or malaria. The Forty-eighth also admitted patients injured in plane crashes and suffering from scrub typhus. In fact, the incidence of typhus became so acute in late 1944 and early 1945 that the U.S. Typhus Commission came to Myitkyina in October to study the disease. The Forty-eighth's Captain Walters called the men with scrub typhus "the most acutely ill patients we have ever nursed. . . . everything possible was done to combat this disease, but in the end it was agreed that good nursing care was the only answer." At one time the Forty-eighth was caring for sixty Americans suffering from the disease.[28]

The Eighteenth General and the Second and Forty-fourth Field Hospitals joined the Forty-eighth Evac in Burma, and in December 1944 the 335th Station Hospital arrived. The latter was a 100-bed unit staffed by African-American medical personnel, including sixteen physicians and sixteen nurses under Chief Nurse Lt. (later Capt.) Agnes Glass. Three of the nurses, including Lt. Daryle E. Foster, had already served in Liberia with the Second Station Hospital. The 335th's enlisted men came to India by ship, but the others flew from New York's LaGuardia Airport to Karachi via Newfoundland, Casablanca, and Egypt. Lt. Nadine Davis Lane, who had joined the Army Nurse Corps in 1942 and spent two years at Fort Huachuca, was among the nurses making the trip. After a four-day layover in Karachi because of inclement weather, they flew to Assam province. For four weeks, the nurses were assigned to the Forty-eighth Evac. "We nursed Chinese troops who were fighting in Burma. Their soldiers had wounds from artillery, tank, land mines, hand-to-hand combat wounds, animal attacks, snake bites, accidents and malaria, combat fatigue, you name it," Lane remembers. They lived in British tents with dirt floors. One nurse remembers the problems this entailed: "Frogs and lizards ran or hopped around the tent floors. My greatest fear was of course snakes. . . . We were to upturn and examine or shake any clothing or supply we left lying about before using it. When my boots were off, before I put them on I threw them across the room. Just in case some creature decided to use them. I wanted whatever was inside to come out a distance from me."[29]

After six weeks the nurses joined their unit in Burma in December 1944. Lane writes, "Our hospital, the 335th, was located at mile 80 along the Ledo road. The site had been General Stilwell's headquarters. We were surrounded by jungle, and the hospital was in a clearing in the jungle. We would say the only thing to do was to 'go up it, down it, or over it.'" She recalls that the nurses lived two to a room, divided by a bamboo wall from two other nurses sharing the other room. "Windows were bamboo that could be opened and propped. Floors were braided bamboo." The hospital was housed in similar structures, except for the surgical building, which had a concrete floor, and all buildings had electric power from generators. Although supplies at the 335th were adequate, the nurses' diet was monotonous. They were able to supplement it with wild turkeys or fish purchased from the native Burmese, who caught the large salmon-like fish by dynamiting the local streams.

The nurses at the 335th worked six hours a day or twenty-four hours if the road to their mountainside quarters washed out. Although they had frequented a Chinese cafe nightly while at Ledo, in Burma the nurses had no club or canteen, but Lane says, "many of us read extensively, played games at a small building we designated as a club." They also became acquainted with some other American officers at a post twenty-five miles away and some Indian officers in an engineering unit who visited from time to time. "We had a five-piece 'musical combo' that rigged up a dance session for us, so we could loosen up a bit." For entertainment, the personnel of the 335th had movies shown in an open-air ampitheater. "The 'mahuts' who worked the the elephants for heavy construction on the Ledo road came to the movie on their elephants," recalls Lane.[30]

Among the other hospitals serving in Burma was the Forty-fourth Field Hospital, which had the distinction of employing a graduate of the Seagrave School who served as a nurse/interpreter on the ward for Kachins. She shared her earlier experiences of the war with the American nurses, including the story of how she and her husband were driven from their home by the Japanese, who "looted her home of all luxuries and even necessities." Her husband had later died of pneumonia.[31]

At the beginning of the war, official U.S. Army policy ruled that Army nurses would not be assigned to hospitals directly supporting combat troops in Burma or China, nor would they be assigned to Chinese hospitals. This policy reflected the Army's fear that the safety and health of American women could not be guaranteed in frontline hospitals that were often in Japanese-held territory. It also reflected General Stilwell's attitude about American women, who "would need special types of housing and require allocations of Hump tonnage to certain modest luxuries such as cosmetics which would be better devoted to the stuff of war." Some theater officials felt that the most compelling reason for the ban on American nurses in China was Stilwell's well-known preference for English-speaking Chinese nurses. Despite this policy, he did agree to allow flight nurses to go to China. Six Army flight nurses from the 803d MAES were escorted to Ku'ming by the squadron commander on December 2, 1943, where they were greeted by newsreel cameramen anxious to record the arrival of the "first American nurses" in China. The nurses went to various airfields for flight evacuation duties.

These airfields were near the front, and nurses serving there were "in harm's way." Lt. Ruth M. "Chris" Smith, ANC, a flight nurse serving in China, recalled her first air raid. Awakened by a Chinese hotel attendant when the raid began, the nurses jumped out of bed and assisted two patients to safety. "It was the first time I ever saw a bomb explode at night," Smith writes. "There was a great splash of fire which showered the area with flaming incendiary particles." A plane strafed the runway and flares lit up the field, but fortunately, she recalls, no large bombers came over. In addition to air raids, flying on medical evacuation flights out of China could be dangerous duty, as one incident clearly illustrates.

2d Lt. Jeanette C. "Tex" Gleason, ANC, earned the dubious distinction of being the first flight nurse to bail out of an airplane in China. Her parachute opened and she landed about fifty miles from Kweilin, sustaining only minor bruises. She spent four days in the mountains before friendly locals rescued her and took her to a village.[32]

Another six flight nurses were assigned to China in July 1944, preceeded in February by the first American nurse contingent, who were allowed to serve at the Ninety-fifth Station Hospital in Ku'ming, China. Eight more nurses arrived with Lieutenant Chevalier at Ku'ming in March and were joined on May 18 by eighteen more nurses from the Twenty-first Field Hospital. By the end of 1944, the Ninety-fifth Station Hospital, with a 750-bed capacity, was fully set up and had a total of twenty-two assigned nurses and another four attached to it.[33]

The arrival of Army nurses assigned to regular army hospitals in China followed two years of controversy. Colonel Tamraz attempted in mid-1942 to have army nurses assigned to medical units in China, but his attempts failed. When the Ninety-fifth Station Hospital took over the facility at Ku'ming in late October 1943, it inherited fifteen Chinese nurses serving at the hospital caring for American patients. Although Army officials felt a need for English-speaking nurses for ward duty at the Ninety-fifth, they were reluctant to request Army nurses. Their stated reason was the lack of quarters for women.

When a need for English-speaking nurses arose at Chengtu, a short distance from Chungking, Colonel Williams was able to wring permission from Stilwell to allow the Chinese nurses to volunteer to be transferred to Chengtu or Kweillin so that Army nurses from the Twenty-first and Twenty-second Field Hospitals could be sent to China to serve at the Ninety-fifth. Three Chinese nurses did volunteer to serve at the Fourteenth Air Force Dispensary at Chengtu and left for that location in mid-May, but when Stilwell learned that Army nurses were being sent inland from Ku'ming he ordered the women be stopped at Chabua and sent back. Stilwell was adamant, and only reluctantly allowed flight nurses to remain on duty at Chengtu and Kweilin when he was assured "their presence at these places was essential for the proper operation of that unit." This incident chastened the staff and prompted Colonel Armstrong to warn Colonel Gentry about allowing Army nurses to serve in other locations in China. "The Boss will have all our scalps," he told Gentry.

Colonel Armstrong labeled the issue of Army nurses in China "the biggest headache we have had . . . since I arrived." As the road to China opened, both he and Stanton urged the transfer of more nurses to China to help care for an increasing patient load, but authorization was dependent upon "Vinegar Joe" Stilwell's response, and few officials were anxious to arouse the peppery general's wrath. The Army's slowness to bring nurses to China was also influenced by the small number of American troops (3,000) serving there in 1944 and by the fact that in the spring of 1944 when Captain Avery visited the hospital Ku'ming she was impressed by the "excellent work" being done there by Chinese nurses. As a result in her report Avery recommended that no Army nurses be sent to China "at the present time."[34]

The only reported shortage of nurses in the theater occurred at the medical facilities at Chengtu serving XX Bomber Command and the Fourteenth Air Force. Patients were treated at a host hospital, where the Chinese nurses were being paid one-quarter of the salary given to Army nurses. Army officials feared the assignment of Army nurses would provoke dissension over the disparity in pay, so in desperation, they grounded three flight nurses for hospital duty at Chengtu. When General Stilwell discovered this attempt to go over his head, he ordered flight nurses to Chengtu only on a temporary basis "and only in connection with their air evacuation duties." Eventually the Army negotiated with the West Union University Hospital there to allow its Chinese nurses to be compensated according to the U.S. pay scale.

Finally, in mid-November 1944, permission was received to send Army nurses to China, but ironically it was now the India-Burma Theater's intransigence that kept nurses from serving beyond Ku'ming for at least another two months. The theater was reluctant to allow nurses to leave for fear they could not get replacements from the States. In May 1945, when replacements began arriving in India and hospitals there began closing, the theater finally agreed to release Army nurses for duty in China, evoking a joyous response from the surgeon general, who said, "After a long dry spell we are now getting as many nurses as we need."

Army nurses did arrive at the main hospital serving the Chinese terminus of the Burma Road at Paoshan in February 1944. Here the nurses lived in tents featuring electric lights, matted floors and walls, and comfortable furnishings. They were heated by charcoal braziers and, in the words of Capt. Tyne M. Tamminen, quarters at Paoshan were "far more comfortable and satisfactory than any [they'd] had in larger cities."[35]

Mary Barbero recalls that the nurses in her unit lived in army barracks. In China, she observed, "the cities were bombed out so in some areas people lived in caves. People seemed to have plenty of food, farmers had good crops—people were not discouraged or down-trodden as in India."[36]

Indeed, at Chengtu, U.S. Army nurses and personnel enjoyed the use of the university hospital's operating rooms, X-ray, and clinical lab facilities. Verna Carruth, a nurse with the Ninety-fifth Station Hospital, recalls: "In Chengtu nurses and doctors lived in two professors' homes near the University of China. We had a maid, a cook, and a 'coolie,' Willie, who drew water from a barrel to carry to both tubs for our baths." She also remembers canned food could not be flown over the Hump. Fresh food was available in Chengtu, but adds, "The fresh vegetables and fruits in China always had to be boiled thoroughly. The ground was considered contaminated. In China we were fed fresh eggs three times a day." Carruth says, "Chengtu is where I first gave penicillin,

30,000 units three times a day. Mainly to seriously ill and patients on 'romance wards' (venereal disease)."[37]

Nurses of the Ninety-fifth were quartered in a house on the beautiful university campus and in good weather were even able to dine on the lawn surrounded by colorful flower beds. These amenities were a far cry from earlier conditions at the Ku'ming location when sixty-nine women including the Ninety-fifth's nurses were crowded into one building and two tents. They had shared the bathroom facilities—two toilets and two showers—and were rationed one five-gallon drum of hot water per day. Their chief nurse, Captain Chevalier, had no office except her quarters and the night nurses had no separate sleeping accommodations. By May 1945, the Ninety-fifth had grown from its original twenty beds to the authorized 750 beds and was caring for a census of mostly American patients with a smattering of Russian, British, and French patients and a few Japanese prisoners. The hospital also admitted civilian patients when beds were available. In 1944 the Ninety-fifth treated a total of 7,250 patients.[38]

Some patients were evacuated out to India by the Air Transport Command, which began operations in China in early 1944. As the Japanese advanced in southern and eastern China in late 1944, Army hospitals, especially forward-area dispensaries, began to receive more combat casualties. These often needed air evacuation, and most of the 1,550 patients flown out of the China theater were evacuated in the last year of the war. The increased level of air evacuations provided flight nurses in China with more work, but compared to other theaters their hours of flight time were minimal. 821st MAES nurses flew about ten to twenty hours a month in 1945, but Maj. Margaret D. Craighill reported their work was limited "because there is very little evacuation of battle casualties or seriously ill patients." The women of the 803d MAES accrued even less flight time, although 2d Lt. Miranda Rast made a few trips to Chabua and one flight to Calcutta from Ku'ming. One of the nurses in the unit had only sixteen hours of flight time on her China tour and another just twelve hours, but according to the official history all of the women did excellent nursing on the ground. One of the 821st's nurses, Lt. Anne M. Baroniak, received the Distinguished Flying Cross for her 300 hours of evacuation time, and all the other nurses were awarded the Air Medal.

Wherever Army nurses served in the CBI, nursing could be a challenge. The official report of nursing in the theater noted "that nurses had to be on the run, especially in the heat, fetching ice packs, sponging, changing linen." Fever cases needed much attention, especially when chills were present. Nurses had to assume a lot of responsibility in diagnosis and in getting I.V.s going, as there were not enough doctors to supervise every case at every stage. The number of patients also made it necessary to train corpsmen to do many nursing tasks "like bedside care, giving drugs, doing I.V.s, and blood transfusions we nurses had taken three years to learn to do."[39]

Mary Barbero adds that although "they often had to improvise furniture, etc. they always had the necessary medical supplies and equipment," and she feels that "considering the number of patients and the type of wounds, nursing care and surgical care during the war was excellent. Everything done for a civilian patient was done for the patients in an army hospital whether in the U.S. or abroad." Nadine Lane of the 335th in Burma adds, "We wasted nothing. We improvised containers for our surgical supplies by using metal cans that butter came in. . . . Our greatest challenge was to keep supplies dry and prevent mildew; it was so humid all the time." Barbero concludes, "Conditions may have been less modern in the tropics, but it served the same purpose and obtained the same results as in state-side hospitals."

The U.S. Army established hospitals during World War II in Karachi, Bombay, Calcutta, and New Delhi, with more at Ramgarh Training Center, Kurmitola, Chakulia, Panagrh, Piaoba, and Kalaikunda, as well as the replacement depots at Angus Mills and Kanchrapara. Air Transport Command also had hospitals, including three evacuation hospitals and three general hospitals, in the Ledo area. Most of the hospitals in India handled primarily disease, accident, and dental cases, but many evacuation and some general hospitals received battle casualties from the fighting in Burma.[40]

Nurses in rear areas in India were usually near airfields and saw emergency cases, especially burned soldiers or those injured in aircraft accidents. Most novel to the U.S. Army nurses were the number of cases of tropical diseases treated in India. This not only gave American nurses an opportunity to learn tropical nursing skills, but gave them a renewed sense of purpose, for proper nursing care was the best cure for many of these diseases.

At the 159th Station Hospital, later the 181st General, the leading diseases were gastroenteritis, dysentery, and fever. 2d Lt. Lucy Wainwright, in an interview, explained, "We had some fly fever, pappataci and dengue fever." Malaria was also a serious problem in India. She said, "We had it all year round. It was supposed to be only in the wet season but when the cold season came around we were not supposed to have malaria but we always had cases."

Lieutenant Wainwright, who had developed a specialty in neuropsychiatry before she went into the army, reported that they had a high rate of neuropysch cases at the 159th, "about 20% of the whole hospital." Many soldiers, she said, arrived in India with psychological problems, but others suffered from domestic troubles at home or had difficulty getting along with their officers. Especially the parachutists. "We had more of them sick than any other group." At first 50 percent returned to duty, but as time went on the rate was more like 15 to 20 percent. "People don't want to get well because they don't like India. A lot of them have been out long, and have lost considerable weight, and they are what we call neurasthenic. We send them back and they will be back in twenty-four hours." Lt. Eleanor Bradley, also at the 181st General, told an interviewer about the neuropsych cases: "My personal opinion is that these patients had made their minds up to be pyschotic. They were afraid of going into the line and being killed. Some broke down as soon as they came to India."[41]

As in other theaters, one of the most prevalent illnesses for American soldiers was venereal disease. "The venereal disease rate was quite high, but I believe it dropped considerably in the last few months," Dorothy Sykes told her interviewer. "When we went there it was 900 per thousand, but it dropped down the month before we left to 104." Lucy Wainwright added that the engineers and ordnance groups and "colored troops" that came out in July 1942 had such a high venereal disease rate that the hospital had to set up a tent colony of 160 beds just for these patients. She explained that the Army put some areas in Karachi off limits, "but the troops still went there." She also said that if a soldier went to the hospital with venereal disease he was not considered on duty so "they treated themselves and sometimes didn't keep up the treatment."[42]

Lieutenant Sykes said the drop in the VD rate was due to the program the Army established which consisted of regular lectures and posters and "pro stations." "The local prophylactic program compelled every soldier to take a pro-phylactic." She said they were not permitted to pass the gate without taking one and were required before going into town to take two sulfathiazole tablets before leaving the base and two within eight hours of their return. She credits the vene-real disease officer with the success of the program and said he "used to go around and visit the various companies and had meetings with the boys." He also had to examine the prostitutes for infection, for the Army decided that with so many areas for the soldiers to go to it was more efficient to allow the women to come near the base where they could be examined.[43]

Although the Army was slow in appointing a theater director of nursing for the CBI, one was finally chosen in November 1944. Her duties were to visit all the bases and hospitals where Army nurses were serving, to supervise the hous-ing, food, rest, leave recreation, and training of theater nurses, and to meet new arrivals to make certain they were given proper orientation. Nurses' morale in the CBI was generally good, but the new director soon discovered that the theater was not without its problems. High on the list of complaints was the lack of proper uniforms and the absence of a rotation policy. Nadine Lane recalls, "There were some lonesome feelings for people who had missed their families." She said four of the nurses in her unit returned to the States, one who married an officer, another who was pregnant and wanted to go home to be with her husband, and two who became very debilitated from bouts with malaria. "The rest of us rolled with the punches," she asserts. "People can become very close to each other in confined areas. When someone received a package from home we officers shared the contents regardless of how small, i.e., sharing a small mustard to perk up the taste of 'bully beef.'"[44]

Some nurses also complained about having to nurse Chinese patients.

Perhaps the most troublesome problem, however, was promotion. Happily, in December 1944, a change of policy made promotion to first lieutenant possible based only on service and merit, allowing 337 Army nurses in India to be promoted. Rotation was a slow policy to develop in the CBI as well, but between October 24, 1944, and May 20, 1945, 301 nurses, six dietitians, and four physical therapists rotated back to duty in the United States.

By V-J Day there were 1,300 Army nurses on duty in the former China-Burma-India Theater, which in late October 1944 had been divided into the Burma-India Theater commanded by Lt. Gen. Daniel I. Sultan and the China Theater under Maj. Gen. Alfred Wedemeyer. In the Burma-India Theater the closure of the Ramgarh Training Center and in China the departure of XX Bomber Command to India and on to Saipan decreased the need for medical support and prompted the closing of some hospitals, such as the Ninety-eighth Station Hospital at Chakulia. The Ninety-eighth enjoyed a beautiful location, but had more nurses than work, and so it closed on May 10, 1945. The low case load at some hospitals created a morale problem for many of the nurses, but at units like the Thirty-seventh Station Hospital nurses and medical personnel were kept busy caring for medical cases and for a few Air Force personnel injured on bombing missions. The Thirty-seventh's most exciting experience in the theater, however, came in March 1945, when a violent windstorm blew roofs off the base buildings. Flying debris killed eight men and injured many others, who were admitted to the hospital for treatment.

At Kungming the Ninety-fifth Station Hospital began caring for Japanese patients after the atomic bomb was dropped and the war ended. Nurse Verna Carruth recalls: "The POWs of Japan—mainly in Manchuria—were liberated and came to the 95th Station Hospital to have their condition (health) improved so they could travel to the U.S." When the Chinese civil war began between the Nationalistis and the Communists, Verna says the hospital evacuated all their patients to India and the nurses' quarters were surrounded by gun emplacements.[45]

With the Japanese surrender in early September 1945, the war in the CBI came to a close. Although some of the recently arrived nurses continued on duty after V-J Day, in the next few months most in the CBI returned to the States. Army nurse strength in China actually peaked at 180 in September 1945, but with the transfer of most Air Transport Command troops to India, the need for medical support dwindled. By November only three dozen nurses remained in China, serving at the one dispensary left in western China and at the 172d General Hospital in Shanghai. The Burma-India Theater was deactivated in May 1946, but even when the U.S. Navy took responsibility for medical care of the U.S. Marines in China, twelve Army nurses remained on duty at Shanghai as a part of U.S. Forces, China.[46]

Perhaps the most revealing statement about Army nursing in the CBI during World War II was the report that matter of factly stated, "In all, no sick or wounded GI was for long inaccessible to a hospital where nurses were serving."[47] Considering that Asia is a vast continent, this is a remarkable statement about the commitment of the U.S. Army in World War II to provide quality, professional nursing care for its sick and wounded soldiers and to allow trained ANC nurses to accomplish that mission.

8

They Also Served

The Army Nurse Corps at Home
and in the Minor Theaters of War

 Although most Army nurses in World War II were assigned to hospital units in the continental United States or in major theaters of war, thousands of nurses served in minor theaters from Alaska to Iceland, Africa, and the Middle East. Their experience, although less well known, was equally valuable and often quite interesting.

The first Army nurses to be sent to foreign soil during World War II were nurses of the Eleventh, Sixty-seventh, and 168th Station Hospitals, who departed by convoy in mid-September 1941 for Iceland. Prior to the nurses' arrival, medical support for the American troops in Iceland was provided by the officers and men of the Army Medical Department, who had debarked at the capital of Reykjavik only a few weeks earlier. They joined U.S. Marines, soldiers of the Fifth Infantry Division, and an Army Air Force P-40 air defense squadron on duty in that large volcanic island as part of the President Roosevelt's "short of war" defense policy. Located on the edge of the Arctic Circle, Iceland was vital to the protection of the Allied lifeline from North America to the British Isles. Before the arrival of American fighter planes, German reconnaissance planes from Norway flew over the island on a weekly basis, prompting Allied authorities to fear that the Germans might invade the island using airborne troops.[1]

Because the British were already on garrison duty in Iceland, the early U.S. Army nurse arrivals shared their assignment with their English counterparts in Queen Alexandra's Imperial Nursing Service. American medical headquarters was at Camp Pershing, near the capital at Reykjavik, and all hospital units came under the authority of the base surgeon, Maj. Charles Beasely. When the United States officially entered the war, the Iceland Base Command (IBC) had seventy-seven Army nurses on duty. Hospital facilities in Iceland varied. For example, the 168th Station Hospital occupied a three-story building built in 1898 by the Odd Fellows as a leper hospital. By the time American nurses arrived in Iceland, the British had expanded the original hospital to 100 beds. The further addition of two large Nissen huts brought the bed strength up to 500 and by the end of 1941 the 168th had admitted 1,800 patients.

The 168th Station Hospital offered a wide variety of in-and outpatient medical care to our troops in Iceland. Dorothy Smith, who was a ward nurse in the ear, nose, and throat clinic at the 168th, told an interviewer in 1944, "I assisted the medical officer in the treatment of patients. We averaged 2,000 patients a month. Our personnel consisted of two medical officers, one nurse, and three enlisted men. The laboratory service was adequate."[2]

The Eleventh Station Hospital was set up in a more isolated location, but one which boasted central heating provided by nearby hot springs. Here American nurses shared bathing facilities with British nurses, but at other hospitals the bathing facilities were at first less than ideal. "All water must be carried quite a distance, but no one seems to mind that. . . . A bathhouse is under construction . . . [and] will be quite conveniently located, but we will still have to go outdoors to reach it," one nurse reported.

Prior to the departure of the British nurses, who graciously left some furniture behind, American nurses had fashioned their own furniture from packing boxes. One nurse recalled, "I didn't realize we had so many carpenters with us."[3] Army nurses in Iceland settled in quickly and "you would be surprised at their enthusiasm in fixing up the house," Lieutenant Umbach wrote to Louise Heyden, whose unit was still in the States but had been scheduled for duty in Iceland. Lieutenant Umbach lived in a Nissen hut with seven other nurses and told 1st Lt. (later Capt.) Heyden that she could hardly look at a packing crate "without realizing its possibilities," and that "Miss Hayenga is stenciling some clever figures on their walls." She said she longed for a Woolworth's and sent Heyden a long list of items to bring with her to decorate her hut—Cretonne for curtains, trunk covers, a mirror, "a teapot and cups for when your British friends call," candles, candlesticks, artificial flowers, cocktail napkins, "and any small gadgets from the dime store you might need in a kitchen. Oh yes, a tea kettle also."[4]

Uniforms were a major concern for those women serving in Iceland's cold, damp climate. Early arrivals came without proper clothing and soon found that requisitioning uniforms and shoes from the Quartermaster Corps in the States was a less than satisfactory solution. Their joy at the arrvial of the first shipment of uniforms turned to disappointment when the suits were all the wrong sizes and not one pair of the seventeen pairs of shoes sent fit! Worse, many of the boxes of fur mittens and caps had been rifled.

Iceland's long winters made proper clothing a necessity, not a luxury. Although winter temperatures on the island were similar to those in New England, the wind was a decisive factor. "It is the wind and rain that makes the winter bad. The wind is especially bad in winter. It will blow for three or four days. At times transportation is grounded because of the wind. A year ago in January the wind reached a velocity of 100 mph. It blew down huts and several people were killed," Capt. Louise S. Heyden, ANC, told an interviewer in November 1943.[5]

"Clothing had always been a sore spot with all of the nurses, primarily because of the overcoat," said Dorothy Smith. This held true in Iceland and was especially evident when her unit went to England: "When we go out on the street wearing the overcoat we are probably the worst-dressed women in England." Fortunately, in Iceland the army parka solved the problem for nurses arriving later in the war. Louise Heyden said, "The parka is a lifesaver because you can wear it practically the year round, especially when one travels on those terrible roads." Nurses on duty in Iceland also wore slacks, "and they are really needed because of the wind. However, one doesn't need a lot of heavy underclothing except when you go out and then they wear what you call 'snuggies.'"[6]

Army nurses in Iceland staffed a general hospital and several station hospitals that provided routine medical care for the troops garrisoned there . They did not receive casualties from combat. According to Lieutenant Heyden they had about 100 nurses, and the medical care consisted of "plain hernias and appendectomies, but there was a great deal of orthopedic work because of bad terrain. Many trucks tipped over and caused many injuries." She also told an interviewer that the hospital had a lot of gastric cases and pharyngitis and some pneumonia. In the summer of 1943 they experienced a jaundice outbreak and had a patient census of 800.[7]

One of the most serious medical emergencies in Iceland was not the result of enemy action, but of fire. Hospital personnel had conducted fire and air-raid drills regularly, so, "when the fire bell sounded a real alarm, they rushed to their designated places." The fire started in the basement of an old wooden hospital building housing almost a hundred patients. Fortunately, one of the army nurses was hospitalized in the building suffering from a cold at the time. Lieutenant Riley hastily dressed and ran downstairs to warn the other nurses in their quarters and they all came running. When the flames shot up, firefighters knew only rapid evacuation was possible before the three-story building was engulfed by fire. Even nurses off duty in town heard the call for help and raced back. "There was no talking, only action and plenty of it," said Lt. Margaret Riley, ANC. Frances Crouch and Genevieve Thorpe took charge of the litter bearers in a frantic effort to remove all the patients in time. Because the hospital had no elevator, patients had to be carried down stairs and removed by ambulance to a nearby general hospital. Men suffering from frozen feet, a victim of a heart attack, and a patient recovering from a recent appendectomy had to be handled with extreme care. Orthopedic patients in traction and those hooked to I.V.s presented a challenge: "They were cut free from their apparatus and all were placed on special mattresses and carried downstairs—some in extra blankets and packed with pillows to prevent the shock of sudden removal." Acting with speed and efficiency, the nurses, doctors, and corpsmen had the burning building evacuated within fifteen minutes, but a shift in the wind also carried the flames to the nurses' barracks, which were destroyed.[8]

In addition to accident victims, Iceland hospitals cared for a high percentage of neuropsych patients, 128 mental cases out of 400 patients. Louise Heyden confessed they had no method of treating them and simply put them in wards. The hospital had two psychiatrists and three nurses trained in neuropsychiatry, but could not evacuate the neuropsych cases back to the States because, Heyden said, "the Navy wouldn't take them." Some were released to their old units, but returned a few weeks later. Many, she felt, were malingerers, but the more violent cases were a real problem: "the buildings or huts were not suited for this work because many patients rammed their arms through the plasterboard. They also managed to break out. All this made their control a problem."[9]

Although Heyden did not speculate further on the reason for so many neuropsych cases, the isolation and tedium of duty in Iceland may have been a contributing factor.

"The big problem was amusement," said Heyden. Nurses and officers had the use of officers' clubs where twice-monthly dances were given, but at first the troops had little entertainment. By November 1943, however, Iceland was receiving USO shows and a good supply of movies, in addition to putting on local talent shows. The nurses held a dance once a month. Compared to some units serving in other theaters this was lavish entertainment.

In addition, many Army camps in Iceland were within commuting distance of the capital of Reykjavik, which had a population of about 45,000. American service personnel in Iceland got along well with the local populace, many of whom spoke English and were very hospitable. An island of great natural beauty, Iceland also offered sports-minded servicemen opportunities for trout fishing, bicycling, horseback riding, and camping in the summer. Later in the war, the Red Cross opened a recreational center, which provided a daily movie, a library, Ping-Pong, billiards, and bowling. During the long summer days in Iceland, the warm temperatures made outings to the mountains, geysers, falls, a wishing pool, and other sights very popular with American troops. By 1945 Reykjavik also had a large PX where nurses and G.I.s could purchase ice cream, popcorn, candy, regular meals, and a variety of items. For troops stationed at remote camps, however, duty in Iceland proved monotonous because the routine of garrison duty lacked the excitement of being in a combat area and contributing directly to the war effort.[10]

In general, Army nurses and other military personnel fared better serving in Iceland than in England or Ireland, where some of the units were transferred later in the war. Lt. Dorothy Smith, who served at the 168th Station Hospital in Iceland and then in England, told an Army interviewer in 1944, "The morale in Iceland was very good, for we had good housing and recreation facilities. . . . In England morale was not so good primarily because of the poor housing and living conditions." She attributes low morale also to the lack of work and to the "male shortage."[11]

American medical units, including Army nurses, also served in Greenland and in Labrador, where troops were stationed as part of the air ferry route that began from Presque Isle, Maine, to Gander in Newfoundland or Goose Bay in Labrador, and then continued on another 775 miles to Iceland. From there, it made its longest flight to Prestwick, Scotland. Dispensaries and small station hospitals were established for many of these arctic and subarctic bases and came under the command of the theater surgeon Capt. Michael Q. Hancock at his headquarters in Winnipeg, Canada.[12]

One of the largest station hospitals in eastern Canada during the war was the 100-bed Sixth Station Hospital, which opened at Goose Bay in April 1943. 1st Lt. Lillian Castleberry, ANC, told an interviewer in 1944 about her experiences serving at the Sixth Station Hospital near the settlement of Northwest River, some 175 miles inland. She recalled that it was "never very warm" in Labrador: the temperatures varied from 40 to 60 degrees Fahrenheit in summer and went to 32 below zero F in winter. More disturbing than the cold weather, according to Castleberry, was the isolation: "There were every few places that one could visit because of the absence of railroads. The only method of transportation was by air." In fact, air links provided most of the hospital's supplies—access by boat was confined to three summer months before ice closed the port.

Castleberry's hospital served a base command of about 100 officers and 1,100 men, mostly belonging to the Army Air Corps. Housed in wooden buildings, the Sixth Station Hospital was home to six doctors, eight nurses, and forty-five enlisted men, and was, she reported, "very nicely furnished inside, far superior to any station hospital . . . in the States." Although they had a capacity of seventy-five beds (reduced from one hundred), the daily census of patients was twenty-five or thirty, for Labrador enjoyed a healthful climate. Most of the hospital admissions were from upper-respiratory infections. Seriously ill or injured cases were evacuated by air to the United States. Most of the Sixth Station Hospital's injury cases were fractures. Labrador had its share of mental cases as well and Castleberry's hospital set aside part of a ward for them. "Most of them needed encouragement more than anything else," she told an interviewer. "The Red Cross helped them quite a bit." Any of the neuropsych cases that could not be returned to duty within thirty days were evacuated to the States.[13]

Army nurses also served in Manitoba, Canada, on the shores of Hudson Bay at the Fourth Station Hospital, three miles from the small settlement and Royal Canadian Mounted Police headquarters at Churchill. Here they experienced the rigors of a frigid climate where, according to Lt. Cora O'Hare, ANC, "the temperature during the winter reached 60 below." Just before her arrival, the Fourth Station Hospital endured a gale with 105 mph winds. "The wind just blows and blows and one wonders if it will ever stop," she told an Army interviewer in January 1944. At first Lieutenant O'Hare's group of nurses wore men's winter clothing, but eventually women's clothing became available and she found it adequate, except for the parka, which needed more protection for the face. Many troops stationed in Canada or Labrador discovered that G.I. clothing was less than satisfactory for the Arctic. Army shoes were quickly replaced by Eskimo mukluks, Indian moccasins, or heavy felt shoes sold by the Hudson Bay Company. As the war progressed, the clothing issue was resolved and Lieutenant Castleberry said, "We have everything that you could think of that one would need in the Arctic." Her only complaint was about the arctic boots, which would not buckle when the nurses wore heavy socks. The Air Force came to the women's rescue by giving them fleece-lined flying boots. The quartermaster also ordered wolverine fur to be sewed on the parkas, which proved a perfect solution: wolverine is the only fur that does not collect ice from the breath.[14]

Although Lillian Castleberry was candid about the problems of serving in such an isolated post and recommended that soldiers be rotated home after twelve to fourteen months, she said her nurses at the Sixth Station Hospital had made a satisfactory adjustment: "They have gone through the hard part and it is their desire to remain there for a time." She had carried out a rigorous training program in medical, surgical, and clinical work for the nurses and reported, "After the training each girl was able to take over anywhere without hesitation or interruption of routine. All of them are very good nurses. . . . They like living together and they get along beautifully."[15]

In addition to the Army nurses and medical personnel serving in station hospitals and dispensaries in the arctic and subarctic regions along the North Atlantic air ferry route, there were servicemen and women manning air bases and stations along the South Atlantic air ferry route, which began in Florida and continued to Natal in Brazil and then across the ocean to Gambia in West Africa. From there pilots flew Lend-Lease planes to Khartoum in the Sudan by way of Nigeria and French Equatorial Africa. A regular transport route was established all the way to the North African Mission in Cairo, Egypt, after the United States entered the war. Liberia became the West African terminus of the route. From there the aircraft ferry and transport service branched into two routes, one leading to Cairo, Basra, and Palestine, and the other to Eritrea and Aden.[16]

When American military personnel began arriving in larger numbers in mid-1942, the mission was changed to U.S. Army Forces in the Middle East (USAFIME). In West Africa, the Army established a separate command for the 2,000 service personnel on duty in Liberia at Roberts Field along the Air Transport Command route and defending the Firestone Tire and Rubber Company plantation. Medical support for the troops in Liberia was the responsibility of the surgeon's office at Roberts Field, east of Monrovia, where the 250-bed Twenty-fifth Station Hospital cared for all medical cases in the command. For eight months 1st Lt. Susan E. Freeman, ANC, served as chief nurse of the Twenty-fifth Station

Hospital, which was an integrated unit of four white physicians serving with black nurses and enlisted personnel. Lieutenant Freeman told an Army interviewer in late December 1943 that the Twenty-fifth Station Hospital had twenty-one medical officers, thirty nurses, and 180 enlisted men. The unit provided medical support for American and Royal Air Force (RAF) troops maintaining the airfield and to a substantial number of natives employed by the command.

Ellen Robinson Page, a lifelong resident of New Jersey who graduated from Phillips School of Nursing in St. Louis and joined the Army Nurse Corps in July 1942, was among the contingent of nurses who reported to the Twenty-fifth. She came from Fort Huachuca with nine other Army nurses and joined the rest of the group from Fort Bragg, Livingston, and Tuskeegee at a staging area at Camp Kilmer, New Jersey. She recalls the frustration of being very near to her family but of not being not allowed to make phone calls prior to boarding a converted luxury liner for the voyage to Africa. "A convoy of thirty ships, of which three left to go to the Mediterranean. Two were sunk, but one did get through. One night the whole convoy was at a standstill because enemy submarines were in the waters," she says. En route to Liberia, Lieutenant Page used her nursing skills as the assistant for an emergency appendectomy. After five days in Casablanca awaiting a pilot ship to take them down the coast of Africa to Liberia, the nurses arrived at Roberts Field. "When we reached Liberia the boat docked approximately one mile from shore, the water was too shallow to go in. Ended up we had to jump from ship to landing craft, which is a scary thing to do," Freeman remembered.

When Lieutenant Freeman and her nurses arrived at Roberts Field, they found a fully functioning hospital constructed of regular army-type wooden buildings with ramp connections. Freeman found "everything was fixed very nicely when we got there," and Lieutenant Page elaborated, "The bathroom was a separate building, mostly thatched, concrete floor, never any privacy. Creatures like lizards and other things of that nature. Sometimes a small monkey would appear there!" There were also very large rats, which sometimes sounded like a herd of animals walking on the hospital ramps. But otherwise the living conditions at the Twenty-fifth were fairly comfortable. Nurses' diets in Liberia were typical army rations supplemented by occasional fishing trips when "sometimes the staff would have good luck and catch fresh fish, a rare treat." The water supply at Roberts Field was safe, but always ran rusty, "but we just used it," Page recalled, explaining that the nurses used rainwater to wash their hair and clothes.

The patient census at the Twenty-fifth Station Hospital ran about 170 or 180 patients, most of them suffering from malaria, but it also received some surgical cases. The prevailing type of surgery was orthopedics: "We had several cast cases most of the time." However, the nurses' mission in Liberia was not only to provide nursing care to Allied troops but also to make friends with the Liberian people. "It was sort of a good will mission," commented Susan Freeman, who felt that their efforts would have been more successful if she had been able to select the nurses who were assigned to the hospital.

Although she admits that the recreation and travel opportunities in Liberia were limited, she remembers the nurses played pinochle, made use of a Ping-Pong table, or attended movies at an auditorium that was a mile from their quarters. "Always we tried to have one of the doctors or a male unit go with us down along the dirt road," she recalled. On rare occasions, the nurses were invited by the American ambassador to come to the capitol at Monrovia, "an eighty mile trip through the Firestone Rubber Plantation." Otherwise the nurses had little chance for sightseeing. They heard that there were leopards nearby and one doctor claimed to have seen one near the latrine. They also saw natives walking in a straight line carrying boa constrictors.[17]

Although Lieutenant Freeman's unit was the only African-American nurse contingent to serve in Africa, Army nurses also served at the Twenty-third Station Hospital at Leopoldville in the Belgian Congo. The hospital was opened in December 1942 to provide medical care for the southern branch of the Air Transport Command route. Kathleen Marren recalled that its nurses sailed for Africa on the former cruise ship *James Parker*. En route, the ship docked for several days at Ascension Island. She writes, "Here we picked up a unit of engineers who had built an airstrip on the island. We visited a British battleship that was docked nearby. We spent a pleasant afternoon of 'high tea' and entertainment." She recalls that the battleship escorted the transport to the mouth of the Congo River and from there the nurses sailed up the river as far as it was navigable and then went by rail to Leopoldville.[18]

Grace Blair Campbell, who joined the Army Nurse Corps in March 1942, was among the nurses serving in the Leopoldville. "Gorgeous flowers, bugs, natives and the tropical illnesses" made Leopoldville a most fascinating assignment for her. Nurses lived in the ABC Hotel until their living quarters were completed in the hospital area. "We then had wooden-screened barracks," she remembered. When they went overseas from the staging area at Fort Bragg the nurses had only woolen uniforms, which they could not wear because of the heat: "Someone bought a second-hand sewing machine and a bolt of beige material. The nurses who knew how to sew made skirts which we wore."[19]

Campbell, Marren, and their fellow nurses and medical personnel spent much of their time caring for patients suffering from tropical diseases, especially malaria. "We learned to nurse malaria and dysentery," Campbell says. Marren points out that the illnesses of central Africa also affected the staff: "We had one nurse die while we were still living in the hotel, and one of the doctors died after I returned to the States." Campbell recalls that the nurse died of bacillary dysentery.

With the exception of these two tragic incidents, the nurses' health in the Congo was good and morale remained high. Opportunities for recreation and travel, however, were few. "Our social life was very limited. We went to dances at the Officer's Club, played bridge, and when off duty tried to get around to do some sightseeing." However, Grace Campbell admits, "Our commanding officer did not give us the opportunity to travel that he could have." Kathleen Marren seconds this: "While I was with the unit we did not have transportation for travel. Later I believe the unit did get more opportunity to travel—We were entertained by the local people."[20]

In April 1943, the Twenty-third Station Hospital was transferred to North Africa when the southern route was abandoned by the Air Transport Command. Kathleen Marren, Grace Blair Campbell, and the other nurses served at Port Lyautey, Morocco, and Oran, Algeria, in North Africa and then went on to Epinal, France. They were overseas a total of thirty-nine months during the war.

At the other end of the Mediterranean, U.S. Army nurses were also serving "Uncle Sam" in hospitals and dispensaries in the Middle East and in Russia. The presence of American nurses in such remote areas of the war effort as Egypt, Eritrea, Iran, and the Soviet Union was dictated by the need to provide quality medical care to U.S. troops assigned to these commands.

Perhaps the smallest number of Army nurses to serve in this part of the world were the dozen women assigned to field hospitals caring for sick and wounded American G.I.s at Army Air Force (USAAF) stations in Poltava and Mirgorod, Russia. In April 1944, the twelve nurses flew from England to Cairo and on to Teheran, where they spent weeks waiting for passports and studying Russian. Capt. Anna Lisa Moline, ANC, who became an assistant to the director of nursing service in the ETO, recalls, "We studied the Russian language under a special tutor and had lectures and special films to orient us to the Russian situation. It was an interesting six weeks."[21]

When Moline and her fellow nurses finally got the go-ahead to enter Russia, they were warned "about the rough living conditions and the possibility of enemy bombing." They were not disappointed—on arriving in Poltava they discovered that headquarters was the only building not ruined by bombing. The hospital was being set up under canvas and the nurses pitched in immediately because shuttle bombing missions by USAAF planes between Italy and Russia were scheduled to begin the next day. The nurses cared for Air Force crews injured flying these brief missions over enemy territory, and Captain Moline said, "It was thrilling to see the 'Flying Fortresses' and fighter planes circle the field and those who wished to land drop their flares."

American hospital locations in Russia varied from the windy plains of Mirgorod, "which made us think of the dust bowl in the Middle West," to a wooded area near a river at Piryatin. These remote hospitals lacked many basic supplies, but the men fashioned basin stands, trays, tables, and bedside screens from boxes and old bomb crates. "A coat of white and Air Corps blue did wonders for all these articles," Moline remembers. While in Russia the nurses enjoyed meeting officers of the Russian air force, who invited them to a concert of Russian folk songs, dances, and gypsy music. The hospital also employed a limited number of Russian women to do laundry.

Dire predictions about enemy air attacks proved quite realistic: German bombers came over around midnight one June evening. Captain Moline and others evacuated their patients into trenches "wide enough to accommodate the stretchers" and tried to be reassuring as the first bombs fell. "The noise was deafening, anti-aircraft shells bursting, bombs exploding, and planes droning," she says. When bombs made a direct hit near one of the hospital tents doctors and nurses rushed out to assist the wounded and brought them back to the trenches for first aid. After the air attack ended, at about three o'clock in the morning, the newly injured were brought into the surgery and shock tents, and the nurses and doctors worked feverishly for hours: "All through the next day it seemed that there was no end to the number of men who were injured." Fortunately, the air attacks did not continue, and although bombed, the Mirgorod hospital had few injuries.

After the first few weeks, the hospitals settled into a routine and the nurses even had time for picnics and swimming in a nearby river. During their time in Russia, the nurses were able to visit Moscow. "We enjoyed the ballet, and saw Red Square, Lenin's tomb, the Kremlin, and the city's modern subway system," recalls Moline. When Air Force bombing missions were halted, the hospitals left Russia but Captain Moline felt the experience had been very interesting and valuable: "We had learned to like the Russians as people and we had a feeling they liked us. We had enjoyed building up our hospital and making a home for ourselves on the Russian plains. Not without regret we left Russian soil where we had learned to know a kindly people."[22]

In North Africa an American military mission was established in September 1941 to help the British with port construction and maintenance of aircraft, vehicles, and locomotives. After our entry into the war, the U.S. Army began sending male medical personnel and equipment to Egypt and Eritrea. Army nurses did not arrive, however, until November 1, 1942, when 105 nurses were sent to the Thirty-eighth General Hospital in the Delta area and sixty to the Twenty-first Station Hospital in Eritrea. The former, an affiliated hospital unit from Jefferson Medical College in Philadelphia, sailed from the United States on September 20, 1942, arriving at Port Tevich in late October via Rio de Janiero after a voyage that resembled a peacetime pleasure cruise. Nurses were very welcome in the Middle East, or as Capt. Willie Alder, ANC, remembered: "We were really met with cheers and shouts of joy. It didn't matter that we were burdened like packhorses and wore our steel helmets; everyone seemed to think we looked all right." Another contingent of Army women reported for duty with the Fourth Field Hospital in Levant in mid-November, followed by sixty nurses for the Nineteenth and Thirtieth Station Hospitals in Iran two weeks before Christmas. By the end of the year there were 245 Army nurses in the Middle East.[23]

Army nurses also served at a number of hospitals in what eventually became designated as the Persian Gulf Command, where a total of 29,500 American troops were stationed during the war. The largest of the U.S. Army hospitals in the command was the 113th, which began in May 1942 as a 750-bed station hospital at Ahwaz in southern Iran, about 100 miles from the gulf. The 113th served not only the servicemen in the area, but also was a clearing house for patients from all over the command who were en route back to the States via the Thirty-eighth Station Hospital in Egypt. The hospital buildings, built from the ground up by Americans using native brick, mud, and stone, were laid out in a radial pattern and eventually covered acres. Other Army hospitals in Iran were located all along the Persian corridor, north from the gulf toward Teheran and the Caspian Sea. The smaller field hospitals sent platoons out to care for troops in more remote locations.

1st Lt. Elsie Schwable, ANC, was the chief nurse of the Twenty-first Station Hospital at Khorramschar, Iran, before being transferred to Teheran in April 1943. At Teheran the hospital served quartermaster troops who transported Lend-Lease equipment form the Persian Gulf to the Russian border. The nurses lived and worked in "very hot" mud and brick buildings, although there were a few air-conditioned wards. "It's very hot," reported one nurse. "Temperature readings in the sun were 187 degrees and in the shade 115 degrees. We were on the 'C' ration and all one had to do to heat the food was to place the can in the sunlight. We slept outside most of the time because it was too hot in the buildings." The Twenty-first cared mostly for malaria cases. Ironically, although 7,000 trucks per day loaded with food and equipment passed through the area en route to Russia, Lieutenant Schwable told an interviewer that hospital "supplies were hard to obtain" and personnel "needed additional refrigeration badly, but could not get the quartermaster to release any units." Most disheartening was the loss in a fire of an entire warehouse filled with "nice refrigerators." Lieutenant Schwable said morale was low at the Twenty-first because of a lack of work and recreational facilities, and few travel opportunities—"there is nothing of interest in Teheran"—and the heat.[24]

There was no active combat in the Persian Gulf Command, but the poor living conditions and variety of diseases there kept American medical personnel and nurses occupied and prompted an Associated Press correspondent, Clyde Farnsworth, to dub the war in the Persian Gulf a "battle without bloodshed." Dysentery, amoebic dysentery, pappataci fever, and venereal disease were prevalent in the Persian Gulf Command, along with common respiratory diseases and accident victims.

Nurses and medical personnel stationed in Iran during the war shared some hardships unique to that region. The official Army medical history called Iran a "land of pestilence," where the local populace was infected with typhus, malaria, venereal disease, intestinal infections, small pox, and a variety of other ailments. "All locations were deplorable as far as sanitation was concerned, and many were at the mercy of the sweltering sun for a good part of the year." Drinking water at bases and hospitals had to be filtered and then boiled or chlorinated, and the monotonous Army diet could only be supplemented from local produce after careful washing or boiling because of the method of fertilizing gardens in Iran. Flies, mosquitoes, and other insects added to the misery of troops stationed in Iran, where nurses and soldiers "struggled in those early days in the freezing weather, the sticky-like glue mud, the dust storms, and the terrific heat of summer."[25]

Halfway across the world, Army nurses were also on duty in the Aleutian Islands and in isolated station hospitals and dispensaries all over Alaska. Although technically not serving "overseas," these nurses experienced many of the same challenges as women working in hospitals in remote areas like Iceland and Africa. The Army considered Alaska, Puerto Rico, and the Philippines as insular posts, and the number of Army personnel assigned to these bases increased steadily in the prewar period. By the end of 1941, 275 reserve nurses were on duty or headed for areas beyond the continental United States.

Some of the first nurses to arrive in Alaska were assigned to bases along the air ferry route to the Soviet Union. Four nurses, including First Lieutenant Beringer, arrived at Fort Richardson near Anchorage on April 19, 1941, and by the time of the attack on Pearl Harbor, the Alaskan Defense Command was employing about fifty Army nurses in four station hospitals. When the United States entered World War II the Army had about 2,000 troops in Alaska under the command of Maj. Gen. Simon Buckner. A small Army force was on duty near Skagway, and the U.S. Navy had civilian contractors working at sites in Sitka and Kodiak. The Navy also maintained a base at Dutch Harbor, which was also defended by Army garrison troops.[26]

Vivian F. Flynn was among the first Army nurses to debark for duty in Alaska. She literally "fell" into Alaska while debarking from the transport at Seward. Flynn broke her arm in the fall and was taken to a civilian hospital to have it set. She and the other five nurses then resumed their journey to their new post. When the war broke out, the hospital had twenty Army nurses, a Red Cross worker, and a dietitian. On the eve of the war, the Fort Ladd Station Hospital also received nurses under the leadership of Chief Nurse Lt. Marie Pace. They reported for duty at Ladd Field in September 1941 and the hospital officially opened in a four-story wing of the Air Corps barracks on December 9. September also brought eleven Army nurses under 1st Lt. Abigail B. Graves to the station hospital at Fort Mears. The hospital was so new that it did not have a supply of operating room linens, and a Navy nurse from Dutch Harbor who arrived to assist in emergency surgical procedures helped sew linens because "the technicians [had] tried their hands at running the sewing machine but with little success."[27]

These early nurse arrivals in Alaska were "pioneers," and like so many military personnel in newly established bases around the globe, they found living conditions somewhat primitive. They soon discovered that cars were useless on the poor Alaskan roads. Often the nurses' quarters were sparsely furnished and the local stores offered little in the way of furniture or accessories to buy. For example, the nurses settling in at Fort Richardson in the fall of 1941 felt an acute need for venetian blinds: they were "practically living in a glass house." By the time a shipment of blinds reached them the war had begun and the windows were already covered with black paper to ensure a secure blackout against enemy aircraft.

Army nurses quickly found the Alaskan countryside made up for the inconveniences, the slow mail service, and the isolation. One nurse wrote: "Alaska's natural beauty is unbelievable. In no place in the world can be found such magnificent sunrises and sunsets. We have a profusion of wild flowers."[28]

After the war began, Army nurses were sent to two new station hospitals, the 203d Station Hospital at Seward and the 204th at Sitka. More women might have been assigned to Alaskan units except for the theater's cautious policy, which the Army attributed more to the "problems of quarters for nurses than enemy activity."

Although the Japanese occupied the islands of Kiska and Attu, Army nurses were never in any immediate danger from Japanese invasions—they served in hospitals far from the scene of enemy action. They were, however, exposed to enemy air attacks on Dutch Harbor and on Fort Mears in June 1942. The hospitals in both locations treated casualties from the air attacks, and at Fort Mears the medical staff worked long hours for several days caring for the wounded. Only three of the sixty servicemen injured in the attack later died. A colonel wounded in the raid reported that the nurses "remained calm and levelheaded under direct fire" and performed their duties tirelessly.

Other than these air raids, there were few combat casualties sent to Alaskan hospitals where Army nurses were assigned. The major combat operations in Alaska during World War II were the American landings on Attu in May 1943. Although Army nurses were moved westward to the 102st Station Hospital at Cold Bay, the 186th Station Hospital at Unimak, and the 179th Station Hospital at Adak Island in the spring of 1943 in anticipation of American operations to reclaim the Aleutian Islands, most of the actual combat casualties from the Attu landings were evacuated to the Zone of the Interior by ship.

One of the most serious emergencies requiring medical care during the war in Alaska occurred on June 23, 1943, when a bomber crashed at Nome's airfield. The plane's bomb load ignited a gasoline dump near the runway and spread shrapnel and flaming fuel over a wide area. Thirty of the wounded were sent to the hospital, which radioed Fort Richardson for help in caring for the wounded, especially for the numerous burn cases. Three officers, two nurses, and a surgical technician arrived the next day by plane with plasma and supplies. The nurses remained at Nome for five days and, according to the ANC historian, "distinguished themselves by their fine work and excellent cooperation."[29]

Except for occasional air crashes or accidents, most Army hospitals in Alaska gave routine care to Air Corps and Army troops stationed nearby. One serviceman in the Aleutians wrote of duty in Alaska, "Nursing at the 328th has nothing about it of the horror of front-line warfare, nor are there the life and action that characterize most wartime hospitals." With the Japanese long gone from the Aleutians, Allied troops were in the "dull and dreary business" of holding what the United States already owned against a possible Japanese attack. One soldier wrote, "Life there is just a succession of lonely, unvarying days piled on end until they equaled two years or more and meant return to the States for reassignment."[30]

Lucille B. Carter, who joined the Army Nurse Corps in 1940 and served in the Aleutians during the war, agrees: "No one was often sick and there were no battles. The nurses spent most of the day trying to make life easier for the soldiers and officers—such as dancing with the officers nightly and cooking [making cookies, etc.] for the soldiers." In the healthful Alaskan climate, fever and disease cases were rare and the nurses cared for cases of respiratory infections, rheumatic fever, and soldiers injured in vehicle or construction accidents.[31]

The real challenge for the nurses in the Aleutians, according to Lucille Carter, was keeping warm and clean. Their bathing facilities were a block from their quarters and the wind blew so hard that the hospital finally had an enclosed trail built between the nurses' Quonset huts and the bath room. Carter and the fifteen other nurses lived two to four women to a hut, but at other hospitals the quarters varied. In 1944 the nurses of the 328th Station Hospital enjoyed small, nicely furnished single rooms in quarters attached to the hospital. They also had a sitting room, a large recreation room, and a dining room nearby.

Morale was a continuing problem in the Alaska Defense Command, especially in remote areas like the Aleutian Islands. There were no small towns, "no diverting natives or civilians, no outside attractions," wrote one G.I. The nurses and medical officers depended on the officers' club, movies, or small dinner parties for entertainment. Outdoor activities in the Aleutians were very limited. In the winter the williwaw winds come up unexpectedly; they would "come in with a roar of an express train" and could knock a person down. Blizzards often buried the huts in snow and closed the roads. In the summer the weather could be dismal as well, with wind, fog, and rain. Servicemen and women in Alaska described the fog as "a gray, wet blanket" and insisted "even the seagulls are grounded in Aleutian fog!"[32]

While American servicemen and nurses fought the cold and the boredom of duty in Alaska, in the continental United States, Army nurses served in scores of Army hospitals. Many of them were assigned to affiliated hospitals or other Army hospital units that eventually went overseas. For example, during the first six months of the war, from December 7, 1941, to July 1, 1942, a total of two surgical hospitals, four 750-bed evacuation hospitals, thirty-seven station hospitals, and fifteen general hospitals were sent to theaters of war ranging from the Panama Canal Zone to Ascension Island. Army nurses accompanied most of these units overseas.[33]

In the continental United States, the number of Army hospitals grew dramatically. Station hospitals, for example, increased from 200 in early 1942 to 425 by June 1943. General hospitals also experienced phenomenal growth, increasing from only fourteen in December 1941 to forty by June 1943. To staff these hospitals, the Army Nurse Corps increased its strength from 7,000 nurses on active duty on December 7, 1941, to 12,000 by June 1942, 36,607 at the end of June 1943, and 52,000 by V-E Day. Army nurses' duties were similar to those of civilian nurses except for the Army's practice of using nurses to supervise and train the enlisted personnel who provided much of the bedside nursing care for sick and injured soldiers. In the continental U.S. Army hospitals, civilians were also employed in numbers as high as 20 percent of their authorized enlisted strength. Most of these civilians were medical technicians, cooks, ward orderlies, janitors, and maintenance men, but in some cases civilian nurses were employed. Until the end of 1942 all female dietitians and physical therapist aides in Army hospitals were civilian employees. By April 1945 Army general hospitals were using 2,000 cadet nurses and 1,000 civilian nurses, as well as civilian aides, orderlies, Red Cross volunteers, and WACs.[34]

Although not on duty in the continental United States, Army nurses did serve during the war at hospitals of the Zone of the Interior to provide medical support for American troops in the Caribbean and in the Panama Canal Zone. For example, thirteen nurses under Chief Nurse Lt. Ina L. Copeland, ANC, were assigned to the station hospital at Barinque Field, Puerto Rico. The original hospital was housed in temporary, single-story wooden structures, but later in the war moved into a new four-story concrete facility. Duty on this tropical island was pleasant, and the hospital's mission was to provide routine medical care augmented by an aggressive program to combat venereal disease, which was found to be prevalent among the civilian popualtion. Across the Caribbean, the 333d Station Hospital was providing similar medical support for troops in the Canal Zone. Redesignated from the 218th S.H., the 333d was a 700-bed hospital located first at Fort Amador and then transferred to a modern facility built entirely from scratch and opened in September 1943 at Fort Clayton. The staff of thirty-three officers, seventy-four nurses, and 369 enlisted men enjoyed good athletic and recreational facilities, including a bowling alley and swimming pool. Although far from home, the 333d's nurses were hardly "roughing it": they had their own dining room and a separate mess that employed civilian help who supplemented the nurses' diet with fresh milk, fruits, and vegetables year round. Nurses at Fort Clayton were aided in patient care by three Red Cross workers and a corps of some thirty Gray Ladies of the local Balboa Red Cross chapter.[35]

One of the most unusual assignments given to Army nurses during World War II was as liaison officers between the U.S. Army and Allied units. For example, Lt. Joella Wallace, ANC, served as a liaison officer to the Medical Section, First Brazilian Fighter Squadron. Graduating from St. Joesph's Infirmary in Atlanta in 1939, she joined the Army Nurse Corps in April 1940 and spent three years in the Puerto Rican Department, where she learned to speak Spanish. In 1943 she was sent to Mitchell Field, New York, to train six Brazilian nurses. She recalls, "These nurses were to be trained to go overseas with the squadron just as we give our nurses in the Air Force training." Lieutenant Wallace gave them a month's basic training similar to American nurses, but conducted the classes in Portuguese through an interpreter. Then she took them to various American hospitals, to Bolling Field to see American flight nurses, and to Washington to meet Army Nurse Corps Director Col. Florence A. Blanchfield.

In September 1944 Lieutenant Wallace and her Brazilian nurses reported to a port of embarkation at Patrick Henry, Virginia, for shipment overseas. After a mixup over cancelled orders, Wallace was assigned to the Brazilian squadron and sailed with them to Civitavecchia, Italy, for duty at an American hospital, the 154th Station. She told an interviewer, "I learned their language on the boat trip overseas, which took nineteen days. I was speaking Portuguese on the boat and the Americans thought I knew the language perfectly. Actually, I spoke Portuguese very poorly, but the Brazilians understood me, and I improved as time went on." Wallace chose to live with the Brazilian nurses who cared for their own patients and worked on American wards, which called for a good deal of liaison between the nurses and the American medical personnel.

After two months Lieutenant Wallace and the Brazilian nurses went to a hospital at Leghorn where they had their own three-ward section. Here, the Brazilian nurses and doctors were isolated from American patients. "This was a very sad thing to the Brazilians and they didn't like it at all. . . . They liked working much better with the Americans. . . . The Brazilians count on the Americans to help them and they like us much more than we realize. I noticed this in Italy and also in Brazil," Wallace confided to an Army interviewer.[36]

In addition to sending thousands of American nurses overseas to every theater of war, World War II brought many important changes to the Army Nurse Corps itself. Of these perhaps none was more important than the congressional legislation affecting the status of the Army Nurse Corps within the U.S. Army. In the early years, Army nurses were auxiliaries without army rank, officer status, equal-pay benefits, or veteran's rights. The reasoning behind this departure from the normal Army hierarchy was explained by Army Nurse Corps Director Blanchfield in an article in *The Army Nurse* in 1944. Colonel Blanchfield reminded readers, many of whom were puzzled or angry, that most Army nurses were still second lieutenants when other women's reservists had been promoted, that when the Army first employed nurses in 1898 they were under contract and paid thirty dollars a month plus one ration a day. "There was no thought of promoting anyone, they were 'just nurses' and had one superintendent." Although some improvements were made for Army nurses following WW I, such as the conferring of "relative rank" or the title of an officer without the military status, comparable pay or allowances of a commissioned army officer, temporary commissions with some retirement benefits awaited the approval of Congress in 1942. Prior to that time, wrote Colonel Blanchfield in 1944, "even after twenty years of relative rank, the nurses had much the same arrangement: one head and the rest of the corps were 'just nurses,' each hospital having one chief nurse and all the others, regardless of their duties and responsibilities or length of service were 'just nurses.'" This concept of equality and dedication was a very strong part of the Army Nurse Corps tradition, but the custom set the nurses apart from other women's reserves, which were organized along combat lines with officers, enlisted women, specialized ratings, and regular promotions. Members of the Women's Army Auxiliary Corps (WAAC), Women Accepted for Voluntary Emergency Service (WAVES), the Women's Reserve of the U.S. Coast Guard (SPARS), and the U.S. Marine Corps Women's Reserve did, however, have status similar to nurses in that they had only relative rank from their founding until legislation authorized them regular rank and privileges.

In 1941, nurses entered the U.S. Army without commissions, although they did enjoy relative rank. As one Army nurse recalled, "We were appointed, not commissioned." In keeping with their auxiliary status, the Army Nurse Corps was headed not by a general officer or even a colonel, but by a major, and she was known by the civilian title of director not commanding officer. On December 22, 1942, Public Law 828 authorized relative rank for Army nurses of second lieutenant to colonel and gave them pay and allowances approximately equal to those of male commissioned officers without dependents.[37]

After two and one-half years of having only relative rank, Army and Navy nurses were finally offered temporary commissions with full pay and privileges of the grades from second lieutenant through colonel by the enactment of Public Law 350 in 1944. Congress extended this new status to military nurses, however, only for the duration of war plus six months. This change in status, which became effective on July 10, 1944, was welcomed by most Army nurses, but over 200 of them refused these temporary commissions, choosing to remain in the Corps under the terms of their original appointment. One longtime Army nurse, Nell Close, is said to have refused her temporary commission because "she felt the Corps was losing some of its dignity."[38]

In anticipation of and preparation for this important change of status, Army Nurse Corps Director Blanchfield worked actively, despite opposition from a "considerable number of doctors" within the Medical Department, to begin basic training courses for new Army nurses. Prior to the establishment of training centers, graduate nurses joining the Army Nurse Corps were assigned to jobs straight from civilian life without any formal introduction or indoctrination to military life, what the military refers to as "basic" or "boot camp." According to Capt. Edith Aynes, who had been reassigned from Hawaii to the Army Nurse Corps director's staff in Washington, Colonel Blanchfield "was well aware of the weaknesses of American nurses' preparation for appointment to commissioned rank in the military." Captain Aynes cited these weaknesses: "the nurses' lack of knowledge of military courtesies or customs of the service, their erroneous conception of their role in military nursing, their inability to accept the leadership-teacher-supervisor, set-an-example relationship with enlisted personnel or other nonprofessionals in the hospital, or, conversely, to assume a superior you-do-the-work-I'm-an-officer attitude of many nurses new to the army. " She felt these shortcomings "precluded nurses' acceptance as officers by medical administative officers, enlisted men, WAC officers, particularly, and even by enlisted women who measured their respect for their officers by military more than humanitarian standards."

Taking a clue from the experience of the Women's Army Corps, which found a basic indoctrination course essential for its enlistees and officers, Director Blanchfield finally managed to convince the Army to start the first basic training course for army nurses at Fort Meade, Maryland, in September 1943. According to Edith Aynes, this basic indoctrination "included two weeks of field training and two weeks of hospital ward management."

In September 1943, the Army Nurse Corps opened training centers at Fort Devens, Massachusetts, Fort Sam Houston, Texas, and Camp McCoy, Wisconsin, to give nurses joining the Army Nurse Corps an orientation to military life. At the training centers, new Army nurses were introduced to military etiquette and administration and given courses on bivouacking in the field, gas injuries, digging foxholes, and purifying water. One trainee recalled, "Our classes were very interesting. They try to cram an awful lot of lectures during those two weeks. We had classes in military courtesy, protection against chemical warfare, several lectures on the care and causes of tropical fevers, sanitation as practiced in the Army (they stress that point very much)." In addition to lectures, the new Army nurses did morning exercises, drilled daily for one hour, and went on two twelve-mile hikes with knapsacks, canteens, and gas masks. On their last day of basic training, the women were required to participate in the Army infiltration course—walking or crawling a distance, part of it under barbed wire, while being subjected to machine-gun fire and explosive charges to simulate actual combat conditions. "The bullets were about thirty inches above our heads and, believe me, everyone kept their nose stuck to the ground while they were firing," wrote one nurse. After dropping repeatedly to the ground as explosive charges went off, the nurses made it to a low trench, "and everyone crawled into that, and then they let go three machine guns all at once." After that experience the women felt the two weeks of ward duty were easy.

Overseas training, however, proved invaluable when hospital units finally got to the battlefront. "Our conditioning at home station stood us mighty well. Our nurses have taken whatever came along in stride and the hardships didn't bother them," said one hospital commanding officer.[39]

The needs of wartime nursing also gave impetus to the creation of the U.S. Cadet Nurse Corps, a program to train nurses for employment in essential civilian nursing roles or in the Army and Navy nurse corps. One of the most innovative programs of World War II in terms of providing opportunities for young American women, the U.S. Cadet Nurse Corps program offered qualified students full federal nurse education scholarships. The decision to create a new program rather than to reinstitute the old Army School of Nursing, was a sharp break with Army Nurse Corps tradition. However, both Congress and the Army felt it would be more efficient and economical to use existing civilian nursing schools and faculties than to create a military structure to provide more graduate nurses for Army nursing and for civilian needs. The Cadet Nurse Corps, established on July 1, 1943, by Public Law 74, was administered by the U.S. Public Health Service and was funded through the congressional appropriations authorized under an act sponsored by Rep. Frances P. Bolton of Ohio. The Cadet Corps recruiting campaign portrayed nursing education as an attractive and affordable option for many young American women who might otherwise be tempted by high-paying jobs in the wartime work force. The Surgeon General of the Public Health Service, Thomas Parran, however, appealed to American patriotism, saying, "Security of the national health demands that this campaign be a success. There have never been enough nurses. Today this shortage has reached the danger point. We need thousands of superior young women enrolled as new student nurses to maintain even minimum hospital service to hold health service at a safe level."[40]

The U.S. Cadet Corps was open to any nursing student who was admitted to a nursing school after January 1, 1941, provided he or she was in an accelerated program lasting twenty-four to thirty months. Cadet nurses were authorized to wear a distinctive outdoor uniform and an insignia that combined the emblem of the U.S. Public Health Service and the Maltese cross. For their first nine months, Cadet Corps students received full maintenance, and after that period students were eligible for scholarships and a monthly stipend to cover the cost of tuition, student fees, books, and uniforms. This financial support had one important catch—cadet nurses were required to pledge to serve the country as military nurses or in essential civilian nursing assignments throughout the war. They were, however, allowed to marry and were assured that the Army Nurse Corps and many other essential civilian nursing jobs employed married nurses. The Corps was a highly successful program, and 500 more women than the first year's quota of 65,000 students responded to the call.[41]

The first cadet students to serve at a military hospital in the United States were thirty-five women who reported to New Station Hospital at Fort Devens, Massachusetts, for a six-month training program. "The girls—most of them around twenty—arrived here in the natty summer uniform of the Cadet Nurse Corps, a gray and white striped seersucker dress, crew hat with a red band, and black pumps. Senior-cadets wear two Maltese crosses, while junior cadets wear only one," reported *The Service Woman* magazine in January 1944. In an interesting note, the article added, "While in training . . . the girls will hold neither civilian nor military status, but will be treated in a manner accorded cadets at West Point Military Academy."[42]

Before recruitment was ended in mid-October 1945, a total of 169,443 students joined the Cadet Nurse Corps. When the program ended in 1948, 124,065 had graduated from 1,125 American nursing schools and 17,475 had served as Senior Cadets during the last months of the program. Not all of them chose to join the Army or Navy nurse corps, but they all contributed to the war effort by working in hospitals as students and by increasing the overall number of American graduate nurses. One example from the thousands of young women trained by the Cadet Crops program, Eleanor M. Lux, served in the first group of cadet nurses at Fort Devens, Massachusetts. Eleanor was in her senior year at Saint John's Hospital in Lowell when she became a cadet nurse. After basic training with Army nurses, she says, "I applied for a Navy commission and spent the six month's period as a Civil Service nurse at a neurosurgical hospital (army), Cushing General, in Framingham. I was commissioned an ensign in the Navy Nurse Corps in April 1945." She served at USNH Sampson, New York, and after the war in Chelsea, Massachusetts, on a transport, and at various Navy hospitals in California before marrying Dr. Hal DeMay, a pathologist, in 1953.[43]

The U.S. Cadet Nurse Corps included African-American students and had a positive effect on encouraging young black women to enter the nursing profession. In fact, federal scholarships provided by the U.S. Cadet Nurse Corps program enabled the enrollment of black nursing students to rise from 10.9 percent of all students in nursing schools admitting black students to 22 percent by 1944. This figure represented about 2,000 black nursing students, the vast majority of them studying at twenty black institutions. The remainder, about 400 students, were attending some forty-two white nursing schools. Because experts predicted that the field of nursing would expand rapidly after the war, especially in the areas of public health nursing, rehabilitation, and education/administration, the availability of scholarships through the Cadet Corps program was of particular value to young black women, who very often did not have the financial resources to pursue a nursing education.[44]

World War II also brought changes to the Army Nurse Corps with respect to the acceptance and employment of African-American nurses. From its inception in 1901, the Army Nurse Corps had been an all-white institution, but when the U.S. Army began a program of rapid expansion in 1940 that necessitated an increase in the size of the Army Nurse Corps, the War Department steadfastly clung to its official policy of racial segregation and continued that policy during World War II despite protests from black leaders and black soldiers. Army officials justified this policy, insisting that the Army was a servant of the state, not an agent of change, and that the most efficient system of race relations would be one modeled after the constitutional ruling of "separate but equal." This policy meant that, in the Army, facilities for blacks and whites would be kept separate, although as historians have pointed out, not always "equal." Nor was the segregated Army efficient or cost effective. Black soldiers were organized into black units, often with white officers, and almost always with separate facilities.[45]

In 1940 the Army Nurse Corps remained an all-white organization. At first the recruitment of African-American nurses was discouraged, but in 1940-41 black organizations put pressure on Congress and on the White House for a change in recruiting policy. The campaign to open the ranks of the Army Nurse Corps to black nurses was led by Mabel Keaton Staupers, RN, the National Association of Colored Graduate Nurses's (NACGN) representative on the National Nursing Council. Politically astute and very determined, Staupers also created the NACGN National Defense Council, with representatives from every region of the country. In October 1940, after a private meeting with Maj. Julia Stimson, she arranged for the council to discuss the future of black nurses in the U.S. Army with Army Surgeon General James C. Magee. Despite the black nurses' position that assigning black personnel to separate black wards was segregation and despite their insistence that exclusion of black nurses from the military was discriminatory, the surgeon general would not rescind his policy. Staupers and other black leaders then took their case to President Roosevelt, saying, "We have prepared ourselves and many of us are holding responsible executive positions, and can see no reason why we should be denied service in the Army Corps."[46]

Enlisting the support of Mary Beth Bethune, First Lady Eleanor Roosevelt, and others, Staupers convinced the surgeon general to accept a quota of forty-eight African-American nurses to be commissioned into the Army Nurse Corps. The quota was only a temporary compromise, for Staupers and others wanted the armed forces opened to African-Americans without a quota system. Over the course of the war, Staupers sent numerous letters to black newspapers objecting to the Army's quota system for black personnel and organized protests and meetings between white and black nursing leaders in an attempt to integrate the Army and Navy nurse corps. [47]

The original quota group of forty-eight women was divided. Twenty-four nurses went to Fort Bragg, North Carolina, and twenty-four to Camp Livingston, Louisiana. When Camp Livingston closed, the unit serving there was dispersed to Fort Bragg and Fort Huachuca, Arizona. These first black Army nurses were graduates of recognized nursing schools and hospitals all over the

United States, including Kansas City General Hospital No. 2, which had the largest number of the original quota of nurses; Provident Hospital, Chicago; Provident Hospital, Baltimore; Lincoln School of Nursing and Harlem Hospital, New York; Freedman's Hospital, Washington, D.C.; and others.

Esther Allen was one of the first black nurses to join the Army Nurse Corps in 1941. "I was working at a hospital on Staten Island and was recruited by the Red Cross. At the time there were only two bases that accepted black nurses— Fort Bragg, North Carolina, and Camp Livingston, Louisiana, which was located twenty miles from Alexandria, Louisiana. I had never been in the South, so this was quite a cultural shock," she recalled. Esther says the nurses lived in a long wooden barracks building. "Each of us had a single room and bath," she told an interviewer, and a maid was assigned to their quarters. "Our wards were barracks that contained forty-four beds. All beds were lined up so that one could imagine a straight line. No bed was out of line. Once weekly our wards were inspected by the white hierarchy. Beware if he turned out to be a 2d Lt. (we called them shave tails and ninety-day wonders)!" The wards that the black nurses were in charge of always passed inspection. Camp Livingston was supposed to have separate, but equal, facilities for black troops and nurses. Allen remembers, "For recreation we had a Ping-Pong table, a record player and a tennis net. Every once in awhile we would send one of our so-called light skinned nurses over to the white nurses' quarters to see if they had anything we didn't."[48]

After the Pearl Harbor attack and America's entry into the war, the quota for African-American nurses was increased. By 1943, 160 black nurses were on active duty with the Army. Eventually over 100 served in hospitals in the continental United States and overseas in Warrington, England; with the 268th Station Hospital in the Southwest Pacific and in the Philippines; with the 338th and Twenty-fifth Station hospitals in the China-Burma-India theater; and with the Twenty-fifth Station Hospital in Liberia. African-American Army nurses also cared for prisoners of war in eight locations in the United States and served at the hospital at Tuskegee Army Air Field in Alabama. By 1944 the Army Nurse Corps included 250 black nurses, and according to Mary E. Carnegie, when the war ended "there were some 500 in the corps, including 9 captains and 115 first lieutenants. They were serving in 4 general, 3 regional, and 11 station hospitals in the United States and overseas."[49]

Prudence Burns Burrell was one of the first black nurses to volunteer for duty following the Pearl Harbor attack. A native of Mounds, Illinois, she received her training at Kansas City General Hospital No. 2 in Missouri. In the fall of 1942, Burrell, who had been working as a public health nurse and attending summer classes at the University of Minnesota School of Public Health, was asked by the Kansas City chapter of the American Red Cross to recruit African-American nurses. On October 20, 1942, she "recruited herself" and was appointed a second lieutenant in the Army Nurse Corps. After being processed at Fort

Leavenworth, she was assigned to Fort Huachuca, where two combat units of black troops, the Ninety-second and Ninety-third Infantry Divisions, were training.[50]

According to official policy, Fort Huachuca was segregated, which meant the Army had to set up two separate hospital facilities. Hospital No. 1 served African-American personnel and their families, and No. 2 cared for other military and civilian personnel. Black medical professionals were found to staff the medical and dental facilities at Fort Huachuca and the first group of black nurses arrived at the remote post in the southern Arizona mountains in July 1942. Nurse Lt. M. Aiken was already on duty at the new hospital when Lt. Susan Freeman and nine nurses reported or duty at Station Hospital No. 1. "That made eleven of us—and the hospital had 700 patients! But we plunged right in and worked like beavers," Susan Freeman said. She told an interviewer that after six months at Huachuca, "the situation is well in hand. . . . These are good girls, well-trained, and some of them have had excellent experience in hospitals of large bed capacity, and with modern facilities." Freeman, who grew up in Stratford, Connecticut, was the head nurse and superintendent at Freedman's Hospital before joining the Army in April 1941. She caused quite a stir at Camp Livingston when she was the first Army nurse on the post to be promoted to first lieutenant.[51]

By early 1943 there were 100 black nurses on duty at Fort Huachuca. "Some of the girls have come from public health work, some from private nursing, and some from work in small and large hospitals," Roy Wilkins wrote in an article. At Station Hospital No. 1, the nurses worked on the wards and in special departments of the hospital, and attended classes in X-ray, physical therapy, anesthesia, and chemical warfare. They also drilled twice a week on a parade ground near their mess hall. Barbara C. Calderon, who served at Fort Huachuca, found the post accommodations "clean, sparse, but comfortable." Elinor Powell Albert recalls that the nurses went through basic training at Fort Huachuca still wearing their civilian clothes, despite the Arizona heat and dust: "We wore civilian clothing until at long last we got our uniforms. I think the distribution was poor because the uniform was just changing from Red Cross nurses to ANC, others said it was because the 'black' army always got what was left."[52]

Although some of the nurses at Fort Huachuca resented the Army's treatment of African-American soldiers and nurses, others thoroughly enjoyed their experience. Lt. Nadine Davis Lane said, "I was ecstatic most of the time I served. The excitement, rumors and uncertainty of what was going to happen next kept me happy." She found army life stimulating, "There were all of the top physical and intellectual people going and coming whom one met and associated with all the time. What more could one ask? I met many of the 'elite' personalities from African-American society. Had a job I loved, danced, played tennis, bowled, rode horseback, golfed and was entertained by most of the the the 'big name bands' at our officer's club at Fort Huachuca. Stars from Hollywood dropped in anytime. I bumped into people from screen and radio at the officer's club any time."

Despite the amenities of life at army posts in the States, many black nurses were hoping to be sent overseas and one, Lt. Chrystalee Maxwell, said, "When I signed up in Los Angeles I asked for overseas duty. I think if our boys can go to the end of the earth to fight, we should go along and do what we can to make it easier for them. The sooner they send me the better." Octavia Tillman Card expressed slightly different reasons for joining the Army Nurse Corps in late 1944: "They [her family] knew I liked to travel and my last year of training had been paid by the U.S. Cadet Corps and I wanted to pay them back. It was a wonderful deal." Card had been visiting her friend Loretta at the time. She recalled, "We decided to join the ANC and went to the American Red Cross in Cincinnati and applied. We were accepted, but there were quotas and I had to go in from Michigan."[53]

Among the nurses assigned to Fort Huachuca was Frances Dyer Edwards, who joined the Army Nurse Corps in 1944 from Columbus, Ohio. Edwards also said that she signed up to go overseas, "but there was quota of African-American nurses at that time and [she] was not called." Instead, she was sent to Fort Huachuca for basic training. Edwards found the training "adequate" and the Arizona post comfortable by 1944. She writes, "Our living conditions were in barracks with 1 or 2 nurses in a room. The food served was well balanced and tasty. The post had an officer's club, tennis courts, movies, bowling alley, cleaning and pressing shop, post office, etc."[54]

The Army's segregation policy disturbed most of the nurses. Elinor Powell Albert, a tall native of Milton, Massachusetts, and graduate of Lincoln School for Nurses in New York, recalled, "I was not naive re: segregation and discrimination but going into a completely segregated situation was constantly a shock to me. I think I stayed angry most of my army career, even though the whole experience was interesting, maddening, frustrating, and even fun." Ellen Robinson Page, who joined the Army Nurse Corps in July 1942 after graduating from Phillips School of Nursing in St. Louis the previous year, found the army's facilities for black nurses "in most instances separate, but for the most part equal." She recalls that the nurses ran into evidence of racial discrimination most often in various cities in the United States, especially at eating places, but Page adds, "if we were not served at times the commander would take charge and make that restaurant off limits for all personnel."[55]

The army's segregation policy also affected white officers at Fort Huachuca. According to Elinor Albert, "It was then a black base with most of the commanding officers white and often low men on the white army totem pole. There was a small group of career American Indian soldiers who lived separately on the old post."

Like many of their fellow African-American nurses, Frances Dyer Edwards and Elinor Powell Albert also served during the war at camps in the United States that housed enemy prisoners of war. According to Elinor Albert, "When the black troops (92nd and 93rd) moved out to go to Italy the nurses were brought together by the C.O. and told that the nurses were going to be shipped to POW camps since there had been too much fraternization between POWs and the white nurses who had been stationed there."

Albert was sent to a POW camp in Florence, Arizona, which had formerly housed Italian prisoners now being repatriated. She recalls, "We had Germans as young as 15. All other personnel on the post were Americans—white officers and enlisted. There were no more than 20-30 nurses there. We were very isolated, with little or no social life—occasionally we travelled to Tuscon, to Phoenix, and back to Fort Huachuca." The Florence camp holds special memories for Albert, who met and later married one of the German prisoners interned there.[56]

The relationship between the nurses and prisoners at POW camps was often an amiable one, despite the language barrier. Frances Edwards believes that the language barrier was overcome by using English-speaking intepreters on the wards. At the POW camp in Ogden, Utah, the prisoners and the nurses even shared the same dining room, "at different tables, of course."[57]

The relationship between white U.S. Army officers and African-American nurses, however, was not always amiable. Many black nurses serving at army posts in the United States experienced racial discrimination right along with the usual rigors of army discipline. For example, at Camp Rupert in Idaho the nurses dined in an integrated mess with white officers. "The C.O. was angry to have to sit with us and said so. I also told him how unhappy I was to have to be there," says Elinor Albert. Sharing facilities with white officers became a source of anger and discontent at other army posts. Barbara C. Calderon, who joined the Army Nurse Corps in December 1942, recalled "the humiliation of not being able to go to the officers club at San Luis Obispo." Another nurse remembers that the commanding officer of Camp Rupert in Idaho treated the nurses worse than he treated the prisoners. For example, she says the prisoners were allowed to walk or loll on the grass, but when the black nurses crossed the lawn the commanding officer would be on the P.A. system to order them off the grass. He also called one nurse into his office repeatedly and once when she was leaving she overhead him say to his secretary, "That's one of those smart niggers. When I see these black she-apes in officers' uniforms it makes me so mad I could puke."[58]

Sadly, racial prejudice was not confined to Army personnel but was shared by some civilians. Barbara Calderon recalls "the hate spewed at [her] by two white civilians while [she was] waiting to board a commuter train for San Francisco." African-American nurses endured these insults and more subtle forms of racial discrimination and in many cases made the best of a poor situation. They took pride in their profession and most of them accepted even the assignment of nursing prisoners of war with grace and dedication. Although nursing POWs was not considered prestigious duty by many nurses, it did have its rewards. Octavia Tillman Card, who served at two such posts, Camp Rupert, Idaho, and Camp Ogden,

Utah, remembers especially the talent of some of the prisoners: one day, "while making rounds on my unit in the station hospital I was presented with a pencil sketch of me and the staff by a patient lying on the other side of the room, it was detailed and the likeness of us was almost like a snapshot." One of the other prisoners was allowed to build a replica of his hometown complete "with miniature buildings, windmills, and etc. I snapped a picture of this scene."[59] On the other hand, the medical treatment given prisoners at some camps was less than ideal. One nurse candidly admitted that the doctors, draftees who lacked practise and experience, were known to order procedures "which would never be ordered in a civilian hospital."

Nursing POWs in the United States and in England was often done by black nurses, but the policy proved controversial. The NACGH received reports of racial discrimination on army posts and became more concerned about equal opportunity for black nurses when they learned that the 168th Station Hospital in England was caring exclusively for POWs. Mabel Staupers also heard from dissatisfied black nurses. One nurse complained, "There is some kind of recreation on the post for everyone but us—Thus every night week after week, and month after month we sit and stare at each other. It is not a normal life for anyone, after spending eight and half hours with the Germans every day." She was especially bitter about the exclusion of black nurses from a reception being given for the new post commander: "It is a command affair and every officer, besides being urged to attend, was given an invitation. That is, all the officers on the post but the five Negro nurses." Staupers took their concerns to Eleanor Roosevelt in November and the first lady expressed her sympathy, but made no promises regarding the Army's policy of assigning the nurses to prison camps. Although there is some evidence that conditions at these camps improved in 1945, black nurses continued to nurse prisoners for the remainder of the war.[60]

Many black nurses also volunteered to go overseas, but after the Pearl Harbor attack and U.S. entry into the war, the Army sent nurse complements to only three hospitals overseas. Back home in the United States, December 7 brought blackouts, rationing, and other changes. Esther Allen remembered, "After the Pearl Harbor attack there were many changes. The base was closed to everyone but military personnel who had to be in uniform at all times, and civilian employees. Once a week all lights were turned off at night at the base and one lonely plane would fly over to check us out." Allen explains that Camp Livingston was a base for training soldiers and for maneuvers, so it did not receive any battle casualties. Many black troops passed through Livingston during the war. Allen says, "I am proud to say that the black soldiers were a joy to watch. Every uniform was immaculate—no wrinkles or tears. When they marched every knee bent at the same time. Lines were straight and no soldier was out of line. When the trainees were transferred, the area where they lived was clean—not even a cigarette butt on the ground."

Entertainment at these army camps was often limited, so the nurses "socialized with one another, went to post movies, cooked in the barracks often." In Idaho, Octavia Card even had her own garden. She read a lot and learned to knit and crochet. "A black unit of soldiers stopped by in Idaho and we conversed with them," she adds. They also enjoyed a visit from the Harlem Globetrotters and were able to visit a Red Cross canteen in Utah and meet the civilians who came there. "Some of the folks remained friends and kept in touch until their deaths," Card recalls fondly. Many of the women made the best of a difficult situation. Elinor Albert says, "I think most of us nurses had good memories of Fort Huachuca, even with segregation—we had a terrific social life since we were so outnumbered by many eligible male officers. We did work long hours then [twelve-hour shifts], but we were young and life was a great adventure."[61]

By the summer of 1944, 225 black nurses were serving with the Army Nurse Corps, and at the time active recruitment for the Corps was discontinued, 440 black nurses were on duty. Many of these African-American Army nurses were graduates of the nation's all-black nursing schools, which during World War II enjoyed a dramatic increase in enrollments. For example, Freedmen's Hospital in Washington enrolled seventy-seven black students in 1939 and 166 students in 1944. According to the *American Journal of Nursing*, "this rapid expansion of the student body is repeated in other Negro nursing schools throughout the country. Only the wartime difficulties of securing adequately prepared instructors and supervisors, as well as housing and clinical facilities, have prevented Negro enrollment from climbing still higher."[62]

Despite positive publicity and active recruiting campaigns to motivate civilian nurses to volunteer for the Army Nurse Corps, by late 1944 the Army was some 8,000 nurses short of its authorized strength of 50,000 nurses. This, combined with the sudden increase in casualties from the fighting on Leyte in the Philippines and during the Battle of the Bulge in Europe, presented the Army Nurse Corps superintendent with a dilemna. She and the Army surgeon general had opposed national selective service earlier in the war, but in September 1944 Colonel Blanchfield wrote to 27,000 nurses classified as eligible for military service but received only 700 replies, "less than a third of the respondents qualified for or able to join the Corps." This survey prompted the Army to assume responsibility of a stepped-up nurse recruiting program that included the assignment of army nurses to Red Cross recruitment committees in key American cities. The Red Cross, in turn, gave up its "former right to distribution of Army [recruiting] material for national coverage" to the Office of War Information, and the Army Nurse Corps made plans for a major recruiting campaign in February.[63]

Meanwhile, American newspapers learned about the nurse shortage and one columnist in particular, Walter Lippmann, brought the problem to the attention of millions of Americans when he wrote a column entitled "American Women and Our Wounded Men." Lippmann told the public, in "military hospitals at home and abroad our men are not receiving the nursing care they must have" and he predicted that with casualties increasing in number and in seriousness, the recovery of many American wounded might be delayed "or even jeopardized." Lippmann blamed the lack of volunteer response on the "combined financial and institutional and what might be called professional trade union pressures upon women to prefer civilian to military service." When the secretary of war read this article and was assured Lippmann had gotten his facts from Gen. Norman T. Kirk and the situation was indeed "nearly hopeless," he decided to request legislation to draft women for military nursing. The proposal was prepared by Col. John R. Hall and Goldwathwaite Dorr, special assistant to the secretary of war, and submitted to the undersecretary of war the day after Christmas 1944.[64]

In his State of the Union message on January 6, 1945, President Roosevelt shocked many Americans by referring to a shortage of Army and Navy nurses. Roosevelt told his audience that the Army had tried to recruit an additional 10,000 nurses but "the net gain in eight months has been only 2,000. There are now 42,000 nurses in the Army Nurse Corps." These figures came as no surprise to Army Nurse Corps officials, but FDR's explanation of the shortage surprised and horrified many Army nurses, especially those in recruiting. He said, "The present shortage of army nurses is reflected in the undue strain on the existing force. More than a thousand nurses are now hospitalized and part of this is due to overwork." Adding insult to injury, FDR went on to tell the American public that Army hospitals were being sent overseas "without a nurse complement" and cited statistics reporting that in the United States the nurse-to-bed ratio had risen from one nurse for every fifteen hospital beds to one nurse for every twenty beds.

The president concluded this part of his speech with a well-meaning, but ill-advised attempt to shame civilian nurses into volunteering: "It is tragic that the gallant women who have volunteered for service as nurses should be overworked. It is tragic that our wounded men should ever want for the best nursing care." Roosevelt then informed the public that 280,000 women were registered nurses practicing in the country and that the War Manpower Commission estimated 27,000 could be made available for the military without interfering too much with civilian nursing needs. He urged the Selective Service Act be amended to "provide for the induction of nurses into the armed forces" and concluded, "The need is too pressing to await the outcome of further efforts at recruiting."[65]

Roosevelt's speech might have been warmly received by the Army Nurse Corps, but it gave the public the impression that nurses "were failing the wounded" and refusing to "nurse the sick" and volunteer for service. Rather than being a blessing, the message created a nightmare for the Army Nurse Corps director's office. Edith Aynes and Evelyn Blewett decided to meet the adverse publicity and what Aynes called the "untrue grapevine rumoring" head on. They called the editor of the *Saturday Evening Post* to urge him to write an article refuting misimpressions of nurse recruitment. He refused, saying that "he was afraid his paper supply might be cut off if he criticized the President's request for a draft," but he volunteered to write an editorial about the problem. On April 25, 1945, the editorial finally appeared, criticizing the War Department for failing to appropriate sufficient funds and personnel for nurse recruitment and then "implying through its demand for a draft that the voluntary system has failed." Using Francis Bolton's words, the editorial then praised American nurses for volunteering for military service in "numbers far beyond the record of any other group." The editorial urged the American public to ask why nurses had been "prematurely singled out for conscription" when women war workers, WAVES, WACS, SPARS, and Women Marines had not been included in the draft proposals.[66]

In the meantime, Rep. Andrew J. May of Kentucky had introduced a bill into the House of Representatives on January 9, 1945, calling for an amendment to the Selective Service Act of 1940. HR 1284 provided for registration, selection, and induction of every nurse between the ages of 18 and 45 who was registered in the practice of nursing by any state or United States territory.[67]

On January 15, 1945, the American Nursing Association's (ANA) Advisory Council met and endorsed the "principle of a draft of nurses as a first step to selective service for all women." When the House Committee on Military Affairs held hearings on the draft legislation, ANA representatives testified before the committee and interpreted ANA policy to the congressmen present. Before testifying they had consulted representatives of the Army Nurse Corps, Navy Nurse Corps, Red Cross Nursing Service, and other government agencies "in order that they might have an up-to-date picture of the nursing situation."[68]

Katherine J. Densford, president of the ANA, testified for an hour on February 13 and at the close of the hearings the committee asked Representative May to reintroduce a new bill with the amendments proposed by the hearings. They included provisions to draft only unmarried women between the ages of twenty and forty-five and draft not only registered nurses but nursing school graduates who were eligible for registration. The new bill (HR 2277) also provided that qualified graduates of the U.S. Cadet Nurse Corps be inducted first, but that Veteran Administration (VA) nurses and others declared essential not be inducted except on release from the VA or from the Procurement and Assignment service.[69]

In mid-March HR 2277 was debated on the floor of the House of Representatives. During discussion of the bill, Representative Charles R. Clason raised the important issue of the supply of male nurses and black nurses. Clason referred to the earlier testimony of Katherine Densford that the Army had enlisted 2,000 male nurses as corpsmen and agreed with her that male nurses should be given commissions as officers and "be permitted to act as nurses just the same as women nurses." He hoped that an amendment could be made to the bill allowing the Army to use male nurses as nurses and then raised the issue of the employment of black nurses, "a matter of great interest to many Americans."

Mabel Staupers had already broached the issue of employing more African-American nurses with Army Surgeon General Norman T. Kirk at a gathering in early January at the Hotel Pierre in New York. Responding to Kirk's announcement that the Army might have to draft nurses, Staupers said, "Of 9,000 registered Negro nurses the Army has taken 247, the Navy takes none." Kirk tried to justify the army's policy by saying that "the average share of colored nurses in the Army is equal to to the total number of Negro troops," but as nursing historians Philip Kalisch and Beatrice Kalisch have argued, the health of the African-American community might have been jeopardized if 10 percent of its nurses had joined the military. Nonethless, the proposed draft set off an outpouring of protest from the black community and on January 20, 1945, Surgeon General Kirk announced an end to the quota system and five days later the Navy Nurse Corps was authorized to accept black nurses.[70]

In the House debate on HR 2277, Rep. George Schwabe of Oklahoma pointed out that the Army had commissioned only 330 of the 9,000 available black nurses and said, "It is unthinkable that the services of these people are not being used." Representative Clason echoed these sentiments and hoped that "the Army and Navy would commission all qualified colored nurses who applied." In addition, he referred to testimony that black nurses who volunteered or were drafted would not be discriminated against.

The debate on draft legislation for nurses engendered some opposition. Schwabe argued that the "same tactics and language" were being used to draft nurses that the Army had employed in trying to pass legislation to draft labor. He argued that HR 2277 was possibly "only another step toward the drafting of all American women for some form of service under bureaucratic dictation and regimentation." Schwabe was adamant that the principle of free labor was being threatened and warned that "drafted nurses will not perform the same service with as much interest and sympathy and effectiveness as nurses who volunteer their services." He further warned that the sacredness of the home "will be seriously impaired" and that the people's morale would be shocked if the United States went from the volunteer system of obtaining nurses to conscription.

Despite these valid concerns, which seriously threatened the longstanding volunteer tradition of the Army Nurse Corps, on March 7, 1945, the House passed HR 2277 and passed it on to the Senate. Another round of testimony followed and the Senate bill was also amended to include exemptions for any woman taking theological or religious training for the purpose of devoting her life to religious service. The clause pertaining to exemptions for women who were married before March 15, 1943, was deleted and the wording on a clause about male nurses was clarified. However, when the Senate finally brought HR 2277 to a vote on April 9, no action was taken. A month later, Germany surrendered to Allied armies. V-E Day took the pressure off the Army Nurse Corps to recruit more nurses, and when HR 2277 again came up on the Senate calendar it was passed over. Acting Secretary of War Robert P. Patterson suggested no further action be taken on the bill. The surgeon general concurred and wrote Densford on May 30, 1945, "Since no procurement of nurses from other sources other than the Cadet Nurse Corps will be necessary at the time, it is suggested that your Association now terminate its efforts to procure nurses for the Army."[71]

Although the United States remained at war with Japan, the War Department did not renew efforts to draft nurses, but the so-called nurse shortage did effect the Army Nurse Corps by prompting the Army to assume responsibility for nurse recruiting from the American Red Cross. The seriousness of this nurse shortage remains debatable. Official sources suggest the number of American nurses available for military service was sufficient to fill this gap, but the War Manpower Commission had classified almost all the nurses in civilian jobs as essential to the war effort. This disqualified many civilian nurses who might have been convinced to volunteer for the Army Nurse Corps. The shortage was also the result of the Red Cross's inability to recruit enough nurses, despite the authorized ceiling for the Army Nurse Corps, which rose to 55,000 in January 1945 to 60,000 by February 6, 1945. The Red Cross had appointed only 2,229 nurses from June to December 1944.

The proposed draft legislation, coupled with the publicity campaign about the need for more nurses, did result in an increase in volunteering, but even with the increase the official total of Army nurses never reached the authorized ceiling of 60,000. On V-E Day it stood at 57,000, but in the summer of 1945 Colonel Blanchfield estimated that with 56,000 Army nurses, 4,800 Cadet nurses, 1,700 civilian registered graduate nurses, 1,000 nurses' aides, 4,000 WAC medical technicians and 5,000 enlisted men on the rolls, there was sufficient medical personnel to support an army of twelve million. Furthermore, the end of the war in Europe had reduced the need for nurses in the ETO and removed much of the sense of urgency that had motivated HR 2277. The end of the war in Europe even prompted the Army to decrease the number of nurses; by December 1945, 27,000 Army nurses had been discharged.[72]

With the demise of HR 2277, the principle of volunteer service for American nurses was vindicated. What one article called the luster of the "magnificent record" of 81,145 nurses who volunteered for military service and were certified between Pearl Harbor and January 1, 1945, was not "dimmed by any slackening of effort." The time-honored American emphasis on the moral obligation to serve, what the early Republic called "public virtue," was once again preserved.

However, the issue of providing nursing care for American soldiers and sailors could have become a serious one if the war in the Pacific had not ended in August 1945. If American armed forces had invaded the Japanese home islands, American casualties would have demanded a high level of medical support, including a large number of Army and Navy nurses both in the Pacific and back in

the United States. A Japanese invasion or combat operations to compel the surrender of Japanese troops in China would have required thousands of nurses.
While some might have been transferred to the Pacific theater from Europe, most
nurses in the ETO were war weary and not anxious to see further overseas duty.
The Army could have ordered nurses from the ETO and CBI to hospitals in the
Pacific, but the nurses' noneffective rate would probably have increased. Clearly
nurses to care for the "Olympic" casualties would have to come from new recruits
or from those nurses who had not already served overseas. Some of the recruits
could have come from the Cadet Nurse Corps graduates, 10,000 of whom had
applied for service with the army by October 1, 1945. But cadet nurse graduates
might not have been enough to fill the vacancies and provide nursing care to
civilians at home and to soldiers recovering in VA hospitals. Another 9,000 qualified African-American nurses were reported to be willing to join the Army Nurse
Corps and serve wherever needed, but their existence and willingess to serve was
not taken into account by the War Department when draft legislation was composed in December 1944. Furthermore, President Roosevelt's dramatic State of
the Union speech ignored the availability of black nurses for service and offended
many of these women and others in the African-American community, who felt
their services and qualifications were being deliberately dismissed. Thus, while
legislation to draft nurses was never passed and signed into law, the debate over a
nurse shortage and the War Department's reluctance to accept black nurses became what historian Darlene Clark-Hine has described as a "catalyst in the struggle,
bringing support and sympathy from both white and black Americans which
ended the quota system and opened both nurse corps to African-Americans."
Only the end of the war in Europe and the dropping of the atomic bomb on
Japan in August 1945 spared the nation from further debate on proposals for
national draft legislation for nurses.[73]

9

PEACE AT LAST!

Demobilizing the Corps

 Although Army nurses remained on duty in the Pacific after the Japanese surrender, V-J Day brought the Army Nurse Corps' World War II experience to a close. All the challenges of the next few months—demobilization, the return of soldiers and sailors to the United States in Operation "Magic Carpet," the occupation of Germany and Japan—belong to the Army Nurse Corps' postwar story. In August 1945, when the Japanese government accepted the terms of unconditional surrender, over 57,000 nurses were serving with the Army Nurse Corps, well over twice the number participating in World War I. During World War II, Army nurses traveled to every theater of the war to help staff army hospitals, dispensaries, and hospital trains, ships, and medical air evacuation squadrons. Two hundred and one Army nurses died in World War II, sixteen of them from enemy action. Another 1,600 were decorated for meritorious service. When their active service came to an end, most Army nurses returned to civilian life: by September 30, 1946, only 8,500 remained in the Army Nurse Corps. Among them was 1st Lt. Agnes C. Rosele, the first Army Reserve nurse to join the Army Nurse Corps in 1940. A second lieutenant in 1940, Agnes served at Walter Reed Army Hospital and at the station hospital at Camp Wheeler before joining the Ninety-second Evacuation Hospital, 108th Station Hospital, and Fifty-first General in the Southwest Pacific theater. She was promoted to first lieutenant on October 8, 1943, and remained on active duty in the postwar period, rising to the rank of captain in 1948 and retiring from active duty in 1950. Agnes Rosele's career was a typical one for Army Nurse Corps nurses. She graduated from nursing school just prior to the war, was in the first reserve in 1940, and went on active duty for the duration of the war. After V-J Day, Rosele chose to make the Army a career, serving at Valley Forge General Hospital and Letterman General in California.[1]

Other Army nurses left the service after the war to marry and raise families and/or pursue civilian nursing opportunities. A survey of Army nurses conducted in 1945 by the American Nurses' Association found that 17 percent of the respondents wanted to remain in the military. Of the 5,000 questionnaires tabulated by October 1945, 73 percent said they expected to remain in nursing upon release from the service. Of these nurses only 3 percent were regular army nurses, but the greatest percentage (41 percent) had been in the army for at least two years. Their average age was 28.5 years. Only a small fraction of the respondents were married and those who had husbands in the service said they would ask for release when their spouses were discharged.[2]

Thousands of former Army nurses took advantage of veterans' benefits allotted them and many attended colleges and universities under the G.I. Bill. In an article in the *American Journal of Nursing* in 1946, Mary Walker Randolph, RN, attempted to explain to the civilian community the concerns and expectations of Army nurses returning to civilian life. As a veteran Army nurse who had served in both the Mediterranean and European theaters, Lieutenant Randolph said, "The nurses of the armed forces hope, pray, and expect that the civilians will greet them with understanding, sympathy, and the spirit of helpfulness to get them back to a normal life."

To assist them in that task, Mary Randolph then tried to define a "veteran nurse." Her comments, made just after World War II ended, are a valuable summary of the experience of Army and Navy nurses during that conflict, written by a nurse who had served for three and one-half years in overseas assignments. Lieutenant Randolph spoke of the similarities of the Army nursing experience saying: "They ate the same food, and will therefore like ice-cream and green salads in the same proportion that they dislike Spam and dehydrated potatoes. They lived the same camp life; a helmet makes a good basin in France or in Leyte. They suffered the same homesickness for the American way of doing things and experienced the same broadening effect of travelling in foreign countries. These things seem to have made more impression upon the Army nurse than the difference in climate or the enemy she faced."[3]

The differences in nurses' World War II experiences were a factor of age, the length of time of service overseas, and the type of hospital in which they served. Mary Randolph predicted that Army nurses who served in field or evacuation hospitals were likely to experience the greatest difficulty adjusting to civilian life, for they had lived and worked in small units with fewer rules and regulations and "had developed, therefore, a sense of independence and initiative which is not typical of the traditional nurse. All this makes this group more weary, more restless, and will make their readjustment more difficult." She felt that nurses who worked in general hospitals where the routine was similar to civilian hospitals, would "settle back into civilian nursing more easily than the field nurse."

Nurses of different ages faced different problems returning to the civilian world. If returning Army nurses were older, they might be tempted to find a nursing job that was less strenuous than their old one; if they were younger, they would be interested in preparing for "broader and better positions" in civilian nursing. And in her opinion, the time a nurse spent overseas would have a profound impact on her attitudes and ability to readjust to life in the United States. After only a year, nurses serving overseas were still enjoying the "adventure, excitement, and enthusiasm" of their assignments, but after two years many were bored and war weary. "Most nurses got a 'second wind' during their third year, but not an American wind. The jokes about being 'naturalized' when returning to the 'old country' had more than a trace of tears. The abnormal life began to seem normal. For those overseas so long, adjustment will be more difficult," Randolph cautioned her readers.[4]

What did Army nurses expect upon their return from overseas duty? Randolph felt that, first of all, they needed time to recuperate from the stress and hectic schedules of field duty and nursing wounded young men—to recover from "the nervous tension and fatigue built up by life in a foxhole and under shell fire." Returning nurses also needed time to get back in touch with American life, to catch up with family and friends, and to enjoy some of the luxuries they missed while in the Army—"a silk nightgown, a bathroom (with plumbing that works), an ice cream soda, and maybe a red dress." With those items attended to—time, rest, and some luxuries—the Army nurse would turn her attention to her next job. Randolph predicted that returning nurses would have greater expectations for their careers in terms of pay and time off. Overseas duty had given many nurses a new view about finances and the value of money. While on duty outside the United States, nurses' obligations at home were covered by their allotments, allowing them to spend their paychecks overseas freely. As civilians, many would also have to adjust to civilian pay scales, which were often less than the generous $166 a month base pay of an Army nurse, to which the military added a 5 percent pay increase after three years and food and housing allowances. Beyond these basic considerations, Randolph felt that many veteran nurses who had enjoyed an active social life overseas would be carefully considering new jobs that allowed them "more life outside their working hours." And lastly, she expected many returning nurses to defer returning to civilian life in order to continue enjoying the benefits, security, and salary of Army life.[5]

For those nurses who chose an Army career, the postwar era provided new opportunities and permanent status as part of the U.S. Army. The Army opened the doors of some of its schools to nurses after World War II. For example, in June 1946, the Army began offering a twenty-six-week program in psychiatric nursing at Brooke Army Medical Center at Fort Sam Houston, Texas. Army nurses were sent to similar courses at St. Elizabeth's Hospital in Washington, D.C. The need for psychiatric nurses during World War II, and the experience and training given Army nurses informally during the war, set a precedent that encouraged the Army to initiate formal instruction in clinical nursing procedures throughout the armed forces after the war. Following the establishment of this course, the Army introduced a fifty-six-week course in anesthesiology for nurses at four hospitals: Brooke Army, Fitzsimmons General, Letterman General, and Walter Reed. The extensive course featured forty weeks of study at an Army hospital and eight weeks in an approved civilian hospital for clinical experience. This course prepared the nurse for the examination to become a certified Nurse Anesthetist. Courses were also established in 1947 in operating room techniques. All of these specialties were similar to those performed throughout the war, especially in field and evacuation hospitals, where nurses proved under the demands of the wartime that they were capable of specialized nursing.[6]

In this postwar period the Army Nurse Corps also secured important gains in its status within the Army. The Eightieth Congress passed legislation in 1947 creating the Army Nurse Corps in the Medical Department of the Regular Army with an authorized strength of not less than 2,558. The Army-Navy Nurses Act of 1947 gave the nurses permanant commissioned-officer status in grades of second lieutenant through lieutenant colonel and made the chief of the Army Nurse Corps a colonel. Congress also established an Army Nurse Corps section of the Officer's Reserve Corps, and active-duty Army nurses who had held relative rank in the ANC were appointed in appropriate permanent grades. Reserve nurses were also given the opportunity to apply for appointment in the regular army and 492 reserve nurses chose to become members of the Corps. On June 19, 1947, Col. Florence Blanchfield was given the serial number N-1 and commissioned in the permanent grade of lieutenant colonel in the regular army. She thus became the first woman to hold a permanent commission in the U.S. Army.

The U.S. Army Nurse Corps had entered World War II in 1941 with a strong tradition of dedication and service reaching back to the female nurses who tended the wounded in George Washington's Continental Army in 1775. In the century and a half that followed the War of Independence, female nurses had played an important role tending the sick and wounded on America's battlefields and on hospital ships and in army camps. The Army Nurse Corps considered their courage and dedication a legacy when the Nurse Corps was established in 1901 as the first nursing service in the U.S. military. From those early days, through the First World War and in the interwar period, the Army Nurse Corps continued to train and employ graduate professional nurses with, but not in, the U.S. Army. On the eve of the Second World War, the Army Nurse Corps' tradition of being an all-volunteer cadre of white, unmarried, female graduate nurses drawn from the registry of the American Red Cross Nursing Service remained intact.

The rapid expansion of the U.S. Army in World War II and the demands of both civilian and military wartime nursing profoundly affected the Army Nurse Corps and strained its traditions to the limit. In some important respects the Corps upheld its prewar traditions during WW II; in other cases, the war modified those traditions, including the original composition of the Corps, the status and rank of Army nurses, and the way nurses were recruited and trained.

Unlike most American men who served in World War II, Army nurses were not draftees but willing volunteers. They entered the Army Nurse Corps for a variety of reasons—patriotism, to make a contribution to the war effort, to travel and seek adventure, to prove themselves to family and friends. Unlike the uniformed women in the other services—the WACs, WAVES, SPARS, and Women Marines—Army nurses entered the service as career professionals and as graduates of nursing schools with credentials and standards. This gave the Army Nurse Corps a uniformity not enjoyed by the other women's reserves, which tried to attract women with civilian skills, but which by necessity had to enlist women from many different backgrounds with a wide variety of skills and education.

Army nurses also came from an established civilian profession. By 1940 American nurses had a distinct identity and a well-defined place in American society. Nursing was an accepted career for young women and a field in which women had long held leadership positions. American women who joined the Women's Reserves in WW II entered a patriarchal military hierarchy and culture that had officially excluded women except in the roles of wives, girlfriends, and mothers, or occasionally, as in World War I, as noncombat personnel. The role of uniformed women in this all-male world was by no means obvious, and military women fought long and hard to be accepted by their male colleagues and commanders. Although Army nurses also had to struggle to gain recognition from male doctors and medical corps officers and to prove their worth in the field, at least they had a military and nursing tradition from which to draw strength and guidance.

World War II Army nurses' status as officers differentiated them from their female counterparts in the WAC, WAVES, SPARS, and Women Marines, which were organized in a traditional military hierarchy, with some women selected as leaders and given officers' commissions and the majority ranked as enlisted women. Officer status not only gave all Army nurses certain privileges, like access to officers' clubs, but helped to define nurses as a group in the military hierarchy. By their designated role in Army hospitals as the supervisors and often instructors of enlisted men, Army nurses assumed positions of leadership. Yet in the chain of command they were accountable to male medical officers who constituted the hospital or unit's commanding officers and to male physicians. Female physicians were not accepted into the Army until later in the war. This place in the hierarchy was similar to that in civilian hospitals, where the chief administrators were usually, if not always, men. Army nurses had, in other words, a "niche" in the Army medical structure similar to the one they had in civilian life. This as a rule was different from the WACs, WAVES, or SPARS, who sometimes found themselves in the position of giving orders to enlisted men, a responsibility most women had not had in American civilian society in the 1930s and early 1940s.

At the same time, Army Nurse Corps nurses were part of the U.S. Army Medical Department, which has been seen over the years by many historians and military men as a separate and sometimes inferior branch of the Army—"a service within a service." The careers of Army medical officers were distinct from their colleagues in the infantry, artillery, or armored branches, or even in the more specialized branches like the Signal or Engineer corps. The officers who rose to leadership positions in the medical corps were physicians with highly specialized training that set them apart from the products of the U.S. Military Academy at West Point, Officer Candidates' Schools, or the nation's numerous ROTC programs. Medical officers and nurses were in a very real sense, "of" but not "in" the U.S. Army and this fact distinguished the participation of Army nurses from that of their fellow servicewomen in the other women's reserves.

Another aspect of the Army nurses' role within the military structure reflected the noncombat nature of Army medical personnel, who did not carry weapons and were not considered "warriors," but healers and health care providers. Army nurses fit neatly into this military category because women in American society were not viewed as warriors, but as nurturers and healers. Although many nurses in World War II found themselves under enemy fire in situations resembling combat, the Army did not classify them (nor did the public see them) as combat personnel, so the issue of women in combat was deferred to another era. Their presence near the frontlines was questioned early in the war, but those questions were quickly resolved when the nurses proved they could cope effectively with the stresses and dangers of field duty. The reports of commanding officers and chief nurses attest time and again to the courage, determination, and coolness of U.S. Army nurses under fire. The example of sixty-six Army nurses who survived three years in Japanese prison camps while continuing to nurse their fellow prisoners confirms the stability and dedication of military women in the most trying of circumstances.

World War II provided American society and the U.S. military with the best example up until that time of the large-scale employment of women in the military. Approximately 350,000 American women served in the U.S. armed forces during the war, about 60,000 of them as Army nurses and another 14,000 as Navy nurses. Although military nurses composed less than one-fifth of all women in the military in WW II, their contribution was highly visible, well publicized, and considered by most Americans as vitally necessary to the war effort. WACs, WAVEs, SPARS, and Women Marines may have "freed a man to fight," but Army and Navy nurses were part of the team from the beginning. The comment of one historian about the Pearl Harbor attack seems appropriate for the war in general: "The first step on the 'Road to Tokyo' [or Berlin] was with the aid of crutches and wheelchairs." Binding up the nation's wounded servicemen and nursing our G.I.s and sailors back to health was absolutely essential to the war effort, both from the standpoint of morale and from that of manpower.[7]

The necessity of employing female nurses to care for the nation's wounded and ill servicemen was not debated in World War II, but the demands of wartime compelled the Army Nurse Corps to reconsider several of its cherished traditions.

The first tradition to fall to wartime necessity was the Army's policy of accepting only unmarried women. In late 1942 the Army Nurse Corps began accepting married women for active duty, a policy change that the Navy Nurse Corps postponed for years. Other major nursing issues included the question of whether African-American women would be accepted and recruited by the military, whether male nurses would be included in both nurse corps, and whether sufficient numbers of nurses could be recruited on a volunteer basis or would have to be drafted.

Ironically, qualified black nurses and male nurses were eager to join the Army and Navy nurse corps, but the military was reluctant to accept black nurses and never accepted males. By 1945 only about 500 black nurses had been accepted. The Army Nurse Corps and the War Department refused to include male nurses in the ranks of the all-female ANC and drafted young males with professional nursing degrees into the military as corpsmen in assignments that often did not take advantage of their professional nurses' training and qualifications.[8]

By late 1944 qualified American young women were not flocking to the colors, and the both the ANC and the WAC were growing concerned about a shortage of women recruits. The movement to draft nurses in 1945, brief and unsuccessful though it was, only highlights the determination of the American public to provide their servicemen with quality nursing care, which meant professional female nurses. National service legislation would have drafted men and women for civilian jobs as well as military service, but in his speech Roosevelt used the nursing shortage as the rallying point for national service. The House of Representatives passed HR 2277 and the Senate might have done so had Germany not surrendered in May 1945. Although nurses were not drafted, the debates over national service legislation did raise public awareness about a shortage of female volunteers for military service, and it prompted many civilian nurses to volunteer for active duty in the ANC, much as the threat of the draft had spurred volunteering from males in America's other wars. The volunteer tradition of the Army Nurse Corps remained intact, and statistics showed that 31.3 percent of all active American professional nurses volunteered and were accepted for military service during World War II, that is 76,000 of the 100,000 who attempted to join both nursing corps.[9]

The war did, however, alter one prewar tradition of the Army Nurse Corps, a custom that led to confusion and inefficiency at the beginning of the war and caused tension throughout the war years—the American Red Cross's semi-official role as the primary agency for recruiting nurses for the Army. By the end of World War II, the armed forces had assumed responsibilty for recruiting women for military service, freeing the Army Nurse Corps from its long-time association with the ARC. This allowed the Army Nurse Corps to develop a separate identity after many frustrating years of depending on the Red Cross for a registry of supposedly "eligible" reserve nurses.

When World War II ended, the Army Nurse Corps remained an all-volunteer, mostly white, female institution. Wartime had compelled the Corps to accept married nurses and black nurses and had secured them commissioned officer status, veterans' benefits, and a more permanent place in the military structure. However, in the final anaylsis the contribution of the Army Nurse Corps to the changing role of women in American society and in the military was not a major one. Although Army nurses lived up to the traditions of the Army Nurse Corps and rendered dedicated, professional service in time of war, they did not contribute to many breakthroughs for American women. Professional nursing was already dominated by women in the prewar years, the Army Nurse Corps was a small, but well-established part of the U.S. Army in 1941, and the American public expected female nurses to serve their country as military nurses, if not as warriors. Americans were less anxious for women to serve in the military services in nonmedical roles, but a manpower shortage and growing political pressure by women's groups secured the establishment of women's reserves in all three branches of the armed forces. In World War II, women enlisted in such large numbers and served in so many job assignments that their acceptance as a permanent part of the peacetime military was assured in the postwar period. The intregation of women into regular army units or on board warships, into service academies, into most specialities and job assignments, and into combat roles, however, remained far in the future.

Although their participation fell short of achieving full equality for women in the American military, after a long wartime struggle Army nurses did secure equal pay and allowances and full military rank. Most of all, in World War II Army Nurse Corps nurses proved beyond a doubt their ability and willingness to serve and to maintain excellent standards of nursing care under difficult and even dangerous conditions in every theater of the war. Most of the Army nurses who saw active duty during the war considered their contribution to the war effort an important one, and a grateful nation greeted the returning veteran nurses with respect and honor. Many veteran Army nurses continued in the nursing profession after the war was over and/or took advantage of the government benefits entitled to them as official members of the armed forces, including education under the G.I. Bill. The vast majority of those Army nurses interviewed for this study said they look back on their wartime service with a sense of pride and achievement. They feel, as did the U.S. Army, that in World War II they had proudly upheld the tradition of the United States Army Nurse Corps.

NOTES

1 MOBILIZATION

1. *New York Times,* October 9, 1940.

2. Philip Kalisch and Bernice Kalisch, *Advance of American Nursing, 258;* U.S. Army Medical Department, *Highlights,* 1-9; Vern and Bonnie Bullough, *Care of the Sick,* 173.

3. Kalisch and Kalisch, *Advance of American Nursing,* 258.

4. Quoted in Kalisch and Kalisch, 329; and Dorothy and Carl J. Schneider, *Into the Breach,* chap. 4.

5. U.S. Army Medical Department, *Highlights,* 10-11; and U.S. Department of Army, Chief of Military History, "Army Nurse Corps History, 1775-1948," draft. Vol.1 covers up to World War I. (Hereafter cited as *ANC History.*)

6. Kalisch and Kalisch, *Advance of American Nursing,* 332.

7. By comparison, in 1902 the Army Nurse Corps' authorized strength was a mere 100 nurses.

8. Julia Flikke, *Nurses in Action,* 63.

9. Kalisch and Kalisch, *Advance of American Nursing,* 496.

10. For a delightful picture of nursing before WW II, see Edith Aynes, *From Nightingale to Eagle.*

11. *ANC History,* vol. 2, 50; Flikke, *Nurses in Action,* 12.

12. *ANC History,* 50. For more information on the Medical Department's prewar problems, see Clarence McKittrick Smith, *Medical Department,* chap. 2.

13. Ruth Evelyn Parks, RN, "Inside Looking Out," *American Journal of Nursing* 41 (June 1941): 642-43.

14. Mary M. Roberts, *American Nursing: History and Interpretation,* 304; and *ANC History,* vol. 2, 7.

15. *ANC History,* vol. 2, 17, Roberts, *American Nursing,* 306. The *ANC History* cites the figure of 173,000 professionally qualified nurses of the 300,000 in United States. See also Pearl McIver, "Registered Nurses in the USA," *American Journal of Nursing* 42 (1942).

16. In June 1940 the American Medical Association had added its weight to the campaign by etablishing a Medical Preparedness Committee designed to cooperate with the Advisory Committee to the Council of National Defense and federal medical agencies. A subcommittee on nursing was started in late 1940. In September the council created a new committee for health and medicine, which soon saw the need for a subcommittee on nursing. Mary Beard was appointed the chair followed by Marion G. Howell.

17. *ANC History,* vol. 2, 17; Bullough, *Care of the Sick,* 178.

18. *ANC History,* vol 2, 23-24; Clark-Hine, *Black Women in White,* 170.

19. Clark-Hine, 167.

20. *ANC History,* vol. 2, 25; Clarence Smith, *Medical Department,* 110-12; and Clark-Hine, *Black Women in White,* 171. For the employment of black troops, see Ulysses Lee, *Employment of Negro Troops;* and for racial policies and army politics prior to WW II, see Fletcher, *America's First Black General.* General Davis was forced to retire in June 1941 because of the Army's retirement policy, but he was immediately returned to active duty and assigned to the Inspector General's Office, where he was to advise the Army on matters pertaining to "colored units in the service."

21. H. Richard Musser, RN, "Nurse or Soldier?" *American Journal of Nursing* 41 (1941): 1449.

22. *New York Times,* February 25, 1941, 9. In the December 1941 issue of the *American Journal of Nursing,* Beard wrote an influential article titled "Mobilization of Nursing in National Defense" (1363). She urged that the enrollment of Army and Navy nurses through the Red Cross be increased and cited the figure of 11,000 more Army nurses for the coming year. Beard also told readers that "it takes five enrollments to get one available nurse."

2 WAR COMES TO THE PACIFIC

1. Quoted in La Forte and Marcello, eds., *Remembering Pearl Harbor,* 226-27.

2. In the general U.S. Army reorganization of October 1941, the Hawaiian Division had been converted into two triangular divisions, the Twenty-fourth and Twenty-fifth Infantry and several nondivision units of antiaircraft artillery and coast artillery. The U.S. Army Air Forces had an additional 6,706 enlisted men and 754 officers on Oahu.

3. Draft of *History of Army Nurse Corps,* "Meeting the Emergency—Hawaii," Army Historical Center, Washington, DC, 49.

4. Travers, *Eyewitness to Infamy: An Oral History of Pearl Harbor,* 99-100; *Army Nurse Corps History, 1775-1948,* unpublished, Army Historical Center, Carlisle,PA, 101 (hereafter cited as *ANC History*). At Schofield and elsewhere, sixteen civilian surgical teams aided in giving medical care. Civilian physicians manned first-aid stations on the island and treated some 422 civilian casualties from the Japanese attack. These innocent victims included eleven youngsters admitted to Children's Hospital in Honolulu with burns, shell fragments, and bullet wounds. Another eighty-eight civilians were taken to Queen's hospital and City Emergency Hospital in Honolulu.

5. Army interview with 2d Lt. Julia M. Martin, ANC, quoted in Buell Whitehouse, "Organization and Administration of Army Nurse Corps, Mid Pacific" in RG 112, Box 249, National Archives, Washington, DC; interview letter from Anna Urda Busby and clipping, "Dec.7 Still Vivid Memory for Ex-Nurse," *Montgomery Advertizer,* December 7, 1977. A native of Jermyn, Pennsylvania, Anna graduated from the Hackensack, New Jersey, Hospital School of Nursing in 1937 and joined the Army Nurse Corps two years later.

6. Interview letter from Nellie Osterlund, 1978.

7. John J. Morehead, M.D., "Surgical Experience at Pearl Harbor," *Journal of American Medical Association* (1942): 712-13. The wounded were immediately given a half grain of morphine if needed and those in shock received whole blood or liquid plasma or infusion of saline-dextrose. Sulfanilamide powder was put on wounds to prevent infection and those cases requiring immediate surgery were rushed to the hospital's operating rooms.

8. Morehead, "Surgical Experience."

9. Christine M. Chesnik, "Army Nurse Corps, Central Pacific Base Command," RG 112, Box 313, National Archives, Washington, DC, 4.

10. Interview letter and correspondence with Eloise Bowers, July 7, 1978.

11. Interview letter from Mary E. Donovan.

12. Interview letters from Eloise Bowers and Nellie Osterlund.

13. Army interview with Capt. Elva Collison, ANC, RG 112, National Archives, Washington, DC; interview letters from Hannah M. Matthews, December 1, 1978, and Eloise Bowers.

14. For information on the Philippines, see Louis Morton, *War in the Pacific;* John Toland, *But Not in Shame;* and Helen Nicolay, *MacArthur of Bataan.* General MacArthur, who had spent six years in the islands as a military adviser, was appointed commander of the newly created U.S. Army Forces in the Far East (USAFFE) on July 26, 1941.

15. 1st Lt. Josephine M. Nesbit, ANC, "History of the Army Nurse Corps in the Philippine Islands," September 1940-February 1945, 2.

16. Nesbit, "History," 2; and *ANC History,* vol. 7, 100.

17. Marie Adams, Field Director, Hospital Service, A.R.C., "Conditions at Santo Tomas," Army interview, June 7, 1945, Office of the Surgeon General.

18. Ibid., 4.

19. Army interview on July 4, 1942, with Lt. Florence MacDonald, ANC, Chief Nurse, Stotsenberg Station Hospital, Philippine Islands on December 8, 1941.

20. Walter Edmonds, *They Fought with What They Had,* 206.

21. Adams, "Conditions at Santo Tomas," 5.

22. Nesbit, "History," 16; and MacDonald interview, 3.

23. Edmonds, *They Fought,* 206. Edmonds describes the retreat of some units as more of a "rout," 232-33.

24. Dr. Alfred A. Weinstein, *Barbed Wire Surgeon,* 10.

25. Philip Kalisch and Beatrice Kalisch, "Nurses under Fire," 410. Tressa Cates kept a diary of her experiences, which she published as *Drainpipe Diary* in 1957.

26. Edmonds, *They Fought,* 203.

27. *ANC History,* vol. 7, 105; and 1st Lt. Brunetta Kuehlthau, Army interview no. 148, RG 112, entry 302, National Archives, Washington, DC.

28. W.L. White, *They Were Expendable,* 27.

29. MacDonald interview.

30. Weinstein, *Barbed Wire Surgeon,* 19.

31. *ANC History,* vol. 7, 107.

32. Kuehlthau interview; Kalisch and Kalisch, "Nurses under Fire," 414.

33. Interview with Lt. Enid Hatchitt, Army Nurse Corps, July 6, 1942, Army Historical Center, Washington, DC.

34. Weinstein, *Barbed Wire Surgeon,* 44.

35. Lt. Col. James Duckworth, Army interview no. 160, RG 112, entry 302, National Archives, Washington, DC. The hospital areas were marked with red crosses, but, Duckworth said, "the Japanese dropped two bombs into the hospital compound on March 29, one morning, and maybe the 2nd or 3rd of April, they hit in there with three, one of which hit in the ward and killed about 50 and then the 6th . . . they dropped 3 more in there."

36. Weinstein, *Barbed Wire Surgeon,* 49; Kalisch and Kalisch, "Nurses under Fire," 417; see also Julia Flikke, *Nurses in Action: Story of the Army Nurse Corps.*

37. Weinstein, *Barbed Wire Surgeon,* 49; James H. Belote, *Corregidor: Saga of a Fortress,* 56.

38. Kalisch and Kalisch, "Nurses under Fire," 419; Juanita Redmond, *I Served on Bataan,* 144-45; Belote, 110.

39. Flikke, *Nurses in Action,* 186-87; Kalisch and Kalisch, "Nurses under Fire," 420; see also Alice R. Clarke, "Army Nurse Return to the Philippines," *American Journal of Nursing* 45 (May 1945): 342-45.

40. Flikke, *Nurses in Action,* 187; MacDonald interview.

41. Morton, *War in the Pacific,* 542; and Kalisch and Kalisch, "Nurses under Fire," 423.

42. *ANC History;* Kalisch and Kalisch, "Nurses under Fire," 423. For Chief Nurse Annie Mealer's story, see Aynes, *From Nightingale to Eagle,* 180-81.

43. Brenda McBryde, *Quiet Heroines: Nurses of the Second World War,* 79-83; Kalisch and Kalisch, "Nurses under Fire," 425. See also Belote, *Corregidor: Saga of a Fortress.* In Hong Kong, conquering Japanese troops, drunk from a night of looting and rape, entered St. Stephens Hospital, shot the civilian medical superintendent when he protested their entry, bayoneted injured soldiers in their beds, and killed one nurse when she threw herself on a wounded man to protect him. The soldiers then locked the nurses in a room and took them away individually all during Christmas Day to rape them. One British woman who escaped from Macao reported the incidents of rape and looting in Hong Kong.

44. Nesbit, "History"; McBryde, *Quiet Heroines,* 79-83.

45. For a list of the nurses interned, see Kalisch and Kalisch, "Nurses under Fire," 424, and *Service Woman* magazine, September 14, 1945: 2.

46. Kuehlthau interview; Kalisch and Kalisch, "Nurses under Fire," 425; Adams, "Conditions at Santo Tomas," 10-13; Nesbit, "History," 38. Lieutenant Nesbit wrote that Ida Hube, a German citizen living at the Manila Hotel when the Japanese arrived and never interned, brought the nurses money and quantities of foodstuffs. For Navy nurses, see Barbara B. Tomblin, "Beyond Paradise."

47. Jessie Fant Evans, "Release from Los Banos," *American Journal of Nursing* 45 (June 1945), 462-63. Eventually, the wives of the married internees at Los Banos were allowed to join their husbands there, and by 1944 the camp held about 1,500 prisoners. Among them were some 500 missionaries who had been free until the summer of 1944, when the Japanese rounded them up.

48. Adams, "Conditions at Santo Tomas," 21.

49. Kuehlthau interview; Adams, "Conditions at Santo Tomas," 22-23; Nesbit, "History," 42-43. Internees' feet became swollen, their eyes sank deeper into hollowed cheek bones, their gait slowed, and each day more were admitted into the hospital. They were cheered, however, by the daily visitation of American planes overhead.

50. Kuehlthau interview; Cates, *Drainpipe Diary,* 221; Kalisch and Kalisch, "Nurses under Fire," 426.

51. Kuehlthau interview; Adams, "Conditions at Santo Tomas," 21, 24.

52. Kuehlthau interview; Kalisch and Kalisch, "Nurses under Fire," 427.

53. Adams, "Conditions at Santo Tomas," 33; Evans, "Release from Los Banos," 62; and Kuehlthau interview.

54. Mary Rose Huntington, paper delivered at the World War II in the Pacific conference, August 1994; Dorothea Davis letter.

55. Quoted in *American Journal of Nursing* 45 (May 1945).

3 Across the Pacific

1. For background information on the early campaigns in the Pacific theater, see John Toland, *But Not in Shame;* John B. Lundstrom, *First South Pacific Campaign;* Edmonds, *They Fought with What They Had;* Samuel E. Morison, "Rising Sun in the Pacific," in *History of Naval Operations in World War II,* vol. 3; and Ronald Spector, *Eagle Against the Sun.*

2. The Seabees' story is well told by William B. Huie, *Can Do! The Story of the Seabees.*

3. Ruth B. Kelley, "Army Nurse Corps, South Pacific," Records of the Surgeon

General, WW II Administrative files, RG 112, entry 31, Box 313, National Archives, Washington, DC; *ANC History.* The hospitals on New Caledonia were Fifty-second Evac, 109th, Ninth, Twenty-seventh, 331st, 332nd, Thirty-first and 336th Station Hospitals, and the Eighth and Twenty-ninth General Hospitals.

    4. *ANC History,* vol. 8, 153-55. The Ninth Station Hospital settled down at its third site in the Dumbea Valley at the end of the year. The 109th S.H. was its neighbor about thirty-five miles north and, north of Noumea, the Fifty-third also settled in to island living.

    5. Interview letter from Dorothy Moore, April 19, 1980.

    6. *ANC History,* vol. 8, chap. 13, 156.

    7. Moore letter.

    8. "Christmas Overseas," *American Journal of Nursing* 43 (December 1943): 1063.

    9. Annual reports, Hospitals in New Zealand and Australia, RG 112, National Archives, Washington, DC.

    10. Ibid.

    11. Maj. Robert D. Heinl, Jr., "Palms and Planes in the New Hebrides," 229.

    12. For more information on atabrine, see Martin Berger, "The War and Innovation: Atabrine, DDT, and Malaria," a paper delivered the Siena College World War II Conference, June 1993. After further investigation, the breeding grounds for mosquitoes on Efate were discovered to be small streams. The mosquito problem was then controlled by the use of the chemical "Paris Green."

    13. Maj. Minnie B. Schell, ANC, "History of the Army Nurse Corps in Subordinate Units West Pacific Base Command, Efate," Army Historical Center, Washington, DC.

    14. Lt. George Mason, "Flight Nurse," 56; *ANC History,* vol. 8, chap. 13, 165-68.

    15. Annual Report of the 142nd General Hospital, National Archives, Washington, DC; and interview letter from Ruth C. Frothingham, September, 1979.

    16. *ANC History,* vol. 8, chap. 13, 161.

    17. Schell, "History of the Army Nurse Corps in Subordinate Units West Pacific Base Command, Guadalcanal."

    18. *ANC History,* vol. 8, chap. 13, 8.

    19. Interview letters from Ruth C. Frothingham, September 1979; Dorothy Moore, April 19, 1980; and Grace Dick Gosnell, July 24, 1979. For nurses in Australia, see also Julia O. Flikke, *Nurses in Action.*

    20. Frothingham letter.

    21. U.S. Army interview no. 14 with 2d Lt. Mary Swain, ANC, October 12, 1943, RG 112, entry 302, National Archives, Washington, DC; U.S. Army interview no. 19 with 2d Lt. Josephine LeClair, ANC, October 30, 1943, RG 112, entry 302, National Archives, Washington, DC.

    22. *ANC History,* vol. 8, chap. 13, 22.

    23. Ibid., 35-38.

    24. Ibid., 40.

    25. Ibid., 44.

    26. Interview letter from Helen Shriver Brundage, November 21, 1978; Myrtle Arndt Roulston interview letter, October 1978.

    27. Wartime letters of Evelyn Langmuir, courtesy of Ms. Langmuir.

    28. U.S. Army interview no. 94 with Capt. Marian Grimes, ANC, September 11, 1944, RG 112, entry 302, National Archives, Washington, DC.

    29. Brundage interview letter.

30. U.S. Army interview no. 97 with Capt. Peggy G. Carbaugh, ANC, September 13, 1944, RG 112, entry 302, National Archives, Washington, DC.

31. Langmuir letters.

32. Grimes interview.

33. Roulston interview letter; Langmuir letters; Grimes interview; Carbaugh interview; and Daily Diary, 166th Station Hospital, March 28, 1944, RG 112, entry HUMEDS, Box 127, National Archives, Washington, DC.

34. Mattie E. Treadwell, *Women's Army Corps,* 425-26.

35. Interview letter from Prudence Burns Burrell, June 1994.

36. Prudence Burns Burrell, "Serving My Country," *World War II Times* 7 (February-March 1992): 16-17.

37. Brundage letter.

38. Miriam Baker Marken interview letter.

39. Interview letters from Helen Brundage.

40. Marken letter.

41. Roulston letter; Brundage letter.

42. Carbaugh interview; Grimes interview.

43. Brundage letter.

44. Langmuir letters.

45. Ibid.

46. Roulston letter.

47. Langmuir letters.

48. For the U.S. Navy Nurse Corps' contribution to medical care of casualties on Tarawa, see Barbara B. Tomblin, "Beyond Paradise," 37-39.

49. Interview letter from Hannah M. Matthews, December 1, 1978.

50. Maj. Minnie B. Schell, ANC, "History of the Army Nurse Corps in Subordinate Units West Pacific Base Command, Saipan," Army Historical Center, Washington, DC.

51. *ANC History,* vol. 8, chap. 13, 250.

52. Ibid. Samuel E. Morison covers the Saipan operation in vol. 8 of *History of U.S. Naval Operations in World War II.*

53. Schell, "Saipan."

54. *ANC History,* vol. 8, chap. 13, 254.

55. Tomblin, "Beyond Paradise." For nursing on a U.S. Navy hospital ship at Iwo Jima, see Patricia Lochridge, "Solace at Iwo." Iwo Jima was officially taken on February 26, 1945, at a cost of 215 Marine officers and 4,339 enlisted men killed and 1,331 who died of wounds. Another 16,496 men were wounded in the fighting for the island and 2,648 were evacuated for combat fatigue.

56. 1st Lt. Kathleen Barrett, "Overseas with a General Hospital," 3-4; interview letter from Mary Sherman.

57. Interview letter from Mary Brennan, June 7, 1978.

58. Schell, "History of Army Nurse Corps, Guam."

59. Schell, "History of Army Nurse Corps, Tinian."

60. Langmuir letters.

61. *ANC History,* vol. 9, "Victory in the Pacific," chap. 14, 1-30; Lt. Col. Nola Forest, ANC, "Army Nurses at Leyte," *American Journal of Nursing* 1 (1945): 44. The Fifth Evacuation Hospital arrived in Tacloban on October 22, 1944, and the Sixty-ninth Field Hospital, Seventy-sixth, and 165th Station Hospitals followed a few days later to support XXIV Corps operations in the Dulag area.

62. *ANC History,* vol. 9, chap. 14, 32-35.

63. Ibid., 32-35. A total of 400 Filipino nurses' aides were trained in the course, which by March 1945 was being offered in five Army hospitals on Leyte. Only one quarter of the graduates were actually employed by the U.S. Army, but the others found work in the civilian sector.

64. Brundage letter; Nellie Burkholder letter.

65. *ANC History,* vol. 9, chap. 14, 92.

66. Interview letter from Margaret C. Hofschneider, September 22, 1978.

67. Ibid.

68. War Diary, USS *Comfort,* U.S. Navy Operational Archives, Washington DC. S.E. Morison, *History,* vol. 14, 244-45, cites slightly different figures on casualties. See also "*Comfort* Survivors Here," *Merrie-Anna,* newsletter of the USN Base Hospital No.18, vol.1, no.5 (May 6, 1945), Navy Nurse Corps Records, series 111, Subject Files, box 11, U.S. Navy Operational Archives, Washington, DC.

69. War Diary, USS *Comfort.* There was a full moon so the enemy aircraft could not have mistaken the ship for a combatant vessel when it buzzed the hospital ship at masthead height, circled, and then crashed into its superstructure.

70. *ANC History,* vol. 9, chap. 14, "Okinawa," 160.

71. Ibid., 167.

72. Brundage letter.

73. Roulston letter.

74. Gosnell and Frothingham interview letters.

75. Interview letter from Teresa DeGuelle Reynolds, May 7, 1979. For more on the U.S.A.H.S. *Marigold,* see Doris Schwartz, "Nursing Aboard a Hospital Ship," *American Journal of Nursing* 45, 996-97.

76. *ANC History,* vol. 9, chap. 14, 261.

77. Roulston letter.

4   THE TORCH IS LIT

1. For information on Operation TORCH, see Morison, *"Operations in North African Waters October 1942-June 1943," History of United States Naval Operations in World War II;* William Breuer, *Operation Torch;* and Carlo d'Este, *World War II in the Mediterranean 1942-45.*

2. Charles M. Wiltse, *Medical Department: Medical Service in the Mediterranean and Minor Theaters,*107. That would be the standard medical maintenance for 10,000 men for thirty days augmented by biologicals and special drugs appropriate for the conditions.

3. Wiltse, *Medical Department.*

4. Capt. Theresa Archard, ANC, *G.I. Nightingale,* 14, 20.

5. Ibid., 19-20.

6. Ibid., 26-28.

7. Ibid., 40-43; and 2d Lt. Ruth Haskell, ANC, *Helmets and Lipstick,* 98-99.

8. Wiltse, *Medical Department,* 113.

9. Archard, *G.I. Nightingale;* see also Annual Report of the Forty-eighth Surgical Hospital, 1942, RG 112, National Archives, Washington, DC.

10. Roberta Love Tayloe, *Combat Nurse,* 3.

11. Ibid., 28-29.

12. Ibid., 32.

13. Ibid., 35.

14. Archard, *G.I. Nightingale,* 60.

15. Ibid., 61-62.

16. Wittler quoted in Annual Report of the Twelfth General Hospital, RG 112, National Archives, Washington, DC.

17. Ibid.

18. Tayloe, *Combat Nurse,* 39.

19. Haskell, *Helmets and Lipstick.*

20. Haskell, *Helmets and Lipstick;* and Archard, *G.I. Nightingale,* 69.

21. Tayloe, *Combat Nurse,* 41.

22. Wiltse, *Medical Department,* 125-26.

23. Archard, *G.I. Nightingale,* 81.

24. Tayloe, *Combat Nurse,* 43.

25. The attack began around noon on February 21, and it progressed well despite a British tank unit. By afternoon Rommel had been forced to withdraw and a battle began in the darkness three miles south of Thala. For hours the outcome of this battle hung in the balance, but the timely arrival of General Irwin's Ninth Division Artillery tipped the scales in the Allies' favor. For more information on the Kasserine Pass battle see Martin Blumenson, *Kasserine Pass;* "Kasserine Pass, 30 January-22 February, 1943," in Charles Heller, ed., *America's First Battles;* and George Howe, *Northwest Africa: Seizing the Initiative in the West.*

26. Wiltse, *Medical Department,* 123-27.

27. Ibid., 129.

28. Ibid., 128.

29. Mae Mills Link and Hubert A. Coleman, *Medical Support of the Army Air Forces in W.W.II,* 369.

30. Interview with Lt. Henrietta "Mike" Richardson, ANC, May 31, 1978. The first class to receive formal air evac training did not graduate until February 18, 1943, and in June 1943 the 349th was redesignated the Army Air Force (AAF) School of Evacuation and placed under the direct control of the Commanding General, AAF.

31. Richardson interview.

32. Link and Coleman, *Medical Support,* 492-93.

33. Annual Report of the Fifteenth Evacuation Hospital, RG 112, National Archives, Washington DC.

34. Ibid.

35. Wiltse, *Medical Department,* 132-33.

36. Interview, letter from Marjorie Willauer, December 1979.

37. Wiltse, *Medical Department,* 183; Army interview with 2d Lt. Catherine M. Rodman, ANC, August 25, 1944, RG 112, National Archives; and McBryde, *Quiet Heroines,* 135.

38. Yvonne Humphrey, *American Journal of Nursing* 43 (September 1943): 821.

39. Ibid.

40. Wiltse, *Medical Department,* 134.

41. June Wandrey, *Bedpan Commando,* 30-31.

42. d'Este, chap 3 and 4; Morison, vol. 9, part 2.

43. Wandrey, *Bedpan Commando,* 43; and Col. Raymond Scott, Annual Report of the Eleventh Field Hospital, 1943, RG 112, National Archives, Washington, DC. Colonel Scott also wrote "Eleventh Evacuation Hospital in Sicily," in *American Journal of Nursing* 43 (April 1944).

44. Wandrey, *Bedpan Commando,* 44-45.

45. Ibid.

46. Colonel Scott, Annual report of the Eleventh Evacuation Hospital.

47. Army interview no. 55 with Lt. Mary Hawalt, ANC, RG 112, entry 302, National Archives, Washington, DC.

48. Annual Report of the Ninety-first Evacuation Hospital, Annual Report of the Fifteenth Evacuation Hospital, RG 112, National Archives, Washington, DC; and Wiltse, *Medical Department,* 168.

49. Army interview with 1st Lt. Muriel M. Westover, ANC, January 10, 1944, RG 112, National Archives, Washington, DC.; and Wiltse, *Medical Department,* 165. On August 1, 1943, the Fifteenth Evac began caring for battle casualties near Nicosia, where it functioned as a holding unit caring for patients that could be sent back to their units within seven days. By now the Fifteenth's original designation as a 400-bed evacuation hospital had been expanded to 950 beds with the assistance of the three companies from the Fifty-fourth Medical Battalion. From Nicosia some patients were taken back to the 128th Evac and then transferred to the Ninety-third. Soldiers who could walk were transported by 2.5-ton truck so that the ambulances could be used for litter cases. In all, the Fifteenth Evac cared for 1,723 disease cases and 285 injured soldiers during their eighteen-day stay at Nicosia.

50. Wiltse,

51. Wandrey, *Bedpan Commando,* 48.

52. Colonel Scott, Annual Report of the Eleventh Field Hospital; Wandrey, *Bedpan Commando,* 48.

53. Wandrey, *Bedpan Commando,* 49.

54. Archard, *G.I. Nightingale,* 152-54.

55. Ibid., 154, 158-59.

56. Wandrey, *Bedpan Commando,* 54.

57. Ibid., 55, 58.

58. Archard, *G.I. Nightingale,* 163.

59. Hawalt interview.

60. Wandrey, *Bedpan Commando,* 62-63.

61. d'Este, *World War II in the Mediterranean,* 74; Morison, *History,* vol.9, 209-18.

5   FIFTH ARMY FIRST

1. For information on Operation AVALANCHE, see Morison, "Sicily-Salerno-Anzio," *History,* vol. 9; Blumenson, *Salerno to Cassino;* Jackson, *Battle for Italy;* and Pond, *Salerno!*

2. Wiltse, *Medical Department,* 224-25. The medical battalions were the Fifty-second, Fifty-fourth, 161st, and 162d. The 400-bed units were the Fifteenth, Ninety-third, Ninety-fourth, Ninety-fifth, Thirty-eighth, Eighth, Sixteenth, and Fifty-sixth, augmented by the Third Convalescent.

3. Wiltse, *Medical Department,* 227-28.

4. "Notre Casa," Nursing Report of Ninety-fifth Evacuation Hospital, 1943, RG 112, National Archives, Washington, DC.

5. Sally Weaks, "The 202d Hospital Ship Complement U.S.A.H.S. *Shamrock,*" RG 112, National Archives, Washington, DC.

6. Ibid.

7. Ibid.

8. Ibid.

9. "Notre Casa."

10. Quoted in "Army Nurse Describes Evacuation Hospital Work," *Service Woman,* January 14, 1944, p. 10.

11. Annual Report of the Fifty-sixth Evacuation Hospital, RG 112, National Archives, Washington, DC.

12. Wandrey, *Bedpan Commando,* 170, 173.

13. Wiltse, *Medical Department,* 236-40.

14. "Notre Casa."

15. Army interview no. 88 with 2d Lt. Catherine M. Rodman, ANC, August 25, 1944, RG 112, National Archives, Washington, DC.

16. Rodman interview. Lieutenant Rodman's statement, shared by other nurses in Italy, contradicts that of historian Ronald Spector, who says, "In World War II, whole blood was rarely, if ever, available even at division-and corps-level hospitals. In Vietnam stocks of whole blood, packaged in styrofoam containers . . . was almost always available in forward areas" (*After Tet,* 56). Spector's source is Maj. Gen. Surgeon Neel, *Medical Support of the US Army in Vietnam 1965-70.* Prepackaged whole blood may not have been available at the front in Italy and other theaters that used blood plasma, but there is evidence that many hospitals had blood banks with whole blood from soldier donors in the area. In the China-Burma-India (CBI) theater one hospital even sent medical units out to get whole blood from Chinese troops for use with Chinese patients.

17. Wandrey, *Bedpan Commando,* 73-76.

18. Morison, vol. 9, 232-33; and de Este, *World War II in the Mediterranean,* chap. 5.

19. Wiltse, *Medical Department,* 268.

20. Annual Report of Nursing Activities, 1944, Second Auxiliary Surgical Unit, Nursing Reports and History, HUMFDS Records, RG 338, National Archives, Washington, DC.

21. 2d Lt. Inis M. Kaufman, "The Argosy of a Army Nurse Who Earned, at Anzio, the Highest of all Nurse Awards—'Thanks,'" clipping in possession of the author; and *Service Woman,* February 25, 1944, p. 11.

22. Interview letter from Virginia Barton, 1979.

23. Headquarters, Fifty-sixth Evacuation Hospital, Medical Historical Data, RG 112, National Archives, Washington, DC.

24. Annual Report of the Ninety-fifth Evacuation Hospital, 1944, by Colonel Sauer; and enclosure of report by Lt. Col. Hubert Binkley, M.C., RG 112, National Archives, Washington, DC.

25. Annual Report of the Thirty-third Field Hospital; and Ruth Y. White, "Anzio Beachhead," *American Journal of Nursing* 44 (April 1944): 370.

26. Interview letter from Jeanne Wells, February 19, 1980, and interview letter from Dorothy Meador.

27. Wells letter.

28. Second Auxiliary Surgical Unit annual report.

29. Medical History of the Ninety-fourth Evacuation Hospital, Semimobile, 1944, RG 112, National Archives, Washington, DC; and Wells letter.

30. Barton letter.

31. Tayloe, *Combat Nurse,* 76-77.

32. Wandrey, *Bedpan Commando,* 76.

33. "Shell Cases Serve As Anzio Altar," *Service Woman,* April 18, 1944, p. 8.

34. Medical History of the Ninety-fourth Evacuation Hospital, Semimobile, 1944, "Anzio Beachhead," RG 112, National Archives, Washington, DC.

35. Kaufman, "Argosy of an Army Nurse."

36. Annual Report of the Ninety-third Evacuation Hospital, RG 112, National Archives, Washington, DC.

37. War Diary, USS *Seminole; Service Woman,* January 28, 1944, p. 3. LSTs could accommodate 100-150 litters or an equal number of ambulatory patients, who were given hot meals and were attended to during the eighteen-hour voyage to Naples by corpsmen from the Fifty-sixth Medical Battalion.

38. War Diary, USS *Seminole; Service Woman,* January 28, 1944, 3.

39. Ernie Pyle, *Brave Men,* 199.

40. Wiltse, *Medical Department,* 295-96.

41. Annual Report of the Ninety-fourth Evacuation Hospital.

42. Wandrey, *Bedpan Commando,* 112-13.

43. Ibid., 113-14.

44. Second Auxiliary Surgical Unit annual report.

45. Wandrey, *Bedpan Commando,* 115.

46. Wiltse, *Medical Department,* 285.

47. 1st Lt. Sidney Hyman, MAC, "The Medical Story of Anzio," RG 112, National Archives, Washington, DC.

48. Lt. Evelyn Swanson, Ninety-fifth Evacuation Nursing Report, RG 112, National Archives, Washington, DC.

49. Annual Report of the Twenty-seventh Evacuation Hospital, RG 112, National Archives, Washington, DC.

50. Ibid.

51. Tayloe, *Combat Nurse,* 120.

52. Annual Report of the Ninety-fourth Evacuation Hospital.

53. Annual Report of the 170th Evacuation Hospital, RG 112, National Archives, Washington, DC.

54. Interview letter from M.E. Revely, October 20, 1979.

55. Annual Report of the Eighth Evacuation Hospital, 1945, RG 112, National Archives, Washington, DC.

56. Eugenia Kielar, *Thank You,* 149.

57. Annual Report of the Fifty-sixth Evacuation Hospital, 1945, RG 112, National Archives, Washington, DC.

58. Ibid.

59. Kielar, *Thank You,* 127.

60. Annual Report of the Eighth Evacuation Hospital.

61. Ibid.

62. Annual Report of the Fifty-sixth Evacuation Hospital.

63. Kielar, *Thank You,* 219.

64. Annual Report of the Fifty-sixth Evacuation Hospital.

6　To the Rhine and Beyond

1. Capt. Margaret Aaron, Annual Report of Activities in Nursing Section, Box 305 (European Theater of Operations), Record Group 112, National Archives, Washington, DC, 5.

2. Lt. Col. Marjorie Peto, *Women Were Not Expected,* 2.

3. Ibid., 9.

4. Interview letter from J. Ada Mutch, May 27, 1978.

5. Peto, *Women Were Not Expected,* 14. Peto writes of the first lady's visit, "Although the nurses knew this was kidding, the bombastic threats sounded dire enough and you could never tell what a wounded G.I., bored with inaction more than suffering, would do just for the merry hell of it."

6. Aaron, Annual Report, 4, 11-12, 14; interview letter from Alice G. Howard, November 21, 1978.

7. Eula Awbrey Sforza, *A Nurse Remembers,* 63-65. Interview letter from Rose Farley Weber, October 10, 1979.

8. Sforza, 76.

9. Aaron, Annual Report. The Nursing Section had grown so large that it was divided into four base sections-Eastern, Southern, Western, and Northern Ireland—with one captain as the director of nursing services in each section.

10. Aaron, Annual Report, 16-17; 168th Station Hospital Annual Report, RG 407, Adjutant General, Medical Department Surgical Hospital (MDSH) 168.02; and 1st Lt. Dorothy Smith, ANC, Army interview no. 115, December 12, 1944, RG 112, entry 302, National Archives, Washington, DC.

11. Aaron, Annual Report; Treadwell, *Women's Army Corps,* 59.

12. Treadwell, *Women's Army Corps,* 387. The first WAC to arrive was a stenographer who was flown to the Normandy beachhead on June 22 to take minutes at a high-level conference. She was followed on July 14 by the first WAC unit, which came ashore in Normandy from an LST to serve with the communications personnel as typists, clerks, and telephone operators. These WACs were followed over the next few months by thousands of Army women, and by the end of 1944 over half of the WACs in the ETO were on duty in France or Belgium. Three thousand women were on the Continent by October 1944, serving with the Normandy Base Section, Air Force units, Quartermaster's office, Transportation, Engineering, Ordnance, and various other units.

13. *ANC History,* vol. 6, 100.

14. Annual Report of the Thirty-ninth Field Hospital, 1944, ETO, RG 112, National Archives, Washington, DC.

15. *ANC History,* vol. 6, 100-101.

16. *ANC History,* vol.6 , 99. *ANC History* says that two field and two evac hospital nurses arrived on June 10, 1944 and one field nurse arrived at Omaha Beach the next day.

17. Annual Report of the Ninety-first Evacuation Hospital, 1944, ETO, RG 112, National Archives, Washington, DC.

18. Ibid., *ANC History,* vol. 6, 103.

19. *ANC History,* vol. 6, 103-104; Annual Report of the Ninety-first Evac.; interview letter from Janice T. Goers-Reilly, January 20, 1994. On June 23, 1944, the 750-bed Second Evac and the rest of the Third Surgical Group arrived, followed four days later by the Forty-seventh Field, thus completing the list of nurses assigned to the First Army.

20. Jean Truckey, "Nurses Prove Their Courage Under Fire of Enemy," article in possession of the author.

21. Mary Virginia Desmaris, "Navy Nursing on D-Day Plus Four," *American Journal of Nursing* 45, 12.

22. Sforza, *A Nurse Remembers,* 78.

23. Interview letter from Jean Foley Tierney, 1978.

24. History of the 806th MAES, courtesy of Jean Tierney.

25. Tierney letter.

26. Ibid.

27. Sforza, *A Nurse Remembers,* 83.

28. Ibid., 84.

29. Ibid.; Graham A. Cosmos and Albert E. Cowdrey, *Medical Service in the European Theater of Operations,* 263.

30. Cosmos and Cowdrey, *Medical Service,* 261.

31. *ANC History,* vol. 6, 109; Cosmos and Cowdrey, *Medical Service,* 264; Lt. Vincoe Paxton, "Army Reinforcements Land in France," *American Journal of Nursing* 45 (January 1945), 13; and interview letter from Kathryn C. Singer, January 20, 1995. Nurse Singer, who enlisted in the Army in February 1942, served in England and Scotland for seven months before being ordered to the Continent.

32. Sforza, *A Nurse Remembers*, 85.

33. Annual Report of the Ninety-first Evacuation Hospital.

34. Peto, *Women Were Not Expected*, 91.

35. Ibid., 93.

36. Cosmos and Cowdrey, *Medical Service*, 303; *ANC History*, vol. 6, 109; Peto, *Women Were Not Expected*, 97. For example, during August and September 1945, Third Army medical units hospitalized 5,400 German prisoners and the Ninth Army's VIII Corps evacuated 4,700 German POW casualties from the fortress at Brest after its capture by Allied forces.

37. *ANC History*, vol. 6, 111.

38. Annual Report of the Ninety-first Evacuation Hospital.

39. Sforza, *A Nurse Remembers*, 90.

40. Peto, *Women Were Not Expected*, 99.

41. Mary Jose, "Night Shift in an Army Hospital," *American Journal of Nursing* 45 (June 1945), 269.

42. Ibid., 267-69.

43. Annual Report of the Hospital Train, Box 301, ETO, RG 112, National Archives, Washington, DC. The longer journeys were due in part to the advances of the Allied armies and to the fact that hospital trains were boarded in some cases as little as fifty miles from the front lines.

44. For detailed information on the invasion of southern France, see Morison, "The Invasion of France and Germany,1944-45," vol. 11, *History of U.S. Naval Operations in World War II*, part 2; d'Este, *World War II in the Mediterranean;* and William Breuer, *Operation Dragoon.*

45. "Army Nurses in Southern France," *American Journal of Nursing* 44 (October 1944).

46. Capt. Evalyn Swanson, Nursing Report, Annual Report of the Ninety-fifth Evacuation Hospital, 1944, ETO, RG 112, National Archives, Washington, DC.

47. Ibid.

48. Wandrey, *Bedpan Commando*, 128.

49. Swanson, Nursing Report, 5.

50 Wandrey, *Bedpan Commando*, 132, 135, 138.

51. Peto, *Women Were Not Expected*, 119.

52. Sforza, *A Nurse Remembers*, 103.

53. Annual Report of the Forty-fifth Field Hospital, RG 112, National Archives, Washington, DC.

54. U.S. Army Medical Department, *Highlights in the History of the Army Nurse Corps,* 25. For more information on Reba Whittle, see Mary E. Frank, "The Forgotten POW: 2nd Lt. Reba Z. Whittle," student paper, Army War College, February 1990.

55. *ANC History*, vol. 6, 148.

56. *ANC History*, vol. 6, 114; and 1st Lt. Imogene Yarbrough, ANC, Army interview no. 123, January 18, 1945, RG 112, entry 302, National Archives, Washington, DC. For details on forward area nursing care, see Lt. Vincoe Paxton, "With Field Hospital Nurses," *American Journal of Nursing,* 1945, 131-32.

57. For more information on the battle in the Ardennes, see John D. Eisenhower, *Bitter Woods: Hitler's Ardennes Offensive;* and Charles B. MacDonald, *A Time for Trumpets: The Untold Story of the Battle for the Bulge.*

58. *ANC History*, vol. 6, 154; Cosmos and Cowdrey, *Medical Service,* 403-404.

59. Cosmos and Cowdrey, *Medical Service,* 396.

60. Annual Report of the Thirty-ninth Field Hospital, December, 1944, RG 112, Box 412, National Archives, Washington, DC.

61. Wandrey, *Bedpan Commando*, 159; and interview with Janice T. Goers-Reilly, January 20, 1994.

62. Mary Jose, "Hi Angels!" *American Journal of Nursing* 45, 267-69.

63. Ibid., 267.

64. Annual Report of the Thirty-ninth Field Hospital; *ANC History*, vol. 6.

65. Sforza, *A Nurse Remembers*, 104-105.

66. Interview letter from Madelene Bateman, January 8, 1980.

67. Interview letter from Kay Yarabinec, March 10, 1980.

68. Peto, *Women Were Not Expected*, 130.

69. Interview letter from H. Jean McIver Kemp, December 4, 1978.

70. Tierney letter.

71. Sforza, *A Nurse Remembers*, 107.

72. Wandrey, *Bedpan Commando*, 186.

73. Ibid., 185-87.

74. Ibid., 187-88.

75. Ibid., 188.

76. Peto, *Women Were Not Expected*, 141. Her description of the celebrations is worth reading. One Flying Fortress swooped so low over the Hotel de Ville that it missed hitting the roof by only a foot. "There were those sober enough to pray the pilot was not drunk," Peto commented. She also says the hospital's French civilians took a two-week leave without giving notice.

77. Kemp letter.

78. Yarabinec letter.

79. Sforza, *A Nurse Remembers*, 118-19.

80. Wandrey, *Bedpan Commando*, 204-205.

81. Ibid., 207.

82. Tierney letter.

83. Interview letters from Vera M. Fields, June 22, 1978; Madeleine Bateman; Jean Tierney; and Helen Graves, November 1978.

84. Kemp letter.

85. Peto, *Women Were Not Expected*, 144. The mines evidently floated in from the sea.

86. Graves letter; Howard interview.

87. Fields letter.

88. Wandrey, *Bedpan Commando*, 234.

89. Sforza, *A Nurse Remembers*, 134.

7   The End of the Line

1. For the official history of the CBI, see Romanus and Sunderland, *Stilwell's Mission to China, Stilwell's Command Problems,* and *Times Runs Out in the CBI;* also Spector, *Eagle Against the Sun,* chaps. 15 and 16; and Tuchman, *Stilwell and the American Experience in China.*

2. Dorn, *Walkout,* 343. See also White, *Stilwell Papers.* For a personable, readable account of the China-Burma airlift, see Thorne, *Hump.* Thorne does not, however, discuss Army medical units or hospitals in his account.

3. 1st Lt. Eleanor M. Bradley, Army interview no. 121, December 30, 1944, RG 112, entry 320, National Archives, Washington, DC; and "Back from 32 Months of Service in India, Lieutenant Marie Rowley, ANC, Describes Hardships, Rewards of Nursing in Karachi," clipping in Army Historical Center files, Washington, DC.

4. U.S. Army interview with 2d Lt. Lucy M. Wainwright, ANC, in Karachi, India, October 25, 1943, RG 112, National Archives, Washington, DC.

5. U.S. Army interview no. 11 with 2d Lt. Dorothy C. Sykes, ANC, at 181st General Hospital, India, October 4, 1943, RG 112, National Archives, Washington, DC.

6. Treadwell, *Women's Army Corps,* 464.

7. Annual Report of the 159th Station Hospital, RG 112, National Archives, Washington, DC.

8. Wainwright interview.

9. Maj. Mary E. Cornelius, ANC, Annual Report of the Twentieth General Hospital, RG 112, Annual Reports of the Office of Surgeon General, CBI, National Archives, Washington, DC.

10. Interview letter from Alma H. Garside, September 11, 1978.

11. For the story of the construction of the Ledo Road, see Leslie Anders, *Ledo Road.* For the story of an Army field hospital in Burma in 1943, see Seagrave, *Burma Surgeon Returns.* Real progress was made on the Ledo Road during the dry, cool weather of the winter of 1942-43. General Wheeler of the Army Engineer Corps hoped to have 103 miles of the Ledo Road finished by June 1943, but when the rains came in May the road had progressed only four miles beyond the Burmese border.

12. Cornelius, Annual Report of the Twentieth General Hospital.

13. Annual Report of the Thirty-second Portable Surgical Hospital, Box 245A, RG 112, CBI, National Archives, Washington, DC.

14. For the war in Burma and "Merrill's Marauders," see Bidwell, *Chindit War,* 82-83 and 252; and Ogburn, *Marauders.* This unit of American volunteers had been formed as the 530th Provisional Regiment and assigned originally to British General Orde Wingate. In January 1944, Wingate offered the unit to Stilwell to beef up his Chinese forces and he appointed Brig. Gen. Frank Merrill to command the unit. The press dubbed the unit "Merrill's Marauders," despite the fact that Col. Charles Hunter was chiefly responsible for their training.

15. Capt. Mary Ellen Yeager, ANC, Nursing Report, Fourteenth Evacuation Hospital, RG 112, CBI, National Archives, Washington, DC.

16. Agnes D. Gress, "The 14th Evac on the Ledo Road," *American Journal of Nursing* 45 (September 1945), 705.

17. Yeager, Nursing Report, 3-5.

18. Gress, "The 14th Evac on the Ledo Road."

19. 1st Lt. James Stone, MAC, "History of Army Nurses, Physical Therapists, and Dietitians in India," RG 112, CBI, National Archives, Washington, DC, 2.

20. Treadwell, *Women's Army Corps,* 469; Bradley interview; and 2d Lt. Adele M. Petraitis, ANC, Army interview no. 13, October 7, 1943, RG 112, entry 320, National Archives, Washington, DC. The WAC pregnancy rate as of May 1945 was zero.

21. Interview Letter from Sylvia Lasser, September 2, 1979.

22. Lasser letter.

23. Interview letter from Lt. Col. Mary L. Barbero, ANC (Ret.), May 19, 1978; interview letter from Nadine H. Lane, December 28, 1994.

24. Barbero letter; Lasser letter; Treadwell, *Women's Army Corps,* 471. Mattie Treadwell says that the allowance made for nurses to wear civilian evening wear in violation of malaria precautions created a serious precedent that resulted in discipline problems later for the WAC troops.

25. Barbero letter; Lasser interview

26. *ANC History,* vol. 10, chap. 15, 66.

27. Ibid. The 803rd flew 5,800 patients out of Burma in May.

28. Annual report of the 48th S.H., RG112, National Archives, Washington, DC.

29. Lane letter; see also Ulysses Lee, *Employment of Black Troops,* 618.

30. Lane letter.

31. *ANC History,* vol. 9, chap. 14, 109.

32. Ibid., 115; and Lt. Ruth M. Smith, "A Day in the Life of a Nurse in China," *Ex—CBI Roundup,* January 1992, 12-13.

33. *ANC History,* vol. 10, chap. 15, 63-64 and 14, 113. Technically, the "first" Army flight nurses in China—Captain Avery in the spring of 1943 and Lieutenant Hilge, who stopped there on an evacuation flight from West Africa—were only visitors.

34. *ANC History,* vol. 10, chap. 14, 137.

35. Ibid., 139-46.

36. Barbero letter.

37. Interview letter from Verna Carruth, February 13, 1995.

38. *ANC History,* vol. 10, chap. 14, 139.

39. Ibid., 155.

40. Barbero letter; Lane interview; *ANC History,* vol. 10, chap. 14, 155. The hospitals were the Twenty-first, Twenty-second, Twenty-fifth, and Forty-fourth Field Hospitals, the Fourteenth, Forty-eighth, and Seventy-third Evacuation hospitals, the Eighteenth, Twentieth, Sixty-ninth, 172nd General Hospitals, and the Eleventh Station Hospitals.

41. Wainwright interview; Bradley interview.

42. Sykes interview; Wainwright interview.

43. Sykes interview.

44. Lane interview.

45. *ANC History,* vol. 10, chap. 14, 131; Carruth letter.

46. *ANC History,* vol. 10, chap. 14, 178-79.

47. Stone, "History," 5.

8 They Also Served

1. *ANC History,* draft, 1987, Army Historical Center, Carlisle, Pa., vol. 7, 65; and Col. James A. Donovan, *Outpost in the North Atlantic,* 4-6.

2. Capt. Dorothy Smith, ANC, Army interview no. 115, December 12, 1944, RG 112, National Archives, Washington, DC.

3. *ANC History,* vol. 7, 69-71.

4. Capt. Louise S. Heyden, ANC, Army interview, November 3, 1943, RG 112, National Archives, Washington, DC.

5. Ibid.

6. Smith interview.

7. Heyden interview.

8. "Heroism in Iceland," *American Journal of Nursing* 45 (December 1943). When Lt. Louise Heyden arrived in Iceland as chief nurse of the 208th General Hospital in the spring of 1942, the Iceland Base Command had seventy-five medical officers, 254 nurses, and 500 enlisted men. By November 1943, her hospital, which was at first a 1,000-bed general hospital, had split into two 500-bed hospitals, one of which was the 227th Station Hospital.

9. Heyden interview.

10. Ibid. Cpl. Luther M. Chovan, USA, "American Soldier in Reykjavik," *National Geographic Magazine* 88 (November 1945), 536-52. Interview letter from Katherine A. Schlegel, 1979.

11. Smith interview. Schlegel letter.

12. Wiltse, *Medical Department,* 18-26, 31; see also George Whitely, Jr., "New-foundland, North Atlantic Rampart," *National Geographic Magazine* 80 (July 1941).

13. 1st Lt. Lillian Castleberry, ANC, Army interview no. 41, January 12, 1944, RG 112, entry 302, National Archives, Washington, DC.

14. 1st Lt. Cora O'Hare, ANC, Army interview no. 44, January 17, 1944, RG 112, entry 302, National Archives, Washington, DC; Castleberry interview.

15. Castleberry interview.

16. Wiltse, *Medical Department,* 65-67.

17. Army interview with 1st Lt. Susan E. Freeman, RG 112, entry 305, National Archives, Washington, DC; interview letter and audio tape from Ellen Robinson Page, December 12, 1994; Lee, *Employment of Black Troops,* 619. The Republic of Liberia honored Lieutenant Freeman's efforts in personal diplomacy by making her a knight official of the Liberian Humane Order of Africa Redemption. Lee says the Twenty-fifth Field's black nurses were replaced by male nurses, but as no male nurses were accepted by the Army Nurse Corps during the war, he may mean corpsmen.

18. Interview letter from Kathleen Marren.

19. Interview letter from Grace Blair Campbell, 1980.

20. Campbell letter; Marren letter.

21. Anna L. Moline, RN, "U.S. Army Nurses in Russia," *American Journal of Nursing* 45 (November 1945), 904-906.

22. Ibid.

23. Wiltse, "The Army Nurse Corps in the Persian Gulf Command," Army Historical Center, Washington, DC.

24. Ibid.; and 1st Lt. Elsie Schwable, ANC, Army interview no. 2, September 7, 1943, RG 112, entry 302, National Archives, Washington, DC.

25. Wiltse, "The Army Nurse Corps," 76.

26. *ANC History,* chap. 7, "Alaska," 60-68.

27. Ibid.

28. *ANC History,* vol. 7, 58.

29. Ibid., 60-62.

30. Froelich Rainey, "Alaskan Highway an Engineering Epic," *National Geographic* 83 (February 1943), 143-68.

31. Interview letter from Lucille Carter.

32. *ANC History,* vol. 7, 63.

33. Smith, *Medical Department,* 144.

34. Ibid., 33, 101.

35. Annual Report of the Station Hospital Barinque Field, Puerto Rico, April 10, 1943; and Annual Report of the 333d Station Hospital, Fort Clayton, Canal Zone, March 27, 1944, HUMED, entry 54A, RG 112, National Archives, Washington, DC.

36. Army interview no. 187 with 1st Lt. Joella Wallace, ANC, RG 112, entry 302, National Archives, Washington, DC.

37. *Highlights in the History of Army Nurse Corps,* 20; Treadwell, *Women's Army Corps,* 219-20.

38. Aynes, *From Nightingale to Eagle,* 260; Elsie E. Schneider, Nursing, Middle Pacific, RG 112, Box 313, National Archives, Washington, DC, p. 7. In the Hawaiian Department, 100 percent of the Army nurses on duty accepted commissions. The WAAC was disbanded in 1943 in order to be formed into the Women's Army Corps (WAC). The new legislation made the WAC part of the U.S. Army, gave the director, Oveta Culp Hobby, the rank of colonel, and gave WAACs ninety days to decide whether to enlist, be

commissioned into the new Women's Army Corps, or accept an honorable discharge. One month later, another piece of legislation authorized women physicians to be admitted to the Army Medical Corps and Major Craighill became the first woman to serve in the U.S. Army.

39. Aynes, *From Nightingale to Eagle*, 234-35; *Service Woman*, May 12, 1944, pp. 10-11.

40. *Service Woman*, January 14, 1944, p. 12.

41. Ibid.; and Lucile Petry, "U.S. Cadet Nurse Corps," *American Journal of Nursing* 43 (August 1943), 704-708. The stipend varied from fifteen dollars a month for the student's first nine months in school, during which she was called a precadet nurse, to twenty dollars for the next fifteen to twenty months, called the junior cadet period. For the remainder of the now senior cadet's training, the institution using the student's service paid thirty dollars a month.

42. *Service Woman*, July 1944, p. 11; and *Highlights*.

43. Interview letter from Eleanor M. DeMay, May 23, 1980.

44. "Negro Students in the U.S. Cadet Nurse Corps," *American Journal of Nursing* 46 (September 1944), 887.

45. Carnegie, *Path We Tread*, 165-66; and Lee, *Employment of Black Troops*. The eighteen WW I nurses were: Marion Brown Seymour, Anna Oliver Ramos, Lillian Ball, Pearl Billings, Susie Boulding, Eva Clay, Aileen Cole, Edna DePriest, Magnolia Diggs, Sophia Hill, Jeanette Millis, Clara Rollins, Lillian Spears, Virginia Steele, Frances Stewart, Nettie Vick, Jeanette West, and Mabel Williams. A larger number of black civilian nurses were also employed by the Army in camps where a total of 38,000 troops were stationed in WW I. For information on blacks in the military in WW II, see also Osur, *Blacks in the Army Air Forces During W.W.II*, 9. See also Sandler, *Segregated Skies*.

46. *American Journal of Nursing* 44, 476-77. Mabel K. Staupers was executive secretary of the NACGN, which was founded in 1908 in New York City with Martha M. Franklin as president. In 1944 the association had 1,000 members and the *American Journal of Nursing* stated there were about 8,000 black graduate nurses in the U.S. and about 2,000 in schools of nursing.

47. *ANC History*, vol. 2, 23-24; Carnegie, *Path We Tread*, 169. Mary Carnegie says there were about 8,000 registered black nurses in the country in 1945.

48. Esther Allen interview, December 11, 1994.

49. Carnegie, *Path We Tread*, 171.

50. Interview letter from Prudence Burns Burrell, June 1994.

51. Roy Wilkins, "Nurses Go to War," 42-44. For black WACs at Fort Huachuca, see Martha S. Putney, *When the Nation Was in Need*, 75.

52. Wilkins, "Nurses Go to War," 43; interview letter from Barbara C. Calderon, November 7, 1994; interview letter from Elinor Powell Albert, November 6, 1994.

53. Wilkins, "Nurses Go to War," 42; interview letter from Octavia T. Card, August 31, 1994.

54. Interview letter from Frances Dyer Edwards, October 5, 1994.

55. Albert letter; and audiotaped interview with Ellen Robinson Page, December 12, 1994.

56. Edwards letter; Albert letter. For letters from black soldiers about black medical officers and medical treatment, see McGuire, *Taps for a Jim Crow Army*, 56-57, 220.

57. Edwards letter.

58. Albert letter; Calderon letter.

59. Calderon letter; Card letter.

60. *ANC History*, vol. 11, chap. 14, 67-68; Darlene Clark-Hine, *Black Women in White*, 176.

61. Interview letter from Esther Allen, December 11, 1994; Card letter; Albert letter.

62. Estelle M. Riddle and Josephine Nelson, "The Negro Nurse Looks Toward Tomorrow," *American Journal of Nursing* 45 (August 1945), 627-30.

63. *ANC History*, vol. 5, chap. 8, 97-103; the Army Nurse Corps created a monthly journal about and for Army nurses, published a pledge and song, and produced a film, *Army Nurse*, as part of its recruitment campaign.

64. Aynes, *From Nightingale to Eagle*, 268; Treadwell, *Women's Army Corps*, 247; and *ANC History*, vol. 5, chap. 8, 102-103.

65. *New York Times*, January 7, 1945, p. 1.

66. Aynes, *From Nightingale to Eagle*, 276.

67. Edith M. Beattie, RN, "Nurse Draft Legislation and the ANA—A Summary," *American Journal of Nursing* 45, 546.

68. Ibid., 547; and "ANA Testimony on Proposed Draft Legislation," *American Journal of Nursing* (March 1945), 172-74.

69. Beattie, "Nurse Draft Legislation," 547.

70. Ibid., 548; and Congressional Record—House, vol. 91, pt.2, 79th Congress, 1st sess., March 6, 1945 and Appendix, A1156-7; and Kalisch and Kalisch, *Advance of American Nursing*, 567.

71. Aynes, *From Nightingale to Eagle*, 271; see also "Recruiting Halted for Army Nurse Corps Members," *Service Woman*, June 22, 1945, which reported that following the acting secretary of war's letter to Sen. Elbert D. Thomas, chairman of the Senate Committee on Military Affairs, that draft legislation was no longer needed, the Red Cross had notified area offices to discontinue active military recruitment. Senior Cadet student nurses "were expected to furnish replacements for attirition and for unexpeceted future needs."

72. Aynes, *From Nightingale to Eagle*, 277.

73. Clark-Hine, *Black Women in White*, 181. Plans for the invasion of Japan estimated the United States might suffer half a million casualties. These were undoubtedly inflated figures, but planners for an invasion of Japan were using General MacArthur's figure of 124,935 by X+120 and Nimitz's figures of 49,000 Navy casualties by X+ 30. These were based on the figure of 100 casualties in the ground and sea forces per division per day. Assuming the invasion of Japan would have used fourteen divisions, a figure of 168,071 would be reached by X+ 120. See John Prados, review, *Journal of Military History* 58 (July 1994), 551. See also Norman Polmar and Thomas Allen, "Invasion Most Costly," U.S. Naval Institute *Proceedings* 121 (August 1995), 51-56.

9 Peace at Last!

1. Biographical information on Agnes Rosele courtesy of Lt. Col. Iris West, Army Nurse Corps historian, August 5, 1994.

2. "5,000 Army Nurses," *American Journal of Nursing* 45 (October 1945), 775-76.

3. Mary Randolph, "What Nurses Expect," *American Journal of Nursing* 46 (February 1946), 94-96.

4. Ibid., 95.

5. Ibid., 96.

6. "Highlights in the History of the Army Nurse Corps," 25-29.

7. Hartman, *Home Front and Beyond*, 32, 48; Campbell, *Women at War*, 57. Army nurses seem to have escaped the worst of the problems of the "slander campaign" against the WAACs, which had also affected British women's reserves. However, rumors of immorality and nurses being used as "geisha girls" did circulate. For more on the deliberate spread of rumors about the morality of WAACs, see Treadwell, *Women's Army Corps*, 206-18.

8. Sources disagree on the total number of black nurses serving in the Army Nurse Corps in WW II. Susan Hartman says 500 by 1945 (*Home Front,* 33). Doris Weatherford cites the figure of 330 from the *Congressional Record*-House, March 5, 1945 (*American Women and World War II,* 20).

9. Hartman, *Home Front,* 32; and Weatherford, *American Women,* 20. Weatherford feels the Senate would have passed the bill and "the President certainly would have signed it" had V-E Day not intervened. She asserts that had the war lasted another two months in Europe "women would have been drafted." This is debatable, but the House passed the bill by an overwheming margin.

BIBLIOGRAPHY

PRIMARY SOURCES

Manuscript Collections

National Archives, Suitland, Md.: Record Group 112, Records in the Office of the Surgeon General (Army)

Reports and Pamphlets

U.S. Department of the Army, Chief of Military History. "Army Nurse Corps History, 1775-1948," 12 vols., draft, n.d.

Highlights in the History of the Army Nurse Corps. U.S. Army Medical Department, 1975.

U.S. Army Interviews[1] and Oral Histories

Marie Adams
Elinor Powell Albert
Esther Allen
Virginia Ballard
Mary L. Barbero
Virginia Barton
Madelene Bateman
Eloise Bowers
1st Lt. Eleanor M. Bradley
Mary Brennan
Helen Shriver Brundage
Nellie R. Burkholder
Prudence Burns Burrell
Anna Urda Busby
Barbara McDonald Calderon
Capt. Peggy G. Carbaugh
Grace Blair Campbell
Octavia Tillman Card
Verna Carruth
Lucille Carter
1st Lt. Lillian Castleberry
Josephine J. Chelenden
Capt. Elva Collison
Dorothea Davis
Eleanor M. DeMay

Mary E. Donovan
Lt. Col. James Duckworth, MC
Marie A. Dull
Virginia Thompson Edkins
Francis Edwards Dyer
Vera M. Fields
Kay Flynn
1st Lt. Susan Freeman
Ruth C. Frothingham
Alma H. Garside
Jeanne B. George
Janice T. Goers-Reilly
Grace Dick Gosnell
Helen Graves
Capt. Marian Grimes
Blanche S. Harffey
Lt. Mary Hawalt
Capt. Louise Heyden
Margaret C. Hofschneider
Alice G. Howard
Bernice Britten Jones
H. Jean McIver Kemp
1st Lt. Brunetta Kuehlthau
Evelyn Langmuir
Nadine H. Lane

Sylvia Lasser
2d Lt. Josephine LeClair
Jean Lynas
Kathleen Marren
Miriam Baker Marken
2d Lt. Julia M. Martin
Hannah M. Matthews
Lt. Florence MacDonald
Margie Buchan McGinley
Dorothy Meador
Dorothy Moore
1st Lt. Ruby F. Motley
J. Ada Mutch
1st Lt. Cara O'Hare
Nellie Osterlund
Ellen Robinson Page
2d Lt. Adele R. Petraitis
Lt. Mary E. Ray
Juanita Redmond
TeresaDeGuelle Reynolds
Henrietta Richardson

2d Lt. Catherine M. Rodman
Myrtle Arndt Roulston
Katherine A. Schlegel
1st Lt. Elsie Schwable
Mary Sherman
Marie J. Showalter
Kathryn C. Singer
Capt. Dorothy Smith
2d Lt. Mary Swain
2d Lt. Dorothy C. Sykes
Jean Foley Tierney
2d Lt. Lucy M. Wainwright
1st Lt. Joella Wallace
Rose Farley Weber
Jeanne Wells
Lt. Muriel Westover
Marjorie Willauer
Alice Wink
Billie Wittler
Kay Yarabinec
1st Lt. Imogene Yarbrough

SECONDARY SOURCES

"ANA Testimony on Proposed Draft Legislation," *American Journal of Nursing* 45 (March 1945), 172-74.

Anders, Leslie. *The Ledo Road.* Norman, OK: University of Oklahoma Press, 1965.

Archard, Capt. Theresa. *G.I. Nightingale.* New York: W.W. Norton, 1945.

"Army Nurses in Southern France," *American Journal of Nursing* 44 (October 1944), 996.

Aynes, Edith. *From Nightingale to Eagle: An Army Nurse's History.* Englewood Cliffs, NJ: Prentice-Hall, 1973.

Barrett, 1st Lt. Kathleen M. "Overseas with a General Hospital." New Jersey College for Women Alumnae *Bulletin* (December 1945), 3-4.

Beattie, Edith M., R.N. "Nurse Draft Legislation and the ANA—A Summary." *American Journal of Nursing* 45 (February 1945), 546-48.

Belote, James. *Corregidor: Saga of a Fortress.* New York: Harper & Row, 1967.

Berger, Martin. "The War and Innovation: Atabrine, DDT, and Malaria." Paper delivered at the Siena College World War II Conference, June 1993.

Bidwell, Shelford. *The Chindit War.* New York: Macmillan, 1979.

Blumenson, Martin. *Salerno to Cassino.* Washington, D.C.: GPO, 1969.

—. *Kasserine Pass.* Boston: 1967.

Breuer, William. *Operation Torch.* New York: St. Martin's, 1985.

—. *Operation Dragoon: The Allied Invasion of the South of France.* England: Airlife, 1988.

Bullough, Vern L., and Bonnie Bullough. *The Care of the Sick: The Emergence of Modern Nursing.* New York: Prodist, 1978.

Campbell, D'Ann. *Women at War with America.* Cambridge, Mass.: Harvard University Press, 1984.

Carnegie, Mary E. *The Path We Tread: Blacks in Nursing, 1854-1984.* New Philadelphia: J.B. Lippincott, 1986.

Cates, Tressa. *The Drainpipe Diary.* New York: Vantage Press, 1957.

Chovan, Luther M. "American Soldier in Reykjavik." *National Geographic Magazine* 88 (November 1945).

"Christmas Overseas." *American Journal of Nursing* 43 (December 1943), 1063.

Clarke, Alice R. "Army Nurse Returns to the Philippines." *American Journal of Nursing* 45 (May 1945), 342-45.

Clark-Hine, Darlene. *Black Women in White: Racial Conflict and Cooperation in the Nursing Profession 1890-1950.* Bloomington: Indiana University Press, 1989.

Clayton, Frederick. "Front-Line Surgical Nurses." *American Journal of Nursing* 44 (March 1944), 234-35.

Conde, Marlette. *The Lamp and the Caduceus.* Army School of Nursing, 1975.

Cosmos, Graham A., and Albert E. Cowdrey. *The Medical Department: Medical Service in the European Theater of Operations.* Washington, D.C.: U.S. Army Center for Military History, 1992.

Cree, Edna M. "Health of the Army Nurse Corps in the ETO." *American Journal of Nursing* 46, 915.

Desmaris, Mary Virginia. "Navy Nursing on D-Day Plus Four." *American Journal of Nursing* 45 (January 1945), 12.

d'Este, Carlo. *World War II in the Mediterranean 1942-45.* Chapel Hill: Algonquin Books, 1990.

Donovan, Col. James A. *Outpost in the North Atlantic: Marines in the Defense of Iceland.* Washington, D.C.: GPO, 1992.

Dorn, Frank. *Walkout: With Stilwell in Burma.* New York: Crowell, 1971.

Edmonds, Walter. *They Fought with What They Had.* Boston: Little, Brown, 1951.

Eisenhower, John D. *Bitter Woods: Hitler's Ardennes Offensive.* New York: Putnam, 1969.

Evans, Jessie Fant. "Release from Los Banos." *American Journal of Nursing* 45 (June 1945), 462-63.

"5,000 Army Nurses." *American Journal of Nursing* 45 (October 1945), 775-76.

Fletcher, Marvin E. *America's First Black General: General Benjamin O. Davis, Sr. 1880-1970.* Lawrence: University Press of Kansas, 1989.

Flikke, Julia. *Nurses in Action: The Story of the Army Nurse Corps.* Philadelphia: J.P. Lippincott, 1943.

Forrest, Lt. Col. Nola. "Army Nurses at Leyte." *American Journal of Nursing* 45 (January 1945), 44.

Frank, Mary E. "The Forgotten POW: 2nd Lt. Reba Z. Whittle." Student paper, Army War College, February 1992.

Gress, Agnes D. "The 14th Evac on the Ledo Road." *American Journal of Nursing* 45 (September 1945), 704-706.

Hartman, Susan. *The Homefront and Beyond: American Women in the 1940's.* Boston: Twayne Publishers, 1982.

Haskell, Ruth. *Helmets and Lipstick.* Arcadia Lodge Press, 1944.

Heinl, Maj. Robert D., Jr. "Palms and Planes in the New Hebrides." *National Geographic Magazine* (August 1944), 229-56.

Heller, Charles, ed. *America's First Battles.* Washington, D.C.: University of Kansas Press, 1957.

Howe, George. *Northwest Africa: Seizing the Initiative in the West.* Washington, D.C.: Office of the Chief of Military History, Department of the Army, 1957.

Huie, William B. *Can Do! The Story of the Seabees.* New York: Dutton, 1944.

Humphrey, Yvonne E. ". . . with German Prisoners." *American Journal of Nursing* 43 (Sepember 1943), 821-22.

Jackson, W.G.F. *The Battle for Italy.* New York: Harper & Row, 1967.

Jose, Mary. "Night Shift in an Army Hospital." *American Journal of Nursing* 45 (June 1945), 430-33.

———. "Hi Angels!" *American Journal of Nursing* 45, 267-70.

Kalisch, Philip, and Beatrice Kalisch. *The Advance of American Nursing.* Boston: Little, Brown, 1986.

———. "Nurses under Fire: The World War II Experience of Nurses on Bataan and Corregidor." *Nursing Research* 25 (November-December 1976), 401-29.

Kielar, Eugenia. *Thank You, Uncle Sam: Letters of a WWII Army Nurse North Africa to Italy.* Bryn Mawr, PA: Dorrance, 1987.

La Forte, Robert S., and Ronald E. Marcello, eds. *Remembering Pearl Harbor: Eyewitness Accounts by U.S. Military Men and Women.* Wilmington, Del.: Scholarly Resources, 1991.

Lee, Ulysses. *The Employment of Black Troops: U.S. Army in WWII.* Washington, D.C.: GPO, 1966.

Link, Mae Mills, and Hubert A. Coleman. *Medical Support of the Army Air Forces in W.W.II.* Washington, D.C.: Office of the Surgeon General, 1955.

Lochridge, Patricia. "Solace at Iwo." *Woman's Home Companion* 72 (May 1945), 4.

Lundstrom, John B. *The First South Pacific Campaign.* Annapolis: U.S. Naval Institute Press, 1976.

MacDonald, Charles B. *A Time for Trumpets: The Untold Story of the Battle for the Bulge.* New York: Bantam Books, 1984.

Mason, Lt. George. "Flight Nurse." *Flying* (March 1944), 55-56,169, 170.

McBryde, Brenda. *Quiet Heroines: Nurses of the Second World War.* London: Chatto & Windus, Hogarth Press, 1985.

McGuire, Philip. *Taps for a Jim Crow Army: Letters from Black Soldiers in World War II.* Lexington: University Press of Kentucky, 1983.

McIver, Pearl. "Registered Nurses in the USA." *American Journal of Nursing* 42 (1942), 16.

Morehead, John J. "Surgical Experience at Pearl Harbor." *Journal of American Medical Association* 118 (1942), 712-13.

Morison, Samuel Eliot. *History of U.S. Naval Operations in World War II.* Boston: Little, Brown, 1954.

Morton, Louis. *The War in the Pacific, Fall of the Philippines, U.S. Army in World War II.* Washington, D.C.: GPO, 1953.

Musser, H. Richard. "Nurse or Soldier?" *American Journal of Nursing* 41 (1941), 1449.

Neel, Maj. Gen. Surgeon. *Medical Support of the U.S. Army in Vietnam 1965-70.* Washington, D.C.: GPO, 1973.

Nicolay, Helen. *MacArthur of Bataan.* New York: 1942.

Ogburn, Charleton. *The Marauders.* New York: Harper, 1959.

Osur, Alan M. *Blacks in the Army Air Forces During W.W.II.* Washington, D.C.: Office of Air Force History, GPO, 1977.

Parks, Ruth Evelyn. "Inside Looking Out." *American Journal of Nursing* 41 (June 1941), 642-43.

Paxton, Lt. Vincoe. "Army Reinforcements Land in France." *American Journal of Nursing* 45 (January 1945), 13-16.

———. "With Field Hospital Nurses in Germany." *American Journal of Nursing* 45 (February 1945), 131-33.

Peto, Lt. Col. Marjorie. *Women Were Not Expected: An Informal Story of the Nurses of the 2nd General Hospital in the ETO.* West Englewood, N.J.: Author, 1947.

Petry, Lucile. "U.S. Cadet Nurse Corps." *American Journal of Nursing* 43 (August 1943), 704-8.

Polmar, Norman, and Thomas Allen. "Invasion Most Costly." U.S. Naval Institute *Proceedings* 121 (August 1995), 51-56.

Pond, Hugh. *Salerno.* Boston: Little, Brown, 1961.

Prados, John. Review of John R. Skates, *The Invasion of Japan: Alternative to the Bomb. Journal of Military History* 58 (July 1994), 549-51.

Putney, Martha S. *When the Nation Was in Need: Blacks in the Women's Army Corps During World War II.* Metuchen, N.J.: Scarecrow Press, 1992.

Pyle, Ernie. *Brave Men.* New York: Henry Holt, 1944.

Rainey, Froelich. "Alaskan Highway an Engineering Epic." *National Geographic Magazine* 83 (February 1943), 143-68.

Randolph, Mary. "What Nurses Expect." *American Journal of Nursing* 46 (February 1946), 94-96.

Redmond, Juanita. *I Served on Bataan.* Philadelphia: J.P. Lippincott, 1943.

Riddle, Estelle M., and Josephine Nelson. "The Negro Nurse Looks Toward Tomorrow." *American Journal of Nursing* 45 (August 1945), 627-30.

Roberts, Mary M. *American Nursing: History and Interpretation.* New York: Macmillan, 1961.

Romanus, Charles F., and Riley Sunderland. *Stilwell's Command Problems.* Washington, D.C.: GPO, 1956.

——. *Stilwell's Mission to China.* Washington, D.C.: GPO, 1958.

——. *Time Runs Out in the CBI,* Washington, D.C.: GPO, 1959.

Sandler, Stanley. *Segregated Skies: All Black Combat Squadrons of W.W.II.* Washington, D.C.: Smithsonian, 1992.

Schneider, Dorothy, and Carl J. Schneider. *Into the Breach: American Women Overseas in World War I.* New York: Viking, 1991.

Scott, Col. Raymond. "Eleventh Evacuation Hospital in Sicily." *American Journal of Nursing* 43 (April 1943), 925-26.

Seagrave, Gordon. *Burma Surgeon Returns.* New York: W.W. Norton, 1946.

Sforza, Eula Awbrey. *A Nurse Remembers.* N.p., 1991.

Smith, Clarence McKitrick. *The Medical Department: Hospitalization and Evacuation, Zone of the Interior.* Washington, D.C.: GPO, 1956.

Spector, Ronald. *Eagle Against the Sun.* New York: Free Press, 1985.

——. *After Tet.* New York: Free Press, 1993.

Tayloe, Roberta Love. *Combat Nurse: A Journal of World War II.* Santa Barbara: Fithian, 1988.

Thorne, Bliss K. *The Hump.* Philadelphia: Lippincott, 1965.

Toland, John. *But Not in Shame: The Six Months after Pearl Harbor.* New York: Random House, 1961.

Tomblin, Barbara B. "Beyond Paradise: The Navy Nurse Corps in the Pacific," Parts One and Two. *Minerva, the Quarterly Report on Women in the Military* 2 (summer 1993), 33-53; 3 and 4 (fall/winter 1993), 37-56.

Travers, Paul J. *Eyewitness to Infamy: An Oral History of Pearl Harbor.* Lanham, N.Y.: Madison Books, 1991.

Treadwell, Mattie E. *The Women's Army Corps.* Washington, D.C.: GPO, 1954.

Truckey, Jean. "Nurses Prove Their Courage Under Fire of Enemy." Article in possession of author.

Tuchman, Barbara. *Stilwell and the American Experience in China, 1911-45.* New York: Macmillan, 1970.

Wandrey, June. *Bedpan Commando: The Story of a Combat Nurse During World War II.* Elmore, Ohio: Elmore Publishing, 1989.

Weatherford, Doris. *American Women and World War II.* New York: Facts on File, 1990.

Weinstein, Dr. Alfred A. *Barbed Wire Surgeon.* New York: Macmillan, 1948.

White, Ruth Y. "Anzio Beachhead." *American Journal of Nursing* 44 (April 1944), 370.

White, Theodore, ed. *The Stilwell Papers.* New York: W. Sloan Associates, 1948.

White, W.L. *They Were Expendable.* New York: Harcourt, Brace, 1942.

Whiteley, George, Jr. "Newfoundland, North Atlantic Rampart." *National Geographic Magazine* 80 (July 1941), 111-40.

Wilkins, Roy. "Nurses Go to War." *Crisis* (February 1943), 42-44.

Wiltse, Charles M. *The Medical Department: Medical Service in the Mediterranean and Minor Theaters.* Washington, D.C.: GPO, 1965.

[1]Military rank given only for nurses interviewed by the Army.

INDEX

Note: Military units with Roman numerals and ordinal numbers greater than one hundred are alphabetized as if spelled out.

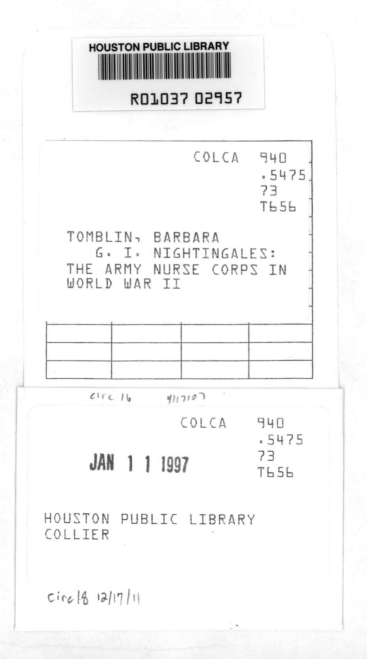

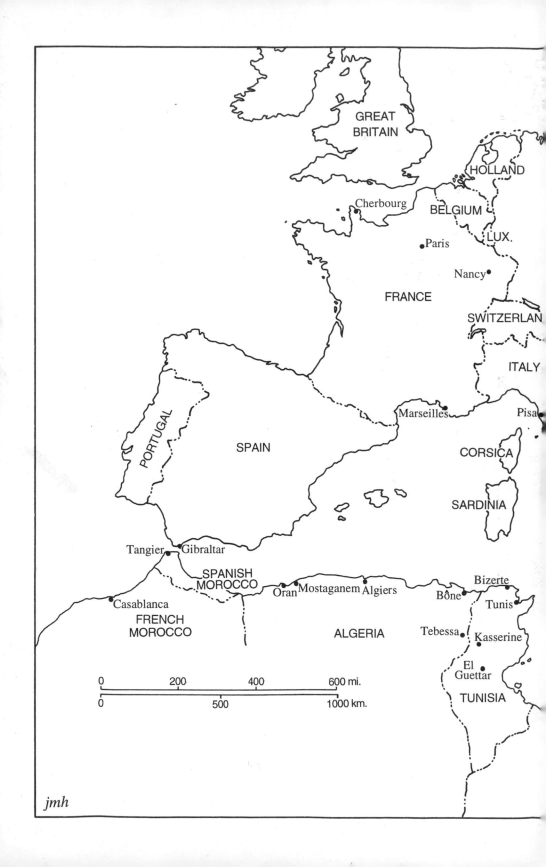